POLITICS AND THE PRESS

POLITICS AND THE PRESS

The News Media and Their Influences

edited by

Pippa Norris

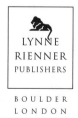

LYNNE
RIENNER
PUBLISHERS

BOULDER
LONDON

Published in the United States of America in 1997 by
Lynne Rienner Publishers, Inc.
1800 30th Street, Boulder, Colorado 80301

and in the United Kingdom by
Lynne Rienner Publishers, Inc.
3 Henrietta Street, Covent Garden, London WC2E 8LU

Library of Congress Cataloging-in-Publication Data
Politics and the press : the news media and their influences / edited
by Pippa Norris.
    Includes bibliographical references and index.
    ISBN 1-55587-670-6 (alk. paper).—ISBN 1-55587-681-1 (pbk. :
alk. paper)
    1. Press and politics. 2. Press—Influence. 3. Broadcast
journalism. I. Norris, Pippa.
PN4738.P55   1997
070.4'49324—DC21   97-3827
                                                          CIP

British Cataloguing in Publication Data
A Cataloguing in Publication record for this book
is available from the British Library.

Printed and bound in the United States of America

    The paper used in this publication meets the requirements
 ∞ of the American National Standard for Permanence of
    Paper for Printed Library Materials Z39.48-1984.

    5 4 3 2 1

Contents

v

Part Three: The Media and Public Policy

Foreword

From its inception about a decade ago, what has been unique about the Joan Shorenstein Center on the Press, Politics and Public Policy is that we have tried to create a common place for both academics and journalists interested in what has become the study of "press/politics." The Shorenstein Center is neither a journalism school nor a government department, but rather an interesting hybrid of the two professions; and though its faculty is dominated by scholars, its Fellows program is broader in scope, welcoming journalists and political practitioners to the table in addition to scholars. This book is the result of their efforts. Every Fellow, whether a scholar or a journalist, a pollster or a politician, writes a paper exploring one of the many sides of press/politics. Each year, a dozen or so Fellows participate in the life and work of the Shorenstein Center, and most of them leave their calling card in the form of a serious paper. We provide the environment for serious scholarship; they provide the product.

For the director of a research center dedicated to the study of the intersection of press and politics in the formation of public policy, this arrangement makes eminently good sense. It means that over time a body of literature, a fledgling library of books, journals, articles, and speeches would be produced that would become the basis for research and teaching in press/politics. *Politics and the Press* is one of a number of books researched and written at the Shorenstein Center that reflect the exploration of the intertwined worlds of press and politics.

This book is divided into three parts: "Gathering the News"; "The Media, Public Opinion, and Elections"; and "The Media and Public Policy." All of the chapters, because they pursue a common challenge, raise a single question: How does the intersection of press and politics affect public policy? This question cuts to the heart of the Shorenstein Center's mandate; it also explains the essence of modern-day governance. It is no longer enough to understand the workings of the three coequal branches of government; now we must also understand the workings of the pollsters, lobbyists, spinmeisters, fund-raisers, and journalists. Imagine a presidential campaign without television, a corporation without public relations, a town without newspapers, a White House without the UPI's Helen Thomas. Impossible? Exactly, so read and appreciate this book.

Marvin Kalb,
Director,
The Joan Shorenstein Center on the
Press, Politics and Public Policy

Introduction:
The Rise of Postmodern
Political Communications?

Pippa Norris

Recent years have seen a rising tide of disquiet about how the U.S. news media cover the political process. Journalists, scholars, and policymakers have voiced increasing unease that the press, far from acting as a bridge linking citizens and the state, has come to act as a barrier to the effective functioning of representative democracy. The public seems to share this concern: according to recent Times-Mirror polls less than a quarter of Americans express a high level of confidence in the press as an institution, and a majority say that the news is too sensational, biased, trivial, and negative.[1] Influential critiques by Neil Postman, James Fallows, Tom Patterson, and Robert Putnam, among others, have generated debate about the appropriate role of the media in the United States.[2] Angst within the mainstream media, fueled by the exodus of readers and viewers, hence falling revenues, has led to controversial innovations, such as experiments with "civic journalism" by some newspapers,[3] although doom-sayers regard such novelties as equivalent to rearranging the chairs on the Titanic.

Commentators have expressed anxiety about many changes in the process of political communications. The main focus of this book centers on three of these concerns: whether traditional standards of journalism have been undermined by technological developments, increased economic competition, and cultural pluralism; whether the process of political communications during election campaigns has produced a more cynical and disengaged public; and whether commercial pressures and "tabloidization" has led to a decline in serious, responsible, and informed coverage of public policy debates. This book provides reflections on these issues from both practitioners and scholars. All these concerns can be understood to reflect deep-rooted changes in journalistic practices produced by the transition from modern to *postmodern* political communications.

Evidence in these chapters suggests that some anxieties about the news media are probably misplaced or exaggerated. Like a hypochondriac stricken by a slight touch of flu, because the news media operate in a narcissistic

1

echo-chamber, the column-inches devoted to "the crisis in journalism" are probably out of all proportion to the nature of the problem. The press is not wholly at fault here; there is often a tendency for many of us to "blame the messenger" for serious and intractable problems found in American society. Nevertheless, although much of the rhetorical angst is overblown, this does not mean that all is well with the world of journalism. The way the news media act as an intermediary institution linking citizens and the state has changed in recent decades, which may have significant consequences for the functioning of democracy. To understand these issues we can start by considering how the process of modernization and postmodernization has transformed U.S. presidential campaigns during the last half century.

From Premodern to Postmodern Communications

To understand the extent of the changes in political communications, contrast the situation facing the average citizen just after World War II with the familiar pattern of campaigning in more recent elections. There are three identifiable stages in the evolution of campaigning in which older forms of communications were supplanted, although not wholly replaced, by newer media, campaign organizations, and communication strategies (see Table I.1).

The 1948 Truman versus Dewey contest exemplified the *premodern* campaign characterized by the predominance of newspapers and radio: a loose organizational network of grassroots volunteers with coordination by local and state party officials; and a short ad hoc campaign run largely by each presidential nominee with a small team of personal advisers. Yet this election also represents the end of an era and the start of the *modern* campaign, typified by the predominance of network television news, the widespread adoption of marketing techniques in strategic campaigns, and the professionalization of political communications. Many campaigns during the late 1970s and early 1980s can be seen to exemplify the modern campaign before this familiar pattern also started to change. Last, the 1996 Clinton versus Dole contest represents the emerging shape of the *postmodern* campaign characterized by a fragmentation of media outlets and audiences, commercial pressures leading to a tabloidization of news, and the evolution of the permanent campaign. There is room for dispute about the precise time line, but the contrasts between the 1948 and 1996 campaigns illustrate the remarkable changes in political communications during the second half of the twentieth century.[4] Each of these elections symbolizes, in its own way, the evolution of significantly different approaches to campaigning.

Table I.1 Changes in Campaigning

	Premodern	Modern	Postmodern
Campaign Organization	Local and decentralized	Nationally coordinated	Nationally coordinated but decentralized operations
Preparations	Short-term and ad-hoc campaign	Long campaign	Permanent campaign
Central Coordination	Party leaders	Central headquarters, more specialist consultants and party officials	More outside consultants, pollsters, and specialist campaign departments
Feedback	Local canvassing	Opinion polls	Opinion polls, focus groups, Internet web sites
Media	National and local press, local handbills, posters and pamphlets, radio leadership speeches	Television broadcasting through major territorial channels	Television narrow-casting through fragmented channels, targeted mail, targeted ads
Campaign Events	Local public meetings, limited whistle-stop leadership tours	Media management, daily press conferences, themed photo ops, TV ads	Extension of media management to "routine" politics, leadership speeches, policy launches, etc.
Costs	Low budget and local costs	Higher costs for producing television ads	Higher costs for consultants, research, and television ads

The Premodern Campaign

The premodern 1948 campaign represented the last hurrah for the old system. The presidential candidates still relied heavily upon traditional, face-to-face retail politics for getting out the message, with whistle-stop railway tours across the country, meetings with party notables and ticker-tape parades in major cities, and keynote speeches before packed crowds.[5] Politics was very much a public spectacle, not a private event experienced in our living rooms, although in the early 1920s the incursion of radio already started to transform the process. In urban strongholds the Democratic machine organized events and turned out supporters at local and state levels. The presidential candidates relied on only a handful of close advisers: Harry Truman's train had an entourage of only about twenty campaign staff, including speechwriters, secretaries, and security details, accompanied by a small group of about forty reporters. Thomas Dewey's campaign organization was similar in size, with about one hundred reporters accompanying his whistle-stop trains.

Newspapers, radio, and movie newsreels provided the main sources of mediated news. The United States had about 1,800 daily newspapers, reaching about a third of the population every day, not including thousands of weekly papers and popular magazines. The partisan press had been in decline for many decades, but newspapers were clearly stacked in the GOP camp in their editorial support: 771 papers (65 percent of all papers) endorsed Dewey, compared with only 182 papers (15 percent) that supported Truman.[6] The Republican edge in terms of circulation figures was even greater, and this partisan bias persisted in every election until the 1960s.

Yet the bias of the newspapers received a counterbalance from the other media. The 1934 Communication Act regulating the airwaves ensured that equal opportunities for access to the airwaves must be provided to all bona fide candidates for public office, forbade the censorship of political broadcasts on the radio, and regulated radio and television stations through the Federal Communications Commission (FCC). Franklin Delano Roosevelt's fireside chats on radio, and later Truman's, reached a national audience, with over 90 percent of households owning a radio set. Radio carried candidate speeches to a wide audience, as well as broadcasting paid ads and special political programs throughout the election.

During the campaign two short ten-minute films of Truman and Dewey played in movie theaters throughout the country, at a time when about 65 million people went to the movies every week. Television was only starting to play a role: in 1948 the party conventions were covered, reaching audiences in New York and Washington, D.C., and this campaign also saw the first paid television appearances by presidential candidates. But the audience was limited: in 1950 only 9 percent of U.S. households possessed a black-and-white television set flickering in the corner of the living room, although the consumer boom of the 1950s rapidly transformed this situation. For the few who watched TV, without cable, the three major networks monopolized the airwaves. In the 1950s, each network broadcast only fifteen minutes of news in the early evening.[7] Almost all commercial television stations were affiliated with ABC, NBC, or CBS.

The balance between the print press and electronic media was already starting to shift by 1952: when people were asked by the National Election Study (NES) about their main source of election information, 39 percent reported following the campaign "regularly" in newspapers, 34 percent listened to "a good many" radio speeches or discussions, but already 32 percent watched "a good many" programs about the campaign on television.[8] The first systematic studies of media use in U.S. campaigns were carried out by Paul Lasarsfeld and colleagues in the early 1940s.[9] In contrast to popular theories about the sweeping influence of political propaganda,

Lasarsfeld found that the "attentive public" who tuned into campaign speeches on the radio, followed the campaign in newspapers, and discussed politics with friends were already the most committed partisans. The inattentive public, drawn from the less well educated and lower socioeconomic groups, were less exposed to news in papers, magazines, and radio.

Most commentators predicted that President Truman was going to be defeated. International problems of the postwar reconstruction led to divisions among the Allies and the start of the Cold War. At home there were difficulties of demobilization. The conversion of the U.S. economy to peacetime needs produced high taxes, labor strikes, and rising prices. Race was to cause more deep-rooted divisions: Truman was sympathetic to black demands for civil and voting rights, and when the Democratic convention strongly endorsed this policy the party split three ways, with Governor Strom Thurmond heading the States' Rights "Dixiecrats" opposed to reform, while on the left former Vice President Henry Wallace led a new Progressive party of pacifists, reformers, and New Dealers. When Governor Dewey was nominated again by the Republicans, in the first convention covered on television, almost everybody expected him to win. Fifty of the nation's top political writers picked Dewey as the winner. After the election, in the first nationwide survey that eventually became the NES, two-thirds of the public expressed surprise at the outcome.

The conventional wisdom about the result was reinforced by the available opinion polls. The first systematic opinion polls based on samples of the population were developed in the mid-1930s. But Truman disregarded the polls and relied instead on his close advisers and the crowds that greeted him at every campaign stop, although Dewey was the first presidential candidate to employ a pollster on his staff. In 1948 the available surveys by George Gallup, Archibald Crossley, and Elmo Roper confidently predicted a comfortable victory for Governor Thomas E. Dewey. Just before the election *Life* carried a big picture of Dewey with the caption "The next President of the United States," and the *Chicago Tribune*'s premature headline was "Dewey defeats Truman." Elmo Roper even discontinued polling on September 9, 1948, when he predicted 52.2 percent for Dewey to 37.1 percent for Truman, because he regarded the result as so inevitable that "no amount of electioneering" could alter the outcome. In the end the pollsters, press commentators, and editorial writers experienced a rout: Truman won about 50 percent of the popular vote and carried 28 states producing 303 electoral college votes, and the Democrats recaptured control of both houses of Congress.

The Evolution of the Modern Campaign

Some of the features of traditional premodern campaigns continue; for example, retail face-to-face politics remains important for presidential candidates in the Iowa caucus and the New Hampshire primary. Nevertheless, if we contrast the Truman-Dewey contest with modern elections, the extent of the revolution in political communications is striking. The evolution of the modern campaign was marked by several related developments in electioneering: the shift from newspapers and radio toward *network television news;* from dispersed state and local party organizations to a nationally coordinated *strategic campaign;* and from party officials and volunteers contributing time and labor to paid *professional consultants* specializing in communications, marketing, polling, and campaign management. The move from amateur to professional campaigns was marked by more frequent use of experts, PR consultants, and professional fund-raisers making decisions that were formerly made by candidates or party officials. These developments have been well documented elsewhere and will not be covered in detail here.[10] The modern campaign evolved into a familiar pattern from the early 1950s until the mid-1980s, with similar, although not identical, changes becoming evident across advanced industrialized societies.[11] One of the major consequences of these developments in the late 1960s and early 1970s was the nationalization of the presidential campaign, with network news programs broadcasting candidate speeches, party conventions, and election events across the country, unifying Americans in a common experience.[12] During this period, in many ways whatever was covered on CBS, NBC, and ABC and the *New York Times, Washington Post,* and *Wall Street Journal* was the presidential campaign, with anchors, broadcast journalists, and reporters for the major papers as figures of unchallenged authority. There was a well-established hierarchy among and within news organizations and a clear sense of professional identity and standards among journalists. Yet the golden days of network news were not to last, producing anxieties about the proliferation of media outlets and messages.

The Postmodern Campaign?

In the last decade we can identify the transition from this familiar world to the postmodern campaign as marked by several related developments: the *fragmentation* of audiences and outlets, with the shift from network television toward more diverse news sources including talk radio, local television news, and newer media like the Internet; the *tabloidization* of news due to fierce commercial pressures; and the move toward the *permanent campaign* with the continuous feedback provided by polls, focus groups, and electronic town meetings to inform routine decisionmaking, not just campaigns. Elections since the mid-1980s exemplify these developments. As a result candidates and mainstream journalists seem to be struggling ever harder to retain control of their message through the traditional channels, but the familiar ground is shifting under their feet, producing the outpourings of anxieties about the media. In the extensive literature that has developed, the concept of postmodernism is complex, open to multiple interpretations.[13] Yet the commonalities of postmodernism are usually understood to include greater cultural pluralism, social diversity, and fragmentation of sources; increased challenges to traditional forms of hierarchical authority and external standards of rational knowledge; and a more inchoate and confused sense of identity. These developments can be seen to represent a new openness and tolerance for alternative views and multiple forms of understanding, as well as a source of anxiety and disorientation as the familiar standards are swept away.

As we approach the end of the twentieth century, postmodernism seems to have swept the news media in the United States. Competition for readers and viewers has become far more intense, with the fragmentation of the mass market into narrower and narrower segments. Partial deregulation of the television industry, the growth of cable television systems and satellite services, and the rise of new networks, videotape recorders, teletext, and communication via the Internet have splintered the competition for news in the marketplace.[14] The networks in 1970 had no rivals: only 10 percent of American homes had cable. By 1980, penetration by this service had only reached 20 percent of households. But by 1994 almost two-thirds had cable (62.4 percent), and three-quarters (77.1 percent) had VCRs.[15] Times-Mirror surveys indicate that in 1995 more than a third of all American homes had computers, while a fifth of all households had computers with modems. Not surprisingly, given these developments, network audience share plummeted from 93 percent in 1977 to 54 percent in 1994.[16] By the mid-1990s, on the average weeknight only 13.8 percent of the population tunes into the early evening news, and only 4.6 percent watch late news, with viewers disproportionately concentrated among the older age groups.[17] The readership for newspapers has experienced a steady hemorrhage for decades, which shows no signs of being staunched. The development of digital technology that multiplies television channels and new sources of Internet information seems likely to accelerate these developments.

The growth of "narrow-casting" means that more and more sources are reaching increasingly specialized audiences. Although a small group of political aficionados can find ever more detailed information about government, public policy, and campaigns through these sources, simultaneously surfing the web and watching CNN and C-Span during the election, many others find it easier to tune out political information by watching MTV, HBO, and *Monday Night Football.* The multiplicity of outlets, stories, and channels has undermined the sense that the network news today can ever sign off with the classic Cronkite phrase, "That's the way it is." The familiar authorities have gone, replaced by multiple realities, for good or ill.

Moreover, when people do watch television news, commercial pressures have encouraged tabloid journalism that focuses on an endless diet of crime, scandals, and sex (preferably all three) and "infotainment." This pattern is particularly clear in local television "news," where one study found that only 40 percent of airtime is actually devoted to "news," and "mayhem, fluff and sports" predominate.[18] These trends have also infected mainstream journalism. "Downsizing" in the networks and major print newsrooms has threatened traditional standards of journalism, and undermined "hard news" about politics.[19] The structural biases in news have become exacerbated by commercial pressures, including the focus on dramatic personalized stories, episodic news, fragmented information, and normalized news representations, all of which makes it harder for viewers to make sense of the world.[20]

Many commentators have argued that as a result of commercial pressures and tabloidization the news media have contributed toward growing political cynicism and apathy among the American public.[21] Media coverage of election campaigns, in particular, is often blamed for the long-term decay in political trust and civic engagement. The way the press publicizes scandals may create widespread mistrust of politicians and have significant consequences for governments. This pattern is by no means confined to the United States: examples include the coverage of Watergate and Whitewater in the United States, the widespread stain of Tangentopoli in Italy, the Recruit and Sagawa corruption scandals in Japan, and the pervasive problems of sexual and financial sleaze afflicting the Conservative government of John Major in Britain.

The role of the press in publicizing such scandals may have changed over time. The proliferation of media outlets may have led to more negative, episodic, and conflict-related news, encouraging the feeling that social problems are intractable and beyond the powers of government intervention. Tabloidization focuses publicity on the personal lives of political leaders, so that personal peccadilloes of presidents or congressional representatives, as well as figures of authority like church or military leaders, that would have remained discreetly hidden a few decades ago are now emblazoned on the front page. The focus on revealing exclusive scandals may have created greater disillusionment about traditional institutions, as well as producing cynicism about general standards of public life.

In a related argument, Tom Patterson concludes that as an institution the press is unsuited to the new powers that it has acquired. U.S. journalistic values, he argues, tend toward an antipolitics bias, are skeptical of the major institutions in society, and focus on campaign strategy (who is ahead, who behind) at the expense of issues. The press overemphasizes change rather than consistency, inside-the-beltway op-ed criticism rather than government success, and questions of personal character at the expense of dry policy debate. Parties tend to be portrayed in an overwhelmingly negative light. Among the public it is argued this produces an excessively cynical, ill-informed, and negative view of politicians, which drives a wedge between candidates and voters and increases mistrust of the political process. As a result, Patterson concludes, voters end up poorly informed and ill-equipped to select the best candidate in a crowded nomination race: "A press-based electoral system is not a suitable basis for that most pivotal of all decisions, the choice of a president."[22] Studies of the role of the media in the 1996 presidential primaries confirm that the network news coverage remains overwhelmingly focused on horse-race rather than policy issues, with a relentlessly negative tone provided by the reporters, in contrast to more positive messages from the candidates themselves.[23]

Last, political leaders face greater difficulties in connecting with voters in a news system characterized by increased fragmentation and tabloidization. Political candidates have to run up the down escalator simply to stay in place. In order to do this, we have seen the evolution of the permanent campaign. The techniques for monitoring the pulse of the public, including focus groups, daily tracking polls, and electronic town meetings, have gradually moved beyond the campaign to become an integral part of governing. Starting with John Kennedy, but developing particularly under Richard Nixon, the White House's sensitivity to public opinion became an enduring institutional feature of the modern presidency. Opinion polling, once fairly ad hoc, became centralized within the White House and organized around routine procedures for monitoring public support.[24] More recent developments have seen changes in the techniques commonly used to measure public opinion and greater sensitivity to the results in framing and communicating public policy options. These developments happened first within the presidency but have subsequently expanded throughout all levels of government so that the techniques for winning elections have become increasingly central to the techniques for governing, and the policy debate in Washington has become part of the permanent campaign.

Concerns About Gathering the News

The first section of this book considers the consequences of these technological, economic, and cultural developments and some effects that flow from the modernization of political communications. In the first chapter Richard Parker examines the future of global television, in particular whether technological developments have transformed international relations around the world. Are we heading toward a universal culture, with the same pictures and programs in Los Angeles or London, New Delhi or Tokyo? Whereas technological determinists suggest that we are on the threshold of entering a new world linked together by television, Parker argues that in practice there are serious limits to the prospect of global journalism. Economic constraints and the tradition of government involvement in public service broadcasting mean that nationally rooted media systems retain their power to determine most of what we see.

Market pressures have not only affected television but also the process of gathering news and selling newspapers. In Chapter 2 Alison Carper, a journalist, considers how far the growth of marketing techniques such as surveys and focus groups has affected the contents and style of many medium-sized and small newspapers. Four arguments—the pedagogical, enticement, democratic, and business imperative ones—are commonly used to justify the introduction of these techniques. Carper concludes that through changing in response to market research and adopting purely profit-seeking objectives, journalists have abandoned their traditional roles and their claim to special status in society.

Reflecting changes in the United States, the profession of journalism has also had to adapt in recent decades to the demands of greater diversity in the workforce and society. The process of modernization has produced greater recognition of the need for social diversity and multiple cultural identities in the press. Journalism has seen the gradual entry of pluralist voices into the newsmaking process, including more women, African Americans, and Hispanics.[25] But at the same time there are strong assertions that the media have not gone far enough in this regard, that gains made during the 1970s consolidated but failed to move ahead in the 1980s, and that dominant news values and traditional structures of news organizations remain unreconstructed.

In Chapter 3, Pearl Stewart, the first African American woman editor of the *Oakland Tribune,* considers how far there have been gains in the employment of minorities in newspapers and broadcasting. Based on personal interviews and a review of the data, she finds that women of color have made some gains at lower levels of the journalistic workforce. Nevertheless, among key decisionmakers, such as editors and newspaper executives, women of color have hit the glass ceiling. The reason, Stewart suggests, is that gender and racial stereotypes continue to affect appointments at corporate management level. This chapter throws light on the debate about the need for affirmative action and the anxieties on both sides of the racial divide.

Reflecting similar concerns, Jorge Quiroga, a television reporter, looks at the way the press has covered the Hispanic community. In Chapter 4 he starts by considering what type of coverage we might expect if news stories reflected the diversity of the Hispanic population in the United States. Quiroga goes on to compare case studies of events in four cities—Boston, Los Angeles, Washington, D.C., and New York—to see whether there was a pattern of coverage of Hispanics. He concludes that news about this community is problematic due to traditional newsroom attitudes and stereotyping, a lack of employment of Hispanic journalists, and weak linkages between the press and Hispanic groups.

Political Communications in Election Campaigns

Just as technological, economic, and cultural pressures have fragmented the process of news gathering, so at the same time developments have also fragmented U.S. politics and increased the power of the media to step into this vacuum. The growth of primaries in the late 1960s and early 1970s fatally weakened party control of the candidate nomination process and allowed the media to play an ever greater role as "king-makers." As discussed earlier, whether this new role is appropriate for the press has been the subject of much soul-searching in journalism.

The second section considers how television ads, campaign news, and candidate debates influence public opinion, the discourse within campaigns, and ultimately the outcome of elections. What is the role of news and TV ads within campaigns? In Chapter 5 Montague Kern and Marion Just look at how voters construct images of political candidates. They draws on evidence from focus groups exposed to news and advertising broadcasts during the 1990 Senate race in North Carolina between Jesse Helms and Harvey Gantt. The analysis considers how citizens construct candidate "schemas," or cognitive structures that integrate new information into existing knowledge. This chapter uses a "constructionist" approach, which suggests that people construct meaning from media messages based on their own attitudes, values, and feelings. Kern and Just conclude that individuals actively participate in the process of evaluating candidates, so that the messages they receive interact with their existing preferences, feelings, and experiences. Moreover, the study found that affectively laden messages in advertising, rather than campaign news, dominated the discourse in focus groups. In particular, negative advertising was widely regarded as credible mainly because it resonated with the widespread belief that most politicians are untrustworthy.

Campaign communications occur through advertising and the news media but also through candidate debates. No matter how stage managed, these debates provide a unique opportunity for voters to examine directly the character and policies of the presidential candidates at length in a live and unscripted session, without the filter of journalistic commentary. Few campaign events attract as large an audience as the presidential debates. Yet their impact on voters has been a matter of considerable dispute, as has the most appropriate format for staging these events.[26] In Chapter 6, based on interviews with a panel of undecided and weakly committed voters, Michael X. Delli Carpini, Scott Keeter, and Sharon Webb describe the reaction to the second presidential debate in 1992. The "People's Debate," as it was known, used a talk show format and was held in Richmond, Virginia. The results suggest that the debate had a clear and fairly dramatic impact on undecided voters, which persisted for the remainder of the campaign and influenced the voting of many panelists. This shift is consistent with the changes in voting intentions monitored by the tracking polls, which also suggest that this event boosted Clinton's support at the expense of Bush. These events suggest that debates will continue to play a significant role in presidential elections, especially in close campaigns.

Debates provide presidential contenders with free air time, but the main way candidates try to communicate their message is through the medium of paid advertisements. The 1996 campaign is estimated to be by far the most expensive, costing in the region of $2 billion at all levels. Television absorbs most of this money: two-thirds or more of presidential campaign spending goes to TV advertising.[27] The press has responded to changes in campaigning in different ways. One innovation, introduced in Britain in 1983 and in the United States in 1990, is Adwatch features in which newspapers and television news deconstruct and evaluate campaign advertisements. This is an attempt by newspapers to provide the electorate with more information, to counter public disgust with negative ads in the wake of the 1988 presidential campaign. Stories that critique a candidate's TV ads have become standard fare, although the effect of this reporting remains a matter of dispute. Some claim that adwatches fail, mainly because they reinforce the candidate's messages, although others dispute the evidence.[28] In Chapter 7 Michael Milburn and Justin Brown discussed adwatches with journalists, and used an experimental design to monitor their effects. During the campaign, they asked subjects to read different newspaper columns, then showed them six different television advertisements. Milburn and Brown found that those who read the Adwatch stories became more critical of the contents of the ads, and the effect of this process was to prevent attitudinal change. They conclude that Adwatch columns have the potential to reduce the impact of illegitimate attempts at political persuasion and also to increase evaluative thinking. Understood in this light, it appears that rather than reinforcing the message of the ads, as some claim, the main effect of adwatches was inoculation. Milburn and Brown conclude that these columns are therefore a useful addition to campaign coverage that mitigates the impact of negative ads.

The Media and Public Policy

Finally, many believe that the combined effect of ever-increasing commercial pressures, fragmentation, and tabloidization has been a decline in serious and substantive press coverage of public policy issues. In network television the displacement of hard news by infotainment, the rise of news magazine shows and the decline of serious documentaries, and the use of episodic rather than thematic frames may lead to less effective public deliberation about the serious policy problems facing the United States. The concluding section of this book considers how television influences the domestic and foreign policy process.

In Chapter 8 the philosopher Sissela Bok explores the influence of television on violence in the United States, particularly among children, and the arguments used in the public debate about this issue. This chapter carefully dissects rationales that are commonly deployed in this debate, such as the way that violence is regarded as endemic throughout American society, so nothing can be done to prevent this problem, or the view that we should not blame television when there are many other causes of the problem. Bok concludes that violence is the result of a complex and interlocking set of causes, and there are no simple solutions. Nevertheless, the weight of evidence clearly indicates that the way the media depict violence on the screen is one contributory factor, and this needs to be addressed in a serious public debate.

The way the media cover the political process affects domestic as well as foreign policy issues. In order to consider this, in Chapter 9 Timothy Cook analyzes the way the press responded to the AIDS health crisis. The news media are often seen as most influential in their agenda-setting role, that is, the way they influence perceptions about the major problems facing society and government. Cook argues that the way newspapers and television covered the AIDS story was problematic, mainly due to standard journalistic practices. The epidemic was downplayed in the first four years mainly because journalists relied on authoritative sources to define the news, they failed to respond quickly enough to new developments, they feared being inflammatory, and they favored certain slants but not others on the AIDS problem. Cook concludes that the media have a critical role to play in informing the public about health concerns, and to fulfill this well journalists need to examine the standard practices that determine the news agenda.

The role of the news media in international conflict has generated an extensive literature focusing on the effects of coverage on public opinion and foreign policy. In Chapter 10 Barrie Dunsmore, an experienced foreign correspondent for ABC News, considers how technology is changing the way television covers international conflict, in particular the ability of TV to cover wars live. This development has major security and political implications, and therefore raises concerns about the most appropriate guidelines under which journalists should operate in these new circumstances. Dunsmore discusses these issues with a range of key leaders in the military, the television networks, and high-level government officials to see whether any sort of consensus would emerge. He concludes that live television of the battlefield is going to happen sometime in the near future, as the technology allows it. The result is likely to be a threat to operational security, since it becomes more difficult for the military to control the flow of information to the enemy, although whether such information is likely to determine the outcome of the conflict is less probable. Dunsmore concludes that the implications of live coverage will produce new problems for journalists and the military, but also that it is unlikely that any guidelines regulating coverage will be agreed upon by all sides in the near future.

The way that international coverage has been influenced by geopolitical developments in the post–Cold War world is the subject of the next chapter. In Chapter 11 Pippa Norris considers how dominant news frames evolve, adapt, and change when confronted by new conditions. After World War II the Cold War frame provided a simple heuristic shortcut to identify the causes, and consequences, of U.S. foreign policy. From 1945 to 1989 the Cold War frame provided a simple story line for journalists to explain complex developments in countries from Hungary to Vietnam, Afghanistan, and Nicaragua. What happens to international coverage in the U.S. media once that frame disappears? To analyze this issue, Norris looks at a content analysis of network television news during three periods: 1973–1989, which is classified as the late Cold War years; 1989–1991, which is defined as the transition period; and 1992–1995, which represents the post–Cold War world. The end of the Cold War might be expected to influence the amount and priority of international news, the regions and countries that are regarded as newsworthy, and the themes of international news stories. The results of the content analysis confirm that the end of the Cold War has had significant consequences for how U.S. network news has framed international news. The end of the Cold War and the transition period were widely regarded as major news. Network news adapted fairly rapidly to the new geopolitical realities of the post–Cold War period, but the result has been a decline in international news, and in recent years those stories that were shown were shorter and further down the running order. The result is that although there are complex ethnic, regional, and religious conflicts in Bosnia, Haiti, and the Middle East and rapid change in new democracies such as South Africa and Russia, there is less opportunity for viewers of U.S. network news to make sense of these developments. We therefore have the paradox of more information than ever before available from conflicts around the globe, but perhaps less ability to understand this information.

Last of all, in Chapter 12 Steven Livingston reconsiders the effects of the media on public policy, particularly the supposed "CNN effect," which many believe has changed U.S. diplomacy and foreign policy. Despite numerous studies of the CNN effect, there remains considerable confusion about the nature and impact of 24-hour TV news on U.S. intervention around the world. In order to clarify this issue, Livingstone suggests that we need to develop a typology capable of distinguishing between several CNN effects, namely television coverage (1) as a policy agenda-setting agent; (2) as an impediment to a desired policy goal; and, (3) as an accelerant to decisionmaking. The chapter goes on to consider how these different CNN effects may have influenced decisionmaking concerning humanitarian operations, from Bosnia and Somalia to Zaire. Livingstone concludes that there are a range of potential media effects on different types of intervention, such as strategic deterrence, peacekeeping, and humanitarian aid, and we need to distinguish between these activities if we are to make any progress in understanding the effects of television coverage on foreign policymaking.

Therefore, this book aims to reconsider how recent developments have affected the gathering of news; the interaction among the media, public opinion, and elections; and the role of the news media in the public policy process. We can conclude that some of the concerns about political communication in the United States are exaggerated, but nevertheless there are some serious anxieties created by the transition to postmodern news. The modernization of political communications has produced a more fragmented and tabloid-like press, making it more difficult for political leaders to use the traditional news media as a bridge to connect with the public. Yet modernization has created new opportunities for a wider range of voices to be heard, as well as new dangers. We often hear the concerns of mainstream journalists, who express unease about these changes, but we hear less commonly from the younger generation who are adapting more easily to these changes and more diverse groups who have gained access through this fragmentation of traditional media. We will have to wait and see whether the anxieties about communications caused by this period of transition are borne out by future events.

Notes

1. Times Mirror Center for the People and the Press, *The People, the Press and Their Leaders* (Washington, D.C.: Times Mirror Center, 1995).

2. Neil Postman, *Amusing Ourselves to Death* (New York: Viking, 1985); Tom Patterson, *Out of Order* (New York: Vintage Press, 1993); James Fallows, *Breaking the News* (New York: Pantheon, 1996); Robert Putnam, "Tuning In, Tuning Out: The Strange Disappearance of Social Capital in America," *PS: Political Science and Politics* 27 (4), 1996: 664–683.

3. Jay Rosen and Paul Taylor, *The New News v. the Old News* (New York: Twentieth Century Fund Press/The Brookings Institution, 1992); Arthur Charity, *Doing Public Journalism* (New York: Guilford, 1995).

4. See Pippa Norris, *Electoral Change Since 1945* (Oxford: Blackwell, 1997).

5. For accounts, see Paul F. Boller, *Presidential Campaigns* (Oxford: Oxford University Press, 1985); David McCulloch, *Truman* (New York: Simon and

Schuster, 1992); Kathleen Hall Jamieson, *Packaging the Presidency* (Oxford: Oxford University Press, 1984); Larry Sabato, *The Rise of Political Consultants* (New York: Basic Books, 1981).

6. Harold W. Stanley and Richard G. Niemi, *Vital Statistics on American Politics* (Washington D.C.: Congressional Quarterly [CQ] Press, 1995).

7. The shift to 30-minute network news became standard only in 1963.

8. Stanley and Niemi, *Vital Statistics on American Politics,* p. 66.

9. Paul F. Lasarsfeld, Bernard R. Berelson, and H. Gaudet, *The People's Choice* (New York: Columbia University Press, 1948); Bernard R. Berelson, Paul F. Lasarsfeld, and William N. McPhee, *Voting* (Chicago: University of Chicago Press, 1963).

10. See, for example, Tom Patterson, *The Mass Media Election* (New York: Praeger, 1976); Jamieson, *Packaging the Presidency;* Wilson Carey McWilliams, *The Politics of Disappointment: American Elections 1976–94* (Chatham, N.J.: Chatham House, 1995); Larry Sabato, *The Rise of Political Consultants* (New York: Basic Books, 1981); Dan Nimmo, *Mediated Political Realities* (New York: Longman, 1990); Frank Luntz, *Candidates, Consultants and Campaigns* (Oxford: Basil Blackwell, 1988); Mathew D. McCubbins, *Under the Watchful Eye* (Washington, D.C.: CQ Press, 1992).

11. David Swanson and Paolo Mancini (eds.), *Politics, Media and Modern Democracy* (New York: Praeger, 1996); David Butler and Austin Ranney (eds.), *Electioneering* (Oxford: Clarendon Press, 1992); Shaun Bowler and David M. Farrell (eds.), *Electoral Strategies and Political Marketing* (New York: St. Martin's Press, 1992); Ralph Negrine and Stylianos Papathanassopoulos, "The 'Americanisation' of Political Communications: A Critique," in *The Harvard International Journal of Press/Politics* 1 (2), Spring 1996: 45–62.

12. Michael Schudson, *The Power of News* (Cambridge: Harvard University Press, 1995), pp. 169–188.

13. See Jean-Francois Lyotard, *The Post-Modern Condition* (Minneapolis: University of Minnesota Press, 1979); Jean Baudrilland, *Simulations* (New York: Semiotext, 1983); Jurgen Habermas, *The Philosophical Discourse of Modernity* (Cambridge: MIT Press, 1987); Krishna Kumar, *From Post-Industrial to Post-Modern Society* (Oxford: Blackwell, 1995).

14. See W. Russell Neuman, *The Future of the Mass Audience* (Cambridge: Cambridge University Press, 1993); Wilson Dizard, Jr., *Old Media, New Media* (New York: Longman, 1994); Michael X. Delli Carpini, "Voters, Candidates and Campaigns in the New Information Age," *The Harvard International Journal of Press/Politics* 1 (4), Fall 1996: 36–56.

15. Stanley and Niemi, *Vital Statistics on American Politics.*

16. Doris Graber, *Mass Media and American Politics,* 5th ed. (Washington, D.C.: CQ Press, 1997), p. 48.

17. Stanley and Niemi, *Vital Statistics on American Politics.*

18. See Paul Klite, Robert A. Bardwell, and Jason Salzman, "Local TV News: Mayhem, Fluff and Sports?" *The Harvard International Journal of Press/Politics* 2 (2), Spring 1997.

19. Penn Kimball, *Down-Sizing the News* (Washington D.C.: Woodrow Wilson Center Press, 1994).

20. See W. Lance Bennett, *News: The Politics of Illusion,* 3rd ed. (New York: Longmans, 1996).

21. For a cogent argument by a journalist, see James Fallows, *Breaking the News* (New York: Pantheon, 1996).

22. Tom Patterson, *Out of Order* (New York: Vintage, 1996), p. 52.

23. Robert Lichter and Ted Smith, "Why Elections Are Bad News: Media and Candidate Discourse in the 1996 Presidential Primary," *The Harvard International Journal of Press/Politics* 1 (4), Fall 1996: 15–35.

24. See Lawrence R. Jacobs and Robert Y. Shapiro, "The Rise of Presidential Polling," *Public Opinion Quarterly,* Summer 1995.

25. Pippa Norris (ed.), *Women, Media and Politics* (New York: Oxford University Press, 1997); David Weaver and G. Cleveland Wilhoit, *The American Journalist in the 1990s* (Mahwah, N.J.: Lawrence Erlbaum, 1996).

26. See James B. Lemert et al., *News Verdicts, the Debates, and Presidential Campaigns* (New York: Praeger, 1991).

27. For discussions of the role of advertising, see Darell West, *Ad Wars* (Washington D.C.: CQ Press, 1996); Stephen Ansolabehere and Shanto Iyengar, *Going Negative* (New York: Free Press, 1995).

28. See Stephen Ansolabehere and Shanto Iyengar, "Can the Press Monitor Campaign Advertising? An Experimental Study," *The Harvard International Journal of Press/Politics* 1 (1), Winter 1996: 72–86; John C. Tedesco, Lori Melton McKinnon, and Lynda Lee Kaid, "Advertising Watchdogs: A Content Analysis of Print and Broadcast Ad Watches," *The Harvard International Journal of Press/Politics* 1 (4), Fall 1996: 76–93; Kathleen Hall Jamieson and Joseph N. Cappella, "Setting the Record Straight: Do Ad Watches Help or Hurt?" *The Harvard International Journal of Press/Politics* 2 (1), Winter 1997.

PART ONE

GATHERING THE NEWS

1

Technology and the Future of Global Television

Richard Parker

Over the past forty years, television has transformed the ways all of us think about the news. Television's immediacy, and the unique quality it has of allowing us to "see" events unfold ten blocks—or ten thousand miles— away, has been unprecedented. But in a century saturated with novelty, that contribution, like so many innovations, has grown commonplace—so much so that few of us ever reflect that the meaning itself of the word, *tele-vision,* derives from the Greek root, *tele,* for "afar." But having absorbed that initial transformation in the way we receive the news, we are being led today to yet another momentous shift. This new transformation goes by several names; most commonly, it's referred to as "global" or "borderless" TV, and a great many newscasters, media moguls, and media critics alike insist "global" represents the future of TV.

But what precisely *is* "global television"? After "seeing" television's coverage of Tiananmen Square or the Gulf War, it's hard to doubt that some sort of transformation *is* going on. Each of these geographically distant events was not only changed by being broadcast "live," but because "we" as an audience were in some sense changed too—aware (as were the event's participants) that what we saw was being seen simultaneously in more than a hundred countries around the world. This new global television coverage—the extraordinary ability to broadcast events into hundreds of millions of homes around the world—has become (as commentators quickly pointed out) a part of the events, an essential in the grammar of change itself—so much, it seems, that the pundits, accepting that change, have been left to reflect on what responsibilities the new global TV journalists and TV news organizations now have toward their massive, cross-cultural audiences.[1]

This idea of "global television," of course, is about more than just news coverage and the enormous size of a mass, universal audience. It includes a technological component—of satellites and home satellite dishes, of cable and a nearly unlimited number of channels, of high-definition

21

reception and virtual reality and digitization and interactivity. It encompasses too a global programming menu of game shows, shopping channels, sports, movies, sitcoms, "soft" news, even "soft" porn. But most important, at its core, it implies the foundations of a common universal culture, in which we will someday see much the same programming no matter where we live—a final, dialectic completion of the late-nineteenth-century notion of "mass culture." Economically, it implies an equally expansive vision of a capitalist sanctum sanctorum, in effect, the ultimate "mass market" not only for global programming but global advertising, global products, and global consumer spending. Linked together through these common invented "vernaculars," proponents tell us we stand literally on the edge of an era when (no matter where we live) we will be able, at the flick of a button, to satisfy whatever interest, appetite, or fantasy we might have. The aim of this chapter is to outline the nature of the debate about the future of global television, to consider the way that economic factors will drive the development of communications, and to conclude that some of the more sweeping claims about the decline of national broadcasting systems and the rise of global television are premature and largely overdrawn.

The Debate About the Future of Global Television

Where are we heading? Are we all about to enter a century when satellites humming above us will bounce back identical and instantaneous information and entertainment whether we're in Kalamazoo or the Kalahari? Can we expect that cabled and digitized high-definition television carrying not just two, or ten, or even a hundred—but five hundred channels—will be universally available by the middle or end of the next century in our homes, our offices, even our cars, no matter where we live on the planet?

There is a strong debate about the future of television, dividing the advocates of the global television revolution, the critics of this development, and those who strike a middle path. For many the promise of global television appears unmistakable, and undeniable facts seem to point toward the accuracy of that promise. For example, CNN International already reaches more than 200 countries, with the overwhelming majority of the world's population; more than 120 communication satellites now beam TV pictures down to every inhabited continent on earth; the number of TV sets now in use exceeds 1.2 billion globally; and that symbolic cornerstone of the internationalized, yet individualized, TV future—the simple "home dish" receiver—may soon be almost as small and inexpensive as a television today. Today a host of anecdotal evidence points toward much the same conclusion, if in sometimes disarming ways.

- In Japanese homes today, TVs are more common than flush toilets.
- During the Gulf War, Iraqi troops carted off an estimated 50,000 satellite dishes—leading some CNN staffers to joke that what the Iraqis wanted was not oil but free TV.
- Filipino troops recently surprised and captured a guerrilla mountain camp because its revolutionary inhabitants were too busy watching MTV.
- *Los Simpsons* is now a top-rated show in Colombia and Argentina, while a Mexican soap opera, *The Rich Also Cry,* is winning massive audiences in Moscow.
- The United States alone now exports more than 120,000 hours of television programming annually just to Europe, and global trade in programming is growing at more than 15 percent per year.[2]

Little wonder, then, that John Eger, a former CBS News executive, could rhapsodize recently on his industry's future:

> [Global TV is] a technology that knows no barriers, no national boundaries and does not recognize any of the artificial divisions between the different people and places of the world. Here is a technology that does not recognize color, creed, race, or nationality. It is a technology that is supernational, acultural, alingual, a technology of sight and sound, of binary digits, that can indeed saturate the world.
>
> It is a technology that creates simply by providing the means—a flow of information and ideas—a force throughout the world that simply will not stop, however we may resist its flow. . . . [Global TV is a] truly vast and revolutionary change, propelled by our technology towards acceptance of the concept that we are indeed one people on Earth, one family living in one home, a family with common problems, concerns, and interests.[3]

But if to its advocates, the emergence of this vast new world holds out unlimited promise, to others the potential has at times seemed more ominous. During the late 1970s and early 1980s, broadcasters, governments, and media specialists alike were riven by the highly charged "New World Information Order" debate. At its height, the United Nations Educational, Scientific, and Cultural Organization's (UNESCO's) director pronounced global information flows "one of the greatest forms of inequality in the contemporary world." Even more condemnatory, Third World media critic Mustapha Masmoudi declared "the flagrant quantitative and qualitative imbalance" in North-South communications equal to nothing less than "a violation of national territories and private homes, and a veritable form of mental rape."[4]

By the early 1980s, the debate over the New World Information Order had begun to recede, faced with an inflamed opposition led by the U.S.

government and many Western media. Issues raised by it, however, have continued to reappear. At the same time, however, major changes in technology—increasing numbers of satellites, the proliferation of television sets, a growing number of channels—plus a new political climate, fed in the West by a movement toward "privatization" and in the Communist world by the collapse of the Soviet empire, have altered significantly the terms of the debate.[5]

But new technologies and regulatory models have not ended debates over television's purported future. Indeed, the two seemingly polar positions above—Eger's "lyric" vision and Masmoudi's "demonic" nightmare, for want of better terms—are well established in most modern discussions of TV's future. In recent years, though, a new, third position has emerged—held, interestingly enough, by some of television's most powerful and informed players. For example, to Silvio Berlusconi, president of the international media conglomerate Fininvest Group (and Italy's richest man), the future for "global television" is decidedly more complicated than Eger or Masmoudi would allow. Berlusconi says he agrees with the broadly popular notion that "the future belongs to global television." But he then quickly insists that its arrival lies off in a distant and uncertain future. "That future will be a long time coming," he says. "Not years but maybe decades, maybe more than a century."

These views find resonance, although in a different key, in Peter Fiddick's assessment of the same unfolding process. Fiddick is editor of *The Listener,* and to him much about the cheerful predictions of "borderless television" conceals a quite nationalistic and corporatist struggle over control of new wealth. To Fiddick, all too much of the talk about "globalization" is a corporate form of "happy talk," as international media giants go about the process of reorganizing and capturing control of new media markets and assets.

> In some cases we see the preemptive strike in action, as some media group stakes out a piece of territory to ensure against having to pay twice the price to retrieve it from a rival at some unknown future date. . . . Others, more versed in the niceties of mediaspeak, talk of the need to form an integrated network—vertically, horizontally, you name it—capable of giving a flexible response to the demands of the 21st century and so forth, when what they are really doing is more to do with getting big enough to be bid-proof.[6]

What both Berlusconi and Fiddick are pointing out is that ultimately global television—whatever its technological origins—seems destined to be profoundly driven by the emerging market economics and the market actors that increasingly shape the industry.

To Americans, acknowledging the role of markets and competition in television might seem a commonplace, unworthy of comment. But, in fact, it is crucial to understand the novelty of market economics shaping global television's development. For much of TV's first forty years (outside the United States),[7] the world of television was fundamentally one of government-owned stations broadcasting frequently on as few as one or two channels. From the 1950s up to the mid-1980s, "economics"—in the sense of competitive market economics—played little or no role, since the governments operated their television systems as public agencies. Sustained by a combination of taxes and viewer fees, advertising and competition between channels played virtually no part in television's global development.

In the future, how will economics shape the emergence of global television and, in particular, development of television news—the medium through which the majority in industrialized countries now get the news? Will competition and privatization of television open up new and competing sources of information? Will direct access by satellite act to erode authoritarian regimes, playing a role similar to shortwave during World War II and the Cold War? Will a handful of corporate owners emerge to dominate the new world? Will the flow of information become so truly diversified that the indictments embodied in the New World Information Order come to have no meaning? Will the average citizen in rural Africa or Asia find herself as able to be "informed" about the events and issues of the day as a government official or stockbroker in Washington, Tokyo, or London?

None of these questions offers simple answers. As we shall see, although competitive market economics has a crucial new role to play, the tradition of government involvement in broadcasting is by no means disappearing. In the following pages, I will argue that the prospects for global television—and especially television news—are neither so roseate as John Eger would have us believe, nor quite so oppressive as many in UNESCO once feared. Drawing on Berlusconi's and Fiddick's insights and on those of professionals in the television industry, I will try to show some of the likely patterns the globalization of television will follow over the next several decades, and both the innovations technological change will bring and the inherent limits—especially those around economics—that will intrude.

How the Economics of Television Works

A starting point for understanding the economic limits acting on the emerging market for global television lies in the history of other wonders of the Industrial Age. Television is by no means the first vaunted "revolution" industrialization has brought us. The electric light, telephone, radio, airplane, automobile, phonograph—all are widely celebrated and widely analyzed examples of earlier technological transformations that form cornerstones of the modern consumer society. Yet despite their "global" technological "availability" (in some cases, for more than a century), Americans especially sometimes forget that well over half the planet's population enjoys no routine access to virtually any of them. Sixty percent of the world's inhabitants, for example, have never even made a phone call.[8]

Consider the automobile for a moment. Mass production of automobiles began in the United States and Western Europe by the eve of World War I. By the mid-1920s, they were in use in virtually all countries around the world—but at widely different levels. Today, seventy years later, the automobile is most certainly "global"—yet still used at widely different rates, if measured on a per capita, country-by-country basis, and with much the same relative ranking of distribution as in the mid-1920s.

What is true of the automobile holds with striking regularity across a host of other modern technological innovations that citizens of the developed West today take for granted. Whether it's washing machines or sewing machines, stereos or dishwashers, the West's common exposure to advertising and the notion of an easily accessible consumer product culture (with its implied belief in the "egalitarianism" of access) is consistently belied by global data on household appliance and consumer electronics consumption.[9] Why, if technology is such a driving force, should this be so? The simplest answer, in economic terms, is that dispersion of new technology follows markets or the lack thereof. In the case of television's development, two crucial elements in market development have shaped dispersion to date: income and government policy.

For most people in most countries, *income* is the first crucial determinant of access to television (or autos, stereos, or other consumer goods). Indeed, most studies of country-by-country ownership of televisions show how simply such ownership correlates with per capita income. High income equals a high number of TVs per capita; low income equals a low number.[10]

But as income plays a leading role in the distribution of basic access to television, the second factor—*government policy toward television*—has been the other chief determinant of television's evolution. As noted, apart from the United States (and two or three other exceptions), virtually every country developed its television broadcast system as a terrestrially based, over-the-air government monopoly. Sometimes the system was considered a direct, ministerial part of the government, sometimes (the BBC is one example) a semi-independent public agency.[11]

In the excited talk about globalization and competition, it's sometimes forgotten how large these public systems still loom. Globally, the majority of people still live in countries where public broadcast monopolies have no domestic private competitors. In Western Europe and Latin America, which in the 1980s began allowing privately owned channels as competitors, these public systems still play a major role in broadcast. In countries with "dual" public-private systems—such as Britain, France, Germany, Italy, or Japan—in fact, the public broadcaster still is more watched than any private competitor. In revenue terms, moreover, the largest public systems (such as the BBC, Italy's RAI, or Japan's NHK) rank in revenue terms with private media giants such as Capital Cities/ABC, General Electric (GE), or CBS, even though the U.S. market is substantially larger.[12]

To date, in more than 160 countries that began with public broadcast monopolies, none of those broadcasters has gone out of business.[13] In the forty or so countries (primarily in Western Europe and Latin America) with dual public-private systems, public broadcasting—despite a great deal of talk in the 1980s about it being a "dinosaur"—shows no signs of withering away. Quite to the contrary, charged with becoming more competitive, these public systems may now accept advertising, use audience research, and generally behave in many ways as if they were private broadcasters.

As a consequence, although European public broadcasters in the 1980s experienced a sharp drop in audience share as new private channels proliferated (similar to the fall U.S. networks experienced, faced with cable), more recent information suggests public stations are now holding their own. With only a handful of exceptions, in fact, the public channels still capture the majority of the viewing audience against aggressive private competition and growth.[14] This survival—and in many countries, continued dominance—of the public broadcasters will greatly influence the evolution of global television patterns. Fundamentally committed to their national audiences, with a more complex mandate and agenda, and now increasingly competitive with private national alternatives, they are shaping the markets—and market entry terms—in a number of crucial ways.

Eli Noam, in his comprehensive *Television in Europe,* underscores this point in a way that fairly describes the complicated interaction of public and private interests over television's future outside Europe as well. Talking about the impact of video cassettes, satellite transmission, and cable technology on Europe's public TV in the 1980s, he cautions against viewing change as simply a product of technological innovation and private entrepreneurship. Noam emphasizes that the role of the public sector is going to loom large for a very long time.

> Clearly media issues are highly political. Broadcast media are part of our cultural reference and they help to set the political agenda-setting role. Competing groups vie for control over culture because it permits them to influence society. Thus, broadcasting institutions are often embroiled in controversy over values and politics.
>
> In the process, however, neither governments nor public broadcasters will become obsolete. The latter continue to have important functions, in particular producing or distributing programs that are not adequately provided otherwise. They are experienced organizations with an important mission and wide support, and they will not vanish. They may even improve as the privileges of their exclusivity vanish.[15]

Government's direct hand in broadcasting is far from the only means by which it is shaping television. As Noam mentions, governments have a myriad of means to profoundly affect the evolution of television well into the next century, at a minimum.

Through their systems, for example, they can directly control (or set standards for) entry and operation of the cable systems that compete with domestic over-the-air broadcasting. Although there are more private satellite operators now (such as Astra and Panamsat), governments—not private enterprises—will most likely launch, operate, and allocate transponder space on the majority of TV-carrying satellites. In addition, through promotion of domestic programming production and limits on "foreign" programming content, they can shape importantly many of the viewer choices their national audiences will have.

National economic policies will also play a crucial hand in the evolution of twenty-first-century television. The hard-fought struggle right now over standards for high-definition television (HDTV) is only one of a dozen seemingly "technical" issues that represent thousands of jobs and billions of dollars for the winners. In the post–Cold War era, with economics as the new centerpiece for competitive national relations, few governments will treat television in isolation. Who produces the new technology, who owns the broadcast systems and programming, and what standards will be accepted are as much an issue today as the once obscure issues of rail track width or electrical voltage standards seemed a century ago—with equally sizable economic implications. Americans who blithely imagine that global television will emerge as part of a Ricardian world of open trade and free competition do so at their own peril.[16]

What Are the Economics of Global Television?

If income levels and government policies are acting as crucial forces shaping the environment for global television, what are the economics of that system itself, especially as it emerges from its history of government monopoly? In theory, any global television system will be composed of several distinct elements, rather than forming a unitary whole. First, there must be a *delivery system*—designated over-the-air frequencies or a satellite or cable network—that can carry a television's electronic signal from point of origin to a television screen. Second, a *broadcast system* must exist—as a network, independent over-the-air or cable channel, or satellite broadcaster—that is capable of organizing programming and ensuring its placement on the delivery system. Third, a *programming system*—whether linked to or independent of the broadcast system—must conceive and create the programming (or organize the news or arrange for sports coverage) that the broadcast system carries. Finally, there must be a *financial payments system* underwriting all this—through advertising, viewer fees, or a tax of some sort—to allow the various systems, directly or indirectly, to operate.

From the early 1950s, when television began, up through the late 1970s, these four requirements were met on a national, not a global level. Governments (again, excepting the United States) generally authorized a single broadcast entity to organize, program, deliver, and financially operate single-nation, over-the-air television systems. Small elements of a global system nonetheless began to appear, however tentatively—programming was purchased from other countries, and there was some international exchange of news footage, sports events, and so on. But all of this was done within a national context, and the delivery of broadcast material between nations was done by sending videotape or film by mail or courier—in the trade, such delivery was called "bicycling," hinting at its simple origins.

However small and technologically primitive by modern standards, the international sale of programming was even so laying a crucial foundation for the modern possibility of global television—a rudimentary international TV market. Government broadcasters around the world operated with limited revenues and saw purchase of foreign programming through this market as a cost-saving measure when ranked against original domestic program production.

But what made such foreign programming so comparatively cheap? In economic terms, it reflected two crucial concepts. The first is the concept of "sunk costs" and applies to the seller: the programming offered in the international market had generally already been produced, shown, and paid for in its original market. Because in television new programming almost always is preferred by audiences to reruns, the economic value of such "old" programming plummets in its originating market. It is not without value—popular series can earn lucrative residual revenues—but profit-maximizing producers generally move on to creating "new" programming to earn greater revenues and profits domestically.

This leaves a secondary, foreign market where the program has not been shown before. Here we can see the second concept at work: how wide disparity in income levels and government dominance of broadcasting historically cooperated to shape the buyer's end of this international programming market.

Program producers sell a product—a single program or series, usually divided into half-hour or hour-long segments, or a movie—to a broadcaster, who in turn shows it to his or her audience. Of course, the seller hopes to sell the program to multiple broadcasters, each delivering (in theory) a national and hence geographically separate nonoverlapping audience. The most striking feature of these distinct audiences is their ongoing variation in value to the seller even today. Table 1.1, drawn from a 1993 industry

Table 1.1 Global TV Program Prices (Range Paid per Half-Hour Program in International Trade)

		Low $$	High $$		Low $$	High $$
North America				**India**	1,000	1,500
Canada	CBC English	12,000	60,000	Indonesia	700	1,200
	CBC French	10,000	25,000	Japan NHK	10,000	40,000
	CTV	10,000	60,000	Commercial	15,000	150,000
U.S.A.	Main network	100,000	2m	South Korea	750	1,500
	Pay cable	50,000	1.25m	Macau	1,400	1,700
	Basic cable	5,000	250,000	Malaysia[a]	1,000	1,600
	PBS network	50,000	250,000	Pakistan	400	600
	Syndication	30,000	100,000	Philippines	1,000	1,700
				Singapore	700	800
Central & South America				Sri Lanka	300	400
Argentina		1,500	5,000	Taiwan	600	750
Bolivia		200	350	Thailand	600	1,500
Brazil		2,500	12,000			
Chile		1,000	6,000	**Oceania**		
Colombia		2,500	6,500	Australia ABC	9,000	45,000
Costa Rica		500	1,500	Commercial	20,000	100,000
Ecuador		1,000	2,200	New Zealand	1,500	6,000
El Salvador		400	630			
Guatemala		330	450	**Middle East**		
Honduras		200	430	Abu Dhabi	500	875
Mexico		2,500	10,000	Bahrain	500	650
Panama		300	660	Cyprus	250	300
Paraguay		140	250	Dubai	600	875
Peru		700	1,200	Iran	750	1,500
Uruguay		300	660	Iraq[b]	800	1,000
Venezuela		5,000	7,000	Israel	500	1,350
				Jordan	600	800
Western Europe				Kuwait	1,000	1,200
Austria		2,600	6,000	Lebanon	300	500
Belgium		3,000	5,000	Malta	100	300
Denmark		2,000	4,500	Qatar	600	875
Finland		1,800	6,000	Saudi Arabia	1,500	2,000
France		6,000	60,000	Syria	400	650
Germany		15,000	80,000	Yemen (North or South)	500	1,500
Gibraltar		200				
Greece		1,500	4,000	**Africa**		
Iceland		600	850	Algeria	200	600
Ireland		1,500	2,000	Angola	200	600
Italy		8,000	60,000	Bophuthatswana	500	700
Luxembourg		1,300	4,000	Egypt	1,000	1,200
Netherlands		3,000	7,000	Ethiopia	200	600
Norway		1,500	5,000	Gabon	200	750
Portugal		2,000	4,000	Kenya	200	750
Spain		7,000	35,000	Mauritius	175	200
Sweden		2,500	5,000	Morocco	300	500
Switzerland		2,500	5,000	Namibia	400	425
Turkey		1,500	3,000	Nigeria	1,500	3,000
UK	BBC/ITV	20,000	100,000	Seychelles	125	175
	Channel 4	15,000	70,000	South Africa	2,000	7,000
	Satellite	1,000	70,000	Swaziland	100	200
	Cable	2,000	4,000	Tunisia	500	700
				Zambia	200	300
Eastern Europe				Zimbabwe	200	250
Albania		200	250			
Bulgaria		500	1,000	**Caribbean**		
Czechoslovakia		600	1,250	Aruba	80	100
Hungary		800	1,000	Bahamas	200	250
Poland		750	1,500	Barbados	200	250
Romania		700	1,000	Bermuda	100	200
USSR		1,000	5,000	Cuba	400	450
Yugoslavia		1,000	1,500	Dominican Republic	200	600
				Haiti	100	200
Asia & the Far East				Jamaica	100	200
Bangladesh		200		Netherlands Antilles	100	200
Brunei		250	500	Puerto Rico	1,500	7,000
China		1,000	2,000	St. Maarten	100	120
Hong Kong		1,000	1,500	Trinidad & Tobago	300	400

Source: TBI.

Notes: a. If telecast prior to Singapore.

b. Prices that could be commanded during normal times.

study, shows the average price range a program producer might expect, selling a single thirty-minute program to various broadcasters around the world.[17]

Note how selling a program to a U.S. network yields the producer as much as $2 million, whereas selling the same program to a French broadcaster nets between $6,000 and $60,000, and to a Chilean station as little as $1,000. Immediately, one can see what is a seminal issue for a would-be global television industry: although the global market for programming sold to multiple domestic broadcasters may be extensive (that is, covering a very large number of separate markets), the value of those broadcast markets varies enormously. Selling to just half a dozen of them, out of more than 160 worldwide, will produce more than 83 percent of all the potential available income globally for a program.[18]

Why is this so? One obvious factor, of course, is a market's size: smaller markets, with fewer people, should earn less than larger ones—other factors being equal. But other factors are not equal. As mentioned earlier, there is wide variation in personal income among these countries, irrespective of size. Thus in Africa, Asia, Latin America, and Eastern Europe, lower per capita incomes—and substantially fewer TV sets (hence smaller audiences)—not total population, account for much of the low price levels paid for programming.

But income and per capita TVs are not fully explanatory either. Western Europe, Canada, and Japan all have high per capita incomes; even adjusting for audience size doesn't explain why a program's value in the United States is four to six times greater per viewer than in other advanced industrial countries. In the United States, with high average incomes, competition among networks and stations, and an advertising-based revenue stream, program producers earn high gross revenues. When dealing with dual public/private systems in countries with similarly high incomes, though, clearly their ability to earn income falls. (When they sell into countries with a traditionally straightforward TV monopoly, little or no advertising, and low average incomes, their incomes plummet.) Why does a continuing government presence in these television markets apparently hold down programmer income?

The television markets of the advanced industrial countries other than the United States today are a public/private mix in which government channels still capture the largest audience share collectively and in which the amount of advertising carried on both public and private channels is strictly regulated. From the 1950s through the 1970s, these governments operated TV monopolies that had no particular reason to bid up the price of programming they purchased, nor to worry particularly about audience acceptance (and hence audience size) for the programs they broadcast. Viewers either watched, or they did not, and program purchase prices stayed low.

The historic fact of government monopoly alone should not presumably explain why in public/private systems today, programmer income is still lower than in the United States. After all, deregulation has existed long enough to approximate competitive, U.S.-style markets—or has it? The reality is that in these dual systems, in which the public broadcaster still relies for much of its income on license fees as well as advertising, an indirect cap is placed on private broadcasters' advertising income. By dividing the market between public and private channels, and with public channels capturing substantial license income, these public channels hold advertising rates below those a private-only market would have. This in turn lowers the income private channels are willing to spend on programming, whether imported or domestic.

Table 1.2 helps illustrate the point more clearly. A 1991 survey of TV advertising spending globally, it shows that spending, both gross and per capita, varies. In the United States, TV advertising approached $30 billion annually, with per capita ad expenditures at nearly $120. Japan, with a dual public/private system dating back to the American Occupation, and hence the oldest public/private competition, has the second highest overall spending ($12 billion) and per capita expenditure ($101). In Western Europe, where private channels basically date only from the late 1970s to the early 1980s, total TV advertising is slightly higher than Japan's (at $17.4 billion), but is spread across a population nearly 3.5 times larger. Per capita ad spending, as a consequence, is significantly lower—at $40, barely a third of that of the United States and Japan.

In Europe, lower per capita ad spending levels are compensated for, at least for public broadcasters, by their license fees. In 1991, gross West European license fees totaled nearly $12.9 billion—even as advertising revenues have grown as a percentage of their total income. Moreover, although private competition had taken off in the 1980s, license fees had risen steadily (both in nominal and real terms) throughout the period, allowing the public systems to hold their advertising rates below what they would have been had the systems been purely advertising-based.[19] This downward pressure on ad rates by the public systems in turn placed an upward cap on the rates the private competition could charge, since the public systems still held major audience share.

Table 1.2 also lets us grasp clearly how advertising plays a role in television outside the United States, Europe, and Japan—a crucial factor in any discussion of the possibilities for global television's success. Note how in Asia, for example, Japan plus Australia (with 6 percent of the region's population) accounts for over 80 percent of TV ad spending, or how all of Latin America, with a population 50 percent larger than the United States, amounts to 6 percent of the United States' TV ad revenues. Or, most striking, how Middle East ad dollars total barely $100 million, or how African TV ad spending (apart from South Africa) is virtually nil.

Table 1.2   Worldwide Television Advertising Expenditures

Region/Country	Population (Millions)	1991 Adv. Exp. (U.S.$M)	Adv. Exp. Per Cap. (U.S.$)	Forecast 1992 Adv. Exp. (U.S.$M)	Forecast Real Growth '92 v. '91 (%)	Forecast Real Growth '93 v. '92 (%)
Africa						
Kenya C	24.4	(3)	(0.1)			
South Africa C	35.3	311	8.8	337	8.3	6.4
Zambia	81.0	(0)	(0.0)			
Zimbabwe C	9.8	(5)	(0.5)			
Total	150.5	311	4.0	337	8.3	6.4
Asia/Pacific						
Australia C	17.1	1,257	73.5	1,231	−2.1	−0.7
China	1,135.0	88	0.1	107	21.4	21.3
Hong Kong C	5.8	485	83.6	507	4.6	6.4
India C	827.1	134	0.2	149	11.2	5.7
Indonesia C	179.3	109	0.6	152	39.5	21.4
Japan PC	123.5	12,466	100.9	12,778	2.5	2.4
Malaysia C	17.9	153	8.5	166	8.2	5.8
New Zeland PC	3.4	204	60.0	214	5.1	4.5
Pakistan C	113.7	(39)	(0.3)			
Philippines *C	61.5	126	2.0	141	11.8	17.5
Singapore C	2.7	112	41.5	127	13.6	7.4
South Korea *C	42.8	880	20.6	1,051	19.4	9.9
Sri Lanka C	17.0	(4)	(0.2)			
Taiwan C	20.4	688	32.7	809	21.1	23.6
Thailand C	57.2	306	5.3	332	8.4	8.4
Total	2,624.4	16,988	6.8	17,763	4.6	4.3
Europe						
Austria	7.6	261	34.3	289	10.6	−2.0
Belgium PC	9.8	397	40.5	412	3.9	1.1
Cyprus	0.7	(2)	(3.1)			
Denmark	5.1	158	31.0	183	15.8	8.7
Finland	5.0	160	32.0	154	−3.7	−0.6
France C	56.4	2,369	42.0	2,393	1.0	1.4
Germany	77.6	2,233	28.8	2,548	14.1	7.3
Greece C	10.0	310	31.0	377	21.5	21.2
Ireland	3.5	92	26.3	94	2.0	1.8
Italy	57.7	3,608	62.5	3,767	4.4	3.3
Malta**	0.4	(4)	(11.4)			
Netherlands C	14.9	385	25.8	407	5.7	4.2
Norway	4.3	39	9.1	61	55.9	71.6
Portugal PC	10.5	228	21.7	248	8.6	7.0
Spain	39.0	2,466	63.2	2,399	−2.7	−0.2
Sweden	8.6	80	9.3	141	76.4	25.3
Switzerland	6.7	153	22.8	153	0.1	2.8
Turkey	58.7	320	5.5	361	12.7	15.9
United Kingdom PC	57.4	4,176	72.8	4,264	2.1	3.7
Total	433.9	17,435	40.3	18,249	4.7	4.2

(continues)

Table 1.2   (continued)

	Population (Millions)	1991 Adv. Exp. (U.S.$M)	Adv. Exp. Per Cap. (U.S.$)	Forecast 1992 Adv. Exp. (U.S.$M)	Forecast Real Growth '92 v. '91 (%)	Forecast Real Growth '93 v. '92 (%)
Latin America/Caribbean						
Argentina PC	32.3	(251)	(7.8)			
Bolivia C	7.3	(47)	(6.4)			
Brazil PC	150.2	(1,826)	(12.2)			
Chile C	13.2	123	9.3	132	7.1	2.8
Colombia C	33.0	272	8.2	392	44.3	0.9
Costa Rica *C	2.8	(38)	(13.4)			
Dominican						
Republic C	7.1	(38)	(5.3)			
Ecuador PC	10.6	(27)	(2.6)			
Guatemala P	9.2	(11)	(1.1)			
Mexico C	86.2	800	9.3	882	10.2	8.1
Panama C	2.4	(32)	(13.3)			
Puerto Rico *P	3.5	316	90.3	302	–4.3	1.0
Trinidad &						
Tobago C	1.3	(9)	(7.2)			
Venezuela C	19.7	335	17.0	402	20.0	25.0
Total	378.8	1,846	11.9	2,110	14.3	8.6
Middle East						
Bahrain **	0.5	(5)	(9.8)			
Israel **	4.6	(20)	(4.3)			
Oman **	1.6	(5)	(3.1)			
Qatar **	0.4	(3)	(8.5)			
Saudi Arabia **	14.9	(50)	(3.4)			
U.A.E. **	1.6	(22)	(13.4)			
Total	23.6					
North America						
Canada	26.5	1,369	51.7	1,435	4.8	4.4
United States PC	250.0	29,580	118.3	29,225	–1.1	0.3
Total	276.5	30,949	111.9	30,689	–0.8	0.5

Sources: The figures in this table have been taken from two worldwide reports of national population and advertising expenditure data. Zenith Media Worldwide figures are without brackets and Starch INRA Hooper figures are in parentheses. NB: All the Zenith figures in the 1991 expenditure column are for 1991, whereas all the Starch INRA Hooper figures in the same column (in parentheses) are for 1990 only. For this reason the latter are not included in the region totals.

Country Codes:

P—Production costs included in expenditure totals, agency commission excluded.

C—Agency commission included in expenditure totals, production costs excluded.

PC—Both production costs and agency commission included in expenditure totals.

**—Neither production cost nor agency commission details are given.

*P—Production costs included, agency commission details not given.

*C—Production cost details not given, agency commission included.

No sign means both production costs and agency commission excluded from expenditure totals.

As we shall see, the size of the ad market outside the so-called Organization for Economic Cooperation and Development (OECD) countries (comprising basically the industrial West, Japan, and Australia) is a minor fraction of the monies spent inside the world's industrial core. Although deregulation is bringing rapid growth to many of these markets, the bases from which they start often are no larger than some city or county television ad markets in the United States. Would-be global broadcasters are by no means wholly dependent on advertising alone for potential revenues, but advertising is no small part of their strategy for profitability. Thus, once again, we are brought back to the realization of the role income and government policy—not just with regard to TV but also economic growth—are going to play in any future for global television. Far from being a matter simply of technology driving a global future, we are forced to wrestle with some of the oldest questions the world has faced.

The Emerging Global or Multinational Market

When Americans talk about "global television," the first image that usually comes to mind these days is CNN International. Now broadcast into more than 200 countries, it seems the very model for what is commonly meant by global television. In fact, it is only one part of the market for single-source, satellite-based, transnational broadcasting. Since CNNI's creation eight years ago, it has been joined globally by the BBC's World Service Television; by MTV's European, Latin American, and Asian efforts; and, on a regional basis, by Rupert Murdoch's Sky-TV and the EBU's Euronews in Europe, by the Middle East Broadcast Center in the Arab world, by Televisa's Eco and NBC's Spanish-language service in Latin America, and by South Africa's M-Net in Africa. In addition, there is almost daily talk of new global or regional satellite-based competitors, ranging from Japan's NHK to French-language broadcasting into Francophone Africa. With so much apparent activity in the global TV field and new entrants seemingly anxious to enter, it's helpful to distinguish at least three separate concepts that often intermingle when global television is discussed.

The first is *international* television, the oldest of the three categories, which suggests simply the transfer of television programming (or program licenses, etc., as distinct from hardware) through sale or barter between at least two countries. This particular form of trade dates back to the mid-1950s.

Second is the idea of *multinational* television, which suggests a more kaleidoscopic set of relations that includes much wider program transfer, coproduction of programming, regional (rather than national) broadcasting, and transnational ownership of broadcasting and production facilities. For the most part, this newer form began in the 1980s, with the technological and regulatory changes that characterized the decade.

Finally, there is the *global* television of the 1990s, with an expansive multinationalism that promises to make all, or at least a great portion, of the planet's TV audience available to a set of individual broadcasters.[20] It certainly includes many of the features of multinational television but in scope vastly transcends the regional ambitions of multinationalism.

The Dominance of International Programming

Global TV may be the topic of the hour, but of the three categories, international television is by far the largest in economic terms. Beginning in the 1950s, the United States built on its experience in theatrical motion picture exports by selling movies (either from studio libraries or, after an appropriate delay, following foreign theatrical release) to foreign broadcasters. In turn, European, Japanese, and smaller markets sought export markets for their own motion picture industries.[21] By the early 1960s, this process gradually began to include trade in television programs, particularly of domestically popular U.S. TV series.

From its inception forty years ago, however, this international trade in programming has been far from global as we commonly use the term. First, it was (and remains) overwhelmingly a bilateral, transatlantic affair, in economic terms. Second, it has been a decidedly one-way trade: measured in dollars, this international market has been one of Europeans buying U.S. exports.

International trade data show this concentration and flow pattern quite clearly. In 1989, for example, total world trade in TV programming amounted to $2.4 billion. Far from being broadly distributed among many trade partners, that trade was concentrated in very few hands: U.S. exports alone accounted for 71 percent of the total. Appetite for those U.S. exports, in turn, was similarly concentrated: Western Europe imported three-quarters (or $1.3 billion) of them. (By comparison, and as a measure of the one-way flow, U.S. imports of all foreign programming, not just from Europe, amounted to barely $160 million. That was just over 10 percent of U.S. exports, and barely 2 percent of U.S. programming hours.)

Put slightly differently, if one ignored the United States and Europe as TV program importers, the remaining 200 or so nations of the world (with nearly 88 percent of the earth's population) together in 1989 made less than $700 million in international programming purchases—barely a quarter of the global total.[22] One could—as some UN analysts and Third World critics have—more rightly refer to this not as international trade, but a dual-level trading system, overwhelmingly dominated by a Euro-American market, with only a distantly secondary global component. Or as one U.S. television executive bluntly put it, "This business is about as 'global' as a one-way New York-to-London plane ticket is a trip around the world."[23]

The market figures in Table 1.3 show in greater detail just how this nominally international television trade has behaved in recent years.

Table 1.3   Estimated International Program Exports, 1987 Projected to 1995

	1987	1989	1991	1993	1995
Exports ($ millions)					
United States	1,119	1,696	2,096	2,521	3,005
Western Europe	161	426	660	910	1,175
Other	194	273	393	566	815
Total	1,474	2,395	3,149	3,997	4,995
% of Total					
United States	76	71	67	63	60
Western Europe	11	18	21	23	24
Others	13	11	12	14	16
U.S. Export Market Share Compared to Other Imports (%)[a]					
In Western Europe	77	79	78	76	74
Outside Western Europe	75	71	62	60	57
Western Europe Export Market Shares Compared to Other Imports (%)[a]					
In United States	68	70	72	73	76
Outside United States	4	10	18	20	24

Source: Adapted from Neil Weinstock, *U.S. and International Programming* (Frost & Sullivan, New York, 1991).

Note: Because of rounding, percents may appear to add up to 101. "Western Europe" includes European Union Countries and Austria, Switzerland, and Scandinavia.

a. Does not include competition from domestic production.

Several things are noteworthy. First, the good news for Hollywood (and U.S. balance-of-payments) is that the aggregate international market for programming is still expanding rapidly—from 1987 to 1995, chiefly as a result of new European channels, the increase was from under $1.5 billion to nearly $5 billion—a more than threefold increase in nominal terms. As in the past, because it continues to purchase more than half the programming sold internationally, Western Europe still drives that growth, as it searches for ways to fill the explosion of total broadcasting hours now available on the continent as a result of the new broadcasters.

Although the United States has overwhelmingly been the beneficiary of this explosion in European television (at the beginning of the 1980s, United States to Europe exports were under $200 million), future market growth is not without major problems for U.S. studios. Within the overall global growth curve, the U.S. share of the total market is declining, even while growing in dollar terms. The significant news is that the most rapid growth of exports is from outside the United States—especially West European exports, which will effectively double their market share over the same period.

It is this shift—of U.S. sales growth, but at a slower rate than the total market, and the appearance of a sizable competitive West European export market—that is prompting new growth in what we have defined as the multinational (as distinct from the international) market for television. The implications, as we shall see, reach well beyond the old transatlantic trade.[24]

The Shift to Multinational Programming

Multinational broadcasting does not by itself imply a leap into a new era of globalism for television. Nor is it simply *replacing* the older international trade. Rather, it is supplementing the older form by forging a new category in television trade among nations. Its emergence in the 1980s directly reflects a tectonic shift in the transatlantic trade that has characterized that older—but very much still ongoing—international market. That shift was caused primarily by two changes in the European TV environment: first, the privatization and commercialization of TV itself (which we've already examined), and second, the rise of the European Community (EC) with its quest for an integrated, continental market.

With the arrival of competitive broadcasting and viewer choice, broadcasters discovered that an old shibboleth—that Europeans readily accepted foreign programming, even when dubbed or subtitled—was little more than a myth. Given the opportunity, viewers showed a decided preference for original programming in their own language, with characters, plots, and styles that reflected national—rather than Hollywood's—culture. (The preference for domestic programming is widely documented, and is discussed later in this chapter.) This discovery, however, presented a challenge to the broadcasters, because the cost of original production was decidedly higher than purchase of U.S. reruns.

A recent Annenberg Center study summarized the cost dilemma facing the new European broadcasters: "If considered as a single unit, the [European Community] may represent the largest media market in the world. . . . However, Europe's media industry is fragmented by culture, language, taste, and regulation . . . [consequently] there is no truly pan-European media market, and European media groups are relatively weak." One significant measure of that market fragmentation, the study notes, is that 85 percent of all European television programs are never transmitted beyond their original linguistic group.[25]

Thus, for the Europeans, a crucial issue in an environment where channels were proliferating and viewing hours growing was how to satisfy popular demand for domestic programming to relatively small audiences. "Coproduction" and "outside production" became the watchwords of the new multinational approach. By dividing costs and responsibilities through coproduction among production divisions or subsidiaries of two or more broadcasters, often from different countries, program producers could divide the costs and hence the risks associated with program production. By using independent producers, rather than the broadcasters themselves, to generate the programming, costs and risks could likewise be reduced for the broadcasters.

Measured in dollar terms, it is easy to see just how significant multinational programming is becoming. In 1992, coproduction and outside production represented more than $2.8 billion of West Europe's programming purchases; imports were $2.15 billion. By 1995, the gap had grown—multinational programming to nearly $5.3 billion, while imports rose only modestly, to $2.7 billion. Another measure of the spread of multinational coproduction comes from a survey conducted by the trade journal *Television Business International,* in association with the William Morris Agency. Conducted in late 1989, the survey—which was extensive, but by no means comprehensive—found seventy-eight active coproductions in France, eighty-two in the UK, fifty-two in Germany, forty-two in Italy, sixty-one in the United States, twenty-five in Canada, and dozens more scattered among the smaller states of Europe.[26]

The mention of sixty-one U.S. coproductions indicates that the new multinational programming wave is far from an exclusively European phenomenon. As European television has grown, U.S. producers—accustomed under international trade to "owning" the market for imported programs—have recognized the threat posed by the multinational alternative, especially since the "multinational" threatened to become, more accurately, "multi-European" in scope.

A second factor has been at play in the U.S. reaction to the growth of multinational production. For years, European cultural critics had denounced the "Hollywoodization" of European cultural life—first through movies, and then through the heavy purchase of U.S. programming by European public broadcasters. One of the most powerful arguments against privatizing European television came from those critics, who feared that more channels would open a floodgate to U.S. sitcoms and melodramas such as *Dallas* and *Dynasty.* The French particularly—personified in then Minister of Culture Jack Lang—goaded the European Community into looking carefully at setting restrictive quotas on further imports of U.S. TV shows. In the end, as set forth in eventual EC reports and guidelines, the threatened "quotas" proved to be far from restrictive and so loosely drawn as to be ineffectual, but the warning was heard on both sides of the Atlantic.[27]

A recent U.S. industry study makes clear the implications that Hollywood took from Europe's change of television regimes in the 1980s:

> U.S-based and other foreign producers who would sell their teleproductions in the Europe of the 1990s must increasingly (a) engage in coproductions with the Europeans; (b) produce their own shows partly in Europe; and (c) help distribute European productions elsewhere, in order to maintain access to their European markets. . . .
>
> Large U.S. producers, eager to extend their sales successes in Europe, can [also] be expected to cooperate with Europeans to produce shows saleable in the U.S., thus changing the long tradition of ratings disasters for foreign shows on U.S. TV. Only those European producers willing and able to work closely with U.S. partners and buyers will achieve this export success.[28]

The result is that multinational programming now is growing quickly—indeed, quite surprisingly so. The consulting firm Booz Allen and Hamilton, examining the dynamics of the coproduction field, estimated that it is expanding at the rate of 30–40 percent per annum, with the increase heavily concentrated—as one would predict—in the cost-intensive film-for-TV, drama, and miniseries segments of the industry. Sampling fifty coproductions, totaling 275 hours of broadcast time, Booz Allen furthermore found that U.S. producers were extensively responding to the "multi-European" threat to their historic market share for programming exports. Although "inter-European" coproductions made up 40 percent of their sample, "European–United States" deals were close behind at 34 percent, with the remainder a mixed bag of "Euro–United States–Other" deals, ranging from bi- to multilateral partnerships.[29]

Conclusion

Why are these two markets—in international and multinational production and trade—so important in understanding the evolution toward a would-be global television village? First, their form—their heavy reliance on the European and U.S. markets—lets us see once again how important income is in shaping TV markets. The affluence of Europe and the United States has meant that, for the past forty years, the international trade has really been primarily a bilateral, transatlantic trade. Nonetheless, international trade, although economically minor, has allowed broadcasters outside this axis to become experienced in program exchange. Thus, the claim of novelty for at least one part of what proponents cite as a "new" globalism is instead well established and quite familiar, even though less important economically.

Second, focusing on multinational programming can also let us see that the new technology and regulatory environment of the 1980s—which supporters cite as laying the ground for globalism—is spawning a process that is decidedly more complex. As European broadcasters discovered in the 1980s, the demand for foreign programming—once a decent quality, locally produced alternative is available—is substantially less than they had imagined and less than critics of "Hollywoodization" had so vocally feared. This represents no small challenge to proponents of a global TV future, because it suggests that rather than serving to *unify* separate national markets, the changes of the 1980s are actually *strengthening national broadcast systems,* even as the number of broadcasters per country grows.

Indeed, too much focus on international and multinational markets can lead us astray from a central fact almost never underscored in the discussion of globalizing television: the vast majority of programming is produced, aired, and remains in a single country. In the United States, of course, this has always been true: barely 2 percent of program hours broadcast come from overseas, mainly British imports. The same has always been true of the lucrative Japanese market as well. As noted earlier, when the EC set out to consider quotas on foreign (i.e., U.S. TV) imports, it in fact discovered—after a decade of channel and broadcast hour proliferation—that 85 percent of all broadcast hours in Western Europe are conceived, produced, aired in—and never leave—their country of origin.

These conclusions are not limited to the huge transatlantic market either. If we look at aggregate programming expenditures globally, we are likewise led—contrary to the image of an emerging globalism—to the same conclusion. By comparison to the $2.4 billion trade in international programming, for example, the sum of spending by broadcasters on their domestic programming is more than $70 billion, measured in U.S. dollars.[30]

In short, on the eve of a presumed new global era for television, domestic—not international, or even regional—broadcasting is surprisingly powerful, if measured in terms of programming. The changes brought by the 1980s may have made foreign programming more technologically available than ever before, but the actual use of such programming in the schedules of most broadcasters is quite small—forty years after the international programming trade was first created.

By itself, this does not refute the idea that a world of more homogeneous programming will emerge—but it does suggest why so knowledgeable an industry player as Silvio Berlusconi could say, as noted at the beginning of this chapter, that global television will be a long time coming. Not years but maybe decades, maybe more than a century. And coupled with the fact (discussed earlier in this chapter) that national public broadcasters remain a powerful force, with large audiences and a strong interest in preserving not only their own roles but an identifiable national TV culture that justifies those roles, this realization of the size of domestic versus international markets is of no small significance. Linked together, local broadcasters will find new and innovative roles to play, unimagined in the global debate that assumed their demise. Stranger things have happened. It wasn't long ago that the giant mainframe computers of IBM and a handful of other multinational giants seemed ready to define the "Computer Age," only to be struck down by the lowly PC. If the "Global Television Age" seems destined to share its time in history with the computer, its companion's experience offers a salutory lesson in the need for modest claims about knowing what lies ahead.

Notes

1. For a sample of commentary on television and the Gulf War, for example, see Thomas Allen et al., *CNN: War in the Gulf* (Marietta, Ga.: Turner Publishing, 1991); Robert Weiner, *Live from Baghdad* (New York: Doubleday, 1992); or Douglas Kellner, *The Persian Gulf TV War* (Boulder, Colo.: Westview Press, 1992). The most excoriating, and informative, is probably John MacArthur, *Second Front: Censorship and Propaganda in the Gulf War* (New York: Hill and Wang, 1992).

2. These anecdotes are from "Tuning In the Global Village," *Los Angeles Times,* October 20, 1992, Section H ("A World Report Special Edition").

3. John Eger, "Prometheus Revisited," Inaugural Address, Institute for Humanistic Studies, Tokyo Institute of Technology, October 7, 1991. Eger is former senior vice president, CBS Broadcast, and managing director, CBS Broadcast International, as well as former director, White House Office of Telecommunications Policy. For a more academically sober but nonetheless highly optimistic assessment of global television's potential, see the late MIT sociologist Ithiel de Sola Pool's *Technologies Without Boundaries* (Cambridge, Mass.: Harvard University Press, 1990).

4. The UNESCO director is quoted in *Final Report: Intergovernmental Conference on Communication Policies in Latin America and the Caribbean* (Paris: UNESCO, 1976), pp. 23–24; Mustapha Masmoudi is quoted in "The New World Information Order," in Jim Richstad and Michael H. Anderson, *Crisis in International News* (New York: Columbia University Press, 1981), pp. 77–96.

5. For a concise summary of the NWIO debate, see George Gerbner et al., *The Global Media Debate: Its Rise, Fall, and Renewal* (Norwood, N.J.: Ablex, 1992). Much of the debate focused on print, rather than television, in fact.

6. Peter Fiddick, "The Global Village," *Gannett Center Journal* (Winter 1989): 92, 99–100. See also Anthony Smith, *The Age of Behemoths: The Globalization of Mass Media Firms* (New York: Twentieth Century Fund, 1992), for a careful and critical look at multinational corporatization of media.

7. U.S. TV, of course, has not been a perfect model of laissez-faire competition, by any means; on the role of the FCC (and the federal government in general) in the economics of U.S. broadcasting, see Bruce W. Owen and Steven S. Wildman, *Video Economics* (Cambridge, Mass.: Harvard University Press, 1992) for a representative account.

8. Cf. Chris Irwin, "Address to the New Delhi Press Club," March 5, 1992 (London: BBC/WST, mimeo).

9. Even in the United States, patterns of dispersal heavily follow income lines. Cf. Anne Wells Branscomb, "Who Owns Information," in Pavlik and Dennis, *Demystifying Media Technology,* (Mountain View, Calif.: Mayfield, 1993), chap. 6.

10. Even in the United States, income has been a crucial factor in rate of dispersal for communications technology; see John Carey, "Looking Back to the Future: How Communication Technologies Enter American Households," in Pavlik and Dennis, *Demystifying Media Technology,* pp. 33–39.

11. Eli Noam gives an excellent summary of this pattern. Cf. Eli Noam, *Television in Europe* (New York: Oxford University Press, 1991), especially chap. 1.

12. In 1991, TV broadcast revenues were the following (in billions): NHK, $3.9; GE, $3.2; Capital Cities/ABC, $3.0; RAI, $2.9; CBS, $3.0; BBC, $1.7. Turner Broadcasting reported $1.14, of which CNN International was only $28 million. Cf. "Top 25 Public Broadcasters" and "Top 25 Private Broadcasters," *TBI Yearbook '93* (London: 21st Century, 1993), pp. 346–347 for size comparisons.

13. Singapore, with the proposed sale of SBC, and Mexico, with the sell-off of Imevision, have become the first. Cf. "Sale of the Decade," *Television Business International (TBI),* May 1993, pp. 24ff, on Mexico, and *TBI Yearbook '93*, p. 161, on Singapore. Brazil, though operating a public system, historically has been dominated by private TV, particularly the giant Globo.

14. Cf. Charles Brown, "Public Service Blues," *TBI,* May 1993, pp. 64–72.

15. Noam, *Television in Europe,* pp. 8–9.

16. For an insightful look at the politics and economics of "technical" standard-setting, cf. U.S. Department of Commerce, *Globalization of Mass Media* (Washington, D.C.: Government Printing Office, 1993), esp. pp. 37–42.

17. "Global Program Price Guide," *TBI,* May, 1993, p. 76.

18. And because sales effort is obviously not cost-free, the rational program producer will concentrate selling efforts in those markets first designed to yield the maximum revenue. The smallest markets will in fact either be ignored, or left to defray the program seller's costs by allowing buyers to initiate contact, either directly or by transacting the sale at some public marketplace where the seller's costs are distributed over multiple potential buyers. Cf. National Acadamy of Television Arts and Sciences, International Council, *1993/1994 Almanac* (New York, 1994) for an extensive listing of the global TV trade fairs each year.

19. Cf. "New Ways of Paying for Television in Europe," *TBI Yearbook '93* (London, 1993), pp. 353–356, for an overview and country-by-country analysis of licensing and advertising for public broadcasters.

20. A more expansive definition of "global" television is offered by Negrine and Papathanassopoulos, although the terminology is slightly different—they use "internationalization" to describe what I call "global." Cf. Ralph Negrine and Stylianos Papathanassopoulos, *The Internationalization of Television* (New York: Pinter, 1990), especially pp. 1–2.

21. Five countries—the United States, France, Italy, Britain, and Germany—account for 80 percent of all films that all countries import for television broadcast. Cf. UNESCO, *World Communication Report* (Paris: UNESCO, 1989), pp. 160–161. The percentage is for nonsocialist countries prior to the collapse of the Warsaw Pact.

22. Of course, given the extremely low sale price of programming to countries outside the industrialized core, low dollar volume in such trade understates the potential audience reached in these 150 or so countries.

23. Off-the record interview with author, May 5, 1993.

24. Cf. Jean-Luc Renaud, "'Fortress Europe' Won't Be What Many Believed," in *Television/Radio Age International* (April 1989): 71–77, for an excellent summary of the shifting European market for U.S.—and European—programming.

25. Anton Lensen, *Concentration in the Media Industry: The European Community and Mass Media Regulation* (Washington, D.C.: Annenberg Washington Program, 1992), pp. 5, 8, 10.

26. Barrie Heads, "Co-productions: A Guide to Who's Doing What," *Television Business International* (October 1989): 126–134.

27. Cf. the EC study, "Television Without Frontiers" (Brussels, 1991), as well as a critical review of EC policy in Lensen, *Concentration in the Media Industry.*

28. Neil Weinstock, *U.S. and International Programming* (New York: Frost and Sullivan, 1991), pp. 9–10.

29. Booz Allen and Hamilton, "Strategic Partnerships as a Way Forward in European Broadcasting" (n.p., n.d.).

30. On Euro programming, see Lensen, *Concentration in the Media Industry;* on global programming, Neil Weinstock, *U.S. and International Programming,* p. 2. Inevitably some small portion of this domestic programming does enter international trade, but the order of magnitude stands.

2

Marketing News

Alison Carper

Journalism in the United States has always had two warring halves. On the one side, it is a public service, armed with staunch principles about the people's right to know. On the other, it is a business, invigorated by hearty profits or by profits' allure. Its success has always depended on keeping both halves strong, because a wound to one side—principles or financial strength—debilitates the other.

Yet, in the past thirty years or so, the business side of journalism has assumed an unyielding dominance. Newspapers across the country have been sold by families to corporations. Motivated by the medium's potential for profits, executives of these corporations have strived to make each quarter's earnings exceed the last. They have struggled to please shareholders. They have labored to make circulation figures meet their guarantees to advertisers. They have fretted about the cost of newsprint and delivery. In more recent years, however, the executives' concerns have changed. Rather than worry about profitability, they have become anxious about their industry's very survival. The reasons for this shift are not hard to discern.

Recessions have undermined the stability of newspapers' advertising base. New sources of information and entertainment have drawn subscribers away. And, most ominously, a declining regard for the written word has eroded the habit of reading. Taken together, these trends seemed to raise the specter of newspapers' extinction. Without drastic reforms, the executives believed, their industry might well disappear.

What to do? Besieged by adverse social and economic trends and plagued by the profit demands of shareholders, the executives went searching for a remedy. They found a plausible one in a prescription offered by industry consultants: use market research techniques to find out what readers want and then give it to them. The very same tools that brought prosperity to manufacturers of soap and automobiles—public-opinion surveys and focus groups—could restore the newspaper industry to health, the consultants advised.

It was, of course, up to editors to adopt this advice—editors who, at one time or another and to varying degrees, were likely to harbor lofty notions about the purpose of their profession. Like all journalists, they had been schooled in the traditions of free speech, and they knew that the liberty they enjoyed was preserved by the Constitution for one reason: newspapers inform the citizenry, and in a democracy, citizens must be informed in order to fulfill the demands of self-governance.

In recent years, then, these editors have faced a need to reconcile two objectives, the fulfillment of their democratic function and the assurance of their own survival. As a result, they have found strong journalistic justifications for using marketing techniques to shape the news. In this chapter, I argue that the goals of marketing are largely in conflict with the role that the press should play in a democracy.

The Growth of Marketing Techniques

Journalism's adoption of marketing techniques has affected nearly every newspaper in the United States. In some cases, editors call upon focus groups for guidance. Sitting behind one-way mirrors, they listen to comments about their newspaper by a dozen or so readers or "potential" readers. An industry consultant, hired by the newspaper, serves as the group's moderator, asking questions and giving shape and order to the discussion. Often, the members of these focus groups are randomly selected from the paper's readership area, but not always. Sometimes they are chosen from a particular demographic group to which the paper especially wants to appeal, such as women or young people. In either case, consultants are obliged to warn editors that no focus group speaks for an entire community. Nonetheless, editors are naturally tempted to generalize from the comments they hear.

Editors also use reader surveys to acquaint themselves with the tastes and sentiments of their community. Again, the newspaper itself, or its corporate headquarters, will often work with a consultant to write the survey. The questionnaires are usually mailed to readers or appear as coupons in the paper. Some newspapers, however, do not undertake research of their own, but use that which has been gathered by others, such as by the headquarters of their parent newspaper chain or consultants who make the results of their work available to the newspaper industry as a whole.

At Knight-Ridder, one of the country's wealthiest newspaper chains, papers carry out their own research. Each of the corporation's twenty-nine papers probes its readership—using a survey or focus group—at least once every twenty-four months. The chain has also conducted concentrated campaigns to find out what readers want. When it redesigned its *Boca Raton News* in 1990, it drew upon more than thirty focus groups for guidance.[1]

At Gannett, all but one of the company's eighty-three dailies is required to adopt a detailed strategy that will allow it to find out what its readers want and give it to them. The exception to the companywide program—known as News 2000—is *USA Today,* a paper that was conceived of and created by the kind of market research that is now saturating the rest of the chain.

Gannett's mandate does give each paper the freedom to execute News 2000's imperatives in its own way. In Washington state, editors at the *Olympian* took steps to satisfy the program's requirements by sending reporters to shopping malls and other public places to pass out surveys that asked readers to rate their news preferences.[2]

In Little Rock, the chain's *Arkansas Gazette* distributed reader surveys that had two columns, one for hard news, one for soft. From column A, readers were asked to check off whether they wanted more news about Europe, the Middle East, the governor, the legislature, or the county, and from column B, whether they wanted more advice on infants, teenagers, dating, retirement, or single parenting.[3]

Gannett owns more papers than any corporation in the United States. Knight-Ridder ranks second. These chains are indeed prominent in the industry. But their embrace of marketing techniques does not encompass the whole movement. Rather, these companies are emblematic of a still larger trend. One can cast a line in any direction to find other newspapers that use marketing methods to shape news content: the *Chicago Tribune, Wall Street Journal,* and *New York Times* are three prestigious examples.

Although these papers do use surveys and focus groups, marketing has, generally speaking, least affected the content of the country's biggest and most prestigious dailies. Yet upon inspection one can see its mark even on some of them. The *Boston Globe,* for example, reaches out to readers by periodically asking them a question on the front page and inviting them to call in their responses. The *Los Angeles Times* prints a local news summary on the left-hand column of the front page of its Orange County edition. And the *Philadelphia Inquirer* sandwiches brief story summaries between the headline of an article and the text. Whether or not these features can be traced to specific surveys by each newspaper, the modifications are consistent with recommendations by market researchers who distribute their findings industrywide.

Many market-driven changes in the biggest papers are modifications in format, such as art and layout, rather than in the content of the news. Yet, there are exceptions. At the *Atlanta Journal-Constitution,* a paper whose Sunday circulation of around 700,000 makes it among the country's largest, a major readership research drive was followed by radical changes in news content, including shorter articles and more briefs and graphics in place of stories.

But generally speaking, it has been at medium-sized and small papers—and primarily those owned by chains—that market-driven modifications have had the greatest effect. The *Orange County Register, Seattle*

Times, and the *Olympian,* for example, have been profoundly influenced by market research. Like the *Atlanta Journal-Constitution,* editors at these papers have shaped news content, not just format, to cater to the demands of the market.

Adherents of the marketing school say surveys and focus groups produce newspapers that respond to the needs of people. This chapter will argue that they have the opposite effect. Gratifying readers' wants is not the same as satisfying their needs, and indeed, I will argue, a preoccupation with the former can disable newspapers from achieving the latter. I also hope to show that in responding to the wishes of readers, editors produce papers that are rigidly formulaic. Using marketing tools, then, does not produce a creative new kind of journalism but rather the newspaper equivalent of paint-by-numbers art.

When did the marketing trend begin? If a single year had to be assigned, it would be 1977, when the American Newspaper Publishers Association and the Newspaper Advertising Bureau joined forces to address what the industry saw as an impending crisis of declining readership. Together the associations created a $5 million Readership Project, and the project turned to market research for its answers. The first major study that the project commissioned drew upon focus group discussions with newspaper readers and prospective readers in twelve cities. Conducted by market researcher Ruth Clark and distributed to the organization's 3,500 members, the study, called "Changing Needs for Changing Readers," had the effect of legitimizing the use of market research in shaping editorial content. It launched the marketing trend.[4] The study suggested that newspapers adopt both format and content changes. It suggested greater use of news summaries, briefs, graphic aids, "coping" stories, and "good" news. And it recommended that papers run less national, foreign, and government news.[5]

Clark believed that the future of newspapers lay in the willingness of editors to cater to the demands of the 1970s' Me Generation, a generation that wanted to hear less about national and world events and was hungry for "news" about the lifestyle issues of people exactly like themselves. In effect, Clark recommended that newspapers draw a curtain over the window on the world that they had traditionally offered their audience and hand readers a mirror instead.

In the years since Clark's report, dozens of publications urging newspaper executives to survey their readers were circulated by the American Newspaper Publishers Association and the American Society of Newspaper Editors. Some bore apocalyptic titles, such as, "Keys to Our Survival."[6] Others were less melodramatic in tone but just as pointed in message, such as, "Readers: How to Gain and Retain Them."[7] The industry publications *Editor and Publisher* and *Presstime* joined the marketing bandwagon with a parade of articles. They appeared under such headlines as "Whoever

Stays Closest to the Customer Will Win"[8] and "Reviving a Romance with Readers Is the Biggest Challenge for Many Newspapers."[9]

Conferences, conventions, and seminars for newspaper executives also became popular forums in which industry consultants tried to persuade editors to use surveys and focus groups.[10] Whether for an industry report, article, or oral presentation, the formula suggested was the same. It included, on the one hand, more "quick reads"; "escape" or upbeat news; entertaining articles; "multiple points of entry," such as graphic aids and sidebars designed to ease the reader into the main news story; and news-you-can-use, or, as communication theorists call it, "immediate-reward news," which generally consists of a health, coping, or lifestyle tip that resonates right away with the reader. On the other hand, it offered less foreign, national, and government news—indeed, with the exception of crime stories, less "hard news" altogether.

The drive to promote the marketing approach has had its effect—both on newspapers and on the minds of their executives. Over the years, even the rhetoric of executives has changed to reflect the new influence. It is not uncommon to hear editors refer to readers as "customers" now. One often hears the newspaper called the "product."

The following statements from a few of the country's publishers and editors are evidence of the depth of the new marketing mentality:

> We must sell ourselves like Chevrolet and Ivory Soap.
> —Wayne Ezell, editor of the *Boca Raton News*[11]

> We try to listen and tailor our product to the marketplace. Our readers tell us, "We don't want to work terribly hard; we don't want to struggle through what you're trying to tell us." They like stories they can use for their coffee-break talk.
> —John Gardner, publisher of the *Quad-City Times* in Iowa[12]

> We're trying to put out a newspaper for a whole new generation of newspaper scanners out there who expect to develop a conversational knowledge of what's in the paper based only on reading the headlines.
> —Dan Hays, editor of the *Quad-City Times*[13]

> The surest way to editorial failure is to impose upon readers our own sense of what they ought to know. We must judge the value of what we publish in *their* terms.
> —Michael Fancher, editor of the *Seattle Times*[14]

> News is what our readers say it is.
> —Steve Crosby, editor of the *Wausau Daily Herald* in Wisconsin[15]

Two kinds of modifications are urged by marketing enthusiasts, and an important distinction must be drawn between them. The first affects newspaper *format,* and while such changes have been dramatic in recent years, the limited scope of this chapter does not allow me to discuss those changes here. The second modification affects editorial *content,* and it is with this that the remainder of this chapter will be concerned because it is the shaping of news content to appeal to an audience's preferences that conflicts with the historical mission of journalism.

One could turn to any number of newspapers to find examples of how editorial content is shaped to correspond to readers' tastes, but the *Atlanta Journal-Constitution* offers a portrait that is more vivid than most, so it is on that paper I will draw for illustrations. On Sunday, April 3, 1994, there were only eleven pages of local, national, and foreign news in the 138-page *Journal-Constitution.* The front page carried only three stories, only one of which jumped. The dominant story was a feature about local churches' preparations for Easter services. The page's lead story, about North Korea's growing capacity to produce nuclear weapons, was only six paragraphs long.

Dominant stories on the front page recently have also included a feature, on a Sunday, that revealed that baby boomers are going to bed earlier.[16] In May of 1992, after a cyclone hit Bangladesh and killed 125,000 people, the story was found inside while the front page included a piece on the opening of a McDonald's at the city's public hospital and a dispute between the city and caterers who provide food in an Atlanta park.[17]

That same year, *Journal-Constitution* editor Ron Martin told the *Washington Journalism Review* that the days when reporters went out, gathered a story, and wrote it up are over. Reporters now work as part of a team, along with editors and artists, and together they come up with news "packages."[18] At the *Journal-Constitution* and elsewhere, government, national, and foreign stories are a frequent casualty of the market-driven approach.

Boca Raton News editor Wayne Ezell acknowledged this with admirable candor in an interview with *Washington Post* media correspondent Howard Kurtz. Asked if he would stop carrying foreign news if focus groups said they were not interested, Ezell said, "That would tell me they're not reading it, so why should I have it? If readers said they wanted more comics and less foreign news, in a market-driven economy, I'm going to give them more comics and less foreign news."[19]

Newspapers that embrace the marketing approach often find themselves practicing a particular kind of formula journalism—the kind that emphasizes format at the expense of content. At the *Boca Raton News,* the drive to have the news fit into a predetermined format has shifted positions of power in the newsroom. Under the old arrangement, a copy editor was subordinate to a reporter. But when the paper's format took precedence over the content of news stories, it was the copy editor—who "pushes, pummels and pounds the writer's words to fit the format"—who gained the upper hand.[20]

The marketing approach to news content also has caused some papers to scale down their emphasis on traditional beats, including government coverage, and create new beats that reflect those topics they believe readers care about most. In Wausau, Wisconsin, editors at the *Daily Herald* consolidated the city, county, and suburban government beats and reassigned the two reporters who lost their beats to general assignments. Steve Crosby, the Wausau paper's editor, said that, in fact, city hall news has become so rare in the *Daily Herald* that "the mayor calls and complains."[21]

In Rochester, New York, readers of the *Democrat and Chronicle* also find less government news in their paper now. Editor Barbara Henry says the paper is "not as nose-to-the-grindstone on city hall and the county legislature [as it used to be]. Yes, we still cover them, but we don't do it in the nitty-gritty way we used to."[22]

Lou Heldman, who directed Knight-Ridder's remake of the *Boca Raton News,* says that his editors have learned that government stories are more expendable than other types of news. They "tend to be the first thing dropped when the space crunch comes," he said.[23]

Meanwhile, at the *Orange County Register,* "shopping malls" and "car culture" beats have been created, as have weekly pet and hobby sections.[24] And, while minimizing government stories, the *Boca Raton News* makes an effort to satisfy readers' demands for "good" news with a "Today's Hero" column, which highlights the heroic side of a local resident each day.[25]

Lou Heldman of Knight-Ridder says he believes that the purpose of the *Boca Raton News* is to do "a good job of explaining the world for people who don't want the world in great depth."[26] The paper is replete with opinion columns, sports a bold front-page box that tells readers where the comics are, and is filled with briefs on everything from local to national to entertainment news. Depth is one thing that is not on the *News*'s menu of offerings.

It is not surprising, then, to find that the paper has a rigid "no-jump" policy for front page stories.[27] Even on the first, dramatic day of the Gulf War, when U.S. forces began bombing Iraq, the lead story did not continue on a subsequent page. As a consequence, it was only eleven paragraphs long.[28] When Wayne Ezell of the *Boca Raton News* told *Washington Post* media critic Howard Kurtz that he would stop carrying foreign news if focus groups said they were not interested, his reasoning was that of a businessman.

Arguments for Marketing

But what of those arguments editors make from their position as journalists? We can identify four, which can be outlined and challenged. Briefly stated, they are:

- The *Pedagogical* Argument, which maintains that marketing tools tell editors how readers learn from the news, and so allow them to craft their newspapers into the kind of products that readers find most accessible.
- The *Enticement* Argument, according to which editors are morally obliged to lure readers into buying the paper, because, the argument goes, once readers have the paper in hand, they will read the serious news.
- The *Democratic* Argument, which maintains that surveys and focus groups are highly democratic in that they allow readers to specify what it is they want. Since newspapers, like government, are a service, then readers, according to this argument, should be able to "vote" for the content of their paper.
- The *Business Imperative* Argument, which holds that if newspapers are in financial trouble, editors must give readers whatever they want, because if they do not, the papers will perish and every opportunity for quality journalism will perish along with them.

The Pedagogical Argument

The Pedagogical Argument is predicated on theories about how people learn from the news. Although editors may base their perceptions of this phenomenon on anecdotes, impressions, and prejudices, academics have rigorously explored the questions of how learning from the news takes place. These explorations have resulted in detailed expositions, the best example of which is found in the book by Russell Neuman, Marion Just, and Ann Crigler, *Common Knowledge*.[29] This book begins with the discovery that traditional newspapers are the least accessible of the news media, that is, that people have more trouble absorbing information from newspapers than they do from television newscasts or weekly news magazines. But, as the book goes on to explain, people's level of difficulty with each medium depends on their cognitive skills. Those with low skills absorb the least from newspapers and, indeed, gravitate toward TV. Those with high skills get the most from newspapers and naturally tend to read them. So, it is primarily for the purpose of capturing those with average skills that the Pedagogical Argument is designed. Those in this group can make efficient use of either medium, although in the absence of papers they find easy to understand, they are inclined to watch TV.

If the goal, then, is to enhance accessibility for those who fall into this middle category, what shall be the means? This is where the authors of *Common Knowledge* and newspaper editors who embrace marketing tools part ways. Neuman, Just, and Crigler believe that format changes (more use of color, art, and graphics) and moderate content changes (more detailed background or context to news stories) are the best ways to make an article more accessible. But market-oriented journalists take a different view. When readers responding to surveys or speaking up in focus groups say that they are not very interested in national, foreign, and government news, editors conclude that if those stories were shorter, they would be easier to digest. If readers are getting little hard news in any event, the editors conclude, then abbreviated bits of news will at least give them something of value.

What are we to make of this reasoning? It is counterintuitive at best. It advocates offering less information in the name of assisting the learning process and maintains that more knowledge will be absorbed if the amount of information available is reduced to accord with the amount habitually absorbed. That is, it argues that the best way to educate is to cut back horizons to meet the field of vision. But how can such an exercise lead to an expanded view of the world?

Cutting back horizons does not promote education; it impedes it. The effect is not an expansion of readers' knowledge of national and world events but a reinforcement of their provincialism. The truncation and oversimplification of the news also inhibits learning in another way as well. Because the message a newspaper implicitly conveys is that its pages reflect the world's most noteworthy events, its failure to reflect those events encourages complacency on the part of readers. Indeed, when the "hard news" is abbreviated, readers who are not inclined to turn to foreign and national stories are no longer even forced to be conscious of what they are missing.

Additionally, an oversimplified newspaper prevents readers from "graduating up" to a level at which they read and understand more complicated news stories. Some readers who are initially disinclined to tackle pieces that are nuanced or complex could eventually use traditional newspapers to work their way up to those stories and thus attain a broader vision of the world. Reducing the news content and simplifying stories prevents them from being able to do so.

The Pedagogical Argument has a familiar parallel in education theory, namely the view that students should not be expected to perform tasks in which they have not already proved their ability. Central to this philosophy is the idea that the primary purpose of education is not to increase stores of knowledge but to raise self-esteem.

There is a danger inherent in this view, however. When the raising of self-esteem becomes the expressed goal of schools, the base on which that confidence is built—mastery of the material—can become something to be sacrificed if it blocks the way. The result is an insecure foundation on which the rhetoric of self-esteem is erected, not a solid one supporting the real thing.

Take the example of the "whole language" approach to teaching reading and writing, a controversial method that is currently in vogue in some schools around the country.[30] Teachers who use it refrain from correcting the spelling of children just learning how to write. If a child spells apple, A-P-L, the teacher, who values the child's self-esteem more than she values her growing store of knowledge, will recognize only the intent behind the misspelled word and praise the child for writing her version of apple. The teacher's expectations are cut back to meet the student's ability; horizons are reduced to accord with present limits of understanding. Just as when newspapers are simplified, learning is not promoted; it is impeded.

Newspaper consultants and editors tend to interpret the results of market research as a call for greater simplification even when the study results are ambiguous. A clear illustration of this is found in a 1991 ASNE readership report, "Keys to Our Survival." The report identifies two types of people who are not loyal newspaper readers but could become so. The first is the "at-risk" reader, a person who dips into the paper a few times a week, scanning it superficially each time. He is someone who feels harried and unable to control his life, tends to retreat into a protected and "provincial" world, and likes news stories that are short and entertaining, the report said.

The other type is the "potential" reader. This is the reader who is seriously interested in news events and prefers newspapers to TV. She is busy but does not feel harried. She is a "deep" reader and wants more detail and explanation in news stories than her local paper now provides. In short, the reason she does not read the paper now is that it has become too superficial to satisfy her needs.

The two types account for equal segments—13 percent—of the newspaper market, the report said. But it is far easier to attract the at-risk reader than the potential reader. It takes less effort to "package" small pieces of information than it does to provide in-depth news. The report, written for newspaper executives, noted all this, and it recommended taking the easier path.

There is nothing wrong with making newspapers accessible to readers. Indeed, making complex events clear has always been the aim of journalistic narrative, but using market research to this end poses serious problems. First, it encourages newspapers to take the most expedient route to accessibility, namely abbreviating news stories. Second, it tends to screen out the preferences of an important minority of customers, those who are intensely interested in the news. Third, it refashions papers in the image of television, since it is in the light of TV's success that editors construe the responses to their own surveys. Helping people understand the events of a complex world is a laudable goal, but eliminating all complexity in the name of teaching defeats the purpose.

The Enticement Argument

According to the Enticement Argument, newspapers must give readers what they want in order to lure them into buying the paper. Once the paper is in their hands, the argument goes, they will read the serious news.

There are several objections to this argument. First, it fails to take account of the impact of a simple fact, that is, every frivolous story that is printed takes up space in the newspaper that would otherwise be used for something less frivolous. But advocates of the Enticement Argument do not recognize this. In their view, the information that people want—as determined by market research—is merely added on top of the standard news fare. Market research, according to this theory, is only meant to enhance, not to change, the content of newspapers.

However, a glance at any newspaper that has adopted the market-research approach proves the Enticement advocates wrong. As we saw with the *Atlanta Journal-Constitution,* stories of the sort that focus group respondents say they prefer—about lifestyle issues and community events—have not been added to the hard news, they have displaced it. In other words, the market-oriented changes have not been used to entice readers to get the informational nutrition they need; rather they have supplanted the old diet altogether.

The *Atlanta Journal-Constitution* also illustrates the second flaw in the Enticement Argument. In order to be lured into reading the serious news, the import of that news has to be clear. In other words, a distinction must be made between stories inserted to gratify readers or get their attention and stories of substance.

Papers have historically maintained this distinction by reserving the front page for the important news and relegating the less substantial stories to inside sections. But once newspapers begin to promote attention-getting stories self-consciously as an "enticement," the hierarchy of news values is overthrown. As the *Atlanta Journal-Constitution* demonstrates, nonnews stories get moved to the front pages, whereas much of the hard news is relegated to subsequent pages, briefs, and indexes. In the name of enticement, editors fail to highlight the news most worth reading. The result is that it is no longer clear what readers are being enticed to read.

The Democratic Argument

According to the Democratic Argument, focus groups and surveys are justifiable because they are democratic tools. Like politicians who defend the use of opinion polls on the grounds that they enable them to enact policy that accords with their constituents' will, advocates of the Democratic Argument argue that focus groups and surveys allow them to produce newspapers that correspond to their readers' needs and desires.

When George Gallup first popularized the opinion poll, he promoted it as a democratic tool; a "sampling referendum," he called it.[31] In *The Pulse of Democracy* (1940), Gallup said that the poll, which a telephone in every home had recently made possible, would allow citizens to voice their views on all issues, something that had not been feasible since the United States' democratic experiment began. For the first time ever, the opinion poll would bring the nation into "one great room," he said. "After one hundred and fifty years, we return to the town meeting. This time the whole nation is within the doors," Gallup wrote.[32]

It was, it would seem, in the interest of democracy—that is, of encouraging journalists to hear the voices in Gallup's great room—that the American Society of Newspaper Editors, in a 1981 report, scolded editors for their general unwillingness to ask readers what kind of news they want. "From time immemorial," the report began, "editors have been blithe spirits—largely untouchable, unteachable, and utterly independent. They listened to the dicta of few except their publishers. Vox populi be damned."[33] The same rebuke is found in a 1992 *Nieman Reports* article by three high-ranking newspaper executives. "Who, if not the reading public, should judge the value of a newspaper's service?" the authors asked.[34]

From Gallup's days to the present, polls have become an increasingly acceptable—even respected—guide for leaders to turn to when making decisions. (Bill Clinton used them liberally in his first eighteen months in office.) The opinion poll, when relied upon to an extreme degree, becomes a referendum on public policy decisions. When polls dictate policy, the boundaries of representational government are breached, and the nation resembles, at least for the moment, a direct democracy. As Gallup predicted, the country is indeed brought into one great room. And, though it is Americans who make up the resulting assembly, the process has a distinctly Athenian flavor. But, is the Athenian model of government an appropriate one for us? Should our government aspire to direct democracy? There are reasons to believe that such an ideal would be misplaced in the U.S. context.

In order for Athenian democracy to function, one needs Athenian citizens—and ideal Athenian citizens at that.[35] What is an ideal citizen of Athens? That is a person whose reason dominates his or her passions and for whom the common good takes precedence over his or her own private interests. Direct democracy demands a nation made up of such citizens. For the Athenian assembly to work, each member must conform his or her behavior to this ethical ideal.

The U.S. political system, on the other hand, is predicated on a very different idea of the citizen. Rather than rely on an ideal of human behavior, the Framers of the U.S. government set their sights lower; they sought an image of "natural man," that is, of how people would behave if they had been stripped of society's artifices and constraints. Influenced by David Hume and John Locke and consulting the record of history, they decided that people do not make natural Athenians. They concluded that we are far too predisposed to place our own interest ahead of the common good.

Whether the Framers' view of human nature does justice to our full humanity is an open question. Nevertheless, it is clear that the U.S. system of government was designed to function even if the Framers' pessimistic view were largely true, that is, even if most citizens never took account of the public good. But, of course, even a country such as ours needs trustees to attend to the commonwealth. For any nation to endure, laws must be enacted that are expressly intended for the common good, even if they conflict with the interests of naturally self-seeking individuals. For example, the raising of taxes is always unpopular, but taxes must occasionally be increased to meet government expenses. Likewise, most citizens do not want to make the sacrifices necessary for cleaning up the nation's air, yet laws must be enacted that require expensive antipollution devices to be installed on cars and in factories. The list could be extended, but the point is clear. In each of these cases, what is good for society as a whole does not reflect the sum choice of individuals acting only in their own interest.

The Framers were conscious of the potential for conflict between the aggregate of citizen's wishes and the common good. So, they built into the constitutional system a number of barriers intended to insulate lawmakers—the popularly selected trustees of the commonwealth—from the people's will. For example, they called for senators to serve what then seemed like very long six-year terms, for presidents to be elected indirectly through an electoral college, and for the members of the Supreme Court to serve lifetime appointments. Each of these provisions was designed, at least in part, to give political leaders the space they need to deliberate about and pursue the common good while being at least somewhat protected from popular pressure.

It is this space for independent deliberation that is subverted by politicians' public opinion polls. When lawmakers blindly follow the dictates of the people through the polls, they relinquish their prerogative of assessing when and how the public good varies from the aggregate wishes of self-seeking individuals. In the same way, when editors believe their duty is to gratify the tastes of readers, they are relinquishing their higher responsibility—their *democratic* responsibility—to make sure the public is informed about the vital issues and events of the day.

Just as direct democracy can only work when citizens place their civic duties or societal interests ahead of their private concerns, so too reader surveys and focus groups can only work to the advantage of the public if the public interest prevails. When they do not exist, readers will ask only for news relating to their private interests and neglect their need for information that will enable them to participate responsibly in the common society, that is, information that will equip them to perform the tasks of a democratic citizen. Rather than ask for more national, foreign, and government news, they will tell consultants such as Ruth Clark that they want more news that affects them, the members of the Me Generation.

Where ideal Athenian citizens are not present, a system that seems to be modeled on direct democracy can paradoxically yield less democratic results. When self-interested people are given the kind of newspaper they say they want, the gulf is widened between those who have enough information to participate meaningfully in the democratic process and those who do not. The result is not democratization but an exacerbated form of elitism. Market-oriented journalism leads, therefore, not to a more equal society, but a more divided one.

The conflict between representative and direct democracy has a corollary in the traditional doctrines justifying press freedom. There are two familiar models of the press that offer justification for the liberties that the First Amendment sanctions, and there are fundamental differences between them. The first is the libertarian model, and the second, the social-responsibility model.[36] As with the distinct ideas about human nature that each form of democracy assumes, each model adopts its own vision of the press.

According to the libertarian model, the press resembles an open marketplace of ideas, a public arena from which no views ought to be excluded. Opinions compete for dominance here, according to the libertarian view, and out of the contest, the truth inevitably emerges victorious.

John Stuart Mill buttressed the libertarian model with four now classic arguments in favor of press freedom.[37] First, he believed that censorship is wrong because in suppressing falsehood, there is always the risk that truth will be silenced. Second, he noted that false opinions, no less than true ones, may be founded on a kernel of truth, and that kernel can lead on to still larger discoveries. Third, he contended that even if a commonly held opinion is true, it is only when those who hold it are forced to defend it that the opinion rises above the level of prejudice and becomes a rationally held belief. And finally, he held that the truth must be challenged from time to time to keep it from losing its vitality and thus its effect on character.

The libertarian model promotes a strictly negative conception of press freedom. That is, that in order for newspapers to carry out their function, they must be free from censorship and control. This model presumes that citizens can find truth in the cacophony of press voices and thus inform themselves about the world. In this way, a high degree of rationality on the part of readers is presumed. Truth can only prevail in the open marketplace of opinions if the public mind is capable of discerning it in a sea of falsity. It is in this respect that the libertarian press resembles direct democracy; the models for both presume that people are guided to their decisions and convictions not by passion but by reason.

Critics of the libertarian model reject this optimistic view of human nature. A person, they observe, "is capable of using his reason, but he is loath to do so."[38] These skeptics doubt that people have the stamina to exercise their rational powers, and indeed, their misgivings seem to find validity in the evidence all around us. The triumph of television is, perhaps, the most vivid proof that we are eager to suspend our powers of reason. TV viewers cheerfully allow themselves to be hypnotized by images—flashes of pseudo-reality that bypass the intellect and directly manipulate the emotions. The rise of docudramas, news magazine shows, and programs in which performers "reenact" sensational news events are evidence of the public's preference for fantasy and entertainment over rational deliberation and discourse.

Critics of the libertarian model reject as unrealistic the notion that people will sort truth from falsehood in the marketplace of ideas. Out of this skepticism emerges the second model of press freedom, the social-responsibility model. This view recognizes that the press has liberties, but it maintains that it also has correlative obligations. Although they grant that journalists must be free from compulsion, the advocates of this model demand that the press must also make a "contribution to the maintenance and development of a free society."[39] In other words, the social-responsibility model requires the press to earn its constitutional protection, not just by speaking its collective mind but by interpreting the day's events, arranging them for maximum comprehensibility, and instructing the public about the issues that they as citizens must confront in the exercise of self-governance. With its emphasis on journalistic discretion and judgment, the social-responsibility model resembles the model of representational government adopted by the authors of the *Federalist Papers*. In both models, the stewards of the community—journalists in the one case and legislators in the other—are obligated to deliberate about how best to serve the commonwealth.

Although the social-responsibility theory had a prestigious sponsor in Robert Maynard Hutchins—the chairman of a committee that wrote a celebrated report advancing the view[40]—it was never universally popular among newspaper executives. There has always been a strain of resistance to the model's suggestion that anything—even the burden of a self-proclaimed duty—should compromise the press's autonomy.[41]

The general hostility to the social-responsibility model is only reinforced by journalism's recent adoption of the use of marketing techniques to shape the news. Editors who use surveys and focus groups, after all, are discouraged from exercising their independent judgment and encouraged to capitulate to the demands of public taste.

Where, then, can one find a justification for freedom of the press? On the one hand, the libertarian model's presumption that people are guided by reason has been decidedly discredited. On the other hand, the social-responsibility model makes demands that the press is obviously unwilling to shoulder. Journalism's adoption of marketing techniques is further proof of the press's repudiation of those demands.

From this vantage point, one can see that the press's adoption of marketing techniques not only widens the gulf between the well-informed minority and the rest of society but also has another alarming effect as well. The acceptance of these techniques represents a decisive abandonment of the social-responsibility model, the final disposal of that model's tattered remains. Without even the threads of the social-responsibility theory to hang onto, the press is left without a reasonable justification for the unrestrained freedom it enjoys.

The Business Imperative Argument

The Business Imperative Argument maintains that if papers do not give readers what they want, they will lose money and possibly go out of business, and if this happens, all opportunity for quality journalism will be lost. As Michael Fancher, Kathleen Criner, and James Lessersohn put the argument in a question in their *Nieman Reports* article, "What quality of service can a newspaper provide if it accepts a long-term decline in financial strength?"[42]

Of the four pro-marketing arguments, editors hold this one most zealously, yet it, too, has significant weaknesses. First, it rests on a tenuous empirical basis. The vast majority of U.S. papers are monopolies in their markets and many are owned by Fortune 500 companies. On the whole, newspapers' pretax profit margins range from 15 to 20 percent. Even throughout the difficult years of the 1980s, profits did not dip below this. Returns in this range make the newspaper business consistently more profitable than most industries.[43]

Second, the Business Imperative Argument substitutes a short-term for a long-term vision. In the short term, it seems to make good business sense to give people what they want. But in the long term, such pandering is likely to be detrimental to a paper's continued commercial viability. Thoughtful readers will perceive immediately that their refashioned newspaper has become impoverished. And sooner or later, even less thoughtful readers will perceive that their paper is not offering them anything that they cannot get, more cheaply and easily, on TV. So, the conscious trivialization of newspapers in the name of appealing to readers may ultimately hasten, rather than retard, the demise that the industry itself now fears.

William Hornby, former editor of the *Denver Post,* described the effect of catering to a public that has lost its hunger for the news in an article in *Quill* in 1976—soon after the trend began. "If the decline in the respect for news spreads, if the hard, spot news of what's happening becomes more and more capsuled in easy doses, between columns of matter on how to take a bath, newspapers will move away from the central human need they particularly exist to satisfy," he wrote. "That can't help but be weakening in the long run. For the truth is—no matter what the marketers of bathing tips say—news is still the basic thing people want from newspapers."[44]

Third, newspaper executives who embrace the Business Imperative Argument fail to take into account the value of their most important commodity, namely their credibility. Papers earn and sustain credibility not only by being truthful but by adhering to the decrees of an unwritten contract between reader and editor, the terms of which state that newspapers must provide an accurate picture of the day's events. This means presenting the news in an order and fashion that reflects a considered assessment of the importance of each story.

It is this credibility that papers that embrace marketing techniques are in danger of losing. Without it, readers' respect for newspapers as a whole will erode. They will eventually turn to other news sources without feeling that they are giving up anything of value. Thus, not only do market-oriented changes fail the test of being pragmatically justifiable, they are also often implemented in suspect and unprofessional ways.

To begin with, newspaper consultants charged with carrying out market research work for individual clients, so, like a lawyer representing a party in a dispute, the "truth" that their research leads them to is not objective, but client-directed. At *Newsday* in Long Island, for example, editors brought in a focus group of women recently to test their hunches about the appeal of a new feature page targeted to the female sex. Editors sat behind a one-way mirror, in the usual custom, and watched a consultant moderate the group's conversation in an adjoining room. The consultant, who had been told in advance about the editors' plans for a women's page, asked the group questions about their tastes in feature articles and wrote responses on a blackboard. But, as one editor watching the proceedings later reported, only the answers that confirmed the editors' theories about why a women's page would be appealing were in fact written down, and it was only these that the moderator pursued in follow-up questions.

Such partiality on the part of the moderator is not uncommon. At the *Orange County Register,* even the pretense of disinterestedness has been abandoned. When focus groups are brought in to discuss the news pages, an outside consultant does not moderate—an editor from the newsroom does. In addition, market researchers often seek to imbue their findings with an aura of scientific validity that the results do not merit. Often their pretenses to scientific rigor are undermined by their own subsequent pronouncements.

Ruth Clark's reports provide a clear example. Five years after her original study, Clark published a second report whose findings opposed the first. While she was criticized after the second study was released for not doing a statistically valid analysis the first time around, Clark maintained that the new findings simply reflected a change in readers' tastes.

Discussing her second report at the American Society for Newspaper Editors convention in 1984, Clark told editors that readers no longer wanted coping stories, they wanted the news. Readers, she said, were now calling for "less advice, more information."[45] "Hard news," Clark declared, "is back in vogue."[46]

Finally, market researchers (and those who adopt their findings) often seek to extend the results of their research to inapplicable contexts. For instance, the results of a national survey may be applied to a local paper, although the preferences of the local community may differ significantly from those expressed by the American public at large. For example, when the *Olympian* was refashioned to accord with Gannett's national findings on reader preferences, story jumps were severely restricted and more briefs, graphics, and news-you-can-use appeared. Local readers saw it and complained. The paper, they told the *Olympian* staff, lacked the in-depth news coverage they liked.[47]

Conclusion

We can conclude that in more ways than one, the newspaper industry holds up a mirror to American culture. What it prints on the front page reflects events as they unfold in the world. Its utilization of marketing techniques likewise reflects a number of currents in the larger society. The first of these currents is the glorification of science. Science has achieved such prestige that our culture makes every effort to bring its methods and presuppositions to bear, even on those aspects of life that seem least amenable to them. In the education and rearing of our children, in the study of society and of human nature, and now also in journalism, "scientific" practitioners, with their statistical methods and claims of infallibility, enjoy the highest authority. Little room is left over for the exercise of independent judgment. The pressure that journalists now feel to conform to the demands of readers—as these have been ascertained with allegedly scientific precision by market researchers—is a clear example of the constraints imposed by putatively scientific techniques on individual freedom, including the freedom to judge. Quantitative studies, with their aura of certainty, are a substitute for the exercise of discretion in many fields. In recent decades, journalism has been added to the list.

The phenomenon of running newspapers according to the results of surveys and focus groups also reflects a second broad trend in American life, the decline in status given to civic responsibility, both among the people at large and the nation's elites. Like politicians, lawyers, doctors, and business executives, editors enjoy a position of privilege in our culture. In the past, it was thought that social privilege carried with it a set of correlative obligations. For politicians, this meant taking the lead in advocating unpopular but necessary programs. For editors, it meant putting out papers that educate and inform the public.

It should come as no surprise that the journalistic establishment is in the process of turning its back on its traditional obligations and viewing itself more purely as a profit-seeking business now. After all, this is what the political, legal, and medical establishments have been doing throughout the 1980s and 1990s. It is part of the zeitgeist.

In blending increasingly into corporate America, journalism—like politics, law, and medicine—is relinquishing its special status in society. Newspapers are no longer, in the words of A.J. Liebling, "a privately owned public utility."[48] Rather, they are commercial enterprises like any other, and as such they have become "more subject to control by managers schooled in profit making than by editors passionate for fierce journalism."[49]

Finally, the specific kinds of changes that newspapers have instituted in response to their market research—shorter articles, more "upbeat" news, more graphics—reflect larger transformations in American society as well. With the printed word ceding power to the televised image, people's capacity for sustained attention to any kind of exposition has radically diminished. Neil Postman has persuasively argued that television has accustomed Americans to expect entertainment rather than argument or information and has taught them to bring this expectation to every activity, including the reading of newspapers.

> Television is the paradigm for our conception of public information. As the printing press did in an earlier time, television has achieved the power to define the form in which news must come, and it has also defined how we shall respond to it. In presenting news to us packaged as vaudeville, television induces other media to do the same, so that the total information environment begins to mirror television.[50]

Newspapers engaged in the act of reinventing themselves have indeed taken on more and more of the properties associated with TV. But acknowledging that newspapers' embrace of the marketing agenda reflects recent developments in American culture does not absolve newspaper executives of responsibility for their actions. Even within the context of the dominant cultural trends, it is possible to be more or less responsible, more or less committed to upholding the traditional standards of one's profession, and more or less honest with oneself about the role one is playing and the consequences of one's actions. What I have argued in this chapter is that the newspaper industry should frankly explore the harm caused to its traditional mission by its adoption of a marketing mentality. Newspapers are too important to the functioning of democracy for there to be so radical a transformation with so little self-examination and self-doubt.

Notes

1. "Boca Watch," *NewsInc* (February 1991): 19.
2. Doug Underwood, "The Very Model of the Reader-Driven Newsroom?" *Columbia Journalism Review* (December 1993): 42–44.
3. Howard Kurtz, *Media Circus* (New York: Times Books, 1993), p. 322.
4. Doug Underwood, *When MBAs Rule the Newsroom* (New York: Columbia University Press, 1993), pp. 7–8.
5. Ruth Clark, "Changing Needs of Changing Readers." Commissioned by the American Society of Newspaper Editors as a part of the Newspaper Readership Project, May 1979.
6. "Keys to Our Survival," American Society of Newspaper Editors, 1991.
7. "Readers: How to Gain and Retain Them," Newspaper Advertising Bureau, 1986.
8. Barbara Cohen and Susan Engel, "Whoever Stays Closest to the Customer Will Win," *Editor and Publisher* (September 14, 1991): 4.
9. Gene Goltz, "Reviving a Romance with Readers Is the Biggest Challenge for Many Newspapers," *Presstime* (February 1988): 16–22.
10. Thomas B. Rosensteil, "Editors Debate Need to Redefine America's Newspapers," *Los Angeles Times,* April 13, 1991, p. A18; and Jim Willis, "The Tyranny of the Apathetic," *Nieman Reports* (Spring 1992): 11–16.
11. Kurtz, *Media Circus,* p. 348.
12. Doug Underwood, "When MBAs Rule the Newsroom," *Columbia Journalism Review* (March/April 1988): 28.
13. Ibid.
14. Michael Fancher, "The Metamorphosis of the Newspaper Editor," *Gannett Center Journal* (Spring 1987): 69–80.
15. Carl Sessions Stepp, "When Readers Design the News," *Washington Journalism Review,* pp. 20–24.
16. Richard Shumate, "Life After Kovach," *Washington Journalism Review* (September 1992): 28–32.
17. Ibid.
18. Ibid.
19. Kurtz, *Media Circus,* p. 348.
20. George Albert Gladney, "USA Today, Its Imitators, and Its Critics: Do Newsroom Staffs Face an Ethical Dilemma?" *Journal of Mass Media Ethics* 8 (1): 17–36.
21. Stepp, "When Readers Design the News."
22. Ibid.
23. Ibid.
24. Ibid.
25. Ibid.
26. Kurtz, *Media Circus,* p. 348.
27. Sally Deneen, "Doing the Boca," *Columbia Journalism Review* (May/June 1991): 15.
28. Ibid.

29. Russell W. Neuman, Marion R. Just, and Ann N. Crigler, *Common Knowledge* (Chicago: University of Chicago Press, 1992).

30. Joseph Berger, "Fighting over Reading; Principal and Methods Are Under Fire," *New York Times,* November 17, 1993, p. B1.

31. George Gallup and Saul Forbes Rae, *The Pulse of Democracy* (New York: Simon and Schuster, 1940).

32. Ibid.

33. Leo Bogart, *Preserving the Press* (New York: Columbia University Press, 1991), p. 147.

34. Michael Fancher, Kathleen Criner, and James Lessersohn, "How Can America's Newspapers Be Saved?" *Nieman Reports* (Spring 1992): 3.

35. Indeed, the historical evidence suggests that the Athenian model of direct democracy did not function well in Athens.

36. For expositions of both models, see Fred S. Siebert, Theodore Peterson, and Wilbur Schramm, *Four Theories of the Press* (New York: Books for Libraries Press, 1956).

37. John Stuart Mill, *On Liberty* (London: Longmans, Green, Reader and Dyer, 1874).

38. Siebert, Peterson, and Schramm, *Four Theories of the Press,* p. 100.

39. The Commission on Freedom of the Press, *A Free and Responsible Press* (Chicago: University of Chicago Press, 1947), p. 18.

40. Ibid.

41. Clifford G. Christians, John P. Ferre, and P. Mark Fackler, *Good News: Social Ethics and the Press* (New York: Oxford University Press, 1993), p. 37.

42. Fancher, Criner, and Lessersohn. "How Can America's Newspapers Be Saved?"

43. Gladney, "USA Today, Its Imitators, and Its Critics."

44. William H. Hornby, "Beware the 'Market' Thinkers," *The Quill* (January 1976): 14–17.

45. Susan Miller, "America's Dailies and the Drive to Capture Lost Readers," *Gannett Center Journal* (Spring 1987): 56–68.

46. Bogart, *Preserving the Press,* p. 143.

47. Underwood, "The Very Model of the Reader-Driven Newsroom?"

48. A. J. Liebling, *The Press* (New York: Ballantine Books, 1961), p. 32.

49. Carl Sessions Stepp, "Access in a Post–Social Responsibility Age," in Judith Lichtenberg, ed., *Democracy and the Mass Media* (Cambridge: Cambridge University Press, 1990), p. 193.

50. Neil Postman, *Amusing Ourselves to Death: Public Discourse in the Age of Show Business* (New York: Viking, 1985), p. 111.

3

Women of Color as Newspaper Executives

Pearl Stewart

Newspapers in general, and especially those in larger cities, have at least cautiously embraced diversity as a positive goal in their attempts to provide fair and responsible coverage of their communities. As a result, most have made modest gains in recent years in employment of minorities at all levels. However, that progress has stalled at the management and executive levels and has not included minority women in numbers proportionate to their representation in the newsrooms. Presently, 8.2 percent of all newsroom executives and managers are people of color. Among those, minority women make up less than a third, despite the fact that minority women outnumber minority men in lower-level newsroom positions.[1]

Research based on existing data and interviews with decisionmakers and women of color at daily newspapers suggests that the daily print medium is deeply steeped at its upper levels in what the Federal Glass Ceiling Commission calls "white male culture." Newspapers have traditionally been bastions of the "old boys network," typified by the truculent, hard-driven practitioners who have dominated the craft since its inception.

The 1968 *Kerner Commission Report* accused U.S. journalism of being "shockingly backward" in recruiting, training, and promoting African Americans, spurring a belated but vigorous effort by the American Society of Newspaper Editors (ASNE) to integrate the nation's newsrooms.[2] The organization set a "Year 2000" goal that seeks to achieve minority representation at daily newspapers equivalent to their representation in the overall population in the United States by the turn of the century. In 1992, when minorities made up an estimated 24 percent of the U.S. population, they composed 7.6 percent of newsrooms. Despite steady progress, from 400 minority journalists nationwide in 1968 to 2,967 in 1995 (out of 53,840), it is clear that ASNE will fall far short of its turn-of-the-century goal.[3]

However gradual, there has nevertheless been improvement. As discussed by Jorge Quiroga in the next chapter, Hispanics have made some strides in the newsroom and in terms of coverage of issues of concern to the

Hispanic community (see Chapter 4). The challenge now, which this chapter seeks to address, is to examine the relative lack of progress by women of color in this field. This chapter examines research that has been done on race and gender in the workplace and uses interviews with journalism professionals to determine the extent of the problem and what can be done about it.

Against All Odds

Wanda Lloyd is, by most standards, a success, In 1995, as senior editor of *USA Today,* she was the highest-ranking woman of color at a major daily newspaper, coordinating the news operations of four sections and serving as chief of administration and long-term planning. With twenty-five years of management and editing experience at some of the nation's leading newspapers, including the *Washington Post* and *Miami Herald,* she was at the top of a male-dominated profession. Her advancement was completely self-propelled. In the early years of her career she wasn't encouraged, piloted, or mentored as many executives are. On the contrary: "After seven years as deputy Washington editor at *The Post,* I became interested in moving up. I was never, ever given serious consideration. . . . The most blatant thing was that when I asked to be considered for a promotion I didn't even get a response."[4]

Karen Wada, assistant managing editor (AME) of the *Los Angeles Times,* is one of the most powerful women in news, with top-level editing and administrative responsibilities at the second-largest metropolitan newspaper in the country. A Stanford graduate who was recruited by the *Times* while she was still a student, she has risen through the ranks over an eighteen-year period from metro reporter to AME. Yet she still has to contend with stereotypes that marginalize the abilities of Asian American women.

> I remember when I was doing a reference check on a woman I was thinking of hiring. I was talking to a white male editor on the phone. He said "she's really smart but you know Asians just aren't suited to our business, they don't make good reporters because they're just too quiet." He said he was going to advise her to take a job in the editorial library. He said she'd do a terrific job there. At the end of the interview I mentioned to him that I and others have disproved that theory.[5]

Karla Garrett Harshaw was born to be a newspaper editor. She convinced the editor of a small black weekly in Dayton, Ohio, to hire her as the paper's teen writer when she was thirteen. From there she moved to Dayton's major paper, the *Daily News,* where she worked as a reporter, assistant city editor, features editor, and assistant business manager before accepting her present position as editor of the Springfield (Ohio) *News-Sun,* one of only two African American daily newspaper editors in the country. Had she taken the advice of her white male supervisors, Harshaw would still be covering city council meetings.

> At the time that I was expressing interest in middle management—I wanted to become an assistant city editor—one upper level manager was pretty candid about telling me that I didn't fit the image of a newsroom manager. One of the things he said was that I laughed a lot, people liked me and that my general personality was very different from people who were in middle management. If you looked around the newsroom at the people who were in middle management, they were young white males. . . . I was energized by that conversation.[6]

The "Two-Fers"

In the complex discourse surrounding diversity and affirmative action, minority women are often viewed as privileged "two-fers"—as members of two underrepresented groups. Of course, this assumes the employers and executives making hiring and promotion decisions are interested in diversity. If they aren't, being a minority woman is simply a double burden. These paradigms—the minority woman as the recruiter's dream, but also as the most formidable threat to the deeply ingrained white male leadership of the newsroom—are in conflict, and that conflict has resulted in the stalled progress of minority women at today's newspapers. The history of race relations in this country would suggest that minority women, black women especially, would succeed at a faster pace than their male counterparts. Diversity consultant and author Edward W. Jones, Jr., has found that white male executives hold negative stereotypes about blacks in general, but that African American women are far more acceptable in positions of influence than men of the same race:

> Black women . . . seemingly have to overcome issues of both race and sex. But these combined drawbacks may cause less resistance than that experienced by black men.[7]
> Black women are not perceived in the same sexual role as white women or in the same racial role as black men. Within a social context, black females are more accepted in roles of influence than black males. White society has historically allowed more assertive behavior from black women than black men because black women are considered to be less dangerous. If personal comfort levels are a main criterion for advancement, black women are far less threatening and therefore more acceptable to white male executives and so will advance faster and farther than black men.[8]

In addition, there was evidence that between 1976 and 1984 African American men actually lost ground in corporate advancement relative to both white women and black women.[9]

And the most widely circulated recent report on women's progress in corporate management, *Good for Business: Making Full Use of the Nation's Human Capital,* better known as the 1995 Federal Glass Ceiling Commission report, states that black women have made more progress than black men in being promoted into managerial, administrative, and executive positions in the communications industry. (However, the report found that white women and all racial minorities, except Hispanics, are underrepresented relative to their percentages of the total population. African American women held 4.9 percent of these top communications positions, and African American men held 3.7 percent. Hispanic males held 3.3 percent of these positions; Hispanic females 1.8 percent.[10])

In television news, for example, there has been considerably more progress in diversifying newsrooms than at newspapers, although in management positions minority women lag far behind all other groups. According to a survey conducted by Ball State University for the Radio and Television News Directors Association, minorities constitute 17 percent of the television workforce and 8 percent of news directors. However, only 1.5 percent of news directors are minority women, whereas 6.4 percent of news directors are minority men.[11]

Among all private sector industries, black women hold 2.2 percent of managerial jobs, and black men hold 2.3 percent of these jobs.[12] However, current data suggest that newspapers have not kept pace with either the modest gains for minority women in the rest of the communications industry or in corporate America at-large. In fact, women of color are almost invisible on the landscape of newspaper management, even though they are entering the field in greater numbers than minority males.[13]

Minority membership in the American Society of Newspaper Editors and the National Association of Minority Media Executives (NAMME), the two major organizations of newspaper managers and executives, reveals a three-to-one and two-to-one ratio, respectively, of minority men to minority women in print journalism management positions.[14]

ASNE reported in 1995 in its annual Minority Survey that minorities make up 8.2 percent of total newsroom supervisors, up less than 1 percent from the previous year. These positions include mid-level and upper-level managers, but there was no breakdown by gender. By race, 4.1 percent of all supervisors were black, 2.3 percent Hispanic, and 1.3 percent Asian American.[15] In order to obtain gender information, some researchers have used membership in the organizations that are considered representative of the industry. Of ASNE's 872 members, all of them editors and newsroom supervisors, 4.36 percent (38) are minorities and 1.1 percent (11) are minority women (see Table 3.1).[16] Among NAMME's print journalism news executives—the organization's members are all minorities—11 are women and 19 are men. (Most of NAMME's print members are also members of ASNE.[17])

Table 3.1   **Proportion of Ethnic Minority Women Editors**

1995 ASNE Members	Number	Percent
All members	872	100
Minorities	38	4.3
Minority women	11	1.1

Source: American Society of Newspaper Editors.

In an industrywide survey of newspaper newsrooms released by ASNE in 1989 (based on 1987 data), "the absence of minorities and women in the ranks of news executives" was cited as an area of concern. (Executive positions were city editor and above.) The survey found that 15 percent of all news executives were women and only 4 percent were minorities. By 1994, according to ASNE, minorities who described their jobs as "supervisors" (assistant city editors and above) constituted 8 percent of all supervisors.

For Hispanics, a crisis has arisen in the nation's newsrooms. A survey of the nation's sixty largest newspapers (circulation 100,000 or above) revealed a 12 percent decline from 1992 to 1993 in the number of Hispanics working in newsrooms, from 634 to 552.[18] And "one of the most striking problems" was the lack of Latinos in management. Only 2.5 percent of the managers at these newspapers were Hispanic, and among them men outnumbered women more than two to one (see Table 3.2), although there were nearly the same number of male and female Hispanic reporters (see Chapter 4). According to National Association of Hispanic Journalists (NAHJ) president Gilbert Bailon:

> The survey represents a retrenchment of hiring and employee retention in an era when Hispanic domestic and international issues frequently carry Page One headlines. The survey also reaffirms that the national newspapers, the most influential periodicals, continue to maintain a marginal to virtually non-existent presence of Hispanics in the newsroom, especially among managers.[19]

Bailon said in an interview that one reason for the apparent decline was that two newspapers that had previously participated in the survey and that have relatively large Hispanic staffs failed to respond to the latest survey. Nevertheless, he said the results were startling.

Among Asian Americans, their numbers in newsrooms and in management remain disproportionately low (1.9 percent of the newsroom, and 1.3 percent of management), prompting the Freedom Forum in 1995 to begin sponsoring executive training workshops for Asian American journalists.

Table 3.2   **Proportion of Hispanics in Sixty Newsrooms, 1993**

Hispanics	Number	Percent
Males	334	2.20
Females	218	1.43
Male reporters	156	2.42
Female reporters	132	2.05
Male managers	58	1.76
Female managers	25	1.43
Male copyeditors	56	2.20
Female copyeditors	44	1.73
Male photo/artists	64	4.38
Female photo/artists	17	1.16
All Hispanics	552	3.63
All newsrooms	15,214	100.00

Source: National Association of Hispanic Journalists.

The Comfort Zone: Minority Women Keep Out

Women and men, minority and nonminority, in the upper levels of newspaper editing and those involved with industry associations tend to agree that minority women are lagging behind all other groups in advancement and promotions. Of the eighteen managers and executives interviewed thus far for this chapter, all said that their own observations led them to concur with the numbers reported by ASNE and NAMME, although some were surprised that minority males, especially African American men, were faring so much better than the women. Those who expressed surprise mentioned the theories referenced above about black men being perceived as a threat.

Among the minority women and men interviewed, most held the view that one of the strongest barriers to minority women, if not the strongest, is the almost impenetrable old boys network, which they feel is more deeply ingrained in the newspaper business than in many other professions. ASNE minority affairs director Veronica Jennings describes it this way:

> It's about trying to get within that inner circle and getting comfortable socially with [the executives] so that they feel comfortable with you . . . and feel that you are someone that they would be willing to promote and take a risk on. But often you don't have the opportunity to interact with them in a relaxed, less formal kind of environment.[20]

This "white male culture," as the Federal Glass Ceiling Commission report calls it, is present throughout the corporate world and is an inhibitor to the advancement of all the excluded groups. As one CEO told the commission:

> The old line companies are run by the white "46 long" guys who practice inappropriate male rituals that are dysfunctional to business. Male bonding through hunting, fishing and sports talk is irrelevant to business. Too much so-called "strategic planning" takes place after the bars close—that kind of male fellowship is irrelevant to business.

Wanda Lloyd assessed the culture at her news organization and decided there was something she could do to penetrate, or at least perforate, this barrier. She noticed that on Monday mornings the white male executives at *USA Today* prefaced their business conversations with an in-depth analysis of their weekend adventures on the golf course. Lloyd had no interest in playing golf, but

> The [executives] here—we call them "the boys"—talk about golf. It's hallway conversation, after-meeting conversation, before-the-meeting conversation. I wanted to be a part of these conversations, because eventually they get around to talking about who should be hired, or what story should go on the cover. . . . So I learned everything I could about golf, I read golf books . . . and I watch as much of the golf tournaments on Sunday afternoon as I can stand to watch, which is not a whole lot. Then I come in on Monday morning and say, "Did you see that shot the Walrus made yesterday?" I still don't play golf. I have no interest in playing. I just talk golf. Why should I learn? They're not going to invite me to play golf with them. They're still "the boys."[21]

To some women this might appear extreme. But it illustrates a way in which one woman, who was continually left out of trivial discussions that often led to executive decisions, attempted to accommodate the dominant culture in her workplace. While this may have worked well for her, it is a method of "playing along" with the long-standing traditions that have enabled white males to maintain control over the executive suites while consciously or unconsciously excluding outsiders. The Glass Ceiling Commission noted that women and minorities have little or no access to these "informal networks of communication," which it called part of the "pipeline barriers that directly affect opportunity for advancement."[22] So rather than acquiescing, critics of these practices, such as the CEO quoted in the Federal Glass Ceiling Commission report, suggest ending it. After all, should traditions that have, in effect, created discrimination be endorsed by complicity?

Although the federal report concluded that male-dominated "informal networks" exist throughout corporate America, some chroniclers of newspaper history say these traditions may be even more emblematic of the newsroom and its tough, hard-driving practitioners who have remained predominantly white and predominantly male. Loren Ghiglione, in *The American Journalist: Paradox of the Press*, writes, "It is difficult to avoid emphasizing white males in a book about journalism—a craft . . . that for much of its history has been inhospitable to women, African Americans and others."[23]

An industry that should have been a catalyst for social change, journalism more often clung to the status quo, opposing the rights of racial minorities sometimes to the point of advocating violence. When legendary journalist-crusader Ida B. Wells investigated the lynchings of black men in the 1890s for her black Memphis newspaper, *Free Speech,* and reported the white press's inaccuracies about the brutality, she was threatened and eventually run out of town. The Memphis *Commercial Appeal* responded to one of her articles: "The black wretch who had written that foul lie should be . . . burned at a stake," after which a mob ransacked Wells's press and threatened to lynch her, causing her to flee to New York.[24]

Another renowned nineteenth-century journalist-activist, Frederick Douglass, was similarly excoriated by the mainstream press for his abolitionist writings. The *New York Herald* urged its readers to "dump Douglass's press into Lake Ontario and banish him to Canada."[25]

Journalism historians Clint C. Wilson II and Felix Gutierrez write that blacks, Asians, Hispanics, and Native Americans have all been subjected to vituperative attacks from newspapers—from the demonizing of Chinese laborers by the *San Francisco Chronicle* in the 1880s to the demonizing of Japanese immigrants in the early 1900s by the same paper.

> *The Chronicle* urged and supported a city-wide boycott of Japanese merchants in San Francisco. The paper charged the immigrants with maintaining loyalty to the emperor of Japan. Mass meetings were held denouncing Japanese immigrants, and acts of assault and other violence soon followed against them.[26]

And in 1954, when the U.S. Supreme Court ruled against school desegregation in *Brown v. Board of Education,* Northern Illinois University professor Orayb Najjar writes, white editors gathered at a specially called meeting of the American Society of Newspaper Editors to discuss the matter. They were treated to a particularly venomous outburst from Harry Ayers, editor of Alabama's *Anniston Star:* "It would be difficult to raise the standard of education in Alabama to the national standards, while carrying on our back at the same time an illiterate and sometimes vicious people. . . . Many Negroes are dirty, are unreliable, are liars."[27] Ayers, it was reported, had also been a member of his state's Board of Education. However, in contrast to the extremist views of Ayers, James Wecshler of the *New York Post* boldly announced that he would bring black journalists into ASNE's membership because "we really don't know what Negroes think."[28]

When that meeting was convened, William Hilliard was just starting out as a "copy boy" at the *Portland Oregonian.* After a couple of years Hilliard became a sports reporter but was pulled off his beat because local whites objected to his presence at private clubs where he was sent to cover swim meets. Hilliard was then switched to the city desk and eventually became executive editor of the 345,000-circulation paper. He also became the first African American president of ASNE.

Now retired, Hilliard believes that many newspapers and ASNE, since the *Kerner Commission Report,* have made a firm commitment to diversity in newsrooms, but he sees white male leadership as a continuing barrier. Hilliard says of some of his colleagues: "They really don't mingle in an environment that gives them the opportunity to run into minorities. . . . They would always tell me they couldn't find any qualified minorities. Of course, [minorities] have never been a part of their network."[29] Hilliard believes these managers should venture outside their traditional social and professional spheres to acquaint themselves with potential writers and editors, as well as to understand groups other than their own. Hilliard recalls that an African American woman on his staff alerted him to growing discontent among the female staff because of their exclusion from informal discussions about job opportunities and promotions. "She said the men would go off and make all the decisions and the women were being left out." Hilliard says he discussed it with several of his male editors, "but there was a lot of resistance and denial. They didn't want to change."

Similarly, Rick Rodriguez, managing editor of the *Sacramento Bee* and one of a steadily growing number of male Hispanic editors, says he recently promoted an "extremely qualified" African American woman to assistant sports editor amid vehement protests from white male staff members. "A man who felt he should have been chosen for the job made totally inappropriate sexist and racist remarks," which resulted in disciplinary action. Rodriguez says it's important for managers to act swiftly in such cases to demonstrate that there is "support from the top" for diversity.[30]

Some minority women contend that entry into this inner circle, where a minority woman could get considered for upper management, is all but impossible because there is no password. Rather, such ethereal qualifications as "chemistry," "the right fit," and "comfort" must be met. What's frustrating to so many women is that this is rarely articulated, and even if it were, there's not much one can do to acquire it. Jacqueline Thomas, Washington bureau chief for the *Detroit News,* puts it this way:

> There appears to be a human trait that you have a higher level of comfort with people who are most like you, have common experiences, values or whatever. . . . Women of color have the problem that very few people making the decisions about their promotions are like them in many ways.[31]

The issue of comfort has been squarely addressed in studies examining impediments to the advancement of women and minorities in both the private and public sectors. Meredith Ann Newman explores it in a 1993 article in which she cites the "lack of fit model of bias."[32] Newman explains,

"Proponents of this thesis argue that the presence of women in management may upset the prevailing comfort zone to the extent that their numbers in the higher ranks remain artificially low." She refers to the "cloning effect" in organizations in which top managers seek replicas of themselves when they make promotion decisions. J. C. Turner's research in the 1980s also suggested that supervisors tend to favor individuals for promotions who belong to their group over members of other groups.[33]

Diversity consultants who advise white male executives recommend that they acknowledge these tendencies and work to overcome them. Walterene Swanston, a diversity consultant and former executive director of the National Association of Black Journalists (NABJ), urges white newspaper executives: "Be aware of your own prejudices and biases and learn how to manage them. Make sure you are comfortable with people who are different from you."[34]

But the problem is, often they are not comfortable, and that lack of comfort can't be dispelled simply by suggestion. Ben Bradlee, in his book *A Good Life,* explains that when he was about to take the helm of the *Washington Post* after the riots of the 1960s, he had to face that reality:

> To be blunt about it, I didn't know anything about blacks, or the black experience, and I was about to become involved in the leadership of the number-one newspaper in a city that was 70 percent black, and a readership that was 25 percent black. I had no black friends growing up. There were no blacks in my boarding school. . . . At *Newsweek* there had been only a handful of black leaders like Roy Wilkins, A Philip Randolph, Louis Martin, but I knew no ordinary black people.[35]

With that realization, Bradlee began attending meetings of "an eclectic group of black men—some former criminals, some solid citizens," who gathered once a week to discuss local issues.[36] His course of action, taken thirty years ago, is the kind of response recommended by diversity experts and others in the field. Many African American male editors and news executives are convinced, from their own experiences, that newsrooms are indeed shrouded in white male culture, which, they tend to agree, doesn't appear to be dissipating.

Bennie Ivory, executive editor of the Wilmington (Delaware) *News-Journal,* views the situation with urgency, citing a near-absence of minority women in the "pipeline" positions. "That's really the problem everywhere [in newspapers]. It's much worse than it was 10, even five, years ago," Ivory says, noting that women are concentrated in the lower-level positions, and increasingly, are leaving newspapers because of "frustration that progress is coming so slowly." The reason, he contends, is that white male executives are reluctant to abandon the security of the old networking techniques. "There's no question about it. People gravitate toward people they're more comfortable with. White males naturally gravitate toward other white males. . . . It's just a reality. It's not fair but I don't know how to get around it."

Academics have examined these practices as they relate to the need for affirmative action. Management professor David E. Terpstra sums up both sides of the argument in a 1995 article for *Employment Relations Today:*

> It has been argued that recruitment practices such as employee referrals, word-of-mouth and the use of "old-boy" networks tend to unfairly discriminate against minorities and women. . . . Numerical goals may force some organizations to broaden their search efforts and employ alternative recruiting methods and sources.[37]

Terpstra also explains that opponents of affirmative action suggest that the "diversity movement" should provide enough positive incentives to organizations to achieve a more balanced workforce—that the goal of "organization success" should be enough incentive to prevent employers from discriminating against minorities and women. Opponents also believe affirmative action prevents employers from using "the most valid selection procedures to identify the best applicants" and that existing legislation, such as Title VII, "affords all the protection needed to individuals who feel that they have been victims of employment discrimination."[38]

> Adjusting for past discrimination against one group by counterdiscrimination against another group may result in a never-ending cycle of compensatory preferential adjustments. Such a system will almost always [be] perceived as unfair by the members of those groups who are not currently granted preferential status.[39]

The favoring of like groups extends to personnel evaluations, which some researchers have found may be clouded by the biases of those who are conducting the evaluations—that supervisors, who in their study were overwhelmingly white and male, tended to favor people of the same race and gender.[40]

In a recent article on racial differences in job performance and career advancement, Magid Igbaria and Wayne M. Wormley note that a "potential determinant" of slow advancement rates for blacks and other minorities is biased assessment of job performance: "Systematic biases in job performance evaluations can place blacks at a distinct disadvantage when being considered for promotions and produce bias in promotion decisions over time. . . . Minorities are evaluated more negatively than their actual performance warrants."[41] So when capable minorities are told they aren't "well suited" or "the right fit" for a position, a manager's prejudice against that person may be playing a part in that assessment. And if the manager is a white male and the worker is a minority female, both race and gender are likely to factor into the determination of suitability.

What contributes to these biases and the lack of comfort? Both practitioners and researchers suggest that the answer lies in stereotypes, misinformation, and ignorance. In 1982 the *Wall Street Journal* conducted a survey of Ivy League graduates in the class of 1957, asking them if they agreed with the statement, "Blacks are as intelligent as whites." Less than half the respondents, who were then in their late forties, agreed: only 36 percent of Princeton grads agreed, as did 47 percent of Yale graduates and 55 percent of Harvard graduates.[42] Diversity consultant Edward W. Jones, Jr., cites this survey to support his position that racial prejudice, which he calls "colorism," can cloud performance evaluations: "Study after study shows that colorism exists among white Americans; whereas they generally have an automatically positive internal picture of whites, they don't have one of blacks. It takes an effort to react positively toward blacks."[43]

Minority women represent two "out groups," if the persons making the promotion decisions are white males. A 1989 ASNE survey of the newspaper industry found that 85 percent of newsroom executives (from city editors up) were male and 96 percent were white. Women of color would therefore be the least likely group to be considered management material by white males who hold biases against minorities and women. A number of studies support the theory that minority women are doubly impacted by barriers in corporate America, including the Federal Glass Ceiling Commission report, which states that minority women "are subject to racial and ethnic stereotypes as well as general stereotypes about women."[44] Sheila Wellington, of a New York–based business research group that contributed to the Glass Ceiling study, discusses stereotypes about the two groups during an interview with the *Tampa Tribune:* "While white women may be labeled unfairly as too timid or emotional, some black women are viewed even more severely as 'two-for-one affirmative action hires or promotions' who are incompetent, hostile and lazy."[45]

Such double stereotyping applies to other minority women. As *Los Angeles Times* assistant managing editor Karen Wada explained, Asian American women may be considered unqualified for certain positions in newsrooms because of assumptions that they are passive and quiet. In an interview with the Bergen *Record,* Alice Min, a partner in Asian Consultants, a multicultural training firm, says Asian Americans are shocked to find that scholarship and good work habits often aren't rewarded: "We've worked hard in school, we contribute to the community, we're good workers and we're still not promoted or paid like white workers with the same or even less qualifications. You see that after playing by the rules, you're still discriminated against."[46]

Attorney Linda Wong told the *Record* that prospective employers at law firms "intimated that an Asian woman couldn't be assertive in a courtroom." Wong became frustrated that she couldn't get past the stereotypes and eventually established her own practice, but the bitterness remains.

"You work 80 hours a week for five to seven years, and just watch people from the old boys network, white men, and now, white women get the good jobs."

The *Sacramento Bee*'s Rick Rodriguez says that just as there was skepticism about his selection of an African American woman as assistant sports editor, there also have been questions about his decision to move an Asian American woman into an editing position. "People are saying she's only getting [the position] because she's one of Rick's proteges and he's trying to move minorities."[47]

Evelyn Vigil, a Latina who is editor and publisher of the 5,000-circulation Los Alamos *Monitor* in New Mexico, says women of color "have to work three times harder than everybody else and that's all there is to it."[48]

Reinforcing the Status Quo

White male culture is sometimes reinforced in workplaces either by overt actions and speech or subtle tactics designed to encourage "outsiders" to leave. In the case of Rodriguez's appointment of an African American woman as assistant sports editor, a white male reacted with racist and sexist invective. Rodriguez said the statements were made in front of other white males. The person making the statements obviously felt comfortable using such language among his white male colleagues. It was Rodriguez who later heard about the remarks and imposed sanctions. Unfortunately, such behavior has long been tolerated in newsrooms, where crass language among "the guys" has been a part of the culture, even when it was racially or sexually insensitive.

Editor and Publisher reported that during a panel discussion at the 1993 convention of the Asian American Journalists Association, Sharon Stewart, an African American reporter, described an incident at her previous paper in which a white editor said he liked his coffee "as black as Sharon's tits."[49] As a result of the lawsuit Stewart filed on the basis of that and other complaints, the paper agreed to upgrade her assignments and to hire more minorities on their editorial staff. But again, the offender was a white male who felt he had the latitude to embarrass and demean a black woman. Another panelist described the atmosphere in her office, a suburban bureau of a large daily, as having a "frat-house atmosphere" where there "were no checks and balances," until more women joined the editing staff.[50]

Terry Leap and Larry Smeltzer, in an article on workplace harassment, suggest that written policies "can go far in preventing racial and ethnic harassment, with all their destructive effects, from taking root." They recommend that the policy include the following:

> Employees have the right to work in an environment free of undue personal harassment, stress and interpersonal friction. Certain types of racially motivated remarks and harassment are contrary to federal and state civil rights laws and can impose a legal liability on the employer as well as tarnish the organization's public image and damage morale.[51]

However, policies aren't likely to address complaints related to the more subtle and perhaps more frequent efforts to discourage or denigrate employees based on race and gender. Tammy Carter, a mid-level manager who edits the television section of the New Orleans *Times-Picayune*, believes that she has been repeatedly tested in her quest for top management. Though she is not a senior manager, Carter is the highest-ranking person of color at her paper and just one of two minorities in newsroom management out of a staff of about 240. The overt harassment came from outside the paper, but she feels her supervisors let her down:

> I was assigned as bureau chief in St. Bernard Parish, a predominantly white area where most of the people are still living in the '50s. I was required to live in that area. . . . Then we did a series on the community's racist attitudes. A lot of readers flooded the phone lines . . . and the calls became threatening. I just felt that I was hung out there to dry because they [the paper] didn't really support me. They moved one of the writers, a white man, out of the bureau right away, but I had to stay out there. . . . It was just a fiasco.[52]

Carter says letters from angry readers criticizing her work were published without her knowledge. Other writers, she noted, are given copies of such letters prior to their publication, the standard procedure at many newspapers.

After several months—and after Carter's house was splattered with raw eggs—she and her young daughter were allowed to move back into New Orleans. ("I refused to put my daughter in school out there, so they said I could move.") Ultimately she was reassigned to her current position. Although Carter is quick to point out that she has never been subjected to harassment on the job, she feels that her employers contributed to the community's attacks by their lack of support.[53]

Like the editors quoted at the beginning of this chapter, Carter has been discouraged from pursuing management positions; also like the others, she continues to strive for career advancement. However, she has realized that she has little future at her current paper, and she is openly seeking opportunities elsewhere in the industry. Other women of color are responding to thwarted attempts at advancement by leaving the industry. A 1995 survey of people who voluntarily quit their newspaper jobs found that African American women are the most disaffected of any demographic group surveyed and that 57 percent cited lack of career opportunity as a "very important reason" for their decision to leave.[54]

The Backlash: Is 8.2 Percent a Threat?

In a profession where whites continue to hold nearly 92 percent of the management positions, one might not expect to find a backlash against minorities, but 1995 saw one of the most strenuous attacks on newsroom integration in the form of a lengthy article in *The New Republic*, entitled "Race in the Newsroom: A Case Study."[55]

Although it focused on one paper, the *Washington Post*, the article reverberated throughout the newspaper community. And although most of the disgruntled white journalists quoted were anonymous and it was unclear how many of them there actually were, their searing criticism of the paper's diversity policies accompanied by vicious descriptions of their minority colleagues' shortcomings caught the industry's attention. Many *Post* staffers allege that in playing the numbers game, the paper has been forced to hire inappropriate people, reporters who lack the skills to do daily newspaper work competently. "There is just a different standard. White people have to knock their heads against the door and be really exceptional. Whereas if you're black they recruit you, they plead with you, they offer you extra money."[56]

Whites also described black staffers as lacking basic writing skills and being "dumb as a post." According to ASNE president Bill Ketter, the widely publicized article "has done more to damage the efforts of diversity [in newspapers] than any other single factor because it perpetuates a myth. What it said about the *Post* simply is not true."[57] Ketter believes the comments of the anonymous whites in Ruth Shalit's article stem from "misunderstanding, naivete and ignorance" about diversity in the newspaper industry despite the efforts of his organization and others, and he says he's "seeing it more often among white women."

Marty Graham, a white female reporter for the now-folded *Houston Post*, explains her own ambivalence about diversity in the wake of the paper's shutdown as she and her colleagues vied for jobs at other newspapers:

> I think most of us support affirmative action and the goal of diversity. Yet more than a few of us have been asked in interviews about our minority colleagues' availability, and more than a few of us fear losing a chance for a job because we are white. This is a fear we fumble to talk about. I'm uncomfortable talking about it for fear of sounding racist.[58]

The writer is among a growing number of white women who are questioning the benefits of affirmative action. In a recent *Newsday* poll, white women were much more supportive of affirmative action programs than white men, but considerably less supportive than blacks and Hispanics.[59] A mere 14 percent of the white women in the survey said discrimination was a major problem for them, and 23 percent said affirmative action programs should be decreased, compared to 10 percent of black women and 47 percent of white males (see Table 3.3).[60]

Table 3.3   Attitudes Toward Affirmative Action

Group	Increase (%)	Keep the Same (%)	Decrease (%)
White female	34	27	23
White male	14	31	47
Black female	46	34	10
Black male	36	49	8

Source: Newsday.
Note: The question was, "In general, do you think we need to increase, keep the same or decrease affirmative action programs in this country?"

In newspapers, most managers continue to be white and male, but the greatest change in the 1980s came from white women.[61] Jones explains that white male executives are likely to favor promoting white women over blacks:

> If the comfort level is a big factor in an invitation to enter the executive suite, it is understandable that white women will get there before blacks. After all, the mothers, wives and daughters of top officers are white women, and they deal with white women all their lives—but only rarely with black men and women.

Part of the problem with the so-called backlash is that some whites are assuming, as Wanda Lloyd's male applicant at *USA Today* did, that whenever a minority is selected for a position for which the white person applied, he or she was passed over because of race, and in the case of minority women, possibly because of race and gender. All too frequently, the assumption is also made that the minority was unqualified.

Minority journalists see the claim of reverse discrimination as the battle cry of the mediocre. "The people who cry the loudest are the marginal performers who feel threatened," contends *News-Journal* editor Bennie Ivory. He says he simply doesn't understand the white backlash as it relates to the newspaper industry. "It's utterly ridiculous if you look at who's in the newsrooms."

Members of the National Association of Black Journalists share that view as it relates to African Americans. In 1993, 59 percent of the 537 NABJ members who responded to a survey believed that blacks must meet higher standards in order to be promoted, and 89 percent said that when blacks enter the business they are as qualified or better qualified than non-blacks hired at the same time. Only 27 percent felt that they were as likely to be given career opportunities as nonblacks.

It is interesting that when the same questions were put to newsroom managers in ASNE, most of whom were white, most of the responses contrasted those of the black journalists by hefty margins. However, on the subject of blacks being qualified, 73 percent of the managers agreed that their black staff members were at least as qualified for their positions as were other staffers.[62]

Research tends to support this. If qualifications include experience and education, black and other minority journalists tend to simulate their white counterparts. In fact, a study conducted by David Weaver and G. Cleveland Wilhoit for the Freedom Forum in 1992 indicates that minority journalists tend be better educated than their white counterparts—proportionately more have attended graduate school. Minority journalists have been in the field an average of three years less than whites. However, a 1989 survey by the same team for ASNE found that among supervisors, the number of years of experience was virtually the same for minorities and nonminorities, suggesting that minorities who get promotions have "paid their dues" in both experience and education.

Whether in newsrooms, corporations, or even academia, the race struggle has intensified, with minorities feeling increased pressure amid accusations that they are incompetent. Black historian Roger Wilkins, writing in *The Nation,* offers a personal anecdote that illustrates this point. Wilkins explains how he was invited to compete for a full professorship and an endowed chair at George Mason University during a time when the institution was under a court order to desegregate:

> I went through the appropriate application and review process and, in due course, was appointed. A few years later, not long after I had been honored as one of the university's distinguished professors, I was shown an article by a white historian asserting that he had been a candidate for the chair but that at the last moment the job had been whisked away and handed to an unqualified black. I checked the story and discovered that this fellow had, in fact, applied but had not even passed the first threshold.[63]

In fact, plaintiffs have lost 75 percent of the federal cases of reverse discrimination filed since 1990, according to a study by Rutgers University law professor Alfred Blumrosen. He speculates that economic insecurities are leading some workers to blame affirmative action or reverse discrimination for problems that may not be related to race.[64]

Just as the aggrieved employee mentioned by Wanda Lloyd believed he was the superior candidate when, in fact, he hadn't even been a finalist, so too had Wilkins's rival concluded that he would have been chosen if Wilkins had not been a minority filling an affirmative action requirement. It's possible that these whites wouldn't believe any minority could actually compete against them and win purely on merit. They may feel, as did the majority of the respondents in the *Wall Street Journal*'s 1982 survey, that certain minority groups—in that case, blacks—just aren't as intelligent. In 1995 we saw a resurgence of debate over racial equality and intelligence in a bevy of right-wing publications, a domination of the radio airwaves by conservative programming, and a "Contract with America" that includes the proposed dismantling of government affirmative action programs.

White male journalists have been among the harshest critics of affirmative action. Paul Craig Roberts, for example, a columnist with Scripps Howard News Service, called the 1995 Federal Glass Ceiling Commission report "out of tune with its time." Complaining that the commission was made up of "power-lunching female dynamos" that included a U.S. Senator, two members of the House, attorneys, and corporate vice presidents, Roberts concluded: "The chutzpah of this report is amazing. The only legally sanctioned discrimination in corporate America is against white males."

Some diversity management analysts have found that white males may be oblivious to their companies' needs for diversity training and even more oblivious to their own racial biases. Mary Pat McEnrue, writing in *Organizational Dynamics* in 1993, provides an example:

> The senior vice president . . . indicated that the recent labor contract ratification meant employees were happy with current conditions. From his perspective, diversity was not necessary. However, this same vice president later described one ethnic group as people who "will steal you blind." He didn't see any irony in his remarks.[65]

Given his views, employees from that ethnic group are unlikely to move into top positions in his company. Yet, according to this senior executive, his employees are "happy."

Down and Out: Downsizing and Layoffs Imperil Diversity Effort

These are possibly the worst of times for newspapers, economically, and therefore the worst of times for minorities at newspapers. As Marty Graham reported in her *CJR* article on the closing of the *Houston Post,* the fact that minorities were being sought out by recruiters only augmented the distress of the hundreds of journalists who had been put out of work. Graham and the other whites who felt they were being passed over gave little thought to the fact that newspapers are still 92 percent white. Within weeks after the *Houston Post* folded, *New York Newsday* did likewise, and although they were among the largest papers to fold in recent years, they were among the hundreds that are in trouble. *Washington Post* media writer Howard Kurtz recently reported: "A familiar list of culprits—soaring newsprint costs, declining circulation and growing competition from television, talk radio, direct mail and on-line services—has combined to make 1995 the most depressing year in recent newspaper history."[66]

Indeed, the *Los Angeles Times, Baltimore Sun, Philadelphia Inquirer* and *Daily News, Miami Herald,* and *Washington Post* all announced downsizing efforts ranging from employee buyouts to straightforward job cuts. The *Los Angeles Times* eliminated 700 positions; the *Sun* cut 125; the Philadelphia papers abolished 230; and the *Hartford Courant* reduced its staff by 16 percent, granting buyouts to 188 workers (see Table 3.4). And they are the larger, more visible publications. At medium-sized and smaller papers the trend is the same.[67]

Table 3.4   1995 Newspaper Downsizing and Closures

Newspaper	Action Taken	Jobs Lost[a]
Los Angeles Times	Staff reduction	700
Baltimore Sun	Staff reduction	125
Philadelphia (2 papers)	Staff reduction	230
Hartford Courant	Buyouts	188
Washington Post	Buyouts	150
Houston Post	Closed	1,500
New York Newsday	Closed	800
Baltimore Evening Sun	Closed	—[b]

Notes: a. Newsroom and non-newsroom positions.
b. Attempted to avoid layoffs by moving most employees to the morning paper.

Graham summed it up in *CJR* when she explained that the fear of losing out to a minority contributed to the overall "resentments and anxieties" associated with being placed in the unemployment line. Graham also noted that reporters who haven't distinguished themselves by winning prestigious awards and who lack "the race card" must "struggle with the notion that prospective employers might only have money for special recruits."

Minorities, however, see it differently. Many journalists of color feel that the shutdowns and cutbacks have a more adverse effect on minorities, especially minority women, because when layoffs occur the most recently hired workers are generally terminated. When downsizing occurs, even fewer minorities are left in the pipeline to be considered for management positions.

Models of Success

If newspapers focus on hiring and promoting women of color, the results are likely to affect profits. Proper management of diversity can increase revenue, lowers labor costs, and enhances customer satisfaction. McEnrue cites Taylor Cox and Stacy Blake, who offered six ways in which managing diversity can serve as a source of competitive advantage:

(1) by reducing costs associated with excessive turnover and absenteeism;
(2) by making it easier to recruit scarce labor;
(3) by increasing sales to members of minority culture groups;
(4) by promoting team creativity and innovation;
(5) by improving problem solving; and
(6) by enhancing organizational flexibility.[68]

Within the newspaper industry, the professionals interviewed cited the large newspaper chains as having been the most proactive in addressing the need for diversity in management. Specifically, Knight-Ridder, Gannett, and the Times-Mirror METPRO programs were generally viewed as successful in training minorities. Knight-Ridder executive Larry Olmstead was quoted in *Personnel Journal* as saying that the corporation provides financial incentives for its individual news organizations to hire minorities and train them for management positions. "We'll make the money available [salary and benefits] to hire above [the individual newspaper's] budget," Olmstead said, adding that the papers had to absorb the cost within a year. He said additional corporate money was being used for a two-year minority management program.[69]

The management training program for minority journalists conducted by the Maynard Institute for Journalism Education was cited by several editors for turning out some of the top minority managers in the field. The Freedom Forum and Poynter Institute were mentioned often for their support of journalism education for minorities at the professional, collegiate, and precollegiate levels. However, most of the existing programs don't address minority women as a group needing special attention due to the double stereotyping and discrimination that have been discussed here.

Outside the industry, a few examples of innovative approaches include the following:

- United Parcel Service every year sends about fifty of its rising managers to cities away from their home towns for four weeks of volunteer work in communities that are culturally and ethnically diverse "to expose them to people and situations they might not be exposed to on an everyday basis."[70]

- The Prudential established in-house task forces to monitor its diversity effort. It includes a "cultural audit" to measure employee attitudes toward the efforts.[71]
- Avon has six grassroots networks that address issues of specific employee groups—women, African Americans, Hispanics, Asians, parents, and long-term employees. Avon also requires its employees to take a "managing diversity" seminar in which employees at all levels participate together.[72]

Conclusion

Clearly, the race- and sex-based discrimination that exists in corporate America against women of color has not escaped newspapers. Traditions of white male culture ascribed to the corporate world are intensified in the newspaper industry, which has a history of overt exclusionary practices both in its employment and its coverage. The minority women who have ascended to positions of authority have exhibited inordinate determination and resilience. They have had to invent methods of circumventing the existing male networking system that has become a trademark of the newspaper business.

If women of color are to become more visible in newspaper management, the culture of the newsroom will have to change. Attitudes against minority women are so firmly rooted in the industry that the change must be planned and organized. Just as ASNE set goals to racially integrate newsrooms, it and other professional organizations should orchestrate a dismantling of the exclusionary networks and practices that impede the progress of women of color. It is likely that increasing numbers of women of color in management will result in weaker all-male networks, and in adverse reaction from some whites—male and female. Thus numerical progress alone won't solve the problem. If the so-called frat-house or old boys club mentality that permeates too many newsrooms persists, minority women who are promoted will simply end up in hostile territory. To avoid this, I propose a series of recommendations to solve the problems outlined in this chapter.

- Just as ASNE and other professional organizations set hiring goals for racially integrating newsrooms, they should also establish specific goals for bringing diversity to management with emphasis on minority women.
- Informal networking that excludes minorities and women should be

strongly discouraged. Discussions about promotions and hiring should not be limited to same-race and same-sex settings.

- White male and female executives should become more personally involved with diverse cultures in their communities. This might range from volunteering in after-school programs at community centers to teaching literacy courses at the local library.
- Newsrooms should participate in diversity training programs tailored to their specific needs and aimed at resolving race-related conflicts and bringing about an understanding of the need for a multi-ethnic workplace.
- Newsroom managers of all races should attend meetings of professional organizations of different racial groups for purposes of recruiting and expanding their social networks.

Notes

1. American Society of Newspaper Editors, *1995 Survey of Minority Newsroom Employment,* March 1995, pp. 1–3.
2. Report of the National Advisory Commission on Civil Disorders, *What Happened? Why Did It Happen? What Can Be Done?* (New York: E. P. Dutton and Co., 1968), pp. 384–385.
3. ASNE, *1995 Survey,* pp. 1–3.
4. Wanda Lloyd, personal interview, September 28, 1995.
5. Karen Wada, telephone interview, October 31, 1995.
6. Karla Harshaw, personal interview, October 12, 1995.
7. Edward W. Jones, Jr., "Black Managers: The Dream Deferred," in *Differences That Work,* Mary C. Gentile, ed. (Boston: Harvard Business Review Press, 1994), pp. 79–80.
8. Ibid., p. 80.
9. Anne B. Fisher, "Good News, Bad News, and an Invisible Ceiling," *Fortune* (September 16, 1985): 29.
10. Federal Glass Ceiling Commission, *Good for Business: Making Full Use of the Nation's Human Capital* (Washington, D.C.: U.S. Department of Labor, 1995), pp. 77–79.
11. Bob Papper and Andrew Sharma, "Diversity Remains an Elusive Goal," *RTNDA Communicator* (October 1995): 18–19.
12. Ibid.
13. "Changing Roles: Professors and Professionals in Journalism," *Black Issues in Higher Education* (August 10, 1995): 27.
14. From the organizations' membership lists. Although ASNE and NAMME don't contain all minority managers, their combined membership is believed to include most of minorities in upper-level management (assistant managing editor and above). For NAMME, which includes both business and editorial managers in print and broadcast media, I extracted the print/editorial managers.
15. ASNE, *1995 Survey,* Table B.
16. ASNE, *1995 Survey,* pp. 1–3.
17. NAMME membership list, 1995.

18. National Association of Hispanic Journalists, "Hiring of Latinos at Newspapers." *Special Report* 22 (February 1995): 1–5.

19. Gilbert Bailon, "Latinos Losing Ground in Newspaper Journalism," *Noticias* (April 1995): 1.

20. Veronica Jennings, telephone interview, October 4, 1995.

21. Lloyd, personal interview.

22. Federal Glass Ceiling Commission, *Good for Business,* p. 8.

23. Loren Ghiglione, *The American Journalist: Paradox of the Press* (Washington, D.C.: Library of Congress, 1990), p. 15.

24. Ibid., p. 51.

25. Ibid., p. 40.

26. Clint C. Wilson II and Felix Gutierrez, *Minorities and Media* (Newbury Park, Calif.: Sage, 1990), p. 74.

27. Orayb A. Najjar, "Minorities in the Newsroom: The American Society of Newspaper Editors and the Newsroom," research paper, Northern Illinois University, 1995, p. 2.

28. Ibid., p. 9.

29. William Hilliard, interview, 1996.

30. Rick Rodriguez, telephone interview, October 31, 1995.

31. Jacqueline Thomas, telephone interview, October 11, 1995.

32. Meredith Ann Newman, "Career Advancement: Does Gender Make a Difference?" *American Review of Public Administration* 18 (January 1993): 56.

33. J. C. Turner, *Rediscovering the Social Group: A Self-Categorization Theory* (New York: Basil Blackwell, 1987).

34. Walterene Swanston, "Angry White Men," *American Journalism Review* (September 1995): 42.

35. Ben Bradlee, *A Good Life* (New York: Simon and Schuster, 1995) p. 282.

36. Ibid.

37. David E. Terpstra, "Reassessing Affirmative Action: Today's Basic Issues and Questions," *Employment Relations Today* 22 (June 22, 1995): 33.

38. Ibid.

39. Ibid.

40. K. Kraiger and J. K. Ford, "A Meta-Analysis of Ratee Race Effects in Performance Ratings," *Journal of Applied Psychology* 70 (1985): 56–65.

41. Magid Igbaria and Wayne M. Wormley, "Race Differences in Job Performance and Career Success," *Communications of the ACM* (March 1995): 82.

42. *Wall Street Journal,* May 21, 1982.

43. Jones, "Black Managers," pp. 72–73.

44. *Glass Ceiling Commission Report,* p. 153.

45. Michele Drayton, "Breaking Through," *Tampa Tribune,* April 17, 1995, p. 8.

46. Elizabeth Llorente, "Asian-Americans Finding Many Doors Closed to Them," *Record,* October 23, 1994.

47. Rodriguez, telephone interview, October 31, 1995.

48. Evelyn Vigil, telephone interview, November 17, 1995.

49. M. L. Stein, "Unwelcome Gender Politics: Female Panelists Say It Still Pervades Newsrooms," *Editor and Publisher* (September 11, 1993): 13.

50. Ibid.

51. Terry Leap and Larry Smeltzer, "Racial Remarks in the Workplace: Humor or Harassment?" In *Differences That Work,* pp. 85–90.

52. Tammy Carter, telephone interview, November 8, 1995.

53. Ibid.

54. Newspaper Association of America, *Preserving Talent: A Study of Employee Departures in the Newspaper Industry* (Reston, Va.: NAA, 1995), p. 4.

55. Ruth Shalit, "Race in the Newsroom: A Case Study," *The New Republic* (October 2, 1995): 20–37.

56. Ibid., p. 23.

57. Bill Ketter, interview.

58. Marty Graham, "Rancor and Romance: In the Rubble of the Houston Post," *Columbia Journalism Review* (September/October 1995): 47–48.

59. John Riley, "Judging It on Its Merits: Affirmative Action Is Up for Evaluation," *Newsday,* June 11, 1995, p. 6.

60. Ibid., chart.

61. ASNE, "The Changing Face of the Newsroom."

62. *ASNE Bulletin,* p. 28.

63. Roger Wilkins, "Racism Has Its Privileges," *The Nation* 260 (March 27, 1995): 409.

64. Riley, "Judging It on Its Merits," p. 24.

65. Mary Pat McEnrue, "Managing Diversity: Los Angeles Before and After the Riots," *Organizational Dynamics* 21 (January 1993): 18.

66. Howard Kurtz, "The Bad News Starts at Work in the Nation's Newsrooms," *Washington Post,* October 30, 1995, p. A1.

67. Ibid.

68. McEnrue, "Managing Diversity," p. 18.

69. Brenda Paik Sunoo, "Tapping Diversity in America's Newsrooms," *Personnel Journal* 73 (November 1994): 104.

70. "Soup Kitchens, Drug Rehab, AIDS Education—Just Another Day in the Life of an APS Manager," *Reputation Management* (September/October 1995): 53.

71. Shari Caudron, "Training Can Damage Diversity Efforts," *Personnel Journal* (April 1993): 50.

72. Ibid.

4

Hispanic Voices: Is the Press Listening?

Jorge Quiroga

It wasn't so long ago that Hispanics in the United States read with great hope that the 1980s would be the "Decade of the Hispanic."[1] Cover stories in weekly magazines and newspapers and on network television examined demographic increases and concluded that Hispanic clout would be felt both in the ballot box and the shopping mall. Certainly Hispanics attained some significant achievements during the 1980s, and their political influence did increase. But the predictions turned out to be vastly exaggerated and the milestones bittersweet. Hispanic political impact on the presidential elections of 1984 and 1988 was not conclusive. The income gap between Hispanics and non-Hispanics increased. And the expanded numbers created a backlash among non-Hispanics that produced the Official English movement and a bipartisan anti-immigration sentiment.

The unfulfilled potential of the 1980s has pushed Hispanics into the 1990s with even greater expectations. The U.S. Census projects that early in the twenty-first century Hispanics will outnumber blacks as the nation's biggest minority. The extension of the Voting Rights Act to include linguistic minorities is promoting the election of Hispanic lawmakers in record numbers. Despite these achievements, the 1990s offer a paradox of increased opportunity and resistance to Hispanic growth in the United States. In California, politicians clamor that the United States has given too much away to its minorities, and Governor Pete Wilson suggests that to save money the government should strip citizenship from the children of undocumented Mexicans born in the United States. In Texas, the federal government orders extra border patrols along the Rio Grande. In Somerville, Massachusetts, which had billed itself as a haven for new immigrants, school officials start demanding passports from students who have noticeable accents.

Hispanics in the United States are at a crossroads of economic and political assimilation. Yet the problems of underemployment, health, and education remain great obstacles that threaten continued marginalization.

How well Hispanics fare into the turn of the century will in part reflect how the press continues to cover their particular issues and concerns. It is the media that shape public awareness and political opinion. As the American humorist Will Rogers said many years ago, "All I know is just what I read in the papers." Add television, and there is still much truth in Rogers's statement.

Despite an occasional flurry of attention, press indifference toward Hispanics seems more the rule than the exception. Conversely, despite occasional attempts to engage public opinion through tactics such as boycotts, marches, or strikes, Hispanics have remained passive in the face of the inadequate press coverage. The problem itself can be traced to the process of reporting on Hispanics. Reporters and editors habitually seem to speak about Hispanics, not to Hispanics. Journalists are blind to the full range of diversity within this community. I call this the transparency of Hispanics before the U.S. press. It is a curious attribute of being noted, not quite completely ignored but not fully seen or counted. As such, the media influences how Hispanics view themselves as well as how Anglos perceive Hispanics.

There is also a correlation between Hispanic communities where there is a lack of political or grassroots development and the lack of qualitative and quantitative press coverage of Hispanics. Where there is a lack of Hispanic clout, the media encourages a homogeneous view of Hispanics.

Louis DeSipio is a political scientist who studies press coverage of Hispanics in the United States. He says, "The press gives the Anglo audience the wrong impression which allows Anglos to do less for Hispanics because they are not seen as distinct populations that need to be socialized into the American culture."[2] The broadest characteristics about the group are taken from the unadorned statistics that describe a Hispanic underclass. Hispanics are regularly presented by the press as uneducated immigrants who are unable or unwilling to help or speak for themselves. Even the better news operations often fail to meet the challenge posed by a changing population. On those rare occasions when the press feels compelled to report on Hispanics, be it Boston or even Los Angeles, the rift between this emerging group and mainstream society seems even greater.

Writing about press coverage of twenty-five million Hispanics in the United States is, in and of itself, a daunting challenge. Although there are many similarities in experiences, it is important to note that there is no steadfast Hispanic monolith. Miami, for example, is one of the most distinct exceptions. There, Cubans are the majority and define their own press coverage by exerting a dominating influence on the city's economy and politics. San Antonio is also notable for its deep-rooted Hispanic heritage. More than half the city's residents are Mexican American, and many can trace their ancestors to the early founding years, one hundred years before the Declaration of Independence. Boston, however, has a relatively small and diverse Hispanic community, only 10 percent of the city's residents.

In this chapter I consider first what we might expect if press coverage reflected the diversity of Hispanics in the United States. The chapter then adopts a case study approach, looking at the qualitative and quantitative coverage of events in various cities—Boston; Los Angeles; Washington, D.C.; and New York—to establish a pattern of coverage of Hispanics as a whole. Some stories became national events, whereas others received only local coverage. I conclude that the factors that weaken the link between the press and Hispanics are newsroom attitudes, limited knowledge about Hispanics, stereotyping, the lack of employment of Hispanic journalists, and inconsistent efforts by Hispanics to hold the press accountable.

The Diversity of the Hispanic
Population and Patterns of Press Coverage

Who is a Hispanic? The answer varies. Nearly 10 percent of the nation's population of 250 million is Hispanic. Although Hispanics live in every state, the majority (nearly nine of every ten) live in just nine states: New Mexico, California, Texas, Arizona, Colorado, New York, Florida, Nevada, and New Jersey. Mexican Americans form the largest group, accounting for 60 percent of the nation's Hispanic population. Puerto Ricans are the second-largest group, representing 12 percent of all Hispanics, followed by Cuban Americans at 5 percent. The remaining fourth, or 23 percent, come from the Dominican Republic and the Spanish-speaking countries of Central and South America.

Almost 23 percent of all Hispanics are foreign-born.[3] Others are multi-generation Americans, and still others have ancestors whose residences pre-date the nation's birth. About 62 percent of the Hispanic population was born in the United States.[4] Influenced by the continued influx of immigration, Spanish is the nation's second language, spoken at home by over 17 million people. Among native-born Hispanics the use of English increases with each generation. Among the native-born, 62 percent of Mexican Americans, 50 percent of Puerto Ricans, and 31 percent of Cubans speak English predominantly or exclusively at home.[5] Felix Gutierrez, a fourth-generation Californian, expresses a common sentiment among many Mexican Americans when he says, "My great-grandparents didn't cross the border. The border crossed them."[6]

For many it is also hard to understand the diversity within a series of groups who hold nationality above ethnicity. Rodolfo de la Garza, a prominent Hispanic political scientist and researcher, writes, "Mexicans, Puerto Ricans and Cubans have little interaction with each other, most do not recognize that they have much in common culturally, and they do not profess strong affection for each other."[7]

Some even see the term "Hispanic" itself as a forced label. Richard Rodriguez writes in his book *Days of Obligation,* "Hispanic is not a racial or cultural or geographic or linguistic or economic description. It is a bureaucratic integer. A complete political fiction." But the reality is that the dictionary definition of Hispanic—as someone with origins in Spain and its language, people, and culture—no longer applies in the United States. Today the term "Hispanic," along with its colloquial synonym, "Latino," refers to people whose origins are traced to the Spanish-speaking countries of Latin America.[8]

Although they acknowledge the bureaucratic birth of the term "Hispanic" in the 1980 census, many feel that, within the context of an Anglo-Saxon majority in the United States, Hispanics' common language and similar history give them more in common with each other regardless of national origin. "A group consciousness is emerging despite our differences," says Raul Yzaguirre, executive director of the National Council of La Raza, the nation's largest Hispanic civil rights advocacy group. "It is all contextual," he adds. "We are talking about these things as though they were in opposition when in fact we are talking about a set of concentric circles."[9]

From Puerto Ricans in Boston and Salvadorans in Washington, D.C., to Mexicans in Los Angeles, from Chileans in Chicago to Cubans in Miami, from every country in Latin America, black, white, Indian, mestizos— Hispanics now account for one of every ten Americans. They are not a single monolithic community but rather a series of communities arranged in concentric circles. It is a distinction lost on the mainstream press.

"I do not attribute a maliciousness or an agenda on the part of the networks to 'dis' Hispanics. I really think there is a genuine pervasive and overwhelming ignorance on the part of the networks toward this community," say Lisa Navarrate, a spokesperson at La Raza's headquarters in Washington, D.C.[10] Navarrate resists accusing the mainstream media of pernicious racism.

> When you talk to the networks they think Hispanics are immigrants, recent arrivals, that we just got here yesterday and that most of us are here illegally. There are all kinds of myths and stereotypes that they take as the Gospel truth. When in reality two-thirds of the vast majority of Hispanics [Mexican Americans] were born in this country. Their roots go back to before the English got here. But we can say that till we are blue in the face and it doesn't quite resonate.[11]

That is certainly the perception among dozens of Latinos interviewed for this report. From different countries of origin, foreign-born or U.S.-born, Spanish- or English-language dominant, from the East Coast or from the West, liberals or conservatives, Democrats or Republicans, there is one consensus: Hispanics are ill-served by the U.S. press. "There is a lack of understanding as to who Latinos are. The press is still very much driven by the black/white equation. They tend to see us in that context. How are we like blacks and how do we differ from blacks? The census tells them we exist but they don't understand us in our own right," says Felix Gutierrez of the Freedom Forum and a former journalism professor.[12]

Louis DeSipio, a research associate with the Latino National Political Survey based out of the University of Texas at Austin, believes the way the press fails to cover contrasts among Hispanics creates a stereotype among Anglos (a loose term for English-speaking U.S.-born whites of European descent). "They get periodic statistics from the Census Bureau that say things are terrible. Or they give a picture that is accurate for just one person," says DeSipio.[13]

From census reports, publishers and editors learn that Hispanics are the fastest-growing ethnic group in the United States. If census projections hold true, at the beginning of the twenty-first century Hispanics will become the country's largest minority group, surpassing blacks. Due to immigration and high birth rates, the Hispanic population grew over seven times as fast as the rest of the nation's population during the 1980s. (Hispanics increased by 53 percent, in contrast to growth rates of 6 percent for whites and 13 percent for non-Hispanic blacks.[14]) Other snapshots show that Hispanics are the least educated, the poorest, and the least likely to be covered by health insurance. Hispanic children are twice as likely to be living in poverty as are non-Hispanic children.[15]

A growing population, extensions to the Voting Rights Act to specific language minorities, and court challenges to district boundaries during the 1970s and 1980s had considerable political impact. De la Garza and DeSipio write that in the Southwest, for example, "By freeing the Mexican American vote, the parties—particularly the Democrats in the Southwestern states—have become dependent upon Mexican-American votes for victory."[16] In New York, Hispanic elected representation to city, state, and Congress doubled from eleven to twenty-two between 1986 and the November elections of 1992. Hispanic representation to the 103rd session of Congress increased 60 percent. The seven new Hispanic seats expanded the Congressional Hispanic Caucus to seventeen members—still only a paltry 3 percent of the 535 seats in the House of Representatives.

The Hispanic political potential continues to be undermined by weak voter participation. Even the record-setting registration of 5 million Hispanic voters in 1992 reported by the South West Voter Registration Project appears to achieve little more than treading water.[17] Voter registrations by definition include only voting-age U.S. citizens. Expand the base to include the influx of new immigrants as well as the younger, poorer, and less educated Hispanics, and there is in fact little proportionate progress in voter participation. Rodolfo de la Garza and Louis DeSipio studied the effects of the Voting Rights Act on Hispanics. They conclude, "Despite significant improvements in eliminating structural barriers to participation and in electing Latinos to office . . . Latino registration and voting rates nationally have not increased beyond pre-1975 levels."[18]

Hispanic political influence is further diminished by the very nature of Hispanics who are elected. In Washington, members of the Hispanic Congressional Caucus represent the full political spectrum—liberals, moderates, and conservatives. Fourteen members are Democrats and three are Republicans. Unlike the Black Congressional Caucus, Hispanics on Capitol Hill rarely vote as a single bloc. Some of today's most pressing national concerns—welfare reform, crime, national health insurance, job creation, substance abuse, immigration, and AIDS—have a disproportionate impact on Hispanics, but in Washington when the national press covers these issues Hispanics are seldom interviewed. Their opinions are rarely sought. George Condon, Washington bureau chief for Copley News Service and the president of the White House Press Corps Association, does not mince words when he says, "The press seeks opinions from those it perceives to have influence, and in Washington Hispanics are not there yet."[19]

Demographic data provided by the U.S. Census has outpaced qualitative information available about this group. We know how many there are, how much they earn, where they live, their occupations, their legal status, and the language they prefer, but we know much less about their opinions, feelings, and values. De la Garza et al. say, "The nation's knowledge about this group has lagged behind its interest in it, and this knowledge gap has become fertile ground for claims and counterclaims about Hispanics—who they are and what their presence portends for the nation."[20] Lacking substantive facts or interest, the press continues to pay minimal attention.

When Louis DeSipio and James Henson looked at the daily newspapers with the largest circulation in forty major cities in the United States over a six-month period, they found that "Overall, approximately 60% of the paper/days reviewed had no coverage at all . . . of the remaining 49%, the average paper contained 1.6 articles. . . . In other words one would see two articles over about a three day period."[21] The population in each of these forty cities was at least 10 percent Hispanic. The sampling included at least 90 percent of the populations of Cuban, Puerto Rican, or Mexican origin.

"I was surprised. I actually thought that was low. I thought that because so many papers served cities with large Latino communities, you'd find more written about Latinos," says DeSipio.[22] The stories written about Hispanics tended to be local. DeSipio and Henson found no "national" Hispanic coverage. Among the papers that do have coverage, few cover the same stories. This finding suggests the absence of explicitly Latino issues that editors uniformly recognize as meeting their papers' criterion for "national" news.[23]

The little coverage Hispanics do receive usually fits the typical definition of "news." Emily Rooney, executive producer of *World News Tonight with Peter Jennings,* is more blunt, saying, "Most news is about conflict."[24] David Shaw of the *Los Angeles Times* wrote, "News, as defined by the people who write, edit, publish and broadcast it, is about the unusual, the aberrant—about triumphs and tragedies, underachievers and overachievers, it's about the extremes of life, not 'normal everyday' life."[25]

"It is only when the majority culture perceives the black cat is crossing its path that anybody says anything about Latinos," says Ray Suarez, host of National Public Radio's *Talk of the Nation.*[26] The former Chicago reporter watches national and local press coverage of Hispanics from his unique vantage point as the only Hispanic host of a national radio show. "I am in pretty exclusive company."[27] Suarez says the conflict-driven nature of hard news offers few opportunities for the public to see Hispanics in a fuller context: "It's either to highlight pathologies, drug sales, gang violence, school drop out rates or to do a Margaret Mead turn on that night's 'Evening News,' by going over to the other side of town to see what those Mexicans are like."[28]

That is not the case for whites or Anglos, who are routinely represented in many different types of news accounts. Journalism professor Erna Smith examined how the mainstream media covered different ethnic groups in the Bay Area. "Whites were sources for all types of stories but this was not true for people of color. People of color were more likely than whites to be news sources of crime stories and as a group were cited more frequently in these crime stories."[29]

The degree of one-sided coverage varies between newspapers and TV news. The Bay Area has a 15 percent Hispanic population, yet, as Smith writes, "On television . . . 12% of the Latinos were sources of crime compared with 14% for whites. In newspapers, 60% of Latinos were sources of crime stories compared with 18% of the whites."[30] The emphasis on news about Hispanic crime carries over from region to region. In San Antonio, Texas, Thomas Llarade looked at specific news coverage on KMOL-TV. "Hispanics were overrepresented in crime stories and were generally portrayed as criminals, or victims. 31% of Hispanic stories were crime related, while 21% portrayed Hispanics as victims of natural misfortunes. Within these stories Hispanics were rarely interviewed."[31]

Of all natural misfortunes afflicting Hispanics, poverty may be the worst. Nationally, more than a fourth (29 percent) of Hispanics live below federal poverty levels. The 3.1 percent increase in Hispanic poverty between 1991 and 1993 is the highest among any ethnic group in the nation. As Hispanic poverty rises, income drops. Per capita income for Hispanics in 1992 was only half that of whites. (Whites earned $15,981, blacks $9,296, and Hispanics $8,874.[32]) Curiously, this emphasis by the press on Hispanic criminality and poverty does not temper an overriding impulse to overlook Hispanics. It is as if they possessed some unnatural quality of transparency so as to be noticed but not seen with certainty. To understand this further we need to consider case studies of coverage of Hispanics—from Boston to L.A.—to see how these patterns develop.

A Cross Burns in Boston

Twenty-three-year-old Marisol Abreu peered out her living-room window and could hardly believe her eyes. There, in the front courtyard of her apartment, a five-foot wooden cross was on fire. "They make me feel like I don't have the right to live here," she said. None of the racial slurs, the hateful stares she'd endured during the time she'd lived in Charlestown hurt as much or seemed as threatening "as the powerful symbol of the burning cross, which is usually associated with the Klu Klux Klan."[33]

That hardened symbol of hate was hardly anonymous. At 7:30 P.M. a crowd of 100 white teenagers shamelessly gathered around the burning cross. Insults, taunts, and racial slurs were directed at Abreu and other Hispanic residents in the public housing projects where she and her three-year-old daughter lived. No, this wasn't the 1950s in the deep South, nor was it the 1970s when court-ordered busing stirred deep racial animosity in many northern cities. This ugly scene took place in 1993, on a raw damp October evening in Boston, a city with its share of unhealed racial wounds.

How the city's newspapers and TV news covered this troubling episode reveals much about the media's detached relationship with Hispanics in the city and the profound degree to which Hispanic leaders perceive themselves alienated by the press. In Boston, the cross-burning incident capped a night of violence following the stabbing of three white youths by a Hispanic teenager as retaliation for alleged harassment. Several hundred angry white residents chased the eighteen-year-old Hispanic suspect into a friend's apartment in the Bunker Hill Projects in Charlestown. As dumpsters were set ablaze, the mob screamed obscenities and racial slurs. Dozens of police were summoned to the rescue. Under heavy security the Hispanic youth was arrested and whisked out of the building into a police vehicle.

The next morning the *Boston Globe* wrote of the brewing racial confrontation, "Police speculated that the stabbings came after some youths had slashed the tires of three cars believed to be owned by the suspect and his friends. White youths are believed to be responsible for the tire slashings."[34] Press accounts dealt with the facts and the racial framework of the violence and the changing demographics in Charlestown's public housing. Once residents in the 1,111-unit complex were all white. Today they are 62 percent white, 17 percent Hispanic, 11 percent black, and 9 percent Asian. No one would excuse the bloody alleged attack of the Hispanic suspect or the frenzied reaction by the white mob. But had this "race riot" involved black victims and a burning cross or Jews and Nazi anti-Semitic graffiti, the press in Boston would have certainly contacted community leaders. The spontaneous reaction from those groups would have also been more fervent.

Curiously, although two Hispanic eyewitnesses were interviewed, reporters did not seek out opinions from Hispanic leaders. It seemed as if there were no Hispanic names in the newsroom rolodex. Reporters who felt the need to speak to Hispanic leaders were satisfied with simply interviewing the Hispanic director of the Boston Housing Authority, David Cortiella.

"Any community that is undergoing transition—where new neighbors are moving in—will have difficulties," Cortiella told the *Boston Herald* as he inspected the projects the next day.[35] Speaking to a WCVB reporter as the city official looking to calm a volatile situation, Cortiella warned, "Don't make it more than what it is. This is kids fighting kids."[36] Later, Cortiella expressed dismay that other Hispanic voices were not sought out by the press. "If this had been a black/white incident, the *Globe* and the *Herald* would have certainly flipped through their rolodexes and invited reaction from a whole range of black community leaders and politicians."[37] Cortiella says that when he didn't read any interviews with other Hispanic leaders in the city, he called the *Globe* reporter covering the story and complained. "I even had to give him the names of three Hispanic leaders, but it was me giving him leads trying to help him write the story."[38] The story Cortiella wanted was not written. Subsequent reports did not mention Hispanics in Boston as representing a larger constituency. It was a missed opportunity to build bridges between the press and Hispanics.

Equally damning was the passivity of Hispanic leaders themselves. Their silence was so deafening that a week later, the *Globe*'s Efrain Hernandez, Jr., one of a handful of Hispanic reporters in the city, wrote an analysis of it. "For many in the city's Hispanic community, the lack of public outrage by Hispanic activists since the cross burning and other racial unrest in Charlestown has itself been an outrage. Some residents saw a lost opportunity to highlight the complex barriers faced by Hispanics in the city because, at least in public, activists remained largely silent."[39]

Hernandez later explained why so many remained so silent. "Latino leaders were hesitant to get involved because they felt the Hispanic kids were no innocent bystanders, that they were partly to blame for the violence that first night. Some activists felt they had to be careful. They were frustrated about the cross burning. They really did not know what to do. It shows people are intimidated by the media."[40] Instead of providing meaningful coverage of Hispanics in the United States, the U.S. press has chosen a passive role, which distances the press and Hispanics from each other. At times Hispanic leaders and organizations have been indecisive in responding to specific events. Sometimes when they do react, they demonstrate a lack of sophistication and knowledge about using the media. The press, likewise, has often shown a broad lack of understanding and awareness of Hispanics even in the aftermath of a confrontation thick with racial overtones, like the Charlestown melee and cross burning. Once again, reporters and editors opted to talk about Hispanics rather than to talk to them. Maybe it seems simpler not to commit time and effort to understand a group that defies easy definition.

Patterns of Exclusion and the L.A. Riots

The L.A. riots—the most racially charged incident of the decade—provides an excellent example of the media looking through the Hispanic community. The 1991 police beating in Los Angeles of twenty-five-year-old black motorist Rodney King and the subsequent riots in the spring of 1992 were described by a Special Committee of the California State Assembly as the "worst multi-ethnic conflict in United States history."

Yet the image left from the news coverage of the riots was not really multi-ethnic. After viewing the police beating of King, the subsequent beating of the white truck driver Reginald Denny, and many other videotaped acts of arson and vandalism during the riots, viewers would be hardpressed not to describe the violence as something other than the rage of blacks against whites and Korean bystanders. A careful look shows that was hardly the case at all. Hispanics experienced a symmetry of exclusion from beginning to end in the press coverage. They were excluded as perpetrators, as victims, and as a community affected by the melee.

The first subtle omission by the press was a failure to consistently report that one of the four "white" officers charged in the beating of Rodney King was of Latino descent. Only one early article in the *Los Angeles Times* noted that as a youth Officer Theodore Briseno was routinely "teased about his Latino heritage by white friends in high school."[41] Peter Skerry, a noted scholar on Mexican Americans, writes of this omission, "Yet in its news columns and editorials the Times has—with this notable exception—consistently referred to Briseno as one of 'the whites' who assaulted King. Indeed, in the continuing furor over this incident Briseno's ethnic background has been almost universally overlooked."[42]

Neglecting to identify one of the officers as a Hispanic, the media framed the conflict from the outset in the familiar black/white U.S. paradigm of racial conflict. This pattern persisted almost a year later, when the L.A. riots erupted following the acquittal of the four "white" police officers by a Simi Valley jury.

On April 29, 1992, TV cameras zoomed in at the intersection of Florence and Normandy Streets in South Central L.A., the epicenter of the riots. From the minute the TV crews went "live" with the images of black rioters venting their anger against their unsuspecting victims, to the trial in October 1993 of the two black suspects accused of beating white trucker Reginald Denny, the perception created by the media belied the facts. The press overlooked substantial evidence that the riot was a "class rebellion as well as a race revolt."[43] Selective reporting and preconceived notions in the press coverage left Hispanics on the cutting room floor. According to *U.S. News and World Report:*

> The problem with the race-tells-all explanation is that it overlooks the central, perhaps even dominant role that Hispanics played in the violence and suffering. According to the Los Angeles Police Department, Hispanics accounted for half of the 8,700 people arrested city-wide during and after the riots; in fact, the L.A.P.D. arrested *more* Hispanics (4,307) than blacks (3,083). Nineteen Hispanics also died during the civil disorders, just three short of the number of black fatalities. And while newscasts featured embittered standoffs between blacks and Korean shop owners, the L.A. mobs ravaged about as many Hispanic businesses as Korean-owned ones.[44]

TV news accounts projected a one-sided picture into living rooms around the world. Looking carefully at how the press framed the story reveals how little journalists knew about the city's neighborhoods and the complexity of urban tension that existed. Being familiar with the coverage of minorities in the press from her research in San Francisco, Erna Smith decided to examine local and national TV news of the L.A. riots beginning April 29, 1992. Her study included a Korean-language news program and the nation's number one Spanish-language TV network, Univision.

> There were significant differences in the coverage on different stations. The network news coverage framed the story more in terms of blacks and whites than did the local stations in Los Angeles. . . . Blacks and whites were the central focus of 96% of the network news reports compared to 80% of the stories aired on stations in Los Angeles. . . . Conversely, Latinos and Koreans were the central focus of 4% of the stories aired on the networks and 18% of the stories aired on the Los Angeles stations.[45]

The visual images and the framing of these news stories contrasts with the actual participants and the ethnic diversity of the affected neighborhoods. The areas of Los Angeles most decimated by the riots were heavily populated by Hispanics: Koreatown (80 percent), Pico Union (70 percent), and South Central Los Angeles (45 percent).[46] Those numbers, according to Smith, correspond with the arrest totals that showed Hispanics "comprised half the rioters arrested in the City of Los Angeles and possibly 30 to 40 percent of the store owners whose businesses were destroyed by the violence."[47] But in TV news the L.A. riots had a vastly different face, which was not Hispanic. Smith found that "Latinos only comprised 17 percent of the residents and 10 percent of the store owners interviewed in the coverage."[48]

The Tomas Rivera Center in Claremont, California, also conducted a comprehensive study of the L.A. riots and their aftermath. This project specifically tracked the Hispanic presence in the fourteen most highly damaged neighborhoods (including Koreatown, Pico Union, and South Central Los Angeles). In this broader geographical area, Hispanics still accounted for 49 percent of the residents.[49] Analyzing the most highly damaged neighborhoods helps trace the roots of Hispanics' omission in news accounts. East L.A. is the city's largest and best-known Hispanic neighborhood. Because it was largely untouched by the violence, there was an initial assumption that "Latinos scarcely participated in and were mostly unaffected by the unrest."[50]

The result is that Hispanics in the newly emerging barrios that were in the eye of the storm were seen but unheard in the news coverage. This type of reporting was a double-edged sword. On one side, the lack of prominence spared Hispanics public and official condemnation. On the other side, the failure to be visible initially kept Hispanics away from the round-table of negotiations after the riots.

As city, state, and federal agencies began work to rebuild South Central Los Angeles, the initial effort mirrored the black/white framework of the coverage. None of the three commissioners who initially headed the Rebuild L.A. Committee was Hispanic. The oversight became so glaring that Hispanic business and social leaders staged a rally outside of City Hall. They complained that Hispanics were being shortchanged in riot aid. The *Los Angeles Times* reports:

> Joe Sanchez, president of the Mexican-American Grocers Assn., said he remains convinced that African-American organizations have received disproportionate attention and post-riot aid because they have stronger ties to City Hall and because the news media often paint riots in a black-versus-white or black-versus-Korean conflict, in which latinos were primarily looters instead of victims.[51]

Magdalena Duran, a spokesperson for the La Raza office in Los Angeles, agrees:

> We were left out of the reconstruction even in South Central L.A. which is nearly 50% latino. It has grown to be a divisive issue. People still see the area as black and resources still go predominantly to Afro-Americans. There is a real lack of comprehension of the demographic changes in these areas.[52]

After one year a Latino was finally added to the commission. Finally, Barbara Cox, an editor for the Tomas Rivera Center in Los Angeles, says:

> When groups started to coalesce and develop strategies [to address the damage and destruction from the riots] the general feeling was that Latinos were not represented to the degree one would expect among groups like Rebuild L.A.[53]

So how is it possible that with a predilection to see Hispanics in stories of criminality and poverty, the press could have left Hispanics out of the L.A. riots story? How could there be no voice given to Hispanics in Los Angeles even when they were in the throes of a riot? Fernando Oaxaca, the owner of an L.A. public relations company, says part of the problem is that, historically, Hispanics have been slow to mobilize and demand public attention. "When you abuse a Mexican he leaves the room because he doesn't want to be where he's not wanted. We've got to wake up the system. . . . We're going to bug everybody. We're here, and that ain't going to change."[54] The pattern of exclusion also reflects the fact that too few of the reporters and news executives listening in the newsroom are Hispanics who know this community and its language.

Washington, D.C.: Does Anybody Speak Spanish in the Newsroom?

It was a typical afternoon in the *Washington Post* newsroom, May 5, 1991, as reporters and editors worked toward deadline. At the assignment desk, the police radios came alive with calls for back-up in the Mount Pleasant neighborhood of D.C. Soon, radio reports told of a major confrontation between police and Hispanic residents. Apparently a cop had shot a Hispanic immigrant and people were angry. "At the *Post* people started to gather around TV monitors when the local stations cut in with live reports from the scene," says Greg Brock, front page editor. "Then someone in the newsroom suddenly asked, 'Think we should send somebody down there?'" Brock says there was no reporter in the city room who spoke Spanish, so the editors called the international desk and borrowed a Spanish-speaking correspondent, who was sent to the disturbance. The *Washington Post,* which prides itself on its national and international reporting, was now covering a local disturbance in its own backyard as a foreign war. The scene is hardly surprising to one of the few Hispanics who worked at the *Post* before 1991. "When I left the *Post* in 1989 I was one of only two Latino reporters and the other one did not speak Spanish," says Zita Arocha, a staff reporter from 1985 to 1989.[55] Prior to her stint at the *Post*, Arocha reported for the *Tampa Times,* the *Miami Herald,* and the *Miami News.* In Washington she specialized in immigration and Hispanic affairs. Arocha says that before she left the paper she warned her Anglo editors that tensions between the city's burgeoning Hispanic community and the police department were near the breaking point. "I spelled it out for my editors that the Latino community was a time bomb for the city and that the *Post* did not have the resources to cover it."[56]

Two years later the lid came off. The violence was set off after Daniel Gomez, a Salvadoran immigrant, was shot by a black female officer trying to arrest him for disorderly conduct. Police say Gomez had been drinking and lunged at the police officer with a knife.

> What began as a largely Hispanic disturbance on May 5 in Mount Pleasant, grew on May 6 into a free-for-all that spilled over into adjoining neighborhoods. At its peak 1,000 police in riot gear were involved and up to 600 black, Hispanic and white youths were engaged in running battles with the police. As of May 8, some 160 adults and juveniles had been arrested. Thirteen police officers had been injured, and six police cars, a handful of businesses, stores, and a city bus were set afire. While the shooting of 30-year-old Daniel Gomez set off the violence, Hispanics claim the eruption was the result of a history of mistreatment and neglect by police and the city administration.[57]

Milagros Jardine, a radio reporter for WMAL who covered the Mount Pleasant riot, says, "The news organizations in general missed the boat on covering the Latino community and didn't take the opportunity to cover it adequately before the riot so that there was no anticipation on the part of the greater community that this could happen."[58]

Jardine was one of several dozen journalists, city officials, and community leaders who met almost two months after the riots to review how well the city's news organizations had responded. There was general agreement that the media had missed the circumstances of the community's rage prior to the event and in its wake.

> Once the reporters got there I think they started generalizing and started taking in lots of theories and sort of projecting what they thought had happened rather than really listening to what the people in the community were telling them had happened. If there is a fault to be placed, it's the fact that the big news organizations have ignored this [Hispanic] community and for some reason don't see it in their best interest, don't see it as an interesting, exciting, stimulating story to cover.[59]

The capital's Hispanic population exploded during the 1980s with the arrival of thousands of Central Americans fleeing political unrest. The biggest influx came from El Salvador. Despite the growth of the city's Hispanic population, politics and demographics remain overwhelmingly black oriented. Apparently there were few reporters who had a working knowledge of the city's newest immigrant groups. Reports during the three-day melee included gross exaggerations, rumors, and misinformation.

TV news reports, during live coverage from the scene, provided the most glaring unsubstantiated misinformation. "Some Anglo journalists went so far as to suggest a link between rioters and Central American leftist guerrillas, reporting that the reason the protestors were so successful in burning police vehicles and doing so much damage was because they had prior training and connections to guerrilla movements somewhere in a foreign land," says Clavel Sanchez of National Public Radio.[60]

Hispanic reporters blamed the misrepresentations of the Mount Pleasant neighborhood on the lack of Hispanic staff in the city's major media outlets. "I think it became very self evident to each of the media organizations just how out of touch they were with this particular community," says Carlos Sanchez, a reporter at the *Washington Post* who was later assigned to cover the disturbances.[61] Even Sanchez's boss could not disagree.

"Our coverage prior to the disturbances in Mt. Pleasant was inadequate," says Milton Coleman, the *Post*'s metro editor. "I think our coverage got much better the day that Carlos Sanchez was assigned to do this full time. Having reporters who were culturally in tune with the community, or who spoke Spanish became a necessity."[62] Coleman says that the *Post* was able to recruit as many as six or seven Spanish-speaking staff to cover the story. "Not all of them were Latino. Many of them were Anglos," Coleman recalls.[63] The *Post* had only two Hispanic reporters at the time. Today, twelve Hispanics work in the newsroom; they make up 2.2 percent of the staff.[64]

The employment picture for Hispanics in the news media twenty-five years after the *Kerner Commission Report* remains bleak despite recent gains. Hispanics argue that more Hispanic journalists in newsrooms minimizes distortions, exaggerations, and misrepresentations of their Hispanic communities because they understand the vast differences and commonalities among them. "Employment is a vehicle toward coverage. The end result of diversifying the newsroom is supposed to be coverage and content, what is coming off the TV screen or pages of the newspaper. If you do not have Latinos working in the newsroom you are not going to be able to influence the coverage," says Felix Gutierrez, a former journalism professor now working at the Freedom Forum.[65]

Hispanic employment in the United States' newsrooms remains a thorny issue. Underrepresentation remains substantial despite modest gains. Even in markets with a large Hispanic presence, Hispanic employment in the newsroom remains low. You wouldn't expect many Hispanics at the *Wichita Eagle* or the *Richmond Times Dispatch*. Yet in New York City, which is 25 percent Hispanic, the *New York Times*'s newsroom staff is 3.6 percent Hispanic. Los Angeles is 40 percent Hispanic, yet the *Los Angeles Times*'s news staff is 6.46 percent Hispanic. Locally or nationally, underrepresentation of Hispanics is broad. The United States is nearly 10 percent Hispanic, yet only 4 percent of the news staff at the top fifty-seven daily newspapers in the country is Hispanic.[66]

"[The increases are] nothing to write home about. The increases should be much higher than that considering the fact that there have been recruitment programs for nearly a dozen years," says Zita Arocha, a freelance journalist who conducts an annual survey and report on the status of Hispanics for the National Association of Hispanic Journalists. She says the typical excuse offered by news managers—that able Hispanic reporters are hard to find—does not hold true any more: "We have many young Latino journalists working in smaller markets who are ready and good enough to get up to the next rung in medium and large market newspapers. All they need is the opportunity."[67]

Hispanic news managers, the decisionmakers in the newsroom, are an even rarer breed. Only 2.3 percent of news managers in the top fifty-seven newspapers are Hispanic.[68] On the broadcast side of news the raw numbers imply Hispanics have made slightly better gains. "The minority share of the newsroom work force edged to a new high in television last year, but moved backward a bit in radio. Hispanics made substantial gains. The Hispanic share of all TV news personnel went up from 3% in 1990 to 5% in 1991 and 6% in 1992," writes University of Missouri journalism professor Vernon Stone, after reviewing employment records from 411 TV stations and 296 commercial radio stations for the Radio and Television News Directors Foundation.[69] Yet Hispanic journalists analyze the same numbers and see in them more than meets the eye. Aggregate industry totals are misleading.

"Before you go out and buy another TV set, consider the fact that the network news still doesn't look like America, and neither does its primetime programming," write Zita Arocha and Roberto Moreno.[70] "The University of Missouri study finds the proportion of Latino employees still smaller among television stations affiliated with the three major networks—ABC, NBC, and CBS—than among 'other' stations sending up Spanish speaking fare generated by Univision and Telemundo."[71] Arocha adds, "The statistics do not break out differences between English and Spanish language TV but it is my gut feeling that a great part of the aggregate increase is due to the recent boom in Spanish language TV."[72] Diane Alverio, a TV reporter in Hartford, Connecticut, says, "Most of us are the only one in the newsroom. And the people in the newsroom making decisions, what stories, what angle and how to cover them are not Hispanic."[73]

Hispanic reporters tell stories that have a familiar ring to other minorities.[74] They say that pushing aggressively for Hispanic coverage beyond crime and welfare is like putting on a "sombrero" in the newsroom that delegates the reporter to the so-called taco beat. "The hardest part is striking a sense of balance in your work. You do not want to neglect the community you care about, but you also have to show that you can cover anything if you are given the opportunity," says the *Boston Globe*'s Efrain Hernandez, Jr.[75]

In most markets where Hispanics have yet to make substantial economic and political gains, Hispanic reporters say the balance they are forced to strike tilts away from Hispanic coverage. "If you are one of those rare Latinos in a newsroom you will also have to make a career decision. You know that to rise in the system you do the front page stories or the lead stories in the broadcast and that Latino stories are not going to get that play," says NPR's Ray Suarez. He adds that many Hispanic reporters choose professional survival. "So there you are; one of the only people on the inside who can pitch for a different look at the news, and if you do that and become perceived as an ethnic novelty act, you limit your own future opportunities. So you either whitewash yourself to get ahead or you become an advocate inside the newsroom and become marginalized."[76]

"[These reporters] are struggling to be mainstream," observes Rita Elizondo, executive director of the Congressional Hispanic Caucus Institute.[77] At the institute it is Elizondo's job to convince reporters to write stories that have a specific Hispanic interest and to include Hispanic opinion in reporting about the U.S. Congress. It is never an easy job, but often Hispanic reporters make it even harder to do, Elizondo says. "They are finally at the *Washington Post* or they are finally at NBC, and they are struggling so hard to be part of the team and the mainstream that they rarely venture out into covering Latino issues because they don't want to be tagged Latino. It is very disappointing because we certainly don't get the coverage from the non-minority reporters."[78]

Without a concerted advocacy inside and outside the newsroom for more complete coverage of Hispanics, the impression and myths perpetuated are of a people lumped together as a monolith despite vast differences; a people unwilling and unable to help themselves. "Indicative of that national mood is a 1990 national poll that found that compared to Jews, blacks, Asians and southern whites, Americans perceive Latinos as second only to blacks in terms of being lazy rather than hard-working and living off welfare rather than being self-supporting. The survey also reports that Hispanics are seen as the nation's least patriotic group."[79] The low opinion of Hispanics makes perfect sense. Most people base their feelings about minorities from what they read or watch on TV.

Hispanic Magazine looked at all stories published by the *Chicago Tribune,* the *Los Angeles Times,* the *San Antonio Light,* and the *Washington Post* during a week in August 1992. Despite the fact that all the cities serviced by these major dailies have sizable Hispanic communities, the authors "had to look carefully in each paper to find any story positive or negative, about or including Latinos. When Hispanics were mentioned in news articles they were more likely to be found in a crime story as the perpetrator, victim or police officer."[80] The survey found a distinct absence of Hispanic political priorities and opinion, either from grassroots or mainstream political leaders.

In another survey, Unabridged Communications of Arlington, Virginia, reviewed 4,000 articles published in seven major newspapers and three news magazines during July and August 1992. Unabridged Communications notes that "there was no coverage devoted to Latino political priorities" and that the stories "failed to reflect positive contributions Latinos are making to society." The study's author concludes, "If you only had the articles that I culled over these two months you would not have a feel for who the [Hispanic] leadership was or what the needs of this particular community of interests were."[81]

Newspapers provide slightly better coverage of the political priorities among Hispanics. DeSipio and Henson's survey found that of those stories with political content relevant to Latinos, 30 percent dealt with electoral politics. But even this figure obscures an underlying indifference. "In one of the largest categories, electoral politics, mention of Latinos was limited to the inclusion of a Latino surname in 41 percent of the coded articles."[82] The overwhelming number of articles made reference to Hispanics in a political context without interviewing Hispanics. That pattern can be detected even in cases where Latino political importance is widely recognized.

New York: From Invisible to a Critical Voting Bloc

January 2, 1993, saw New York City covered with bright blue skies as the thermometer dipped below freezing. In Times Square sanitation crews swept away the last remnants of 1992. Across the city the novel calm of New Year's Day gave way to the usual traffic din. For many New Yorkers the luxury of a long holiday weekend and the prospect of bargain shopping during postholiday sales tempered the day's chill. For the city's mayor, David Dinkins, however, this was not a day free from politics.

Three thousand miles away, Mayor Dinkins scorched under a tropical midday sun during the inauguration of Pedro Rosello, Puerto Rico's newly elected governor. "For two hours the Mayor sat in the hot mugginess on a dais facing the sea behind the domed marble capitol in San Juan," the *New York Times* wrote describing how the mayoral race had taken a brief detour to the Caribbean.[83]

In fact, for Dinkins, a jaunt to San Juan was hardly out of the way. This was his third trip to the island in less than a year. Preparing for a rematch with former U.S. Attorney Rudolph Giuliani, Dinkins was vividly aware that New York City's black and white voters were sharply divided over his performance during his four-year term in office. The schism left the city's burgeoning Hispanic electorate in a position to make or break his reelection. By the beginning of 1993, 15 percent of all registered voters in New York City were Hispanic, with the overwhelming majority, 80 percent, being Puerto Ricans.[84] This time around, the "voto cafe con leche," or brown vote, would not be taken for granted.

So there Dinkins sat in San Juan, listening to speeches in Spanish. The final election was still eleven months away, but in the political game of symbolism it is the image that often prevails. In the pursuit for Hispanic support another Dinkins trip to Puerto Rico seemed as natural as a ride across the Brooklyn Bridge. The mayor told reporters, "How can you not come? Politics aside it would have been an affront for me not to come."[85] That was the flattery of a politician who already sensed he was vulnerable among key constituents.

The 1993 New York mayoral race was the political coming of age for the city's 2 million Hispanics, who found themselves in the right place at the right election. "We know that all the candidates are salivating for the Latino vote, and it's not clear how that vote will go," said Angelo Falcon, president of the Institute for Puerto Rican Policy, a nonpartisan think tank based in New York City.[86]

As the *Washington Post* observed, this was an election where "race ripples just beneath the surface of the contest . . . and the electorate remains sharply polarized. . . . The overwhelming percentage of blacks support Dinkins, while an almost equally high percentage of whites support Giuliani."[87] In this highly charged setting, the city's newspapers began writing about Hispanics as a "swing vote," as a "weak link" in the Dinkins coalition, or as a "crucial bloc" needed for either Dinkins or Giuliani to win. By the time the final election neared, *Newsday* wrote, "Latinos are not a formidable voting block, but in this close contest it can make a difference," adding: "As the election approaches, Latinos are being intensely wooed by both candidates—bombarded by television and radio ads in Spanish and English and with a direct-mail campaign."[88]

When Angelo Falcon noted, "Ten years ago we were invisible. Now it is almost like we are being over-hyped," he was referring specifically to the barrage of appeals from Dinkins and Giuliani.[89] But Falcon could just as easily have been talking about Hispanic press coverage during the 1993 campaign. And he only had to go back four years, not ten, to note the dramatic difference. If in 1993 Hispanics were overhyped in news accounts, they were nearly invisible in 1989 when Dinkins received 70 percent of the Hispanic vote, helping him eke out a 2 percent victory over Giuliani. (In 1989 13 percent, or one of every eight voters in the Democratic primary, were Hispanic.[90])

As part of the research for this chapter, nearly 500 articles written about the 1989 and 1993 New York mayoral campaigns were reviewed. The articles appeared in the *New York Times* and *Newsday* and were written between January 1 and the November final election of each year. In 1989 Mayor Ed Koch was upset in the Democratic primary by the then Manhattan borough president, David Dinkins. Dinkins then defeated former federal prosecutor Rudolph Giuliani in a rancorous final election. In 1993 the bitter rematch was won by Giuliani.

The contrast in press coverage of Hispanics in the two elections is significant. In 1989, 209 articles made specific mention of the candidates and their respective campaigns. Of these, 153 articles (73 percent) mentioned Hispanics in the context of the election. At first glance, this figure suggests a high degree of inclusion in the press coverage. Upon closer examination one detects a transparent if not invisible quality in the way Hispanics are covered and presented.

In 127 articles (60 percent) the reference to Hispanics was so limited, the term was used only as a noun or adjective, such as in "Hispanic voters," "Hispanic leaders," "Hispanic neighborhoods," "Hispanic police officers," "Hispanic community," "Hispanic agenda," "Hispanic teen-agers," and the distinctive "non-Hispanic white Catholics." For example, when David Dinkins announced his candidacy, a reporter wrote Dinkins made "a special appeal to Hispanic Democrats, whose votes are likely to be critical in the September 12 primary."[91] And when Koch began to lose ground, another reporter wrote of "drastic disaffection coming from the Hispanic community."[92]

Articles like these did not quote Hispanics. Their opinions were ignored. They included no analysis of the Hispanic vote or descriptions suggesting how the varying Hispanic communities fit into the fabric of the city politic. Such omissions are glaring given the fact that Hispanics are a very visible segment of the city. Two million New Yorkers, or 25 percent of the population, is Hispanic.

Only 26 articles (8 percent) of the 209 reviewed included interviews with Hispanics or analysis. Even here, on closer examination, these articles presented a limited range of Hispanic voices. Some of these interviews offered little more than brief quotes about support or endorsements, such as this comment from Bronx Borough President Fernando Ferrer, a Dinkins backer: "In the main Latinos would rather cut off their right hand than reach for a Republican lever";[93] or this quote from a Koch sympathizer along a parade route: "To me he is a great man," said Jaime Hernandez of Brooklyn.[94]

A few insightful articles however, included sharp observations about the fragile character of Dinkins's Latino/black voter base. After Dinkins's primary victory, the *New York Times* wrote, "His coalition included Hispanic voters who . . . finally decided economic or class interest was more important than their political competition with blacks."[95] The subsequent fraying of the rainbow coalition would change both the quantity and the quality of the coverage about Hispanics four years later.

In 1993 over 300 articles appeared in the *New York Times* and *Newsday* that mentioned Hispanics in the framework of the mayoral election. This represented *more than twice* the number of articles mentioning Hispanics in 1989. During the same period the percentage of Hispanic voters increased only slightly, from around 13 percent to around 15 percent.

Not only were Hispanics referred to more often by the press in 1993, but there was also a spectacular contextual difference. Day-to-day reading of newspapers left the distinct impression that Hispanics carried more political clout. Of all the articles that mentioned Hispanics, *ninety articles* (30 percent) referred to them as a critical "swing vote" in the election. And forty-five provided interviews with Hispanics or analysis of the Hispanic voting bloc. These articles included more detail and insights and far more interviews with a broader range of Hispanic politicians, pundits, political scientists, partisan voters, businesspersons, and neighborhood residents. One commentator wrote about the new demographic changes within the Hispanic community, saying that "the city where Latinos once meant 'Puerto Rican' is however in the process of a staggering redefinition" because of the huge recent influx of Dominicans who were mounting an economic and political challenge of their own.[96]

Political and social attitudes were explored. A poll of Hispanics reported, "There are a lot of worms in the Big Apple for many Latinos. . . . More than 84% believe race relations are 'not so good in the city.' . . . About 61% say police mistreat Latinos. . . . More than 64% oppose the teaching in public schools of tolerance of gays and lesbians."[97]

The Latino/black rift was written about in lengthy articles that included rich detail and history. One reporter observed, "Perhaps the strongest indication that Latino politicians do not want to be taken for granted by their black colleagues came during the recent race for State Comptroller," when the Hispanic delegation refused to support the black candidate.[98] Dinkins eventually received the backing from most of the city's Hispanic elected officials, but the endorsement was lukewarm, according to another article: "Critics say there has not been enough progress in appointments, jobs, and city contracts for Hispanic people."[99]

The striking transformation from a voting bloc largely ignored by the press in 1989 to one covered consistently in 1993 reveals two important changes: a new level of sophistication among Hispanic political activists and an increase in the employment of Hispanic reporters willing and able to recognize a good story in their own community concerning the city's politics. The reemergence of Herman Badillo, the Democratic, Puerto Rican–born, former Bronx borough president and congressman also added to the mix. Badillo ran for city comptroller on a fusion ticket with Giuliani.

Hispanic politicians appreciated that the dynamics in 1993 were ideal for the emergence of a new political force. The highly publicized confrontations between blacks and Jews in Brooklyn's Crown Heights neighborhood and the mayor's acknowledged mishandling of the incident had left the city racially polarized. Hispanic activists vied to fill the middle. State Assemblyman Roberto Ramirez says, "There was a new story to be told. The white/black dichotomy had been played out in the press."[100]

Two years earlier, the bitter struggle over redistricting had left Hispanics disenchanted with the depth of commitment from a black-dominated alliance. Assemblyman Ramirez says, "Reapportionment brought out a lot of tensions between latinos and blacks. Some of the mayor's appointees suggested that the goal was to work toward a final map that maximized black districts even at the expense of latinos."[101]

By the time the 1993 mayoral election came around, the Latino/black alliance was weakened, even after the final redistricting plans had given Hispanics greater representation.[102] Hispanic politicians said they were not going to be taken for granted again. "We got stiffed again after 1989 by the so-called Rainbow Coalition," says City Councillor Antonio Pagan. "Dinkins wins with the promise of equal access to Latinos and we got shut out."[103]

The final election on November 2, 1993, was a mirror image of the 1989 match between Dinkins and Giuliani. It was just as close, but this time it was Giuliani who eked out a win by less than 4 percentage points (47,000 votes). Giuliani carried the narrow victory with more than a third of the Hispanic vote (38 percent), an 8 percent increase from 1989. The shift in this electorate confirmed the swing vote and demonstrated that Hispanics are learning to play one candidate off the other. They also learned the art of ticket splitting. The same Hispanics who helped elect an Italian American mayor rejected Badillo, his Puerto Rican running mate for comptroller.

Hispanic pundits say the changed Hispanic profile in 1993 was the result of two factors: timing—a city in the throes of racial tension—and effort—an organized Hispanic political agenda. Pagan says, "Latino politicians and activists made a concerted effort to show the political establishment well before the '93 Mayoral election took place that Latinos could be and would be a significant swing vote."[104]

The New York mayoral election was an example of how the city's Hispanic political community, representing a small voting bloc, maximized its own stature and significance. Hispanics in New York today believe that they were able to influence the campaign agenda and press coverage by establishing a strategy to position Hispanics as the hard-to-assess but crucial swing vote. They understood the political synergy of the moment: the more the candidates perceived Hispanics as a voting bloc that could decide the election, the more they actively campaigned in that community and the more the press would cover issues important to Hispanics. The increased media coverage reinforced the candidates' decisions to woo Hispanic voters. The lesson learned from the New York campaign is that a media strategy is crucial to the success of Hispanic political interest groups, whether they are national, citywide, or community-based.

Conclusion

These case studies illustrate the diversity—and yet the similarity—of press coverage of Hispanics in different communities. When Hispanics reach 10 percent of the population it means they are found everywhere from the unemployment line to the corporate office. Yet the disparities between Hispanics and non-Hispanics remain significant and pose important public policy implications for the future in employment, education, and political empowerment. The Hispanic population is younger and has higher birthrates. Political researcher Robert Brichetto predicts that improvements in their social and economic condition are critical to the country's well-being. "Hispanics in the United States will represent a larger share of the work force, of school enrollments and of the electorate. Non-minority whites will be a greater proportion of the elderly population."[105]

Public policy decisions are influenced by the quality and quantity of media coverage. Whether it is riots, a cross burning, a mayoral election, or a commission's findings on the status of Hispanics, governmental response may be framed by media reporting. Hispanic political development occurs apart from news coverage and sometimes despite the negative or slanted reporting. When there is an increase in Hispanic political clout, the press, being a reactive medium, reflects it in both the quantity and quality of the reporting. There are several steps that both the press and Hispanic groups can take to improve the range of Hispanic voices heard in U.S. newspapers and TV news. In particular, these steps could be seen as a move in the right direction.

- The press must increase employment of Hispanics in print and broadcast newsrooms.
- Editors must promote as priorities Hispanic coverage and inclusion of Hispanics in stories that are not specifically about a Hispanic community.
- Editors must encourage Hispanic reporters to explore their community without fear of being professionally tracked or stereotyped.
- Hispanic political and social interest groups must learn more about the nature of the press and how it functions.
- Hispanic political and social interest groups, national or local, must develop a well-organized press strategy and give it high priority in promoting the "cause" the group is working for.
- Hispanic groups must develop a consistent and on-going media strategy.

Notes

1. For the purpose of this chapter, the term "Hispanic" is interchangeable with "Latino," and no political or social implication is intended.

2. Louis DeSipio, interview, September 24, 1993.

3. Ibid.

4. *Hispanic Americans Today,* U.S. Department of Commerce, Bureau of the Census, 1993.

5. Rodolfo de la Garza, Louis DeSipio, P. Chris Garcia, and Angelo Falcon, *Latino Voices: Mexican, Puerto Rican and Cuban Perspectives on American Politics* (Boulder, Colo.: Westview Press, 1992).

6. Felix Gutierrez, interview, October 21, 1993.

7. De la Garza et al., *Latino Voices,* p. 14.

8. Richard Rodriguez, *Days of Obligation: An Argument with My Mexican Father* (New York: Penguin Books, 1993). De la Garza et al. report, in their 1992 survey of Latino political attitudes (*Latino Voices*), little preference among survey participants for the pan-ethnic terms "Latino" or "Hispanic." They write, "More respondents prefer to be called 'American'" (p. 13). National-origin terms such as "Mexican," "Puerto Rican," or "Cuban" are the preferred identity choice among respondents.

9. "Who Is Latino," *Talk of the Nation,* National Public Radio, Washington, D.C., October 11, 1993.

10. Lisa Navarrate, interview, October 20, 1993.

11. Ibid., October 20, 1993.

12. Gutierrez, interview, October 21, 1993.

13. DeSipio, interview, September 19, 1993.

14. *Hispanic Americans Today,* U.S. Department of Commerce.

15. Ibid.

16. Rodolfo de la Garza and Louis DeSipio, "Save the Baby, Change the Bathwater, and Scrub the Tub: Latino Electoral Participation After Seventeen Years of Voting Rights Coverage," *Texas Law Review* (June 1993): 1494.

17. The 5 million in 1992 is an increase from 4.4 million Hispanics registered to vote in 1988.

18. De la Garza and DeSipio, "Save the Baby," p. 1501.

19. Seminar, Shorenstein Barone Center, Harvard University School of Government, September 28, 1993.

20. De la Garza et al., *Latino Voices,* p. 2.

21. Louis DeSipio and James Henson, "Newspaper Coverage of Latino Issues in Forty Cities," paper delivered at the meetings of the South-West Political Science Association, Fort Worth, Texas, March 28–31, 1990.

22. DeSipio, interview, November 11, 1993.

23. DeSipio and Henson, "Newspaper Coverage of Latino Issues in Forty Cities."

24. Emily Rooney, interview, October 20, 1993.

25. David Shaw, "Minorities in the Press," *Los Angeles Times,* 1990.

26. Ray Suarez, interview, October 14, 1993.

27. Ibid.

28. Ibid.

29. Erna Smith, "What Color Is the News?" San Francisco State University, December 1991, p. 4.

30. Ibid., p. 5.

31. Thomas Llarade, "News Coverage of Hispanics," Policy Analysis Exercise, Harvard University School of Government, April 13, 1993.

32. "Latino Poverty Rises, Income Drops," *Hispanic Link Weekly Report* (October 11, 1993) (from U.S. Census Bureau data released October 4, 1993).

33. Judy Rakowsky and Zachary R. Dowdy, "Burning Cross Placed Outside Hispanic Home," *Boston Globe,* October 21, 1993.

34. Zachary R. Dowdy and Indira A.R. Lakshmanan, "Melee Follows Stabbings, Arrests in Charlestown," *Boston Globe,* October 20, 1993.

35. David Cortiella, *Boston Herald.*

36. David Cortiella, quoted on WCVB-TV, Boston, *NewsCenter Five at 6,* October 21, 1993.

37. David Cortiella, interview, November 2, 1993.

38. David Cortiella, interview, November 16, 1993.

39. Efrain Hernandez, Jr., "Hispanic Activists Decry Silence on Cross Burning," *Boston Globe,* October 28, 1993.

40. Efrain Hernandez, Jr., interview, November 17, 1993.

41. Peter Skerry, *Mexican Americans: The Ambivalent Minority* (New York: Free Press, 1993), p. 9.

42. Ibid.

43. Mike Tharp and David Whitman, with Betsy Streissand, "Hispanics' Tale of Two Cities," *U.S. News and World Report* (May 25, 1992): 40.

44. Ibid., p. 40.

45. Erna Smith, "Transmitting Race: The L.A. Riot in TV News," Shorenstein Paper, Cambridge, Mass., Harvard University, October 10, 1993.

46. Erna Smith, "When the Subject Turned to Race: How Was It Covered?" presented at the Washington Press Club, October 22, 1993, based on her research project, "Transmitting Race: The L.A. Riot in TV News."

47. Ibid.

48. Ibid.

49. Manuel Pastor, Jr., *Latinos and the Los Angeles Uprising: The Economic Context* (Claremont, Calif.: The Tomas Rivera Center, 1993).

50. Ibid., p. 6.

51. Bob Baker, "Latinos Shortchanged in Riot Aid, Group Says," *Los Angeles Times,* September 15, 1992.

52. Magdalena Duran, interview, November 8, 1993.

53. Barbara Cox, interview, November 10, 1993.

54. Ibid.

55. Zita Arocha, interview, November 2, 1993.

56. Ibid.

57. *Hispanic Link Weekly Report* 9, no. 19 (May 13, 1991).

58. Transcript from conference at the National Press Club, Washington, D.C., sponsored by Hispanic News Media Association of Washington, D.C., June 20, 1991.

59. Ibid.

60. Ibid.

61. Ibid.

62. Ibid.

63. Ibid.

64. Zita Arocha and Roberto Moreno, *Hispanics in the News Media: No Room at the Top, 1993* (Washington, D.C.: National Association of Hispanic Journalists, 1993).

65. Gutierrez, interview, October 21, 1991.

66. Arocha and Moreno, *Hispanics in the News Media,* p. 1.

67. Zita Arocha, interview, November 8, 1993.

68. Arocha and Moreno, *Hispanics in the News Media,* p. 1.

69. Vernon Stone, "Good News, Bad News," *Communicator* (August 1993).

70. Arocha and Moreno, *Hispanics in the News Media,* p. 31.

71. Ibid.

72. Zita Arocha, interview, November 4, 1993.

73. Diane Aluerio, interview, November 8, 1993.

74. See *Muted Voices: Frustration and Fear in the Newsroom (An Analytical Look at Obstacles to the Advancement of African-American Journalists),* National Association of Black Journalists Task Force Report, August 1993.

75. Hernandez, interview, November 17, 1993.

76. Suarez, interview, October 14, 1993.

77. Rita Elizondo, interview, October 20, 1993.

78. Ibid.

79. Tom Smith, "Ethnic Survey," *GSS Tropical Report* 19, National Research Center (1990), cited in de la Garza et al., *Latino Voices,* p. 2.

80. "Bad News," *Hispanic Magazine* (November 1992).

81. "Media Notes," *Hispanic Link Weekly Report,* (October 1992).

82. DeSipio and Henson, "Newspaper Coverage of Latino Issues in Forty Cities."

83. "Mayoral Race Detours to Puerto Rico," *New York Times,* January 3, 1993.

84. Elaine Rivera, "Pols' Trip Kicks Off Race for Latino Vote," *Newsday,* December 31, 1992.

85. "Mayoral Race Detours to Puerto Rico."

86. Rivera, "Pols' Trip Kicks Off Race for Latino Vote."

87. *Washington Post,* September 26, 1993.

88. Elaine Rivera, "Serenading Hispanic Voters," *Newsday,* October 20, 1993.

89. Ibid.

90. Rossana Rosada, "Latino Voters: Up for Grabs," *Newsday,* August 24, 1989, p. 70.

91. Frank Lynn, "Dinkins Joins Mayoral Race Against Koch," *New York Times,* February 15, 1989.

92. Larry Rivers, "Koch Continues Slide in Poll: Hispanic Support Plummets," *Newsday,* May 7, 1989.

93. Evelyn Hernandez, "Giuliani Leads Puerto Rican Parade in the Bronx," *Newsday,* August 7, 1989.

94. Michael Powell, "Sun, Salsa, Samba: A Day to Woo Voters," *Newsday,* June 12, 1989.

95. Sam Roberts, "Victory Recipe: Labor, Resolve and a Rainbow," *New York Times,* October 18, 1989.

96. Howard Jordan, "Latino Mayoral Vote: The Margin of Victory," *Newsday,* October 24, 1993, p. 29.

97. Elaine Rivera, "Latinos Would Give Dinkins 43% of Votes Tomorrow," *Newsday,* May 19, 1993, p. 7.

98. Nicholas Goldberg, "Mayor Marches to a Latin Beat: Community May Be Crucial Swing Vote," *Newsday,* May 23, 1993, p. 24.

99. Mireya Navarro, "Dinkins Seeks Hispanic Forgiveness," *New York Times,* October 28, 1993.

100. Roberto Ramirez, interview, December 3, 1993.

101. Ibid.

102. After reapportionment in 1990–1992, the number of New York City Hispanics elected to office, from City Council to State Assembly to Congress, doubled from eleven to twenty-two.

103. Antonio Pagan, interview, December 2, 1993.

104. Ibid.

105. Robert Brichetto, "Making a Milestone," *Hispanic Business* (October 1993): 9.

PART TWO

THE MEDIA, PUBLIC OPINION, AND ELECTIONS

5

How Voters Construct Images of Political Candidates

Montague Kern & Marion Just

The voting literature has belittled the impact of campaigns on electoral outcomes, focusing instead on the greater contribution of partisan alignment[1] and retrospective judgments of governmental performance[2] as key predictors of the vote. But some recent evidence[3] and much popular press are devoted to the power of campaigns to sway the electorate. As discussed in subsequent chapters, much attention by the candidates is devoted to planning television ads and debates (see Chapters 6 and 7). If there is agreement between these two schools of thought, it centers on the impact of the campaign on marginal voters and on the role of the campaign in influencing candidate evaluations and highlighting resonant issues.

The extent to which public discourse during a campaign centers on issues favoring one candidate as opposed to another is considered a good predictor of recent election outcomes. A case in point is the success of the 1988 George Bush presidential campaign in directing discourse to patriotism (the Pledge of Allegiance) and crime (prison furloughs, Willie Horton). The best kind of candidate issue, as illustrated by the 1988 campaign, is one that not only casts the sponsor in a good light ("Bush is tough on crime") but at the same time casts the opponent in a bad light ("Dukakis is soft on crime"). Emphasizing agenda variables over partisan predisposition or economic preordination points to the active role of voters in campaign communication. Issues are only important in the campaign agenda when they resonate with voters and shape their assessments of the candidate.

The research for this chapter was designed to investigate the role of news and advertising in stimulating discourse about campaign issues and in the formation of candidate images. The vehicle for the study is a series of focus groups exposed to news and advertising broadcasts during the 1990 Senate race in North Carolina.

This analysis of issue resonance and candidate image formation uses concepts drawn from schema theories of learning and memory, which increasingly have been tested experimentally.[4] A schema is a "cognitive structure that represents organized knowledge about a given concept or type of stimulus" that enables individuals to integrate new bits of information.[5] So, for example, individuals who know that Jesse Helms is a Republican and Harvey Gantt is a Democrat can employ party schemas in constructing mental images of the two candidates. They will expect the candidates to hold typical partisan views, and they will revise their candidate schemas as they receive new information that confirms or contradicts the images of the candidates they have provisionally constructed from party identification.

Our purpose here is not so much to show how schema aid in information acquisition as to show the dynamics of schema construction. This should prove a useful enterprise from a theoretical standpoint because schema theory is often criticized for taking the schemas as given and offering no explanation for their origin.[6] In this exercise we took two groups of individuals who were essentially unfamiliar with the 1990 North Carolina Senate race and showed them news and political advertising from the climatic weeks of the campaign. We observed how individuals employed their values, beliefs, prior information, and experiences (i.e., schemas) in elaborating new minischemas for Jesse Helms and Harvey Gantt.

Methods

The focus group methodology itself is relatively new and presents a number of analytic problems.[7] The standard size of a focus group (eight to ten people) is too small even for the kinds of validity tests used in experimental research. In addition, focus groups are not in any sense random samples. The participants are generally recruited to meet target criteria (in our case, middle- and working-class Democrats). The culturally and economically homogeneous groups that we constructed for this study participated comfortably and relatively equally in the discussions. The aim of our analysis was to explore not only individual processes but the social construction of meaning. Therefore, we looked at the group discourse as the object of study and analyzed the patterns of expression over time. We note in the reports of other focus group researchers[8] that individual participants often do not hold consistent positions over time. Researchers generally blame the norms of civility and the pressures for consensual outcomes in small groups[9] for some of the variation. We have dealt with the problem of pressure to conform in two ways. First, we have asked each individual to record a response prior to the discussion in order to anchor opinions in the minds of the individuals and provide a cross-pressure for consistency between the discourse and the written opinion. We expect our participants to be more likely to "stick to their guns" because they had committed themselves in writing. Second, our analysis focuses on the trends of discourse, especially shifts in the consensual view as represented by lines of discourse or mean responses. This emphasis allows us to observe the social construction of meaning, which is a major advantage of the focus group method.

The participants were exposed to televised ads and news coverage in the sequence in which they were presented during the last stages of the general election campaign between incumbent Senator Jesse Helms and challenger Harvey Gantt. Because we wished to examine the formation of candidate images, the participants were drawn from outside the state of North Carolina. We expected these "naive" voters to be more open to persuasive messages by and about the candidates than would have been possible in North Carolina itself.

As is typical in the construction of focus groups, the participants were chosen to be ethnically and socioeconomically homogeneous in order to make them as comfortable as possible in expressing their views to a roomful of strangers. The target population was white, middle-class, weak Democrats and independents in southern New Jersey. Our choice of target population was based on our need to find a group relatively unfamiliar with the North Carolina campaign and coincidentally to test the appeal of Helms's anti–affirmative action message to swing voters outside the South. To further enhance the flow of conversation, we conducted separate discussions with men and women. Evidence from the discussions that resulted supports our view that homogeneity on these various dimensions allowed for frank disclosure of views on such highly charged issues as race, homosexuality, and politics. Here we detail the analysis of the men's group in order to illustrate the development of particular schema. The women's group expressed similar sentiments and came to essentially similar conclusions, but emphasized themes somewhat differently from the men. In subsequent studies, we analyze the gender divergences in political discourse.

The focus groups were structured as quasi-simulations. By way of introducing the simulation and stimulating interaction in this group around political topics, in the initial phase (Phase One) the participants were asked to respond to the general question, "Is the country off on the right track or the wrong track?" Race emerged as the most important issue. The participants were then asked to imagine that they were voters in the election between Helms and Gantt and to use the information in the video segments in making up their minds how to vote. Subsequent discussion segments in Phases Two through Seven followed exposure to a brief selection of news and advertising and the neutrally framed question, "What's going on here for you?"

Transcripts of the group discussions were analyzed line-by-line for their topics and cognitive and affective elements. As is common in ethnographic analysis, many lines were multiply coded. Quantitative indicators convey only relative emphasis in the discourse and are used to compare across phases of the discussion or across groups.

The video segments represent two- to three-day periods of news coverage and new candidate advertising, drawn from the final ten days of the Helms-Gantt contest, when opinion shifted away from Gantt and toward Helms. We were interested in seeing whether the structure of news and advertising exposure could help us to understand how opinions shift and how candidate images are reshaped in response to new information. Points of opinion change were primarily assessed from the group discussion. However, analysis of the discourse was aided by a parallel analysis of written, scaled evaluations of the candidates that the participants provided immediately after exposure to each video segment.

Our coding of the discourse arises from a constructionist approach to communication, which holds that individuals construct meaning from media messages based on their own attitudes, values, and affects.[10] We assumed that our participants would assess media messages through the prism of their own information, understanding, and judgments. In charting the discourse we specifically acknowledged when remarks arose in response to the media stimuli and when they were grounded in the information or values of the participants. Following the constructionist tradition, our analysis takes account not only of opinions but also of the critical interpretation of information, behavior, issues, and events. The group discussions analyzed here illustrate that individuals can learn politically relevant information from even brief media exposures and that they interpret that information in the light of their own constructions of political reality.

Advertising and News Stimulus Materials

In examining spot ads in their news environment, this study builds on a research tradition designed to replicate the pattern of candidate presentation actually found on the airwaves.[11] Most studies of voter response to candidates concentrate either on ads or news. The purpose of this research is to understand how voters build candidate images based on a range of information choices. The focus group was offered information in discrete phases, on the theory that the temporal order of messages and their relationship is important in the image formation process.

The news stories and most of the ads are taken from broadcasts in Winston-Salem and Greensboro in North Carolina's three-city Triad (Winston-Salem, Greensboro, and High Point) from the final ten days of the 1990 Gantt-Helms Senate race. This race was notable for the fact that a moderate black Democratic candidate, Harvey Gantt, the former mayor of

Charlotte, challenged conservative Republican incumbent Jesse Helms and ran even with him (with 10 percent of the voters undecided) up until the last ten days of the election. Gantt's strategy involved running on "middle-class" issues, such as education and health, and values, such as self-help. He did not raise the issue of affirmative action or try to protect himself against attacks in this area. In the final ten days, Helms engaged in a series of sharp attacks on Gantt, including the famous "Wringing Hands" ("Crumpled Paper") commercial, which portrayed a rejected white job applicant and attacked affirmative action for minorities. Helms won the election with 53 percent of the vote to 47 percent for Gantt.

The stimulus material was taken from this final ten-day period, which began as Helms came back from Washington to commence a tour of the state's media markets and stepped up his advertising attack. In order to introduce the candidates to the New Jersey audience, the initial video exposure included two of each candidate's positive ads taken from an earlier period in the campaign. These early ads gave the participants in the simulation an opportunity to see the initial self-presentations of the candidates. Otherwise the ads and news used as stimuli were presented in the sequence in which they were broadcast during the final ten days of the race (see Table 5.1). Although the order of exposure faithfully followed the campaign, some news stories have been omitted, and ads that were aired repeatedly in the campaign were shown only once in the focus group exposures.

Table 5.1 News and Advertising Stimuli

Phase 2	The candidates define themselves with a positive ad from earlier in the campaign, and each other with an attack ad.	
	Helms:	"Tiananmen Square" (positive character ad)
	Gantt:	"SAT Scores Worst" (issue-based attack ad)
	Helms:	"Gays/Special Interests" (emotional attack ad)
	Gantt:	"Bio (Self-Made Man)" (positive character ad)
Phase 3	Network News:	ABC, "Mudslinging"
	Gantt:	"Missed Vote" (issue-based attack ad)
	Local News:	WXII, Helms stumping, from Reidsville
Phase 4	Helms:	"Dr. Ellis Paige" (talking head attack ad)
	Gantt:	"Helms Record" (issue-based attack ad)
	Local News:	WFMY, Helms stumping with Republican senators
Phase 5	Helms:	"TV Deal/Racial" (character and issue attack ad)
	Local News:	WXII, Gantt and Helms stumping
	Gantt:	"Don't Be Taken In by the Smears" (talking head response ad)
Phase 6	Helms:	"Education—Link with Quotas" (talking head attack ad)
	Gantt:	"SAT Worst in the Nation" (new version, issue-based attack)
Phase 7	Helms:	"Wringing Hands" (emotional attack ad)

Replicating the pattern of ads and news that reached the voters in the North Carolina Triad meant that Helms's "Wringing Hands" spot (the ad that gained national attention for raising the affirmative action issue in a racially charged contest) was not shown in the focus group until the end of the race. The ad first aired in North Carolina only on the Thursday before the Tuesday election, after most of the other messages on our tape were broadcast. We made a point of including the network news story ("Mudslinging") about campaign advertising, which aired during this period, because we hypothesize that it might have framed subsequent exposure to ads and may have been used by voters in the process of constructing their images of the candidates. The remaining news stories are drawn from local news, which is the primary source of information about Senate campaigns available to viewers. (It is rare for local races to be covered on network news, except as part of national "trend" stories such as "Mudslinging.")

The local news stories in the last ten days of the Helms-Gantt race all deal with strategy and the "horserace." There was a significant "spin" on the news that in this case favored the incumbent, Jesse Helms. The incumbent-orientation represents the norm for local campaign coverage.[12] In the case under consideration, local news not only followed the incumbent but amplified his message. No news stories were developed on journalist reportorial initiative either concerning the issues in the election or the serious charges that Helms raised against Gantt during this period. In particular, there was no analysis of Gantt's alleged misuse of a Federal Communications Commission (FCC) affirmative action program while he was mayor of Charlotte. Instead, major news stories replicated campaign themes, especially those that Helms raised in his ads. In this, they cooperated in a "media blitz" campaign strategy, which involve developing a coordinated message for use in political ads and news soundbites. New information was developed and presented around such simplified, single themes (on the negative side, links with special interests and misuse of office; on the positive side, "he stands up for principle" and represents the voters in office).[13]

Participants in our focus group simulation were initially favorable to Gantt, but they did not find confirmation of their first construction of Gantt in subsequent ads or news stories. Just like real voters, they had to make continual choices, using their own values and experiences to select information to assist them in constructing images of the candidates.

Discourse Analysis

Analysis of the discourse of the focus group was used to facilitate an understanding of the individual frames through which participants evaluate candidates and to assess the extent to which various messages stimulated discussion. In examining the discourse, we considered whether messages of one candidate have a greater impact than those of another and whether some messages reassert themselves in the course of group discussion with a sleeper effect, as individuals crystallize their images of candidates on the basis of new information coming from the media and from other members of the group. The discourse was read by several coders who noted two major components of the discussion—discourse introduced by participants and discourse stimulated by media exposure.

Discourse Introduced by Participants

The first category to emerge was discourse introduced by participants, without reference to information contained in the news and political advertising. Participant-generated discourse was further categorized according to the following operational definitions:

Values: Overarching valued concepts, or norms, that is, standards of behavior against which individual behavior is judged.
Preferences: Expressions of favor or opposition, particularly in relation to issues.
Beliefs: What people think about the world; included are "for" and "against" statements that apply values to real world problems.
Affect: Statements carrying emotional valence around such general concepts as trust, caring, hopefulness, fear, anxiety, distrust, and powerlessness.
Experience: Discourse arising from the life experience of the voter.
Information: A voter's own prior information about the topics under discussion enters the discourse, or information needs are expressed.

Discourse introduced by participants without reference to information contained in the news and ads represented 340 lines or 57.6 percent of the 590 lines of discourse. Its most prominent element was on the affective side: distrust of politicians (29 lines). In other areas, tolerance for African Americans (24 lines) was also important, along with negative attitudes toward racial quotas (24 lines), negative experience with quotas (18 lines), and the need for further information to evaluate campaign messages (32 lines). Prejudice against gays was a significant, if less vocal, submotif (8 lines).

Discourse Evaluating Candidates (Minischema)

The candidate response component comprised a significant portion of the total discourse, 42.3 percent. This discourse, through which candidates were evaluated positively or negatively in response to media stimuli, fell into a number of categories that were found to be related:

Character:	Like and dislike statements about character in general, often referring to *personal qualities* of empathy and caring.
	References to candidate's *records* and *accomplishments*.
	Remarks about ties to special interests.
	Statements about the candidate's credibility.
Campaign:	References to candidate's negative *campaigning*.
	Remarks that the candidate uses *negative advertising*.
Issue Positions:	Statements favoring or disfavoring the candidate's stands on the *issues*.

This analysis enables us to understand the multiple elements of a candidate image (or minischema) as expressed in voter discourse while impressions of a candidate are being formed. It is clear that character is the most significant category of minischema, representing 32.2 percent of the total discourse. Campaign-related candidate schema, including "uses negative advertising," ranked a distant second, at 5.5 percent. Issue-based candidate evaluations lagged even farther behind, at 3.8 percent of the total discourse. The main issue mentioned was education, which was raised in the advertising messages.

Elements of character schema relate to such areas as candidate credibility; the ability to represent everyone; and the negative side of the representation coin, association with "special interests." The results indicate that independence, or lack thereof, from what are taken to be "special interests" has become an important part of voter schema, through which information that comes from the media and through intergroup dialogue is evaluated in the construction of candidate images. Overall, three-fourths of the character-related schema were negative (150 lines of negative to 46 lines of positive discourse).

We find that the way candidates campaign, including their use of negative advertising, is also used by voters in constructing candidate images. Interestingly, however, it is much less significant than the character-related aspect of schema. An opposing aspect, failure to respond to attack, coexists as a frame through which candidate images are constructed. Overall, as Figure 5.1 illustrates, negative character schema predominated within the discourse.

Which Media Stimulated Discourse?

The response component was further analyzed to indicate which message stimulated discourse. The line-by-line analysis of the response discourse

Figure 5.1 Difference Score for Discourse About Helms and Gantt

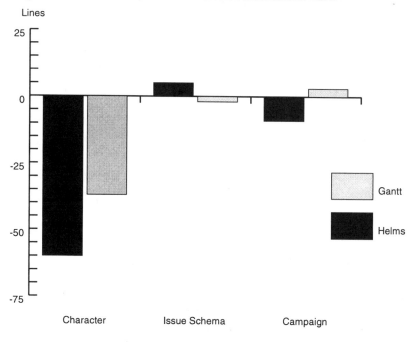

was coded for the specific origin of the information: national television news, local television news, ads and news stories, Helms's ads, Gantt's ads, and both candidates' ads. Table 5.2 summarizes the findings in this area. It also indicates that voters far more frequently selected messages in advertising as topics of discourse than news. Two hundred and ten, out of the total of 273 lines of discourse, are in the reaction to ads-only categories. Table 5.2 also indicates that Helms's ads were the most generative form of expression. Approximately half of all of the discourse coded in the media-stimulated category represented a reaction to one of his ads alone.

The Building of Candidate Images

This research allows us to understand the construction of a candidate image through time, albeit much foreshortened. Individuals actively participate in the process—their values, opinions, judgments, feelings, experiences, and frames for evaluating candidates come into play alongside candidate messages. The interaction between the message, the audience evaluations of the messengers, and resonance with personal values and experience constitutes the message received.

Our special concern is the early stages of the construction of an image

Table 5.2   Lines of Discourse Containing Images of Candidates

PHASE	2	3	4	5	6	7	
		Ad,				Ad	
		Local,	Ads,	Ads,		and	
	Ads	Nat'l	Local	Local		Local	
	Only	News	News	News	Ads	News	Total
TV News								
National	0	11	0	0	0	0	11	
Local	0	14	4	0	0	0	18	
News Subtotal	0	25	4	0	0	0	29	10.6%
Ads and News	0	3	12	11	0	8	34	12.5%
Ads								
Helms	30	20	18	45	3	17	133	
Gantt	35	10	10	1	6	0	62	
Both	11	0	0	0	4	0	15	
Ads Subtotal	76	30	28	46	13	17	210	76.9%
Total							273	100.0%

of an unknown candidate, Harvey Gantt. His image evolves more than Helms's, in this discussion, perhaps because the New Jersey voters in our focus group did not have an image or schema for Gantt at the outset of the discussion. They had to evaluate him exclusively on the basis of the video messages provided for the group. In the case of Helms, some voters had prior schema: expressed by one, for example, as "I don't like Jesse Helms." Distrust of Helms and his messages was stated from the beginning and continued throughout the discussion. Yet just as change occurred in the evolving image of the less well known candidate, it also occurred in relation to Helms's image. Helms was viewed more positively by participants at the end of the focus group than at the beginning.

The change in the evaluations of the candidates is illustrated in Figure 5.2. Over the whole period of the analysis, participants constructed an extremely positive image of Gantt in Phase Two, with thirty lines of positive evaluation and two of negative evaluation, to an evaluation of him in Phase Seven that involved fourteen lines of negative evaluation, comparable to the negative evaluation of Helms. The nadir for Gantt was in Phase Five, with thirty-two lines of negative discourse to Helms's six.

Significantly, the overall feeling thermometers taken for the two candidates point to the same results. As Figure 5.3 illustrates, they reflected the discourse, dropping from a high of seventy-three for Gantt at the outset to sixty-one at the end. Helms's overall rating was about fifty on the 100-point scale, both at the beginning and at the end of the discourse.

After the initial positive evaluation of Harvey Gantt, the discourse went through three main phases as participants brought their values,

Figure 5.2 Difference Score for Campaign Ads and News

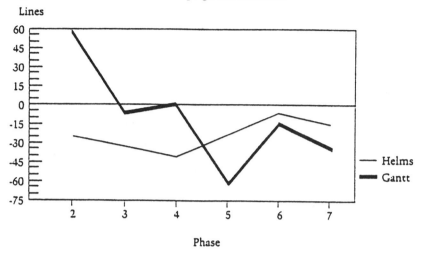

Phase

Figure 5.3 Focus Group Feeling Thermometers

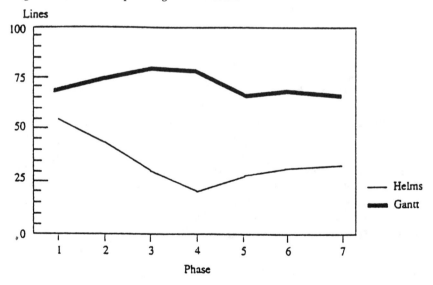

Phase

affects, issue preferences, and experiences to bear on their construction of his image. Gantt's honeymoon stage in Phase Two is examined later as an example of the discourse method of analyzing image construction. At this point (after the first sequence of ads, which are analyzed in detail later) it was clear that voters liked Gantt because his messages resonated with their values of tolerance and individual initiative/self-help. Gantt also had the advantage on the issue of education, which, however, was not an issue of cutting concern in the male focus group.

In contrast, Helms was evaluated with nine negative lines on character and two on negative advertising in Phase Two, as he had introduced an ad linking Gantt with homosexual special interests. Anti-incumbency sentiment was targeted in his direction both during this phase and the next, as voters selected messages from the news stories that corroborated their view that he was an incumbent who had been there a mighty long time, and was probably, therefore, no longer representative of the people. Because Helms was depicted in the Phase Three news stories with older people, and most of the men in the group were middle-aged or younger, one participant said he did not think Helms represented younger people or the working class.

It is interesting, however, that the participants did not apply issues in their negative evaluation of Helms. One person stated, "I don't like him." But no one said, "I don't like his stand on the National Education Association or homosexuality." Voter schema about negative advertising, however, hurt Helms in Phase Two and in the next phase. In Phase Two the main focus was on a local news story that amplified Helms's charge that Gantt was secretly airing negative ads on black radio stations, running a "Secret Campaign." Voters evaluated Helms negatively in Phases Two and Three for his attacks on Gantt.

The participants' frequently expressed value of tolerance and their view that the candidate shared their values of individual initiative and self-help contributed to their positive evaluation of Gantt. Anti-incumbency sentiment and distrust of politicians was targeted in Helms's direction until Phase Six, when it was only Gantt who was evaluated negatively, while Helms was evaluated neutrally. In the final phase, the Gantt and Helms negative evaluations were equally high, but Helms had gained a clear convert, and few Gantt supporters remained.

The Construction of a Positive Image: Phase Two Examined

We examine Phase Two in some detail, paying particular attention to coding categories and the construction of positive imagery of Harvey Gantt as it survived the process of group dynamics. The role of the moderator in facilitating discussion is also illustrated. Phase Two demonstrates that the types of ads that offer the greatest amount of useful information to the voter are those that involve emotional rhetoric, character-related information, and issues that are self-explanatory or relate to readily understood individual experiences. M. Kern says, "In such ads issues are now personified through the use of visual and aural effects." Sound and visuals are blended, or "dovetailed" around a story or situation, exemplifying the values and issues expressed.[14]

In this phase four political ads were introduced as stimuli. Two of them offered information that voters used in their construction of candidate images: a Helms negative emotional attack ad ("Gays/Special Interests") and a Gantt positive emotional biography ad ("Self-Made Man"). The other two ads were largely ignored.

Overall, the dynamics of Phase Two had short-range as well as long-range consequences. The short-range consequences are voter construction of a positive image of Gantt and a negative image of Helms. The long-range consequence, however, is that only *one* of the four ads was a "sleeper," generating discourse and contributing to the ongoing evolution of candidate imagery in subsequent phases. The "sleeper" was Helms's negative attack ad, "Gays/Special Interests."

The ads. Four ads are introduced during Phase Two of the campaign simulation. Two are positive ads, which enable the candidate to make his best case: his character, issues, and record are presented. The two included in this analysis are from early in the race rather than during the final ten days. They were introduced in order to allow the New Jersey voters to see at least one aspect of the positive side of the candidates, which North Carolina voters had already seen. The first of these is a Helms ad in which he compares himself to a courageous Chinese protester who stood up alone in Tiananmen Square against a tank. The second ad is Harvey Gantt's positive emotional "Bio (Self-Made Man)," in which he dovetails the story of his life as a self-made man with the values of individualism and hard work and their implied policy consequences: no government waste or "handouts." He says the driving force behind his campaign is helping to build a nation in which all who strive and work hard can similarly achieve.[15]

The Gantt attack ad is largely informational. It focuses on a series of facts about the state: that its SAT scores rank forty-ninth in the nation, that its children drop out of school, that there are 900 toxic waste sites, and so on. Declarations are presented in text on the screen, for example, "For 18 years Jesse Helms has voted against Education." The ad concludes, "North Carolina Can't Afford Another Six Years of the Jesse Helms Way: It's Time for a Change." The only character message is the record of Jesse Helms. There is no stylistic "dovetailing," or blending of visuals around a story or situation, exemplifying the values and issues expressed. For example, in a recital of toxic waste statistics, there are no tales told about harm to real people. The same is true in relation to the dismal "facts" about education.

The Helms attack ad is of a different sort. In the academic literature all ads that attack an opponent are frequently defined as negative. There are, however, emotional negative ads that utilize harsh sounds and affect-laden symbols to connect the opponent with negatively perceived "others." Helms's "Gays/Fundraising" ad falls into this category. Homosexuals are the negatively perceived "other." The ad's message: Is Gantt indebted to special interest groups? Is he trustworthy?

Although the two ads are very different, both present Helms's and Gantt's issues with emotional rhetoric—such as the role of special interests in contemporary politics, or the need for the United States to return to a self-help ethic. Together, these two ads were the subject of most of the discourse, as the voters in Phase Two constructed their initial images of the candidates.

Gantt's "Bio" offered themes that were congruent with New Jersey's middle-class values as expressed by focus group participants: individual initiative, the work ethic, and tolerance for blacks. "Bio" stimulated positive discourse, with several participants contributing to the construction of a positive image for Gantt, based on information about his character, his stands on an issue—education, which he not only favored, but which his life story as presented in the ad exemplified—and his record. Two voters, who expressed their own concern about education, also used "SAT Scores Worst" to help construct a positive image of Gantt. The positive image construction survived a challenge from one voter, Ken, who based it first on the value of "needing more information" and subsequently on the emotion, "distrust of politicians." It also survived a challenge from another voter, Ralph, who drew from his own experience with the unpopular Governor Jim Florio of New Jersey and indicated that he had seen nothing from either candidate. The dialogue follows, along with an illustration of the coding process and the group dynamic that evolved, including the role of the moderator.

Arnold: He [Gantt] is for people. He's got his *beliefs* [+IMAGE: GENER-AL]. He's doing a lot of things right. I already mentioned he's doing *education* [+IMAGE: ISSUE]. [Coded as a response not only to "Bio" but to "SAT Scores Worst" as well, because education is mentioned.]

Moderator: You say he's for people. Why do you think he's for people?

Arnold: Well, the things that he's done, built schools, and, you know, had a business [+IMAGE: RECORD].

Ken: [disagreeing] How do you know he's doin' them. Did somebody [else] start them [the schools and business]? Is he *finishing* them? [INFOR-MATION LACKING.]

Arnold: Well, you can't tell from all this, but you can tell a lot more than the other guy [INFORMATION LACKING].

Moderator: One at a time, one at a time, folks.

Ken: I was just stating I can't tell that much from looking at the TV [INFORMATION SEEKING]. Politicians have not really been known to tell the truth in my lifetime. That I know of [AFFECT: DISTRUST OF POLITICIANS].

[Ken continues with further distrust of politicians, distrust of the news media, and so on.]

Bob: [disagreeing, enters the discussion, taking it back to the original construction, adding his own interpretation to it] . . . I mean, like he said, he started up, you know, from a poor black kid, you know and he's tryin' for education. [Coded as a response not only to "Bio" but to "SAT" as well because education is mentioned.] You know, at least what he said is "I want everybody to earn. I want them to earn what they work for. Not to give it out" [+IMAGE: CREDIBILITY].

Moderator: So you like that.

Bob: Well, that's what caught me there. At least he came out and said, "I'm not gonna give it out to you" [+IMAGE: GENERAL]. It doesn't necessarily mean, later on, down the road that he's going to do it. But at least he came out and said it. There's a statement, he made it on TV and everybody's gonna hold him accountable for it [+IMAGE: ISSUE].

Moderator: Let me go to Ralph and then let me go down there. Ralph, what are you thinking?

Ralph: You're asking people in New Jersey. This is [not] South Carolina. We're more metropolitan. We're more suspicious. We went through a campaign for governor in which we were veritably, we were deceived to no end. . . . He hasn't shown me anything yet [OWN INFORMATION; AFFECT: DISTRUST OF POLITICIANS].

[The dialogue shifts to Tom, who ranks Gantt favorably on positive campaigning (+IMAGE: POSITIVE CAMPAIGN) and concludes that Helms's negative attack ad must "mean that he can't attack him for what he's saying he did. So that puts some credibility on his advertising" (+GANTT IMAGE: CREDIBILITY; –HELMS IMAGE: NEGATIVE ADS.)]

Thus the image survives several challenges until the topic turns to the subject of the nature of the negative advertising that Helms is using. Tom expresses tolerance for gays who "should not be mistreated." Another participant disagrees, and interprets the information in Helms's ad in the terms described in the ad, as representing special interest group support for Gantt:

Ken: I don't know . . . the fact that if you have one single interest putting in that much money. What's this guy got to give back to these people? [–IMAGE: SPECIAL INTEREST, GAYS.]

Gantt's positive image survives during this phase as he developed it in his advertising, as middle-class male voters construct a candidate image using their own values of tolerance and individual initiative to select related bits of information from the ads. The discourse is more about values than about issues, although education is mentioned. Self-help is frequently stated in terms of values. What emerges is the image of a "people"-oriented candidate whose life reflects the values that participants care about. But Gantt has scored no points against Helms. And the Helms ad has sown a seed in a climate of distrust of politicians and a submotif of prejudice against gays, which is clearly expressed in the next segment of the campaign simulation, Phase Three, as the Gantt image is sullied with the special interest group connection. This seed germinates in later phases of the campaign.

The overall image of Helms, who launched the attack in Phase Two, is negative, and is expressed in the following remarks:

Ray: He's been in the Congress and the Senate for awhile, and is therefore less connected to "the people" [–IMAGE: SPECIAL INTERESTS].

[later]

Ray: He [also] blasted the gay community . . . and if he's against this one specific group he's probably against the middle class and he's probably against blue collar, and everything else [–IMAGE: NEGATIVE ADVERTISING].

Ralph: [disagreeing] Why not bring a negative to light. If it is negative. I mean, that's politics [+IMAGE: NEGATIVE ADVERTISING].

Voters disagreed on the degree to which the use of negative advertising affected their candidate evaluations. Few of them "liked" Helms. But his message got through.

After the "Honeymoon"—Media and the Construction of a Negative Image

Following the "honeymoon" in Phase Two a negative image of Harvey Gantt began in Phase Three, when the sleeper effect of Helms's, as opposed to Gantt's, commercials became apparent. Although they denounced Helms for his "Gays/Special Interests" ad in Phase Two, the participants transferred their reservoir of distrust for politicians from Helms to Gantt in Phase Three. They selected themes from the "Gays/Special Interests" ad, amplified in news stories, as the main topic for discourse. The amplification of the Helms ad occurred in this period not only in the network news story ("Mudslinging"), which ran visuals of the "Gays/Special Interests" ad, but in a local news story that repeated a Helms charge that Gantt was running a "secret" campaign. In the process of selecting information from the media campaign to talk about in the group discussion, participants drew on prior distrust of politicians, as well as prejudice against gays. A question emerged of whether Gantt was gay and why he had gone to San Francisco to raise money. Both points came to be generalized around the idea that Gantt was linked to special interests. This possibility was amplified in news stories containing Helms's charges to this effect, which provided confirmation of voter discomfort.

In Phase Four, Gantt attempted to regain control of the agenda with a return to an issue ad focusing on Helms's poor record in regard to the children of the state. This ran along with Helms's response ad, "Dr. Ellis Paige." The Helms ad focused the education issue around voter distrust of government and politicians. Helms argues he had voted against the federal education bills as charged by Gantt in order to reduce the federal role in education. This assertion brought into play generalized distrust of government and politicians. Here is Tom, a key Gantt supporter:

Tom: Well, I'm starting to be a little confused at this point. You know, Helms is now attacking Gantt and what I have in my mind is what he said about the education issue. You know, the fact that money's being wasted. Being controlled by the federal government rather than . . .
Moderator: You think that could be true.
Tom: Yeah, it's creating a question in my mind. So at this point I'd have to look into the issue further. . . .

In Phase Five, with seeds of doubt sown on education, Gantt's key issue, and concern about whether Gantt did in fact represent the values of individual initiative and self-help, Helms introduced a new message in his two "TV Deal/Racial" ads, accompanied by amplifying news stories. The "TV Deal/Racial" ads charged that Harvey Gantt, as mayor of Charlotte, used an affirmative action program for personal gain. At this point, the reservoir of distrust voters have for politicians was targeted at Gantt and anti-Gantt sentiment overwhelmed the discourse. Opposition to quotas as an issue emerged, as did much discourse relating to personal experience with quotas. Helms had introduced his racial advertising message in a fashion that connected with voter character-based schema for evaluating candidates. He had also introduced it to a group that was deeply concerned about race issues. During Phase One, in response to a question concerning whether the country was on the right or the wrong track, virtually all the participants had selected the latter response, and many identified race as the issue that was the most significant. Five times as many lines of discourse (seventy-five) were devoted to race as to the next most salient issue, drugs (fifteen). Other issues, including taxes and government waste, did not even come close. Subthemes in this dialogue about race concerned the need for tolerance (twenty-nine), interracial marriage, and dating (nineteen) (see Table 5.1). The upshot for Harvey Gantt in Phase Five was not that voters said they were going out to vote for Jesse Helms. Instead, they said, "apathy has set in."

In Phase Six the sleeper effect of the "Dr. Ellis Paige" commercial was apparent. This ad dovetails opposition to a federal role in education, because of federal support for quotas, with the visage of a kindly university professor speaking directly to the camera, bathed in a halo of light. Two stimuli were introduced in a further dialogue on the social issues: a Gantt ad in which he attempts to redirect the campaign agenda back to the Helms voting record on social issues, particularly education ("SAT Worst in the Nation") and a Helms talking head ad in which he reaffirms the message of the "Dr. Ellis Paige" ad, explaining that he opposes a federal role in the area of education because he opposes quotas. The group rejected this second record-based Gantt advertising message ("SAT Worst in Nation") and wondered about the *context* of the bills that Helms voted against. One participant said, "What exactly was the context? There's all these add-ons all the time. There's always, things are grouped together." Others agreed. With "Dr. Ellis Paige" the Helms campaign again produced an ad that, like "Gays/Special Interests" and the "TV Station Deal" ads, was a sleeper (one that comes back into the dialogue) and offers information to which voters return in their ongoing evaluation of candidate messages.

In Phase Seven the "Wringing Hands" commercial was introduced. In it the quota issue is brought away from the workplace (of television station deals) into the home of the individual viewer. A pair of white hands hold a job rejection slip because a job was unfairly given to "a minority." At this point high levels of negative discourse are targeted at both Gantt and Helms, as voters sum up their overall negative evaluation of the candidates. Gantt's negative evaluations include a link with special interests; Helms's include a lack of credibility. The voters' overall conclusion reaffirms their earlier statement: apathy has set in.

The focus group also illustrated the frustration of voters with campaigning and with the content of campaign messages. The participants reiterated their doubt about the veracity of charges and the need to "check out" TV news and advertising information with other sources, specifically newspapers. They complained continually that charges went unanswered and wished there were other forums in which the candidates would be forced to respond to one another (such as debates). From what we know of popular behavior, it is unlikely that dissatisfaction with campaign discourse actually leads to information-seeking behavior, but it suggests that frustration may be a factor in deepening the distrust of politicians, the media, and election campaigns and also contributes to the sense of voter confusion and power-lessness.

This discourse permitted us to make some tentative judgements about the relative weight accorded to different categories of evaluation as they relate to voter construction of candidate images. How significant is "ties to special interests" or credibility, for example, in relation to a variable such as "uses negative advertising"? From this analysis, it is clear that although voters did not like the negative advertising, they used information con-tained in the ads to evaluate the candidate against whom it was targeted.

The bottom line is that charges, such as "ties to special interests" and "misuse of public office for personal gain," were important in voter schema. As individuals slowly constructed and reconstructed their image of Harvey Gantt, they used the available information, particularly negative ads, which were confirmed in news stories.

It is also important to recognize that voters have collateral sources of information. Even in this simulation, which was structured so that the par-ticipants would be naive about this specific campaign, the members of the group were able to bring to bear relevant information about the 1988 presi-dential campaign, local politicians, and the cost of government programs. They used this information to validate or discount the messages conveyed by and about Helms and Gantt. The simulation, therefore, illustrates the active interpretation of new messages in the light of what is already known, which characterizes the electorate's participation in the campaign process.

The analysis of each phase of the discourse, summarized in Figure 5.3, indicates that the broad outlines detailed above do not convey the intricate forward and backward movement, the assessment and reassessment that characterizes candidate evaluation. Images of both candidates were revised over the course of the simulation as voters selected information for atten-tion according to their individual values, affects, and preferences. This analysis also indicates both the greater immediate impact of the Helms ads in stimulating discourse throughout the course of the campaign simulation and their greater "sleeper" effect as they came back into the dialogue at later phases in the simulation, after the media had moved on to other mat-ters. "Learning" occurred as voters selected message elements, according to their own cognitive and affective schema, and used information to con-struct images of the candidates.

Conclusion

In this chapter we demonstrate that the relatively new focus group method can be linked to a more traditional method, simulation, to produce a power-ful new tool for analyzing campaign discourse. The focus groups not only demonstrated the development of candidate images but showed how those images were extended and revised in the light of new information. The participants' individual responses written down on paper were evidence of the shifts in individual opinion in response to campaign stimuli, and we were also able to take advantage of the focus group discourse to identify how the campaign messages operated in the group process.

Analysis of the focus groups indicates that concern about race, which emerged early in the discussion, did not appear to decrease Gantt's initial support—he was actually favored by the New Jersey focus groups at the outset of the simulation. But race concerns clearly were tapped by the Helms "TV Station Deal" ad, which called Gantt's character into question but also raised the issue of minority set-asides and affirmative action.

The "TV Station Deal" example, however, is only one of the several messages that resonated with significant shared values and produced an evaluation or reevaluation of the candidates. As we showed in the analysis of Phase Two, Gantt profited from the norm of self-help (the work ethic) and tolerance. His "Bio" ad made an important contribution to the image that emerged of Gantt as a man who had "pulled himself up by his bootstraps." This image of Gantt as a self-made man enhanced the credibility of his issue message on education. The reasoning was that a person who had made it up from poverty to become an architect really understood the value of education. The Gantt "Bio" spot and the Helms "TV Station Deal" ads demonstrate how ads that powerfully affect candidate evaluations operate through their resonance with significant shared values.

Analysis of the discourse also reveals how one candidate can both disarm and discredit another by mobilizing widely shared beliefs. Helms was able to undermine Gantt's best issue, education, by using advertising to shift the focus to the role of the federal government in education. Here Helms drew on a generalized distrust of "big government" to neutralize Gantt's attack on his education record. This tactic was coupled with an even more powerful assault on Gantt's credibility as a fresh face in politics. Responding to a series of Helms messages, the "Gay/Special Interests" ad, the "gets most of his money from gays" news soundbite, and most effectively in the "TV Station Deal" ad, the participants began to doubt Gantt's honesty and his ability to represent them fairly. The result was that all of Gantt's initial support faded away and the campaign simulation ended in apathy and disgust with the electoral process.

These instances also demonstrate two important findings of our analysis, which are, first, that advertising messages were far more likely than campaign news to stimulate discussion and, second, that advertising dominated the discourse by activating widely shared affects and values. In general, references to news in the discourse about candidates concerned instances in which candidates reiterated campaign messages (e.g., Helms's soundbite repeating his charge that Gantt got "most of his money" from gays).

The focus group simulation provides evidence for the origin and dynamic revision of candidate "minischema" and opens a window on the way information is interpreted and utilized. Most messages appear to slide right past the audience, some messages are stored and may be activated later, and some are immediately inserted into candidate schema. We have seen that the more affectively laden messages embedded in advertising are more likely to figure in the construction of candidate schema, particularly as the messages link up with larger schema such as education or politicians.

One troubling aspect of our analysis of the news sample from this period of the Helms-Gantt campaign was that it showed a painful tendency to amplify Helms's messages at the expense of Gantt's. Helms was given a number of long, unchallenged opportunities to attack Gantt in the news, whereas Gantt was shown on the defensive, denying Helms's attacks. The television journalists made no independent corroborations of the charges, nor did they ask probing questions about the evidence that Helms offered for his attacks.

On an equally dismal note, the simulation demonstrates the wellsprings of distrust that negative advertising activates in candidate attacks; that is, negative advertising is believable precisely because people believe that most politicians are not worthy of their trust. From the standpoint of democratic theory, the distaste for candidates and politicians that results from negative campaigning is particularly troublesome. The problem is circular. Negative ads are believed because politicians are distrusted, and politicians are increasingly distrusted by people who believe negative ads. The most serious aspect of the problem is the tendency for people to want to withdraw altogether from the political process, or, as our simulation participants put it, "apathy just set in." It is not clear that a vibrant exchange of views on critical issues of policy that is essential to democratic debate can be maintained in the face of this level of public distrust.

Notes

1. Paul F. Lazarsfeld, Bernard Berelson, and Hazel Gaudet, *The People's Choice: How the Voter Makes Up His Mind in a Presidential Campaign* (New York: Duell, Sloan and Pearce, 1944).

2. M. P. Fiorina, *Retrospective Voting in American National Elections* (New Haven: Yale University Press, 1981).

3. See M. Hershey, "The Campaign and the Media," in Gerald Pomper, ed., *The Elections of 1988* (Chatham, N.J.: Chatham House, 1989); M. Pfau and H. C. Kenski, *Attack Politics: Strategy and Defense* (New York: Praeger-Greenwood, 1990).

4. See J. Crocker, S. T. Fiske, and S. T. Taylor, "Schematic Bases of Belief Change," in J. R. Eiser, ed., *Attitudinal Judgement* (New York: Springer-Verlag, 1984); W. H. Crockett, "Schemas, Affect and Communication," in L. Donohew, H. E. Sypher, and E. T. Higgins, eds., *Communication, Social Cognition and Affect*

(Hillsdale, N.J.: Lawrence Erlbaum, 1988); S. T. Fiske and S. E. Taylor, *Social Cognition* (Reading, Mass.: Addison-Wesley, 1984); D. A. Graber, *Processing the News: How People Tame the Information Tide,* 2nd ed. (White Plains, N.Y.: Longmans, 1988); R. H. Wicks, "Applying Schema Theory to News Information Processing," paper presented at the 36th Annual Convention of the International Communication Association, Chicago, Illinois, 1986; Wicks, "The Relationship between Involvement and Medium in News Information Processing," paper presented at the 73rd Annual Convention of the Association for Education in Journalism and Mass Communication, Minneapolis, Minnesota, 1990; and Wicks and D. C. Drew, "Learning from the News: Effects of Message Consistency and Medium on Recall and Inference Making," *Journalism Quarterly* 68, nos. 1–2 (1991): 155–164.

5. Fiske and Taylor, *Social Cognition,* p. 139.

6. See J. Kuklinski, R. C. Luskin, and J. Bolland, "Where Is the Schema? Going Beyond the 'S' Word in Political Psychology," *American Political Science Review* 35, no. 4 (1991): 1341–1356;

7. See K. Lewin, "Frontiers in Group Dynamics," *Human Relations* 1 (1947): 2–38; R. Merton, M. Fiske, and P. Kendall, *The Focused Interview* (New York: Bureau of Applied Social Research, Columbia University Press, 1956); R. Krueger, *Focus Groups: A Practical Guide for Applied Research* (Newbury Park, Calif.: Sage, 1988); L. C. Lederman, "Assessing Educational Effectiveness: The Focus Group Interview as a Technique for Data Collection," *Communication Education* 38 (1990): 117–127; Lederman, "An Exploration of the Modification of the Focus Group Technique: Participants Trained to Bring Information with Them," paper presented at the 40th Annual Conference of the International Communication Association, Dublin, Ireland, 1990; M. X. Delli Carpini and B. Williams, "The Method Is the Message: Focus Groups as a Means of Examining the Use of Television in Political Discourse," paper presented at the Annual Meeting of the International Society for Political Psychology, Washington, D.C., 1990; Delli Carpini and Williams, "Defining the Public Sphere: Television and Political Discourse," paper presented at the Annual Meeting of the American Political Science Association, Washington, D.C., 1991.

8. Delli Carpini and Williams, "Defining the Public Sphere."

9. Janis, *Groupthink* (New York: Houghton Mifflin, 1982).

10. See W. Gamson, "A Constructionist Approach to Mass Media and Public Opinion," *Symbolic Interaction* 11, no. 2 (1988): 161–174; W. R. Neuman, M. R. Just, and A. N. Crigler, *Common Knowledge: News and the Construction of Political Meaning* (Chicago, Ill.: University of Chicago Press, 1992).

11. See T. Patterson and R. D. McClure, *The Unseeing Eye: The Myth of Television Power in National Elections* (New York: Putnam, 1976); M. Kern. *Thirty-Second Politics* (New York: Praeger-Greenwood, 1989).

12. See E. Goldenberg and M. Traugott, *Campaigning for Congress* (Washington, D.C.: Congressional Quarterly Press, 1984); M. Robinson, "The Three Faces of American Media," reprinted in D. A. Graber, *Mass Media and American Politics,* 2nd ed. (Washington, D.C.: Congressional Quarterly Press, 1984); Kern, *Thirty-Second Politics.*

13. See Kern, *Thirty-Second Politics;* M. Kern, "The Advertising Driven 'New' Mass Media Election and the Rhetoric of Policy Issues," in R. Spitzer, ed., *Mass Media and Public Policy* (Westport, Conn.: Praeger, 1993).

14. Quotation in Kern, *Thirty-Second Politics,* pp. 208–209; regarding individual experiences, see Kern, "The Advertising Driven 'New' Mass Media Election."

15. The Gantt campaign made a deliberate decision not to run as a minority

candidate. He defined his character and issues in general terms. The result was that he did not address issues relating to race early in the campaign. The Pfau and Kenski discussion in *Attack Politics* of "inoculation" strategies implies that candidates should introduce difficult issues in order to neutralize later attacks.

6

The Impact of Presidential Debates

Michael X. Delli Carpini,
Scott Keeter & Sharon Webb

Testifying before a March 1924 congressional hearing on the regulation of radio, William Harkness, assistant vice president of AT&T, proposed a debate between the Democratic, Republican, and Progressive presidential candidates, to be broadcast to the few million listeners around the country who then owned receivers.[1] His suggestion was ignored, and, despite subsequent efforts over the years, it was not until the "Great Debates" of 1960 that the candidates for the highest office in the nation faced each other in such a forum. After a hiatus of three elections, however, presidential debates have since become the highlight of most campaign seasons.

The importance of debates is both civic and strategic. As a means of public education they offer citizens a unique opportunity to hear (and see) the candidates in an unedited, less-scripted setting than that offered by most other mass-mediated forums. In the age of soundbite politics, even the most structured debates allow for longer, potentially more thoughtful, ruminations about issues of policy, leadership, or character than is the norm. They also serve, along with the nominating conventions and election night itself, as focal points for the campaign, drawing public attention to national politics in a collective way that is far too rare in the United States.

For the candidates, debates serve a more instrumental function. Few campaign events are as publicly anticipated, attract as large an audience, or generate as much media coverage and subsequent analysis as presidential debates. They provide one of the primary sources of information about candidates, supplementing television ads and news (see Chapters 5 and 7). Thus, debates present both the opportunity to get a faltering campaign back on track and the danger of derailing an already successful one. Although the evidence that debates significantly affect the outcome of elections is equivocal,[2] political folklore points to several defining moments that have emerged from these direct exchanges: Richard Nixon's poor physical appearance in the first debate of 1960; Gerald Ford's gaffe regarding Soviet dominance in Eastern Europe in 1976; Ronald Reagan's controlled, "presidential" performance one week before the 1980 election, and his self-deprecating humor in the second debate of 1984; and Michael Dukakis's emotionless response in the last debate of the 1988 campaign to the question of how he would stand on the death penalty if his wife were raped and murdered.

The 1992 presidential campaign offered a number of new or altered approaches to mass-mediated electioneering, most of which involved strengthening the direct interaction between the public and the candidates (and thus challenging the gatekeeping role of traditional journalists). This new trend was reflected in the second presidential debate, held on October 15 in Richmond, Virginia. Dubbed "The People's Debate," it utilized a unique talk show format, in which members of an audience of 209 randomly selected, undecided voters asked questions of the candidates, assisted by newscaster Carole Simpson in a role more akin to a host than a journalist.

The poor performance of George Bush and the strong performances of Bill Clinton and Ross Perot in "The People's Debate" may very well be added to the list of defining moments recounted above. But to what extent did this debate influence the opinions and ultimately the voting choice of the public? We attempt to answer this question by examining the impact of this debate on a panel of 104 randomly selected undecided and weakly committed voters from the Richmond area, who assembled to watch the debate on television at Virginia Commonwealth University. Our study entailed three waves of interviews with panelists: immediately before and after the event and by telephone after the presidential election. The interviews are supplemented by "continuous response" data collected during the debate and by two focus groups conducted approximately thirty minutes after the debate.

Methods and Data

To recruit the panel, we identified likely voters using a telephone survey of residents of the Richmond, Virginia, metropolitan area.[3] Likely voters who were undecided in the presidential election or who said they might change their minds were recruited to participate. Out of 1,859 individuals screened, 626 met the selection criteria. Of these, 150 individuals agreed to attend and were sent packets of information. On the night of the debate, 104 arrived at the university in time to complete the preelection questionnaires and be included in the data collection.[4] At the conclusion of the debate, panelists completed posttest questionnaires. Fifteen also took part in two focus groups. Postelection telephone interviews were conducted with ninety-nine of the panelists, ninety-six of whom reported voting in the presidential election. Because of missing data on key items, the usable sample size for most analyses involving the vote is seventy-nine.

The participants were generally representative of all voters who met the screening criteria (see Table 6.1). It was, according to many measures, a receptive audience looking for reasons to support a candidate. Despite the fact that Republicans outnumbered Democrats (as they do more generally in the Richmond area), and that nearly two-thirds had voted for Bush in 1988 (three-fourths among those who voted), Bush's support was weak (only 6 percent approved of his performance in office). At the same time, Clinton was distrusted by nearly half of the panelists, and another 15 percent were neutral on the question of whether he was sufficiently honest to be president.

Table 6.1 Profile of Eligibles and Participants

	All Study Participants (N = 104) (in percent)	Group for Vote Analysis (N = 79) (in percent)	All Eligibles in Recruitment Survey (N = 626) (in percent)
Race			
White	77	80	73
Black	16	13	18
Other	7	8	9
Party ID			
Democrat	24	23	27
Republican	35	34	37
Independent and other	41	43	36
Predebate candidate preference			
Bush	27	32	37
Clinton	29	29	33
Perot	7	8	5
Undecided	36	32	25

Findings

The debate had a number of immediate and rather dramatic effects on the panelists. Many of these effects appeared to persist through the election and were detectable in the postelection telephone survey.

Knowledge of Candidate Positions on the Issues

Previous research suggests that presidential debates provide valuable opportunities for voters to learn about the candidates' substantive issue stands.[5] However, demonstrating that learning occurs during debates is often a difficult task for social science. The validity of inferences based on a comparison of what debate viewers and nonviewers know about the candidates is threatened by various confounding factors. Studies that avoid this difficulty by comparing debate viewers' knowledge before and after the debates must successfully anticipate what topics will be discussed.

We chose four issues for a before-and-after test of knowledge; three of the issues received at least brief discussion in the debate: the death penalty, health care reform, and taxes.[6] On two of the three, there were notable gains in knowledge. Table 6.2 shows these data. The most dramatic increase was in awareness that President Bush supports the death penalty. Prior to the debate, only 52 percent of the panelists correctly identified Bush's position; after the debate, 89 percent did so.[7] Bush's reference to the death penalty during the debate was brief and oblique and came during a discussion of gun control. In arguing for stronger anticrime legislation, the president said, "I'll probably get into a fight in this room with some, but I happen to think that we need stronger death penalties for those that kill police officers."[8]

Table 6.2   Change in Knowledge of Candidates' Issue Positions

	Predebate (in percent)	Postdebate (in percent)	Postelection (in percent)
Aware that Bush favors the death penalty	52	89	80
Aware that Clinton favors the death penalty	25	25	47
Aware that Clinton favors raising taxes on the wealthy	93	96	99
Aware that Clinton favors requiring most employers to provide health insurance coverage for their workers	81	90	92

A more modest increase in knowledge was seen in awareness of Clinton's position that employers should be mandated to provide health insurance to their employees. Prior to the debate, 81 percent of the panelists said Clinton favored such a mandate. During his discussion of health care reform, Clinton said, "Employers would cover their employees; government would cover the unemployed." After the debate, 90 percent said Clinton favored employer mandates.

One other issue we asked about was mentioned briefly in the debate: whether or not taxes on the wealthy should be raised. Bush made a general comment about his opposition to any new taxes, and Clinton twice mentioned "asking the wealthiest Americans" to pay a larger share. We saw little change in knowledge of these positions, however, because over 90 percent of the panelists already knew them. The percentage correctly identifying the candidates' position rose three points for Clinton (from 93 to 96 percent) and one point for Bush.

Perhaps the knowledge gains we document are unsurprising. The audience paid close attention to the debate and was alerted to the significance of the specific issues by the predebate questionnaire. However, the relevant statements on each issue by the candidates were exceedingly brief, and could easily have been missed. Furthermore, most of the gains in awareness persisted through the election. And, of course, there were many issues discussed that we did not anticipate or have space in the surveys to accommodate. For some of these—term limits, North American Free Trade Agreement (NAFTA), education reform, gun control—one or more of the candidates stated his views quite distinctly, and it is quite likely that many viewers learned from these statements.

Ratings of the Candidates

Most of the necessary preconditions for communication-induced attitude change[9] were present in our study: exposure and attention were elemental to the event; comprehension of the messages, although not guaranteed, seemed likely given the characteristics of the panelists, who were somewhat more knowledgeable about politics than the average citizen in Virginia.[10] The possibility that panelists might yield to the messages was inherent in the chief criterion for their selection to participate: lack of a firm voting commitment. However, this did not mean that the panelists lacked strong opinions about the candidates; indeed, some of their indecision or weakness of commitment resulted from antipathy toward most or all of the candidates.

The debate had a substantial effect on the panelists' impressions of the candidates (see Table 6.3), with ratings of Clinton and Perot rising substantially. These changes are consistent with the audience's "real time" reactions to the debate, as recorded by the continuous response system.[11] The mean on-line ratings for Perot and Clinton (4.99 and 4.73 respectively) were considerably higher than for Bush (4.29) and were also higher than their mean predebate ratings. Not surprisingly, mean postdebate favorability ratings rose for Clinton (from 4.01 before the debate to 5.04 after it) and Perot (from 4.16 to 4.78).[12] Bush's ratings rose modestly, from 4.01 to 4.15. All three candidates experienced a small decline in ratings from the postdebate to the postelection measurement.

The data support the notion that the candidates' performances in the debate had a stronger impact on the postdebate ratings than the predebate ratings had on the panelists' evaluations of the performances. Table 6.4

Table 6.3   Mean Ratings of the Candidates in Each Wave

	Before the Debate	Immediately After the Debate	After the Election
Clinton	4.01	5.04	4.65
Bush	4.01	4.15	3.99
Perot	4.16	4.78	4.63
Total number	79	79	79

Table 6.4   Correlations Between Candidate Ratings in Each Wave

	Predebate	During the Debate	Postdebate
Clinton			
During the debate	.50		
Postdebate	.45	.65	
Postelection	.46	.50	.67
Bush			
During the debate	.39		
Postdebate	.54	.67	
Postelection	.57	.38	.52
Perot			
During the debate	.39		
Postdebate	.48	.58	
Postelection	.39	.34	.45

presents the simple Pearson correlations between measurements at different waves. The pattern for all three candidates is similar. The correlation between the mean rating during the debate (taken from the continuous on-line response) and the postdebate rating was much stronger than the correlation between the rating during the debate and the predebate rating.[13] For example, the correlation between the postdebate rating of Perot and the rating of his debate performance was .58, compared with .39 between the debate rating and the predebate rating.

Echoing the general shifts in impression were changes in specific views about the candidates' weaknesses. In the predebate survey, 44 percent of the panelists believed, with greater or lesser certainty, that Clinton was not sufficiently honest to be president. This percentage declined to 27 in the postdebate survey. Similarly, prior to the debate only 38 percent believed that Perot could work effectively with Congress if he were elected president; after the debate 49 percent believed he could. However, Bush made little headway against the perception that he did not have a viable plan for dealing with the economy's problems. Prior to the debate, 37 percent believed Bush had an effective economic plan; after the debate, the portion holding this view rose only slightly—to 41 percent.

Whose impressions were changed? Nearly all panelists shifted their impressions of one or more candidates, and half moved a total of at least four scale points in their ratings of the three candidates. In general, change was greatest among older panelists, the less informed, and those who said (prior to the debate) that they thought presidential debates were a fair and unbiased source of information about the candidates.[14]

Voter Preference

Consistent with the change in impressions of the candidates, the debate occasioned a substantial swing in candidate preference among the panelists (Table 6.5). Two-thirds of those completely undecided before the debate expressed a candidate preference after the debate, whereas one-fourth of those who were initially leaning toward a candidate altered their choice or became completely undecided. In all, 39 percent of the participants gave different answers to the candidate choice question before and after the debate.

Table 6.5   Change in Candidate Preference, Pre- to Postdebate

Predebate	Postdebate									
	Clinton		Bush		Perot		Undecided		Total	
	%	N	%	N	%	N	%	N	%	N
Clinton	83	(25)	0	(0)	10	(3)	7	(2)	29	(30)
Bush	7	(2)	64	(18)	18	(5)	11	(3)	27	(28)
Perot	11	(1)	0	(0)	78	(7)	11	(1)	9	(9)
Undecided	41	(15)	5	(2)	19	(7)	35	(13)	36	(37)
Total	41	(43)	19	(20)	21	(22)	18	(19)	100	(104)

Note: Percentages, except for totals, are row percentages; number of cases is in parentheses.

Bill Clinton was the beneficiary of much of this change, picking up the votes of 41 percent of those initially undecided, as well as a few votes from Perot and Bush supporters. Meanwhile, he held on to 83 percent of those who favored him in the pretest. Ross Perot gained the votes of 19 percent of the undecided and also took 18 percent of Bush's supporters. Bush retained only 64 percent of his initial supporters and added only two voters from among the undecided. These changes were largely consistent with the participants' judgments as to who "won" the debate: 37 percent chose Clinton, whereas 34 percent picked Perot. Only 6 percent thought Bush did best.

The postelection telephone survey found that nearly 90 percent of Clinton and Bush's postdebate supporters had voted for them (see Table 6.6). Perot lost a third of his postdebate supporters but made up for these defections by capturing some of Clinton's and Bush's leaners. The postdebate undecided panelists gave Bush 40 percent, Perot 33 percent, and Clinton 27 percent. Overall, two-thirds of those who switched during the debate voted for the candidate to whom they had switched.

Table 6.6   Change in Candidate Preference, Postdebate to Postelection

Postdebate	Postelection							
	Clinton		Bush		Perot		Total	
	%	N	%	N	%	N	%	N
Clinton	88	(28)	3	(1)	9	(3)	41	(32)
Bush	0	(0)	89	(16)	11	(2)	23	(18)
Perot	21	(3)	14	(2)	64	(9)	18	(14)
Undecided	27	(4)	40	(6)	33	(5)	19	(15)
Total	44	(35)	32	(25)	24	(19)	100	(79)

Note: Percentages, except for totals, are row percentages; number of cases is in parentheses.

Although these data suggest that the debate had a lasting effect on the panelists, they may understate its impact. Changes in candidate impressions may also have had consequences for the ultimate vote choices, even if the effects were not manifested in immediate changes in candidate preference. To disentangle the debate effects from other influences on the vote (including predispositions toward the candidates, issues, and campaign effects that occurred after the debate), we constructed multivariate candidate choice models and used logistic regression to estimate the parameters. Logistic regression is appropriate for use with dichotomous dependent variables (e.g., 1 = voted for Clinton, 0 = voted for someone else). The coefficients express the change in the log odds of the dependent variable associated with a unit change in the independent variable. Since there were three candidates in the race, a single model of choice between the major party candidates was inappropriate; accordingly, three models—each predicting the vote of a single candidate—were constructed.

Slightly different models were created for predicting each candidate's vote. The differences were minor, and reflected a desire to model the influences parsimoniously by including only those variables demonstratively related to the vote. The principal aim of the analysis was to gauge the effect of *changes* in candidate ratings during the debate on the actual vote choice, relative to other influences. To accomplish this, we constructed a baseline model (for each candidate) that included predebate candidate ratings, opinions on issues, ideology, selected demographic characteristics, and respondent opinion as to which candidate did best in the third debate. Variables with nonsignificant coefficients were dropped from the model.[15] The overall explanatory power of this model was compared with one that included these variables plus a measure of change in the candidate ratings during the debate. If the debate had a lasting effect, the model including the debate change should provide a more powerful prediction of the vote. Furthermore, the coefficients for change in candidate ratings during the debate should be significantly associated with the vote. Table 6.7 shows the results from these models.

Table 6.7   Candidate Choice Models at Three Time Points (N = 79)

	Predebate Model		Postdebate Model		Postelection Model	
Clinton						
Clinton predebate rating	.68	(.22)**	2.03	(.56)**	4.58	(1.58)**
Change pre- to postdebate			1.43	(.45)*	3.68	(1.35)**
Change postdebate to postelection					2.34	(.88)**
Bush predebate rating	−.50	(.20)**	−.24	(.23)	.41	(.43)
Perot predebate rating	−.39	(.20)*	−.57	(.26)*	−1.07	(.45)*
Opinion on government jobs issue	−.58	(.28)*	−1.10	(.43)*	−2.25	(1.00)*
Constant	3.22	(1.86)	−2.35	(2.69)	−11.47	(5.40)*
Pseudo r-squared	.62		.76		.88	
% of cases predicted correctly	83%		85%		92%	
Bush						
Clinton predebate rating	−.68	(.23)**	−1.70	(.48)***	−2.21	(.64)***
Change pre- to postdebate			−.76	(.29)**	−1.24	(.43)*
Change postdebate to postelection					−1.09	(.44)*
Bush predebate rating	.97	(.29)***	1.17	(.40)**	1.04	(.48)*
Perot predebate rating	−.26	(.22)	−.81	(.35)*	−.98	(.44)*
Change pre- to postdebate			−1.00	(.35)**	−1.04	(.46)*
Family income	.93	(.37)*	1.49	(.47)**	1.49	(.58)**
Constant	−5.95	(2.39)*	−2.39	(2.82)	.16	(3.31)
Pseudo r-squared	.64		.79		.86	
% of cases predicted correctly	85%		90%		94%	
Perot						
Perot predebate rating	.48	(.21)*	1.17	(.41)**	2.47	(.91)**
Change pre- to postdebate			.86	(.34)*	2.19	(.74)**
Change postdebate to postelection					1.02	(.38)**
Bush predebate rating	.05	(.17)	.37	(.24)	.66	(.38)
Change pre- to postdebate			.54	(.27)*	1.18	(.47)*
Respondent's age	−0.7	(.03)**	−.08	(.03)**	−.09	(.04)*
R thought Perot did best in 3rd debate					2.92	(1.15)*
Constant	−.75	(1.49)	−5.56	(2.60)*	−14.44	(5.92)*
Pseudo r-squared	.33		.53		.75	
% of cases predicted correctly	80%		83%		89%	

Notes: Cell entries, except model summary statistics, are logistic regression coefficients. Standard errors are in parentheses. Asterisks indicate significance level of coefficient: * $p <$ .05; ** $p < .01$; *** $p < .001$. The pseudo r-square statistic is based on the corrected Aldrich-Nelson measure described by Timothy M. Hagle and Glenn E. Mitchell II. "Goodness of Fit Measures for Probit and Logit," *American Journal of Political Science* 36 (1992): 762–784.

For all three candidates, the explanatory power of the models improved substantially when the variables for debate-induced change in candidate ratings were included. The pseudo r-squared rose by .14 for Clinton's model (from .62 to .76), by .15 for Bush's (.64 to .79), and by .20 for Perot's (.33 to .53). Change in Clinton's rating was a significant predictor of both Clinton's and Bush's vote, whereas change in Perot's rating improved the prediction of Bush's and Perot's vote. Debate-related change in Bush's rating was a significant predictor only of Perot's vote.

Postdebate factors also played a substantial role in the decisions of the panelists. The postelection models in Table 6.7, which include change in candidate ratings after the postdebate measurement, all manifest improved predictive power. The pseudo r-squared for Clinton's model rose by .12 (from .76 to .88), by .07 for Bush (.79 to .86), and by a whopping .22 for Perot (.53 to .75). Postdebate change in Clinton's ratings was significantly related both to his vote and to Bush's. Change in Perot's ratings was a significant predictor of his vote. In addition, respondents' belief that Perot won the third debate was also independently related to his vote. However, it should also be noted that the variables for changes in ratings induced by the second debate remained significantly related to the vote, even in the presence of measures of postdebate phenomena.

A Closer Look at the Impact of "The People's Debate"

The results of our three-wave panel suggest that viewing the Richmond debate significantly influenced the candidate ratings and, ultimately, the vote choices, of undecided and weakly committed voters, independent of their predispositions about the candidates. These effects persisted despite important postdebate events, advertising, news commentary, and other communications. Clinton received the clearest boost, both in ratings and votes, but Perot was also helped.

What was it about the debate that led to this impact? We noted earlier that common wisdom suggests that debates are won or lost through particular "defining moments," rather than because of the cumulative effect of the information and affect generated during debates. Although, as in the case of Gerald Ford's 1976 misstatement about Eastern Europe, this key moment may not emerge until the commentary that follows a debate,[16] one would expect to find some evidence of these critical junctures in the "real time" reactions of viewers and listeners.

Our data do not allow us to directly address the link between an individual's response to specific moments of the debate and shifts in his or her postdebate evaluation of the candidates, but we can, through the use of a "Continuous On-Line Audience Response" (COAR) system, identify the aggregate, moment-by-moment reactions of the audience to the candidates' performances.[17] COAR systems are the sophisticated stepchildren of the "Lazarsfeld-Stanton program analyzer" developed in the mid-1940s for determining audience reactions to radio broadcasts and films. As noted above, our panel watched the debate in an auditorium equipped with a large-screen television. Each individual had a small "dial box" with a knob and seven settings. The settings corresponded to a scale from 1 (strongly dislike) to 7 (strongly like), with 4 being neutral. During the debate, their responses were summarized every two seconds and plotted on a graph, which was superimposed on the video being watched and taped by the researchers.

Two general points about the audience's reactions emerge from an analysis of the video. First, there is a fair amount of movement in the audience's response throughout the debate, with the mean score on the seven-point scale dipping as low as 2.94 and climbing as high as 6.08. Second, although those initially leaning toward a particular candidate usually had the most positive reactions to their candidate's comments, *all* four groupings (the candidates' leaners and those completely undecided) generally reacted to the same comments in the same way—in very few instances during the ninety-minute debate did supporters of one candidate react positively to a comment while supporters of another candidate reacted negatively.

What, specifically, were voters reacting to during the debate? A brief examination of some of the candidates' high and low points is instructive. As noted earlier, George Bush had the lowest average rating of the three candidates, ending with a cumulative mean score of 4.29 (the mean of all audience responses while he was speaking). Bush seldom connected with our panelists: his highest score was 5.48, reached when, in response to the question, "please state your position on term limits," he stated forcefully that "I strongly support term limits for members of the United States Congress." By comparison, Bill Clinton exceeded that score during four of the fourteen opportunities he had to speak, and Ross Perot exceeded it during ten of his fourteen opportunities.

However, three of the four lowest scores recorded during the debate occurred while Bush was speaking, and for ten of his fourteen opportunities, Bush's highest rating was lower than *both* those of Clinton and Perot. Significantly, the two lowest ratings of the night—both received by Bush—were on topics that defined the 1992 campaign. Throughout the campaign, voters had expressed their displeasure with what they considered to be "mudslinging" by the candidates. This theme was reiterated early in the Richmond debate when an audience member remarked that the "amount of time the candidates have spent trashing their opponents' character is depressingly large." Figure 6.1 shows the audience's reactions to the candidates' discussion of this comment.

Figure 6.1   Debate Audience Reaction to Candidates' Discussion of "Character Trashing"

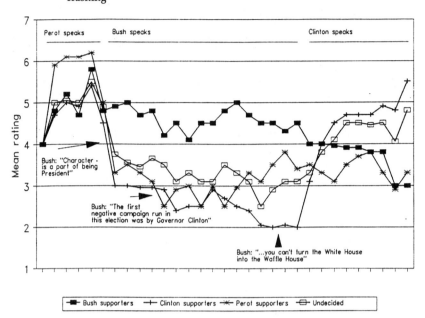

Rather than accepting the questioner's premise—that the campaign would be better off with less mudslinging—Bush tried to defend his actions, arguing that "the first negative campaign run in this election was by Governor Clinton, and I'm not going to sit there and be a punching bag." Throughout his defensive answer, his ratings plummeted, dropping nearly two full points to a score of 2.94 (Figure 6.1 shows ratings broken down by predebate candidate preference). The significance of this moment for our panelists was further documented in one of our focus groups. In response to a question regarding what they thought of the debate format, the following exchange occurred:

Barbara: I think [the candidates] learned from the reactions to the previous debates. I feel they were less likely to be combative. . . .

John: But Mr. Bush tried to get his shot in the beginning.

Barbara: I know he *tried.*

John: He tried, yes he did. He should try to give up on that.

Barbara: But nobody else [responded negatively]. I think it showed that [Clinton and Perot] are better than Bush. He was just trying to do everything the same way he has done it before.

Bush had an equally dramatic slide about forty-five minutes later, in response to an audience member's question as to how the nation's economic woes had personally affected each of the candidates. The question, although simplistic, brought together the public's concern about the economy with their desire for evidence that whoever led the country understood the impact of the bad economic times on the lives of average folks. What was clear, however—again playing into a theme that had emerged much earlier in the campaign—was that Bush "did not get it," fumbling first to try to understand the question, then depersonalizing the issue by stating that "everybody cares if people aren't doing well."[18] Notably, when asked in the postelection telephone survey to describe the most memorable moment of the debate, a dozen panelists mentioned this exchange (the largest number of references to a single event). Postdebate commentary by the media doubtless contributed somewhat to the retrospective salience of the moment, but its significance was also apparent to at least some of the panelists when it happened, as this comment from the focus groups indicates:

Marvin: Can I say something? It was really funny when that girl asked the question about how [the recession] affects you, and Bush avoided the damn question. How come he didn't answer the girl's question? Clinton got up; I don't know whether he answered the damn thing but he made some kind of effort to answer it. Mr. Perot, he answered the question. But Bush had to ask, "could you ask the question again," you know; it was like I wanted to say "don't you hear, don't you understand what the lady's trying to say?" She was trying to find out if it is hitting home to you personally. There ain't no way in hell it's hitting home personally to him.

Bill Clinton's average rating over the entire debate was 4.73, nearly half a point higher than Bush's and three-quarters above the neutral point on the scale. Nonetheless, during only four of his fourteen opportunities to speak did his peak rating exceed that of both Perot and Bush. His high point of the evening, and the only point at which he topped 6.0 on the seven-point scale, was when he stated his strong support for anticrime legislation in general and the Brady handgun control bill in particular. His single low point in the debate came in response to the same question for which Bush received his highest rating—his stand on term limits. Figure 6.2 plots the responses of the panelists during the candidates' discussion of this issue. Clinton followed the president's strong endorsement of term limits by saying "I know they're popular, but I'm against them." He then went on to summarize his opposition to them, and as he did so the graph superimposed on the television screen recorded the audience's disapproval. By the time he had completed his explanation his rating had dropped to an average of 3.17, nearly two and a half points below Bush's peak just moments before. But then, saying, "Let me tell you what I favor instead," he offered an alternative to term limits. Laying out a plan for strict limits on "how

Figure 6.2   Debate Audience Reaction to Candidates' Discussion of Term Limits

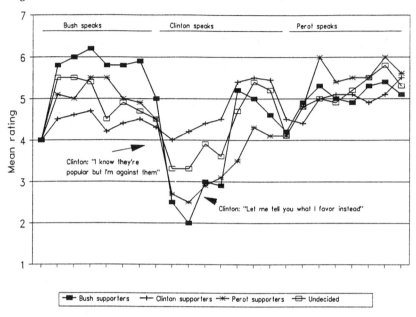

much you can spend running for Congress, strict limits on political action committees, requirements that people running for Congress appear in open public debates like we're doing now," Clinton argued for elections that would put incumbents and challengers on an equal footing. Thus, "the voters could make up their own mind without being subject to an unfair fight." The audience reacted positively to this counterproposal, steadily increasing their favorable responses to a peak of 5.38—nearly that achieved by President Bush on the same question.

Taken as a whole, the pattern of rising and falling support as different points were made suggested an audience that was grappling with difficult issues and that, although having opinions that shaped their initial reactions, was open to reasonable counterarguments. We cannot say whether anyone's opinion on term limits was changed by this exchange, but it is clear that the audience actively followed Clinton's argument and recognized its merits. The focus group conversations following the debate suggested that the audience reacted positively to Clinton's willingness to go into detail on his issue stands. Annette liked the fact that "he went into a little more depth than I had heard, about some of the specific programs that he would try to implement." And according to Meredyth:

Meredyth: Clinton has always sort of looked like a package, a really nicely packaged product that you can find in a gourmet shop. . . . That has always made me leery of him. . . . But tonight he stated some of the specifics that he wanted to do, unlike Bush who just seemed to skate around and not really give us any specifics. It made me think that Clinton knew a little bit more about what was going on than I thought before.

At least as measured by the panelists' instant reactions, Ross Perot was the clear favorite in the Richmond debate. His cumulative mean score was 4.99, three quarters of a point better than Bush, a quarter of a point better than Clinton, and nearly a point above the neutral score. Perot achieved this relatively high rating in part by having few bad moments: unlike Bush or Clinton, at no point did he drop dramatically below the neutral 4.0 point. More impressively, Perot "peaked" higher than either of his opponents during ten of the fourteen opportunities he had to speak. Three of the five most highly rated moments in the debate belonged to Perot, including the two highest ratings of the evening. Significantly, both of these occurred on the same topics on which George Bush had foundered and that were defining issues of the campaign. Perot received a rating of 6.0 with his request, "Let's talk about the things that concern the American people," thus playing to the public's expressed desire to avoid mudslinging and address the issues. And he received the evening's highest rating in response to his promise that "putting our people back to work will be my number one priority."

Despite Perot's strong showing, when asked directly who they thought "won" the debate, more of our participants selected Clinton than Perot. Similarly, more participants shifted their support to Clinton than Perot. The reason for this seeming inconsistency lies in part in the role voters apparently saw Perot as playing. They reacted positively to him and felt he added a great deal to the campaign but did not necessarily see him as a viable candidate. The following comment is typical of those found in the focus groups:

Roberta: I think Ross Perot has added a dimension of being more truthful, in a sense, to the process. I think he's sincere, but I don't know how far he could get. His vice presidential candidate, well, I don't think he's the person to be vice president. I think one thing Perot did, though, was make the other [candidates] come to the issues.

And consider the following exchange:

John: [Perot] adds a little levity to the whole process. It's nice to laugh occasionally instead of being serious all the time.
Michael: But he actually brings out a lot of good points.
Nancy: Yeah—through his humor he really hits the nail on the head.

And Marvin colorfully expressed the views of several of our conversants when he said, "It would be nice to get [Perot] elected, but if he did get elected and he was president, Congress would [expletive] him to death. He would not get anything he wants done."

Conclusion

The second presidential debate in the 1992 election had a clear and fairly dramatic impact on our panel of undecided and weakly committed voters. The effects of the debate appear to have persisted through the remainder of the campaign and affected the voting of many panelists. Considering both the composition of the panel and the nature of the study itself, these measurable effects are perhaps not surprising. The panelists were receptive, and—unlike average voters watching at home—they focused intently on the entire debate, rating its every moment. What, if anything, can be said about the external validity of the study? Do our findings justify a conclusion that the debate had an impact nationally? With appropriate caveats, we believe that they do.

First of all, a large number of citizens nationally had not yet made a firm decision about how to vote and thus were susceptible to influence by the debates. For example, among citizens interviewed by the National Election Study October 1–15, 10 percent of likely voters were completely undecided, and another 30 percent said their candidate preference was "not strong." Thus, individuals similar to our panelists in their level of commitment to a candidate constituted a sizable minority of the electorate.

Second, the debate attracted a huge television audience, with over 51.2 million homes tuned in to the major networks—not including the audiences for PBS and C-SPAN.[19] A majority of the electorate was exposed to some or all of the second debate.

Third, there is substantial evidence that national audiences perceived the relative performances by the candidates in the same way as our Richmond panelists. According to a CBS News poll, the second debate—compared with the others—produced the clearest consensus on a winner: 54 percent of those who watched or listened said Clinton won, compared with 25 percent for Bush and 20 percent for Perot.[20] Furthermore, tracking polls by three organizations found changes in vote intentions after the debate that were consistent with the changes noted in our study (see Table 6.8). Clinton gained 5 points in two of the polls (and 1 point in the other), Perot gained slightly in all three, and Bush lost 3–4 points in each of them. Of course, unlike our study these polls also included firmly committed voters and were not restricted to debate viewers; thus the debate's impact on the undecided or weakly committed debate watcher is probably understated in these data.

Table 6.8   Pre- and Postdebate National Tracking Polls

	Bush	Clinton	Perot	Undecided	Sample
Gallup/USA Today/CNN					
Predebate (Oct. 13–15)	34	47	13	6	1,041 registered voters
Postdebate (Oct. 16–18)	30	48	15	7	1,000 registered voters
ABC News					
Predebate (Oct. 14–15)	34	44	12	10	869 likely voters
Postdebate (Oct. 16–18)	30	49	13	8	1,263 likely voters
Greenberg-Lake/Tarrance Group					
Predebate (Oct. 11–14)	35	41	14	10	1,000 registered voters
Postdebate (Oct. 15, 18–20)	32	46	17	5	1,000 registered voters

Source: The American Enterprise Public Opinion and Demographic Report, *The Public Perspective,* November–December 1992, p. 101.

None of the national data available allow us to gauge the persistence of the second debate's effects. The third debate followed just five days later, and all three candidates campaigned hard during the final two weeks. Complicating the effort to distill the significance of this single event— albeit an important one—is that much of what occurred in it epitomized the major themes and tendencies of the larger campaign and so doubtless reinforced them. Clinton was fluent and at ease in a format well suited to his talents; conversely, Bush was uncomfortable personally and did not have a receptive audience for his strongest message, which was to raise doubts about Clinton. Perot displayed skill in working the audience, though he was unconvincing regarding his ability to effect change in Washington singlehandedly. The second debate provided an outstanding opportunity for a citizen to observe these particular strengths and weaknesses of the candidates, but the same observations could have been made at numerous other times during the campaign.

Pundits derided the second debate as a "softball" affair, and policy wonks found little new in what was said. The candidates were not forced to reconcile conflicting versions of their views, as journalists would have preferred. But our panelists very much liked the format: three-fourths rated it as better than the ones they had seen before, and two-thirds said they learned at least "a fair amount" about the candidates' stands on the issues. Significantly, perhaps, the national audience for the third debate was at least as large as the one for the second, contrary to the predictions of many. If anything, the second debate whetted the electorate's appetite.

We certainly make no claim that the format of the "People's Debate" was preferable to other debate formats. The third debate, which involved the skillful questioning of the candidates by journalist Jim Lehrer, was more focused and intense and probably more informative. The larger conclusion from a consideration of the debates of 1992 is that they appeared both to reflect and contribute to the high level of public interest in this election. Notably, 1992 saw a rise in turnout and an increase in the percentage of the public reporting great interest in the campaign. It left many observers, including us, believing that there may still be some life left in the U.S. polity. The cast of players in 1992 (especially Ross Perot) was partly responsible for this, but the debates and other nontraditional venues for campaigning and campaign reporting were important, too.

Notes

1. Edward W. Chester, *Radio, Television, and American Politics* (New York: Sheed and Ward, 1969), p. 21.

2. See, e.g., Saul Ben-Zeev and Irving S. White, "Effects and Implications," in *The Great Debates: Background, Perspective, Effects,* ed. Sidney Kraus (Bloomington: Indiana University Press, 1962); Steven H. Chaffee and Sun Yuel Choe, "Time of Decision and Media Use During the Ford-Carter Campaign," *Public Opinion Quarterly* 44 (1980): 53–69; John G. Geer, "The Effects of Presidential Debates on the Electorate's Preferences for Candidates," *American Politics Quarterly* 16 (1988): 486–501; Gladys Engel Lang and Kurt Lang, "Immediate and Mediated Responses," in *The Great Debates: Carter vs. Ford, 1976,* ed. Sidney Kraus (Bloomington: Indiana University Press, 1979); David J. Lanoue, "One That Made a Difference: Cognitive Consistency, Political Knowledge, and the 1980 Presidential Debate," *Public Opinion Quarterly* 56 (1992): 168–184.

3. Likely voters were those who said they were registered to vote and "definitely will vote" in the presidential election.

4. A reminder call was made to all recruits the night before the debate. Those who attended were paid $20.

5. See Lee B. Becker, Idowu A. Sobowale, Robin E. Cobbey, and Chaim H. Eyal, "Debates' Effects on Voters' Understanding of Candidates and Issues," in *The Presidential Debates: Media Electoral, and Policy Perspectives,* ed. George F. Bishop, Robert G. Meadow, and Marilyn Jackson-Beeck (New York: Praeger, 1980); Steven H. Chaffee and Jack Dennis, "Presidential Debates: An Empirical Assessment," in *The Past and Future of Presidential Debates,* ed. Austin Ranney (Washington, D.C.: American Enterprise Institute, 1979).

6. The fourth issue was abortion.

7. The 52 percent figure for knowledge of Bush's position on the death

penalty may seem low, but was nearly identical to the percentage who knew this in a late September statewide survey of likely Virginia voters.

8. This was a curious comment, since both Clinton and Perot were supporters of the death penalty. However, few voters knew this, with only 25 percent of the panelists saying that Clinton supported the death penalty. Clinton did not state his position during the debate, and the postdebate measurement was identical. In the postelection survey, 47 percent of the panelists correctly identified Clinton's position.

9. William J. McGuire, "The Nature of Attitudes and Attitude Change," in *The Handbook of Social Psychology,* vol. 3, 2nd ed., ed. G. Lindzey and E. Aronson (Reading, Mass.: Addison-Wesley, 1969).

10. This comparison is based on telephone surveys of the general public in Virginia surveyed in 1990, 1991, and 1992.

11. The audience provided continuous ratings of the debate via the seven-point scale on their dial boxes. The computer recorded the dial box settings every two seconds. The cumulative rating scores are the means for all dial box settings while each candidate was speaking.

12. These data are from the 79 individuals for whom we have complete records, including their vote choices. However, data for the full panel of 104 were nearly identical.

13. Due to a computer malfunction, individual data from the on-line audience response are available for only thirty minutes of the debate.

14. There were significant differences ($p < .05$) across groups in the mean total change in candidate ratings (pre- to postdebate).

15. We did not expect issues and demographics to be particularly significant in these models, given that much of their effect was already reflected in the predebate ratings of the candidates. The three variables that survived (government jobs in the Clinton model, income in the Bush model, and age in the Perot model) exhibited persistent and strong independent effects on the vote.

In a few instances, a candidate's predebate rating was not significant but was retained in the model. This occurred where one of the variables for the *change* in rating was significant in the current model or a subsequent one. The change variables are meaningful only when the baseline rating variables are included as well.

16. Frederick T. Steeper, "Public Response to Gerald Ford's Statements on Eastern Europe in the Second Debate," in *The Presidential Debates: Media Electoral, and Policy Perspectives,* ed. George F. Bishop, Robert G. Meadow, and Marilyn Jackson-Beeck (New York: Praeger, 1980); Thomas E. Patterson, *The Mass Media Election* (New York: Praeger, 1980), pp. 122–123.

17. In theory, an individual's instant reactions *can* be tied to his or her specific responses on the three-wave survey instrument. However, as noted earlier, because of a computer malfunction we have these individual-level data for only thirty minutes of the debate. Furthermore, the periods for which we have data include the beginning and end of the debate, which (from our perspective) were less substantively interesting.

18. In fairness to Bush, the question was a little confusing, in that the questioner asked about the personal impact of the "national debt" but, as Carole Simpson pointed out, probably meant the impact of the recession. Interestingly, Ross Perot was the first of the candidates to address this question, and while his response did not speak to the personal impact of the debt, it received good ratings from the panelists.

19. Wendy Zeligson Adler, "The Debates: The Day After," *The Finish Line:*

Covering the Campaign's Final Days (New York: The Freedom Forum Media Studies Center, 1993), pp. 35–45.

20. Kathleen A. Frankovic, "Public Opinion in the 1992 Campaign," in *The Election of 1992: Reports and Interpretations,* ed. Gerald M. Pomper et al. (Chatham, N.J.: Chatham House, 1993), pp. 110–131.

7

Adwatch:
Covering Campaign Ads

Michael Milburn & Justin Brown

Political campaign advertisements in the 1992 election were a very big business. ABC took in $24 million from political advertisements, six times what they expected to make.[1] Perot was spending about $1 million per day on ads between October 4 and election day, putting up a total of $40 million on advertising.[2] For the last three days of the campaign, Perot bought $4.2 million of advertising, Clinton $2 million, and Bush $1 million.[3]

Consistent with the considerable emphasis that candidates give to political advertising, as shown by Montague Kern and Marion Just in Chapter 5, ads continue to be for most Americans an important source of information about political candidates, particularly for their first impressions. A Times Mirror Center survey of 3,500 Americans found that 62 percent of the respondents reported that they first learned about political candidates from television ads.[4]

In addition, surveys show that a sizable proportion of the electorate reports being influenced by campaign advertisements. A survey conducted at the end of the campaign found that 38 percent of the respondents said that the candidates' commercials were either "very helpful" or "somewhat helpful" in making their voting decision.[5] A *New York Times*/CBS News poll in October found that close to half of respondents reported that their choice for president was influenced at least somewhat by political advertisements.[6]

The public's level of exposure to political ads during the campaign was fairly high. During the month of October, a series of Times Mirror surveys found that between 60 and 68 percent reported seeing Bush ads in the few days prior to the survey, and between 57 and 64 percent had seen Clinton ads. In a late October poll, 62 percent said they had recently seen Perot ads.[7]

In their book *The Unseeing Eye,* Patterson and McClure argued that political ads in the 1972 election could be differentiated into two types: "image" ads designed to produce an emotional response, and "issue" ads to communicate information about candidate positions. In her review of political advertising in the 1980s, Kern observes that this earlier distinction between image and issue ads has become blurred, and that most recent ads, whether they are designed to deliver information or not, attempt to evoke emotional responses. Kathleen Hall Jamieson presents a detailed analysis of the use of emotionally evocative dramatic images in political advertisements in the 1988 presidential campaign that she argues produced false inferences among viewers about the candidates' positions.[8]

Partly in response to the highly emotional negative ad campaign against Michael Dukakis in 1988 masterminded by Roger Ailes, many television stations and newspapers developed "Adwatch" features designed to educate viewers/readers about political ads in the 1992 election campaign and hopefully to limit the efforts of the campaigns to manipulate voters with inaccurate and misleading information. Brooks Jackson of Cable News Network dubbed his effort in this regard the "Ad Police." How do Adwatch analyses of political ads affect the way in which viewers respond to the political advertisements, and how does Adwatch affect the persuasiveness of the ads? Additionally, how do Adwatch columns affect viewers' political efficacy and involvement in the electoral process?

The intended effect of Adwatch on the electorate can be understood as consistent with McGuire's inoculation message theory. Inoculation is an attempt to increase resistance to persuasive messages and attitude change. Successful inoculation is believed to require two components: threat and refutation. Adwatch presents the candidate's message and then critiques it. In this respect, Adwatch is similar to the two-sided messages with which Lumsdaine and Janis first discovered the inoculation effect.[9]

In an ideal representative democracy, candidates offer leadership by presenting cogent arguments on issues relevant to governance. These arguments in turn should help voters elaborate their own political thinking and their expectations of political leaders. The Elaboration Likelihood Model may help explain why elaboration of political thought is often difficult to realize.[10] Elaboration of thought requires cognitive resources that often are needed for other activities such as managing the daily contingencies of life. Petty and Cacioppo explain:

> By *elaboration* in a persuasion context, we mean the extent to which a person thinks about the issue-relevant arguments contained in a message. When conditions foster people's motivation and ability to engage in issue-relevant thinking, the "elaboration likelihood" is said to be high. This means that people are likely to attend to the appeal; attempt to access relevant associations, images, and experiences from memory; scrutinize and elaborate upon the externally provided message arguments in light of the associations available from memory; draw inferences about the merits of the arguments for a recommendation based upon their analyses; and consequently derive an overall evaluation of, or attitude toward, the recommendation.[11]

Because elaborating political thought requires cognitive resources, voters may prefer to devote their cognitive energies elsewhere. As a result, candidates may find that they are most persuasive when relying on peripheral cues that demand few cognitive resources.

Televised campaign advertisements usually contain peripheral cues such as music and visual images. Viewers are likely to be influenced by peripheral cues such as the expertise or attractiveness of the message source,[12] the number rather than the quality of reasons supporting an argument,[13] a "placebic" reason,[14] pleasant music,[15] the visual prominence of a speaker,[16] or even food.[17] Peripheral cues are processed more rapidly and with less effort than the substance of a persuasive argument.[18] As a result, voters whose intentions are shaped by peripheral cues would be expected to be more susceptible to attitude change and have less stable political preferences than voters who more carefully scrutinize political messages.

Adwatch attempts both to refute any false claims made by a candidate and to deconstruct an advertisement's peripheral cues, thus encouraging voters to evaluate the substance of a persuasive message and reducing the influence of peripheral cues. By evaluating the veracity of a candidate's message, Adwatch focuses on the quality of the candidate's argument. By deconstructing the dramatic and visual content of a message, Adwatch encourages voters to think about peripheral cues rather than allowing these cues to influence them unaware.

We wanted to know whether Adwatch had the intended effect on voters. If successful, Adwatch should increase the elaboration of political thought, which should in turn increase the stability of voters' political preferences and reduce their vulnerability to attitude change. In order to assess the effects of Adwatch, we employed a dual strategy, interviewing a number of political reporters who covered political advertisements during the 1992 campaign and conducting an experimental test of the effects of Adwatch.

Journalists' Reaction to Political Advertising and Adwatch

The Times Mirror Center for the People and the Press conducted a series of surveys during the 1992 election campaign that focused on journalists' assessment of the political ad campaign and on the public's utilization of information from political advertisements. In June of 1992, a survey of more than 400 local and national journalists revealed some skepticism about the effectiveness of the Adwatch approach, with nearly 40 percent of the respondents saying that "press coverage of the campaign commercials has not made them [the commercials] more honest."[19] At the same time, however, 85 percent of the journalists interviewed saw the press coverage of commercials as having a positive effect.[20] In a survey conducted in the final weeks of the campaign, a high proportion (77 percent) of a different sample of journalists (n = 250) also felt the press coverage of campaign ads had had a positive effect.[21]

We conducted interviews with television and newspaper journalists involved in Adwatch efforts during the 1992 campaign. Included in our sample were reporters from CNN, the *Boston Globe,* the *Los Angeles Times, USA Today,* and the *New York Times.* We asked three primary questions: (1) What were your specific goals when you produced the Adwatch information? (2) How well do you feel you accomplished those goals? and (3) What would you do differently in the future?

The goals of the various journalists were pretty much the same. First and foremost, they wanted to check the facts in the ad to make sure they were correct, to "identify lies as lies." In addition, they wanted to assess whether the overall impression communicated by each ad was misleading, even if the facts were technically correct. Some important facts might be left out: "That's not the whole story," Brooks Jackson (CNN) would often say. Several reporters pointed out that the campaigns would try to "twist facts" to suit their arguments, not always in a dishonest way, but the facts nevertheless could be twisted and distorted.

Going beyond simple fact checking, Leslie Phillips (*USA Today*) wanted to "deconstruct" the ads, to analyze the use of drama and visuals and the role they played in the overall process of manipulation. This is, however, a difficult task, particularly under the time pressure that all the reporters felt to do the Adwatch as quickly as possible following broadcast of the specific ad. Jamieson's careful analysis of the Willie Horton ad and the way the juxtaposition of visuals, words on the screen, and voice-over were designed to lead to several misleading and erroneous conclusions was not done under the pressure of a news deadline.[22] Nevertheless, all the reporters agreed that this was an important area of concern for Adwatch.

All the journalists were satisfied that they were able to accomplish their primary goals and that those who were exposed to the Adwatch coverage received important information. Additionally, Renee Loth (*Boston Globe*) noted that Adwatch became part of the campaign discourse, with Adwatch columns from the *Washington Post* cited in the Clinton response ad (forty-eight hours after the Bush ad). Campaigns were much more careful this election to limit the overtly dishonest content in ads because of the Adwatch (one producer said they tried to include in the ads source references to claims made in the ads). Independent expenditure groups such as the one that produced the Willie Horton ad were virtually nonexistent in the 1992 campaign. This development lends support to the civil libertarian argument that the best way to confront an unwanted type of speech is to develop ways to encourage opposing types of speech, rather than outlawing the unwanted speech.

The primary difficulty with the Adwatch effort was one of obtaining copies of each ad in time to analyze it. Richard Berke (*New York Times*) noted that this was a way the campaigns could manipulate coverage of their ads, to leave limited time for journalists to cover their ads, although in part this may have been due to the disorganization of the campaigns. Some reporters had the additional problem of fighting with their editors for the space to include their Adwatch analyses, although most had their editors' full support.

The journalists had several recommendations for future Adwatch efforts.

1. *Be more systematic.* Brooks Jackson (CNN) felt that the press needs to develop an intelligence network in order to see all the ads. As it was, journalists were completely dependent on the campaigns for the ads, and many ads, particularly those shown only in specific regions, were not given to the press. Some sort of pooled coverage, comparable to the pooled exit poll results as was the case on election night in the New Hampshire primary, might be effective.

2. *Broaden the ad coverage.* Coverage of ads from House and Senate races was very limited. Examples of ads from these races, even if not from a person's own state, can educate voters about forms of manipulation.

3. *Expand truth squad efforts.* Ads are not the only venue in which influence attempts are made and misleading facts are presented. Thomas Rosensteil (*Los Angeles Times*) suggested that the Adwatch approach should be extended to all forms of political speech, for example, candidates' sparring with each other, candidates' stump speeches, and thirty-minute infomercials. Leslie Phillips (*USA Today*) noted that politicians are often ahead of journalists. Clinton, she observes, has figured out ways to go around the traditional press with electronic mail and cable channels, and the press needs to be responsive to new developments in candidates' communication.

A corroborating perspective on Adwatch is provided by the media consultants who produce the advertisements. Ken Swope, who produced ads in 1992 for Tom Harkin in the Democratic presidential primaries and for Leo McCarthy in California, who ran for the Democratic nomination for the U.S. Senate against Barbara Boxer, feels that Adwatch had a "chilling effect" on the content of ads produced, but a positive chilling effect. Ad professionals knew they had to avoid making any wild and unsubstantiated charges, and they also had to avoid innuendo for which they could be called on the carpet.

An Experimental Test of the Effects of Adwatch

In addition to assessing journalists' reactions to Adwatch, we conducted an experimental test of the effects of watching political ads following exposure to Adwatch information.

Method

Fifty-seven subjects were recruited from introductory classes in psychology and sociology at the University of Massachusetts at Boston. All subjects received a chance to win $500.[23]

We established two conditions, the Adwatch condition and a control condition. In both conditions, subjects watched two political ads from the Bush campaign, then two ads from the Perot campaign, then two ads from the Clinton campaign. Before seeing the ads for each specific candidate, the subjects read newspaper articles about the ads they were about to see. The two conditions were distinguished only by having two different forms of the questionnaire; each questionnaire contained one of the two different sets of newspaper columns, described in more detail later.

We conducted the experiment in the week immediately prior to election week in November. Subjects signed up for one of seven different experimental sessions. For each session the questionnaires for the two different conditions were alternated when passed out, thus randomly assigning subjects to one of the two experimental treatments.

We informed subjects that they would be watching several political advertisements and that prior to watching each ad they would be reading a newspaper column about the advertisement. We also told subjects that they would be asked to write down all the thoughts that occurred to them while they watched the ads. We knew that after the first ad, subjects would anticipate this question being asked of them for ads two through five, so we wanted our measurements for ad one to be the same.

We exposed subjects to the political commercials in groups rather than individually because of our need to balance two constraints. First, we needed to wait a sufficient amount of time into the campaign to acquire ads from the three principal candidates and to obtain Adwatch columns about these specific ads. Second, we felt it was important to conduct the experiment *prior* to the election because we felt the frame of mind of subjects viewing the political advertisements would be considerably different following the election. We were unable to distinguish any significant differences across the different group treatment times.

Political Advertisements

All the subjects watched six political advertisements, two ads from the Bush campaign, two Perot ads, and then two Clinton ads. Detailed information on the ads is presented in the appendix to this chapter.

Adwatch Content

In the Adwatch condition, subjects read newspaper columns from the *Boston Globe* written by Renee Loth, the political reporter assigned to cover political advertising in the 1992 presidential campaign. These columns contained the scripts of the ads themselves, an analysis of the accuracy of the information in the ads, and an assessment of the likely effectiveness of the ads.

In the control condition, prior to viewing the ads the subjects read a column from *USA Today* that mentioned the ads they were to see, but that contained no information about the arguments or content of the ads.

How similar was the content of the *Boston Globe* Adwatch columns to treatment of the same ads in other newspapers? We compared *Boston Globe* columns to Adwatch columns for the same ads from other newspapers, including the *New York Times,* the *Los Angeles Times,* and *USA Today.* The *Boston Globe* columns were comparable to newspaper coverage of the same ads in the number of arguments used and the points made, sometimes including more arguments than columns in other papers, sometimes less.

For example, for the Clinton ad titled "Curtains," the *Boston Globe,* the *New York Times,* and the *Los Angeles Times* all pointed out that the announcements about the unemployment rate and the economy were juxtaposed with comparable Bush statements that were taken out of order and hence misleading. The *Globe* column included additional points, observing that although Bush vetoed unemployment compensation bills, he then supported two extensions and didn't veto any after March 1992, as the ad implies.

In a Bush ad, "Guess," the *Globe, USA Today,* and the *New York Times* all included three arguments/statements about the ad, and the *Los Angeles Times* included seven. The *Boston Globe* Adwatch appears to be generally representative of national newspaper Adwatch coverage, at times somewhat more extensive in its analysis, at times a little less.

Questionnaire

Before watching any advertisements and then again after watching all the ads, subjects completed "thermometer scale" ratings on the candidates. On these scales, we asked subjects to rate on a drawing of a thermometer how warm or cold they felt toward each candidate from 0 to 100, with 50 being neither warm nor cold.

After viewing the two ads for Bush, again after viewing the two Perot ads, and also after viewing Clinton's ads, subjects responded to the instruction: "List all the thoughts that came to your mind as you watched the advertisements for _____."

A coder blind to the experimental hypotheses and conditions coded each protocol for issue-focused thoughts, strategy-focused thoughts, positive thoughts, and negative thoughts. Thoughts for each candidate were coded in terms of their reaction to that candidate's message. For instance, in the protocol asking for thoughts about candidate Clinton, negative thoughts toward candidate Bush would be coded as positive and positive thoughts toward candidate Bush would be coded as negative. For each thought-listing protocol, three measures were computed: proportion of issue-focused thoughts, proportion of positive thoughts, and number of evaluative thoughts both positive and negative.

Finally, after the ads, subjects completed a series of political attitude questions, including measures of political efficacy, political interest, media exposure, and basic demographics.

Results

Attitude change.   To assess whether Adwatch inoculated subjects against attitude change, we computed the absolute value of the change in favorability for each candidate and then averaged across candidates for each subject. This average attitude change value provided a measure of subjects' vulnerability to persuasion. A marginally significant effect for subjects' sex was obtained in which males' attitudes (amount of change = 7.0) changed more than females' (amount of change = 2.33) ($F_{(1,53)} = 3.71, p < .06$).

Inoculation.   We hypothesized that Adwatch would inoculate subjects against attitude change. As predicted, subjects' attitudes toward the candidates changed less in the Adwatch condition (amount of change = 1.9) than in the control condition (amount of change = 6.0) ($F_{(1,53)} = 5.02, p < .05$). One would expect that the benefit of the Adwatch inoculation would be greater for those with greater vulnerability to attitude change. In this case, males would be expected to benefit more from Adwatch than females. The interaction between Adwatch and subjects' sex approached significance ($F_{(1,53)} = 3.06, p < .09$). As seen in Figure 7.1, males in the control condition changed the most. Both the main effect for males and the interaction can be attributed to the substantial attitude change for males in the control condition.

Listed thoughts.   Inoculation theory proposes that the threat to attitude change contained in the inoculating message motivates an audience to

Figure 7.1   Effect of Adwatch on Attitude Change After Viewing Political Ads

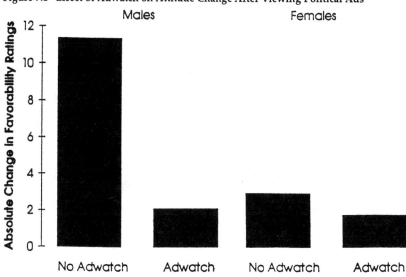

generate counterarguments. In this study, counterarguments would be measured as negative thoughts about the candidates' advertisements. Controlling for subjects' initial level of negative thinking, we found no evidence in the thought-listing procedure that Adwatch increased negative thoughts in the postadvertisement measure ($F_{(1,53)} = 0.58$, $p = .45$). However, the premeasure indicated that subjects' thinking about the election already was predominated by 77 percent negative thoughts.

The Elaboration Likelihood Model proposes that the elaboration of thinking (i.e., an increase in both positive and negative thoughts) indicates allocation of cognitive resources to the quality of a message. As a result of this elaboration, viewers should be less vulnerable to persuasion through peripheral cues and more attentive to the substance of a candidate's message. Controlling for subjects' initial level of evaluative thinking (both positive and negative thoughts), we found that Adwatch elicited significantly more evaluative thoughts (average = 5.5) than the control condition (average = 4.7) ($F_{(1,53)} = 4.21$, $p < .05$).

We also obtained a significant interaction between the subjects' sex and the Adwatch effect for evaluative thinking ($F_{(1,53)} = 5.07$, $p < .05$). As seen in Figure 7.2, Adwatch increased evaluative thoughts substantially more for males than for females. In fact, the main effect for Adwatch can be attributed almost entirely to male subjects.

The attitude change data examined earlier suggested that males were most vulnerable to change in response to the candidates' messages (see Figure 7.1). This vulnerability was substantially reduced by Adwatch. The number of evaluative thoughts corresponds closely to the attitude change

Figure 7.2   **Effect of Adwatch on Evaluative Thoughts After Viewing Political Ads**

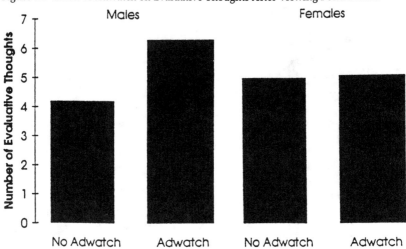

data. This suggests that the stability of preferences produced by Adwatch occurred primarily because subjects elaborated their thinking about the candidates' messages.

Many of the positive and negative thoughts in reaction to the ads that subjects reported related specifically to the arguments in the ads. For example, as a positive statement following the Bush ad, one subject wrote, "Bush has many future plans. The job improvement, export, education [build schools] makes me feel he can do the job as president." Another wrote, "The second one [ad], is probably so true it is pathetic. I think Bill Clinton will increase every tax he can think of and a few if he thinks hard enough he wants to increase." This was coded as a positive thought since it supported the position taken in the Bush ad.

The negative thoughts most often did not follow directly from the arguments in the Adwatch columns. For example, coded as a negative thought in reaction to the Bush ad, one person wrote, "What a jerk," and another wrote, "Lies, lies, lies, lies, lies. George Bush is for the rich in this country and not the poor or the working class." It appears that rather than simply providing a set of arguments that the subjects mimic back while watching the ads, the columns have primed for many people an oppositional frame of mind that allowed subjects to generate or retrieve reactions to the ads that were not included in the Adwatch columns.

Adwatch had no effect on subjects' issue-orientation ($F_{(1,53)} < 1$, not significant). Thus, Adwatch did not increase the extent to which individuals thought about issues when asked to list their thoughts following viewing the ads. This suggests a potential limitation of Adwatch that will be discussed more fully below.

Perceived political efficacy and voting intention.   We asked two questions about political efficacy, each on a 0 to 6 scale. The first question asked subjects how much effect they felt they had on government decisions. The second asked subjects whether they felt elections increased or reduced government indifference. We found that the two questions were not strongly correlated ($r = -.08$), and so we analyzed the responses to these two questions separately. We labeled the first question "perceived personal efficacy" and the second question "perceived government indifference."

There was a significant main effect for gender, with women (average = 5.3) reporting substantially greater personal efficacy than men (average = 3.8) ($F_{(1,53)} = 6.19, p < .02$). Although personal efficacy was greater in the Adwatch condition (average = 5.1) than the control condition (average = 4.5), the difference was not significant ($F_{(1,53)} = 2.70, p = .11$). A significant interaction on personal efficacy was obtained between subjects' sex and the Adwatch manipulation ($F_{(1,53)} = 4.76, p < .04$). As seen in Figure 7.3, Adwatch increased personal efficacy in males but had no positive effect on females. By increasing personal efficacy in males, Adwatch effectively eliminated the gender difference found in the control condition.

As with perceived efficacy, there was a significant interaction between subjects' sex and Adwatch for perceived government indifference ($F_{(1,53)} = 6.96, p = .01$). As seen in Figure 7.4, Adwatch increased perceived government indifference for females and decreased it for males. Neither the Adwatch manipulation nor subjects' sex had a significant effect on perceived government indifference ($F_{(1,53)} = 0.96, p = .33; F_{(1,53)} = 1.98, p < .20$, respectively). In fact, the means were in the opposite direction from the personal efficacy question, with women and subjects in the Adwatch condition reporting a greater perception of government indifference.

Although voting intention was somewhat stronger in the Adwatch condition (average = 7.6) than in the control condition (average = 6.8), the difference was not significant ($F_{(1,53)} = 1.39, p < .25$).

Discussion

The results of our experiment indicate that Adwatch columns have the potential to be effective in reducing the impact not only of illegitimate attempts at persuasion but also of political campaign advertising in general. Prior exposure to Adwatch helped protect subjects against attitude change. Adwatch did not increase negative thoughts toward candidates' messages, nor did it increase subjects' issue orientation. Instead, Adwatch elicited an increase in evaluative thinking. This suggests that peripheral cues and not

Figure 7.3   Effect of Adwatch on Perceived Political Self-Efficacy

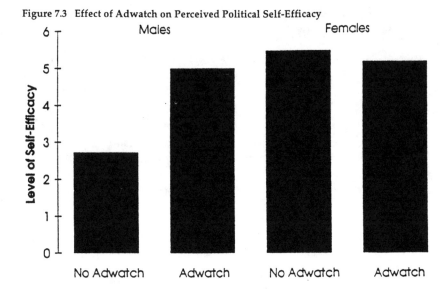

Figure 7.4   Effect of Adwatch on Perceived Government Indifference

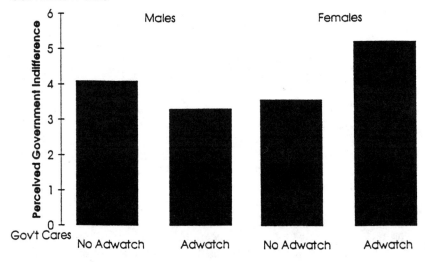

the quality of the candidates' arguments elicited attitude change in the control condition. When subjects in the Adwatch condition allocated more cognitive resources to the advertisements, they were less likely to be influenced by the candidates' messages.

In this study, men were more vulnerable than women to the persuasive effects of political advertisements. We can only speculate about why this occurred. The greater stability of women's preferences may be a consequence of the "gender gap," the strong tendency of women to vote for Democratic candidates. In the final weeks before the general election, more women than men may already have decided on how to cast their votes. As a result, they would be less vulnerable to attitude change.

Whatever the source of male vulnerability to attitude change in the general election, it appears to be the cause of several interactions between subjects' sex and the Adwatch manipulation. Men benefited from Adwatch more than females in terms of reduced attitude change, perceived government indifference, increased critical thinking, and perceived personal efficacy. Since women showed less susceptibility to persuasion than men, there was less potential for Adwatch to reduce susceptibility among women.

The experimental situation we used, however, was an optimal situation for obtaining effects of Adwatch: viewers reading the Adwatch columns, immediately afterward seeing the ads, and then being asked to formulate their thinking about the ads and the candidates. We wondered what the actual effect would be during the 1992 campaign, when there was almost always a time lapse between exposure to Adwatch information (if there was exposure to Adwatch) and viewing the campaign advertisements. Surveys conducted in Los Angeles by the Just, Crigler et al. Democracy '92 Project indicated that Adwatch information from the *Los Angeles Times* was a frequently recalled piece of campaign information. In a survey of 601 Los Angeles citizens between October 26 and October 31, they found that 28 percent of the respondents said they had seen newspaper coverage of political ads in the previous week.[24]

A possible alternative explanation for our experimental results is that subjects were less influenced by the campaign ads in the Adwatch condition because the revelations about the ads' influence attempts alienated them from the electoral process. We do not believe this to have been the case, particularly given the results presented in Figure 7.4 concerning changes in political efficacy. Males increased significantly in their feelings of political efficacy in the Adwatch condition compared to the control condition, whereas females increased slightly, although not significantly. If our attitude change results represented merely increased alienation, we should not have found these increases in feelings of self-efficacy. Nevertheless, the increased feelings of governmental indifference among females suggest that while Adwatch may have stimulated viewers to think more about the ads, engaging in cognitive counterarguing while watching the ads, the information in Adwatch may also have stimulated feelings that there is so much misuse of facts that all politicians care about is getting elected.

Conclusion

Our experimental test of the effects of Adwatch columns on individuals' reactions to political campaign ads indicates that Adwatch reduces the influence of the ads. The Adwatch columns increased the amount of thinking about the ads, allowing subjects to access information and feelings about the candidates and the ads that did not come to mind when they simply watched the ads. Adwatch also increased subjects' feelings of political efficacy, particularly for males.

Adwatch appears to be one of the most important journalistic developments in covering political campaigns in recent years. It has considerable potential for the future of campaign coverage, but journalists and news departments must continue to expand their efforts as candidates find new ways (e.g., thirty-minute infomercials, talk show appearances) to communicate potentially misleading information to voters. This will necessarily involve news organizations committing greater resources to coverage of campaign ads and campaign information, but the benefit to the campaign process appears well worth it.

Despite the apparent benefits of Adwatch, however, our study indicates several potentially negative consequences of Adwatch. Adwatch did not, as anticipated, increase viewers' amount of issue thinking when viewing the ads. In addition, Adwatch increased women's perception of government indifference.

In an ideal democracy, the press has a responsibility to hold political leaders accountable while at the same time not undermining their capacity to lead. Although the press may be doing more to hold political leaders accountable, little is gained if the press at the same time increases feelings of governmental indifference.

Some modification of Adwatch may be required to focus voter attention on issues relevant to governance. In an analysis of the 1952 presidential election, Dahl offered this foresightful warning:

> It must be remembered that a great many voters do not really perceive a choice between candidate A and candidate B; for many people the only perceived alternatives are to vote for one of the candidates or not to vote at all.[25]

Since 1960, there has been a consistent decline in voter turnout.[26]

Ideally, voters select the candidate whose policies best match their own political attitudes.[27] Unfortunately, it is not clear that most voters' political thinking is sufficiently elaborated to allow them to make a meaningful choice between candidates. Krosnick and Milburn found in national surveys that expression of political opinions has declined consistently over the past thirty years.[28] Given our finding that Adwatch did not increase the subjects' issue orientation, this suggests that the press should embed Adwatch information in the context of a more thorough discussion of the issues raised in the specific political advertisements. Adwatch may not have been perfect, but it is nevertheless a significant advance in election coverage.

Appendix:
Political Advertisements

The subjects in both conditions viewed the following six ads:

Bush Ads

Ad title: "Win"
This ad was taken from an economic address that Bush delivered. It started with Bush saying, "The world is in transition. The defining challenge of the '90's is to win the economic competition. To win the peace, we must be a military superpower, an economic superpower, and an export superpower." In the ad, Bush stresses support for free trade, education, and legal reform.

Ad title: "Guess"
In this ad, an announcer says, "To pay for his increased spending in Arkansas, Bill Clinton raised state taxes. And not just on the rich. He increased the sales tax by 33 percent, imposed a mobile home tax, increased the beer tax. He assessed a tourism tax, created a cable TV tax, supported a tax on groceries. And now if elected president, Bill Clinton has promised to increase government spending by $220 billion. Guess where he'll get the money?"

Speeded up images of Bill Clinton give a humorous and frenetic pace to the ad.

Perot Ads

Ad title: "Kids"
An announcer begins this ad by saying, "Our children dream of the world that we promised them as parents, a world of unlimited opportunity. What would they say if they knew that, by the year 2000, we will have left them with a national debt of $8 trillion?"

Images of children fade into each other as Perot's economic message about the deficit is presented.

Ad title: "Red Flag"
Again using an announcer instead of Perot, the voice-over says, "While the Cold War is ending, another war is now upon us. In this new war, the enemy is not the red flag of communism, but the red ink of our national debt, the red tape of our government bureaucracy."

Throughout the ad, a red flag waves on the screen and the spoken words appear written on this red background.

Clinton Ads

Ad title: "Change"
The announcer says, "Something's happening. People are ready. Because they've had enough. Enough of seeing their incomes fall behind and their jobs on the line. Enough of a government that just doesn't work. They're ready for change. And changing people's lives, that's the work of his life."

This is a recitation of Bill Clinton's economic accomplishments as governor of Arkansas.

Ad title: "Curtains"
This ad juxtaposes video of Bush making statements such as, "Thirty million jobs in the next eight years" and "I'm not prepared to say we're in a recession," with an announcer saying, "1990—America's jobless rate hits a three-year high" and "March 1992—Jobless rate hits a six-year high."

Notes

1. B. Carter, "Projected Network Loser in Presidential Race: CBS," *New York Times,* November 2, 1992, Section D, p. 1.

2. P. Widder, "Money, Approach Setting Apart Perot's Ad Effort," *Chicago Tribune,* October 30, 1992, p. 17.

3. Richard L. Berke, "What Is Scarier Than Halloween? Tune in to Candidates' Ads and See," *New York Times,* October 31, 1992.

4. Times Mirror Center for the People and the Press, July 8, 1992, p. 2.

5. Times Mirror Center for the People and the Press, "Campaign '92: Voters Say 'THUMBS UP' to Campaign, Process and Coverage," November 15, 1992, p. 23.

6. Richard L. Berke, "Volleys of Data Replace Blatant Attacks of 1988," *New York Times,* October 29, 1992, Section A, p. 24.

7. See Times Mirror Center for the People and the Press, "Air Wars II," October 15, 1992; Times Mirror Center for the People and the Press, "Air Wars III," October 22, 1992. Times Mirror surveys released on October 8, 15, and 22 found the following percentages for exposure to Bush and Clinton ads:

	10/8	10/15	10/22
Seen Bush Ad	68%	66%	60%
Seen Clinton Ad	64%	59%	57%

8. See T. Patterson and R. McClure, *The Unseeing Eye* (New York: Putnam's, 1976); M. Kern, *Thirty-Second Politics: Political Advertising in the Eighties* (New York: Praeger, 1989); and K. H. Jamieson, *Dirty Politics: Deception, Distraction, and Democracy* (New York: Oxford University Press, 1992).

9. Regarding inoculation message theory, see W. J. McGuire, "The Effectiveness of Supportive and Refutational Defenses in Immunizing and Restoring Beliefs Against Persuasion," *Sociometry* 24 (1962): 184–197. Regarding threat and refutation, see D. Papageorgis and W. J. McGuire, "The Generality of Immunity to Persuasion Produced by Pre-Exposure to Weakened Counterarguments," *Journal of Abnormal and Social Psychology* 62 (1961): 475–481; G. R. Miller and M. Burgoon, *New Techniques of Persuasion* (New York: Harper and Row, 1973); M. Pfau and M. Burgoon, "Inoculation in Political Campaign Communication," *Human Communication Research* 15 (1988): 91–111; Pfau, H. C. Kenski, M. Nitz, and J. Sorenson, "Efficacy of Inoculation Strategies Promoting Resistance to Political Attack Messages: Application to Direct Mail," *Communication Monographs* 57 (1990): 25–43; Pfau, "The Potential of Inoculation in Promoting Resistance to the Effectiveness of Comparative Advertising Messages," *Communication Quarterly* 40 (1992): 26–44; A. A. Lumsdaine and I. L. Janis, "Resistance to 'Counterpropaganda' Produced by One-Sided and Two-Sided 'Propaganda' Presentations," *Public Opinion Quarterly* 17 (1953): 311–318.

10. R. E. Petty and J. T. Cacioppo, "The Elaboration Likelihood Model of Persuasion," in L. Berkowitz (ed.), *Advances in Experimental Social Psychology* (New York: Academic Press, 1986).

11. R. E. Petty and J. T. Cacioppo, *Communication and Persuasion: Central and Peripheral Routes to Attitude Change* (New York: Springer-Verlag, 1986).

12. On the expertise or the attractiveness of the source, see S. Chaiken, "Heuristic Versus Systematic Information Processing and the Use of Source Versus Message Cues in Persuasion," *Journal of Personality and Social Psychology* 39 (1980): 752–766; C. I. Hovland and W. Weiss, "The Influence of Source Credibility on Communication Effectiveness," *Public Opinion Quarterly* 15 (1951): 635–650; H. C. Kelman and A. H. Eagly, "Attitude Toward the Communicator, Perception of Communication Content, and Attitude Change," *Journal of Personality and Social Psychology* 1 (1965): 63–78; Kelman and C. I. Hovland, "Reinstatement of the Communicator in Delayed Measurement of Opinion Change," *Journal of Abnormal and Social Psychology* 48 (1953): 327–335; R. E. Petty, J. T. Cacioppo, and R. Goldman, "Personal Involvement as a Determinant of Argument-Based Persuasion," *Journal of Personality and Social Psychology* 41 (1981): 847–855; Petty, Cacioppo, and D. Schumann, "Central and Peripheral Routes to Advertising Effectiveness: The Moderating Role of Involvement," *Journal of Consumer Research* 10 (1983): 134–148.

13. On the reasons supporting an argument, see A. H. Eagly and R. Warren, "Intelligence, Comprehension, and Opinion Change," *Journal of Personality* 44 (1976): 226–242; R. E. Petty and J. T. Cacioppo, "The Effects of Involvement on Responses to Argument Quantity and Quality: Central and Peripheral Routes to Persuasion," *Journal of Personality and Social Psychology* 46 (1984): 69–81.

14. On placebic reasons, see E. J. Langer, A. Blank, and B. Chanowitz, "The Mindlessness of Ostensibly Thoughtful Action," *Journal of Personality and Social Psychology* 36 (1978): 635–642.

15. On music, see G. Gorn, "The Effects of Music in Advertising on Choice Behavior: A Classical Conditioning Approach," *Journal of Marketing Research* 46 (1982): 94–101.

16. On the visual prominence of the speaker, see E. Borgida and B. Howard-

Pitney, "Personal Involvement and the Robustness of Perceptual Salience Effects," *Journal of Personality and Social Psychology* 45 (1983): 560–570.

17. On food, see I. L. Janis, D. Kaye, and P. Kirschner, "Facilitating Effects of 'Eating While Reading' on Responsiveness to Persuasive Communications," *Journal of Personality and Social Psychology* 1 (1965): 181–186.

18. R. E. Petty and J. T. Cacioppo, "The Elaboration Likelihood Model of Persuasion."

19. Times Mirror Center for the People and the Press, "The Campaign and the Press at Halftime," June 4, 1992, p. 37.

20. Ibid., p. 47.

21. Times Mirror Center for the People and the Press, "The Press and Campaign '92: A Self Assessment," December 20, 1992.

22. Jamieson, *Dirty Politics.*

23. Although college students in general can be a nonrepresentative group of respondents, the population at the University of Massachusetts at Boston is much more diverse than at most universities. The average age of our sample was twenty-five, with a range between eighteen and forty-nine, and only 33 percent of the subjects' parents had gone to college. Thus, they make up a reasonably representative sample. Our confidence in the results we present here is strengthened by the fact that when past studies have asked the same questions of a sample of U. Mass./Boston undergraduates and of a probability sample of Massachusetts residents, the results have been virtually identical. See L. Jussim, M. A. Milburn, and W. Nelson, "Emotional Openness: Sex-Role Stereotypes and Self-Perceptions," *Representative Research in Social Psychology* 19 (1991): 3–20; M. A. Milburn, S. Conrad, F. Sala, and S. Carberry, "Childhood Punishment, Denial, and Political Ideology," paper presented at the annual meeting of the International Society of Political Psychology, Cambridge, Massachusetts, July 1993.

24. D. E. Alger, M. Kern, and D. West, "Political Advertising, Infotainment, the Information Environment, and the Voter in the 1992 Presidential Election," paper presented at the annual meeting of the International Communication Association, May 1993, Washington, D.C.

25. Robert A. Dahl, *A Preface to Democratic Theory* (Chicago: University of Chicago Press, 1956), p. 127.

26. Kinder and Sears, 1985; Milburn, 1991.

27. Jon Krosnick, "The Role of Attitude Importance in Social Evaluations: A Study of Policy Preferences, Presidential Candidate Evaluations, and Voting Behavior," *Journal of Personality and Social Psychology* 55 (1988): 196–210.

28. Krosnick and Milburn, 1990.

PART THREE

THE MEDIA AND PUBLIC POLICY

8

TV Violence, Children, and the Press

Sissela Bok

The last decade has seen growing concern about the role that television violence plays in the lives of U.S. children and adolescents. Much press coverage of this issue, however, has remained at a level of superficiality that helps to inhibit, rather than to facilitate, informed public debate. In this chapter I explore the role—in the press as elsewhere—of certain familiar rationales that serve thus to inhibit discussion and consider the special challenges for the press in facilitating and contributing to debate about the urgent public policy issues related to violence in the United States.

Spotlight on Television Violence

Television violence and the development of our youth are not just another set of public policy problems. They go to the heart of our society's values. The best solutions lie with industry officials, parents, and educators, and I don't relish the prospect of Government action. But if immediate voluntary steps are not taken and deadlines established, Government should respond, and respond immediately.

—Attorney General Janet Reno, testifying before
the Senate Commerce Committee, October 20, 1993[1]

No sooner had Attorney General Janet Reno spoken out about risks from television violence to U.S. children and adolescents and in turn to the larger society, than the scoldings by press and television industry representatives began. Few commentators bothered to report with care on the actual bills under consideration at the Senate Commerce Committee meeting where Reno testified or on the research data on which she drew. The counterarguments focused, rather, either on the relative insignificance of risks from TV violence or on the overriding danger of government censorship regardless of any such risks.

- The *New York Times* editorialized against "Janet Reno's Heavy Hand," warning that although it is foolish to "try to stop a bullet like Schwarzenegger or swing off a mountain like Stallone, . . . most foolish of all is Janet Reno's dangerous embrace of a very seductive form of censorship."[2]
- In *USA Today,* Michael Gartner, former president of NBC News, declared that television violence imitates real world violence, not the other way around, and that attempts to "mess around with anybody's views, opinions, thoughts, words" were far more dangerous than any effects of TV violence: "I know you don't like the fact that Beavis and Butthead play with matches, Ms. Reno. But you're playing with fire."[3]
- An editorial in the *Chicago Tribune* concluded that "Americans who think TV violence is dangerous have the simple option of turning it off, which is fine. What isn't fine is for the government to take over a responsibility that ought to rest with free individuals."[4]
- TV industry representatives insisted that the amount of violence on television was exaggerated by politicians and critics and was nowhere near as linked to street violence as family breakdown and the erosion of values.[5]
- The Comedy Central cable network prepared a thirty-second advertisement purporting to instruct "Dear Janet" about the difference between "real blood" and "stage blood" and claiming that those who "play with [the latter] on stage . . . celebrate life and give people a rage to live."[6]

Why such immediate, summary, and often condescending dismissal in so many quarters? Why bypass Reno's call for *all* concerned—parents, educators, industry officials, and, as a last resort, government—to come to grips with television violence as one of several interlocking factors linked to escalating youth violence? The press, after all, sees as part of its public responsibility to report in depth on similarly interlocking factors when it comes to, say, traffic injuries, drug addiction, or AIDS. Why, then, did so few newspapers bother, in covering Reno's testimony, to analyze diverging claims about the role of television violence in exacerbating youth violence?

It is not as if there were a dearth of data on which to base such reporting. By now, many hundreds of studies have concluded, as have surveys of these studies, that exposure to television violence does affect a number of children for the worse.[7] Two months before Reno's testimony, the American Psychological Association (APA) issued a major report on the research on violence involving children and young people.[8] (See Box 8.1.) Its conclusions regarding the risks to children and to society from television violence were unequivocal.

Little reportorial initiative would have been needed to refer, in

---

Box 8.1   Exposure to Violence in the Mass Media[9]

Nearly four decades of research on television viewing and other media have documented the almost universal exposure of U.S. children to high levels of media violence. Ninety-eight percent of U.S. homes have at least one television, which is watched for an average of twenty-eight hours per week by children between the ages of two and eleven and for twenty-three hours per week by teenagers. Children from low-income families are the heaviest watchers of television.

There is absolutely no doubt that higher levels of viewing violence on television are correlated with increased acceptance of aggressive attitudes and increased aggressive behavior.

Children's exposure to violence in the mass media, particularly at young ages, can have harmful lifelong consequences. Aggressive habits learned early in life are the foundation for later behavior. Aggressive children who have trouble in school and in relating to peers tend to watch more television; the violence they see there, in turn, reinforces their tendency toward aggression, compounding their academic and social failure. These effects are both short-term and long-lasting: a longitudinal study of boys found a significant relation between exposure to television violence at eight years of life and antisocial acts—including serious violent criminal offenses and spouse abuse—twenty-two years later.

---

covering Reno's testimony, to the research surveyed in the APA report—research on which she expressly drew in preparing her remarks. Nor would it have been difficult to report on remaining disagreements among experts. These differences rarely concern the possibility, now widely acknowledged, of harm to children from exposure to television violence, but about what degrees and types of harm are at issue: the degree to which different forms of entertainment violence may affect children for the worse; what proportion of children are harmed by exposure to any of them; the degree to which other factors, such as witnessing violence in the home, contribute to the likelihood of children being adversely affected by exposure to TV violence; the degree to which such effects are temporary or lasting in nature; and the degree to which they are related to aggressive conduct and greater acceptance of violence later in life.

To document these controversies, reporters could have taken a second look at the proceedings of a landmark conference on television violence held in Beverly Hills, California, in August 1993. For the first time scholars, politicians, actors, and industry representatives met face to face to exchange views about the effects of television violence, the available research, and alternative policies to adopt. The brief press reports at the time conveyed only the starkest outlines of conflicting positions, but journalists referring to the C-Span transcript of portions of the proceedings would have had little difficulty in finding more substantive analyses and policy proposals.[10] Referring to them would also have helped underline Reno's special concern with the role of TV violence in the lives of children: a concern that takes on added significance in the light of the sheer amount of such violence that many young children witness. (See Box 8.2.)

Box 8.2

Before finishing grade school, the average child will already have watched, on the average, 8,000 murders and 100,000 acts of violence on TV.[11]

Children tend to watch equal quantities of daytime and prime time television programs and make up 6 percent of the viewing audience even after 10:30 P.M.[12]

Even two-year-olds in the United States are estimated to spend, on average, sixty days a year in front of the TV set.[13]

Obstacles to Public Policy Debate

Not all press coverage of the debates about television violence and about entertainment violence more generally is as spotty as much of what followed Reno's testimony or the earlier conference. *Newsday,* for example, presented different viewpoints regarding the issues taken up by Reno during the week following her testimony; earlier, the *Boston Globe* provided front-page coverage to the August report on *Violence and Youth* by the American Psychological Association and has continued to cover related issues in depth.[14] Anyone with the time and resources to do a literature search could turn up thoughtful, informative articles on TV violence in one newspaper or another over the past few years. Most readers, however, have no access to such diverse sources; many live in communities with very limited news coverage in the first place—let alone access to thorough discussions of the problems related to TV violence. As a result, it is far harder than it need otherwise be for informed public policy debates about these problems to get under way.

In spite of such barriers to informed policy debate, public concern about the role of TV violence in our society is rising. A Times Mirror survey reported in March 1993 that a majority of those interviewed in the survey indicated that they thought there was too much violence on TV and that this bothered them. An even greater majority (80 percent in 1993 as compared to 64 percent in 1983) felt that TV was harmful to society, and just 15 percent felt that TV was harmless in this respect.[15]

The contrast between high levels of public concern and weak policy debates is neither new nor uniquely attributable to inadequate press coverage. Past commissions and panels of experts, even when appointed in the wake of great public concern about violence in society and on TV, have been short on policy proposals. They have tended, after careful research and documentation, to bring forth only the feeblest suggestions for dealing with the risks that they have so amply documented.

Thus, for example, the National Commission on the Causes and Prevention of Violence, appointed by President Lyndon B. Johnson in 1968, commissioned a report on the mass media and violence. After a thorough review of the evidence available at the time, the authors of the report concluded that it was probable that mass media portrayals of violence were one factor that "*must* be considered in attempts to explain the many forms of violence that mark American society today," and that television violence in particular had the greatest potential for short- and long-term effects on audiences.[16] The "television world of violence," the authors maintained, is neither an accurate reflection of the real world of violence as experienced by adult and teenage Americans nor what the majority of adult and teenage Americans want, and it is dominated by norms for violence that are inconsistent with those espoused by these citizens.[17] Yet the report's primary recommendation for how to deal with this problem was only that the mass media create a publicly sponsored and supported "Center for Media Studies" to conduct further research about the matter.

A quarter of a century later, in the spring of 1993, a panel of experts issued a report on violence for the National Academy of Sciences. The panel had commissioned yet another study of the evidence to date of the role of TV violence, this time with much more extensive experience and research on which to base their conclusions. The authors of that study had concluded that "exposure to television violence resulted in increased aggressive behavior, both contemporaneously and over time."[18] Yet the panel mentions no policy suggestions regarding exposure to TV violence in its report, nor does it even include the need for further research about such exposure in its list of recommendations.[19]

By the fall of 1993, however, the climate of debate may have shifted more decisively than in the past. It has been influenced by congressional hearings in 1992 and 1993 by Senator Paul Simon of Illinois, Congressman Edward Markey of Massachusetts, and others, and in turn by testimony such as that by Attorney General Reno. Ever more striking evidence of escalating violence on the part of and victimizing young people has also led to a new determination to inquire into all the factors that might possibly play a role in this slaughter of the young. (See Box 8.3.)

Box 8.3

Arrests for violent crimes per 100,000 youths ages 10–17 went from 215.9 in 1970 to 430.6 in 1990.[20]

The rates of gun-related deaths among 15 to 19-year-olds, which had been rising gradually through the late 1960s, kept on doing so during the 1970s and early 1980s; then doubled from 1985 to 1990.

For all black teenage males, firearm homicide rates nearly tripled during that period, reaching 105.3 deaths per 100.000. Rates among white teenage boys rose rapidly over the same period, largely in the Hispanic community, but much more among blacks.

Homicide is the second leading cause of death of all persons 15–24 (auto crashes are the first) and the leading cause among African American youth.[21]

In 1992, the U.S. Surgeon General cited violence as the leading cause of injury to women ages 15 to 44.[22]

It is becoming harder to ignore television violence as one potential factor, linked not only to the ravages of youth violence but to the still larger toll taken by violence in U.S. society more generally—a toll that is increasingly seen as constituting a public health crisis of epidemic proportions.[23]

Eight Rationales

The heightened awareness of the risks associated with TV violence may yet recede, as so often in the past, after a sputtering but inconclusive debate. If there is to be a more serious and informed public policy debate about these risks, the press will have a crucial role to play. It will need to do a better job of providing the necessary background and analysis, but to do so, it will have to guard against overquick acceptance of certain commonplace but stunted lines of reasoning that help short-circuit debate. Often called *rationales,* these lines of reasoning serve a double function: they offer simplistic *reasons* for not entering into serious debate about a subject, and thus provide *rationalizations* for ignoring or shielding ongoing practices from outside scrutiny and interference.[24] When it comes to violence on and off the TV screen, the following rationales are especially common:

1. America always has been and always will be a violent nation: violence is as American as cherry pie.
2. Why focus the policy debate on TV violence when there are other, more important, factors that contribute to violence?

3. How can you definitively pinpoint, and thus prove, the link between viewing TV violence and acts of real-life violence?
4. Television programs reflect existing violence in the "real world." It would be unrealistic and a disservice to viewers as well as to society to attempt to wipe violence off the screen.
5. People can't even agree on how to define "violence." How, then, can they go on to discuss what to do about it?
6. It is too late to take action against violence on television, considering the plethora of video channels by which entertainment violence will soon be available in homes.
7. It should be up to parents, not the television industry, to monitor the programs that their children watch.
8. Any public policy to decrease TV violence constitutes censorship and represents an intolerable interference with free speech.

All eight of the rationales bring out points worth making. They represent natural forms of hesitation and caution with respect to a cluster of problems many have come to think intractable. But all eight are taken too far when used to dismiss or foreshorten debate about television violence. All fall especially short when used to set aside questions of how to deal with the risks that such violence poses to children.

1. *America always has been and always will be a violent nation: violence is as American as cherry pie.*

H. Rap Brown's metaphor has entered the vernacular. Many take it to be an accurate comment, looking at the United States' present levels of violence against the background of a history of slavery, frontier violence, labor strife, racial conflict, crime, and warfare domestic and international. Although this claim offers a *reason* for taking the United States' history of violence into account in debates concerning all forms of contemporary violence, it cannot, however, suffice for setting aside the debates themselves. When it is used to support such a conclusion, it becomes a falsely fatalistic *rationalization.* Just as "slavery is as American as cherry pie" might have seemed to some an accurate characterization of U.S. society in 1850, it would have been similarly inadequate as a reason for believing that slavery could not be overcome.

The rationale invoking perennial U.S. patterns of violence, when used thus, helps deflect inquiry into explanations for present levels of violence, into contributing factors and remedies. Historical references alone cannot account for the unprecedented sharp rise in recent decades in child and adolescent violence. Nor can they account, more generally, for what a French researcher calls "the very special case of the United States" when it comes to homicide: the fact that its homicide rate is now between four and ten times higher than those of other industrialized nations, with correspondingly disproportional levels of rape, child abuse, and every other form of violence.[25] In 1962, the United States' homicide rate had come down to 4.5 per 100,000 from 6.9 per 100,000 in 1946, following the downward patterns of other industrializing nations; it then began a prolonged upward move to reach 9.4 per 100,000 in 1972.[26] By 1991 there were over 10 homicide victims per 100,000 in the United States, compared to 2 in England, 1.8 in Germany, and 1.2 in Japan; but by 1996, the U.S. rate had declined to 7.5.

The power of this rationale and of the fatalism that it supports may help to explain why the high levels of violence that still mark daily life in the United States have, so far, generated nothing like the determination to bring about change engendered by the Vietnam War. Even though more Americans died of gunshot wounds alone during 1986 and 1987 (or any other two years in the past decade) than in the eight and a half years of that war, this bloodshed has not provoked anything like the amount of political engagement and public policy debate with respect to that war.

The rationale, finally, is singularly inappropriate when it comes to television violence, which is, precisely, not as perennially American as cherry pie. It is only four and a half decades since a few U.S. households acquired their first television sets. By now, 98 percent of U.S. households have television, and many have several sets in different rooms. Television is a presence in children's lives from infancy on, consuming more hours each year than school. The amount and forms of violence to be found on television programs have also mounted to levels that few could have predicted in the 1950s.

A fatalistic rationale about our nation's imperviousness to change with respect to violence may be a natural first reaction to the sense of the intractable nature of the problem.[27] It may result, too, from a sense that we simply do not know enough at present to be able to devise adequate policies in response. As in the case of slavery, however, such a rationale serves also as a rationalization for doing nothing—as an excuse for those who won't be bothered and a shield for those in the weapons, entertainment, and other industries with vested interests in the status quo.

2.   *Why focus the policy debate on TV violence when there are other, more important, factors that contribute to violence?*

This is a natural first reaction to expressions of concern about the role of TV violence in U.S. society, especially for anyone convinced that TV violence is dwarfed by some one other causal factor such as poverty, family breakdown, the availability of firearms, or substance abuse. Why not begin with what is truly important, rather than waste time and energy on the contents of TV programming? Perhaps TV violence is even a scapegoat, "much easier to attack," in the words of the director Michael Mann, "than the imponderables of why there's so much violence in this culture."[28]

Such questions are valuable insofar as they caution against undue stress on the one factor of TV violence alone, or, indeed, on any one other factor by itself.[29] There is clearly reason to address the role of each and every factor that may contribute to violence. To concentrate only on TV violence, in an effort to understand violence in the United States more generally, would be not only mistaken but dangerous, in that it would allow neglect of other, often more direct causes of violence.

But this second rationale is itself mistaken, and indeed dangerous, when it is used to block any concern with TV violence (or any other risk factor such as family breakdown or firearm availability) until all other factors linked to societal violence have been adequately dealt with. We do not usually address complex, multidimensional human problems in this manner. Take heart disease: few critics maintain that, just because a number of risk factors such as smoking or heredity or cholesterol enter into the prevalence of this disease, there is reason not to focus on any one of them. On the contrary, research and inquiry has to continue regarding each one, including those of lesser magnitude.

In the past few years, scholars, advocates, physicians, and government officials working to address problems of violence have increasingly adopted a public health perspective there, too, as with heart disease, cancer, and other major causes of death and disability. It is a perspective that allows the most wide-ranging and integrated ways to explore the incidence, the risk factors, and possible approaches to prevention with respect to different forms of violence.[30] Such a perspective serves as a refreshing antidote to any urge either to address complex problems in terms of only one risk factor or to dismiss concern with any one factor on the grounds that it is not the only one or even the most significant one. In the absence of such a differentiated perspective, it will remain tempting to counter concerns about entertainment violence by conjuring up improbable one-dimensional scenarios—as in asking, with Sam Donaldson, whether people "watch movies, then grab their guns to go out to do mayhem."[31]

Even if there were no TV violence, this would obviously not wipe out the problem of violence in the United States. The same can be said for poverty, drug addiction, the proliferation of firearms, and each of the other risk factors. As Deborah Prothrow-Stith puts it, "It's not an either or. It's not guns or media or parents or poverty."[32] All contribute to the problem of violence in the United States. Yet television serves in a unique way to acculturate Americans to violence. Children learn by imitation, and television provides ample models of persons who seem to personify the power, the brutality, and, too often, the imputed glamor of violence. To mention but one example of societal changes that have been attributed in part to television modeling, the rate of serious crime by children under fifteen increased by 11,000 percent between 1950, when TV was in its infancy, and 1979; since then it has shot up still further.[33]

So long as a focus on entertainment violence is not seen as the only one needed, moreover, the claim that it represents "an easy way out" and is therefore undesirable is beside the point. Why *not* work at the easier as well as at the harder aspects of the problem? It will doubtless be easier to reduce the harmful effects of TV violence on young children than to affect the consequences, say, of family breakdown or domestic violence. Far fewer persons are required to bring about changes in television programming than to reduce poverty, addiction, and other social ills that burden many families in the United States. It is urgent to work to alleviate all of these ills; but there is no reason to delay bringing about change in television programming until this work has been carried out.

The second rationale serves a useful purpose, then, insofar as it warns against a unique focus on any one factor such as that of television violence. But it functions as a rationalization as soon as it is used, instead, to ignore the risks from TV violence or to draw attention away from them; and, as with the first rationale, it can, thus used, serve to prolong silence and inaction with respect to the problem of TV violence as well as to shield those who have the most to gain from such programming.

3.   *How can you definitively pinpoint, and thus prove, the link between viewing TV violence and acts of real-life violence?*

This question challenges the assumption that exposure to television violence constitutes a risk factor in the first place. It is a challenge familiar from the debates concerning the risks associated with tobacco smoking. Representatives of the tobacco industry argue that because, in their opinion, there has been no conclusive proof of a causal link between tobacco and lung cancer, there is no reason to take action against smoking. Nor is there any moral reason for curtailing sales efforts at home and abroad. (See Box 8.4.)

Media representatives similarly claim that until conclusive proof can be produced that TV violence causes harm to viewers and indirect harm to third parties, there is no reason to consider public policy measures to reduce the harm linked with exposure of children or other viewers to violent programs.

Once more, such arguments serve a double purpose. They function as reasons, first of all, to examine with scrupulous care the evidence held to support claims that TV violence harms children, numbing many of them to violence and rendering some among them more likely to commit violent acts. It is clearly the case that more needs to be done to scrutinize different research designs, sampling methods, and possible biases of studies support-

---

Box 8.4

Sworn testimony with Andrew Tisch, chairman and chief exeutive of Lorillard Tobacco Company, taken by Stanley Rosenblatt, an attorney representing a group of flight attendants in a class-action lawsuit against leading cigarette makers:[34]

Q. As far as you're concerned, Mr. Tisch, as the chairman and chief executive officer of Lorillard, this warning on the package which says that smoking causes lung cancer, heart disease and emphysma is inaccurate? You don't believe that is true?

A. That's correct.

Q. Because if you believed it were true in good conscience you wouldn't sell this to Americans, would you, or foreigners for that matter?

A. That's correct.

---

ing such claims and to ask about the steps of reasoning leading from particular research findings to conclusions.

But the arguments also serve as rationalizations as soon as they are used to dismiss existing research and to disparage public concern as alarmist until conclusive proof has been achieved. To ask for some demonstrable pinpointing of just when and how TV violence affects individual children for the worse before debating public policy sets a dangerously high threshold for what is to count as adequate justification in such debates. It would require knowledge about the physical and psychological development of individuals so detailed as to be unattainable. We may never be able to trace, retrospectively, the specific moments at which and reasons for which TV violence contributed to a particular child's desensitization with respect to violence or provided believable models for aggressive conduct. The same is true when it comes to the links between tobacco smoking and cancer, drunk driving and automobile accidents, and many other risk factors presenting public health hazards. Yet our inability to carry out such pinpointing has not stood in the way of discussing and promoting efforts to curtail cigarette smoking and drunk driving; it is not clear, therefore, why it should block such efforts when it comes to TV violence.[35]

An approach to causation more commonly used in considering how to counter public health hazards is that of probabilistic causation. It is not necessary that a factor, such as the cigarette smoking that is thought to play a causal role with respect to lung cancer, produce that effect in all or even most cases, nor that it be the only or the greatest cause of that effect, but only that it "increases the incidence of the effect for a population and increases the likelihood of the effect in an individual case."[36] Using the same approach for TV violence, the link between such violence and the incidence of violent acts in real life need not be individually pinpointed—something that would be as hard to do for TV violence as for cigarette smoking, considering the years that it takes for the effects to come to evidence.

An important question that a public policy debate has to take up concerns, therefore, the levels of certainty regarding causative factors and the amounts and kinds of victimization that would count as risks large enough for debating forceful and concerted responses. How certain must we be of risks to large numbers of people before discussing what action to take?

Although it will always be difficult to produce specific numbers of persons who have been victimized by any one of the risk factors at stake in the United States' exceptional levels of violence, different approximate estimates have been made. Brandon S. Centerwall, a Washington, D.C., psychiatrist, has concluded from large-scale epidemiological studies of homicide in the United States and abroad that "if, hypothetically, television technology had never been developed, . . . [v]iolent crime would be half of what it now is."[37] If so, there would be 10,000 fewer homicides today, he suggests, 70,000 fewer rapes, and 700,000 fewer injurious assaults. Others have estimated that television programs may contribute incrementally to 10 percent of violent crime.[38] Clearly, however, even a lower estimate—say 5 percent—ought to be taken into account in considering the level of certainty desired before action is taken against damage traced to the effects of television violence.

4. *Television programs reflect existing violence in the "real world." It would be unrealistic and a disservice to viewers as well as to society to attempt to wipe violence off the screen.*

According to this rationale, television violence does not add to real world violence so much as mirror it. Leaving it out of programs would offer a saccharine and utterly false view of reality that could not, in the long run, serve either individual or social needs. Newscasts, in particular, report on military combat, bombardment, arson, rape, murder, and other forms of violence throughout daytime and evening hours. Wouldn't reporters deny their primary purpose if they consented to sugarcoat the news or blot out the uglier facets of history in the making? What would it say about us as viewers if we maintained that we would be better off not knowing about the ethnic cleansing in the former Yugoslavia or the starvation in Somalia? To water down news programs benefiting all citizens because of possible effects on child viewers would surely be a betrayal of journalistic integrity. It would deprive society of information indispensable to understanding world events and so make possible errors and abuses that could turn out to be far costlier than any damage to television viewers.

The most horrifying image sequences, moreover, sometimes serve to mobilize public opinion as little else can, as when television coverage brought the famine and slaughter in Somalia to the world's attention. What is wrong with news coverage of crises around the world is not that it exposes inhumanity and victimization and the anguish of mourners, but rather that it does not always do so completely enough or in a sufficiently fairminded way: we should learn about the horrors perpetrated in Somalia, but we should also learn about equally extensive suffering in the Sudan and elsewhere. Amartya Sen has pointed out that great famines, such as that of 1958–1961 in China in which close to 30 million people are estimated to have perished, have only taken place in societies in which there is no free press to disseminate the news of such developments.[39]

The rationale, thus interpreted, offers persuasive reasons against any blanket rejection of projections of violence on the television screen. But if it, in turn, is taken as a blanket rejection of all criticism of levels and forms of televised violence, it serves, instead, as a rationalization for temporizing about debating even the most exploitative programs. With respect to newscasting, first of all, the rationale papers over the concern increasingly felt in media circles concerning the blurring of the line between news and entertainment in so called "infotainment programming." And it fails to take into consideration the drift toward increasingly sensationalized news programming that in no sense mirrors the life of a community or society. "If it bleeds, it leads" is a familiar motto well worth questioning. Disasters, fires, rapes, and murders are now being covered in proportions that bear no relation to reality. As one report on television news coverage in New York City put it,

> Another night, another nightmare.
> The teenage killer gives way to the subway slasher. The mob slaying segues into a spot on kids with guns. The face of a weeping mother dissolves into a close-up of a blood-stained shirt. House fires become "raging infernos." Traffic snarls. Kids fall out of windows. Babies die in random shootings. Manhunts are commonplace. . . .
> Welcome to New York. Day after day, from 4 P.M. to midnight, at almost any time, the nation's largest city is probed, poked, tossed, and turned in quick-cut images projected to a potential viewership of some 18 million people, a population about the size of Iraq's. . . .
> In more than eighty interviews over several weeks, journalists, scholars, and other New Yorkers, ranging from janitors to teachers to corporate executives, described New York—as portrayed by television—as a grim wasteland that bears almost no relation to their lives. The city thus exposed is a sustained scream—a bloodied mess.[40]

Whatever the "real world" is that the fourth rationale claims that television reflects, such news coverage clearly conveys only distorted and disjointed aspects of it. The metaphor of mirroring is even less apt when it comes to entertainment violence. The amount of televised homicide, rape, arson, and torture bears no relation to the frequency with which these actually occur. Although industry representatives may speak of television mirroring the real world, many producers and writers would disown such a comparison as inconsistent with the creative freedom they require. For some, the opposite claim is closer to the truth: that their productions differ so radically and so self-evidently from reality that viewers could not reasonably respond to the violence they contain as if it were in any way connected to their lives. As Joel Silver, the producer of the blockbuster *Die Hard, Lethal Weapon,* and *Predator* films, said, in response to criticisms when his film *Lethal Weapon 3* opened two weeks after the April 1992 Los Angeles riots:

> I mean it's a western, it's entertaining, it's good guys versus bad guys. In that scene in "The Searchers" when John Wayne went after all those Indians, was that genocide? Was that racist? When James Bond dropped the guy in a pond of piranhas, and he says, "Bon appetit," we loved that. That's a great moment. Movies are not *real*.[41]

Silver's movies and others like them are common fare on television. The notion that the violence they portray is not real to viewers is as naive as the metaphor of violent television programs passively reflecting reality. When used to ward off debate, both function as mutually reinforcing, however inconsistent, rationalizations. They downplay, in so doing, the intense, unmediated, and far from passive reality that television violence has assumed for many viewers.

Children, in particular, cannot distinguish between the reality of the violence they see on and off the screen. They are unable, through at least the age of three or four, to distinguish fact and fantasy; even older children rarely manage to keep "real life" violence and vicarious violence in watertight compartments.[42] Because children tend to watch equal quantities of daytime and prime time programs and make up 6 percent of the viewing audience even after 10:30 P.M., they are hardly insulated from programs aimed at older viewers;[43] still less from the sensationalized, concentrated violence of "promos" for violent nighttime programs or movies, since such commercials are often run repeatedly during sports programs and other programs that appeal to young audiences, at times including children's shows.[44]

As a result, children are exposed, before they are in any position to distinguish fact from fantasy, to amounts and levels of violence more brutalizing than many adults—parents, scriptwriters, and TV producers among them—realize. The children most affected are those who also have had personal experience of violence in their family or neighborhood. For them, the violence that they witness around them reinforces the realism that they attribute to the violence they see enacted on the screen, and their view of the world around them is in turn strongly influenced by what they see on television.[45] As the authors of an article on children who witness violence put it: "The young child's attempts to master the age-appropriate fears of monsters under the bed are severely undermined when the child needs to sleep under the bed to dodge real bullets or attempt to screen out the violent fights of his or her care-givers."[46]

The extremes of violence in some television programs are known to affect not only children but to be cited by adolescents and adults carrying out so-called copycat rapes, serial killings, and other forms of assault.[47] James Gilligan, a psychiatrist who has studied mass murderers, has concluded that certain violent TV programs in the United States are no less sadistic than the films used by the SS to desensitize and indoctrinate Nazi torture squads and death camp guards.[48]

Viewers of all ages, moreover, far from experiencing television as somehow either utterly cut off from reality or passively mirroring it, know that it addresses them actively—as consumers, as citizens, as moral agents—for better or worse. They know, too, that this influence goes in both directions, and that news coverage mediates, in this process, between the "real world" and entertainment programs. Those who produce or otherwise shape violent television programs can be guided by and sometimes learn from events covered in news programs, just as criminals can model themselves on and learn new techniques from television programs. Scholars and others urging more careful, analytical debate about TV violence claim that it is worth asking how and when such reciprocal learning takes place and what, if anything, makes it escalate.

5. *People can't even agree on how to define "violence." How, then, can they go on to discuss what to do about it?*

One of the quickest ways to short-circuit serious reflection about TV violence or any other form of violence is to employ some version of the "definitional fallacy": to claim that it is impossible to define violence specifically enough for policy debates. Just as the claim that "one person's terrorist is another person's freedom fighter," if left unexamined, does much to delay serious discussion of political violence, so "one viewer's violence is another's dramatic action" has a superficially plausible ring that invites discussants to give up in confusion rather than attempt a fruitless search for a common definition.

If we refused to debate topics because of doubts or disagreements about definitions, we would have little to talk about. The philosopher John Searle has pointed out that "one of the most important insights of recent work in the philosophy of language [has been that] most non-technical concepts in ordinary language lack absolutely strict rules" according to which one can definitely state when they do and do not apply.[49] This is as true of concepts such as promising or lying as of killing and other forms of violence. All present problems of line-drawing. Yet with respect to none would it make sense to postpone analysis and debate until complete agreement had been reached on definitions and line-drawing questions.

To be sure, the case is different when it comes to specific proposals to establish a system of rating violent programs or to limit the types and degrees and amounts of violence in particular programs or at specified times of day. At such times, definitions of what is to count as violence, gratuitous violence, and the like must be established, along with procedures for resolving differences of view. Much can be learned, in this regard, by comparing the definitions and the procedures used in the rating systems already in place with respect to motion pictures in the United States and abroad, as well as by studying the rules limiting violent television programming in different nations.

Insofar as the fifth rationale reminds us of the difficulties in drawing distinctions between types, degrees, and amounts of violence, it offers a reason to proceed with caution when it comes to legislation. But it is patently in error and serves instead as a rationalization as soon as it is used to undercut discussion of any and all efforts to deal with the effects on children of exposure to television violence. Consider the *Oxford English Dictionary*'s core definition of violence as "the exercise of physical force so as to inflict injury or damage to persons or property."[50] It is hard to think of anyone whose preferred definition of violence would not cover at least such injury. Agreement on such a core definition offers a basis for discussing the effects on children of watching the rapes, shootings, and disgorgements that constitute daily TV fare.[51]

With such a basis, it is then possible to consider further whether the relevant definition of violence should include further distinctions: those, for instance, between intentional harm and unintended or negligent actions resulting in such harm; between actions and omissions leading to harm; between harm done only to persons and to nonhuman living beings or property; between harm done to others and to oneself, as in self-mutilation or suicide; between harm that is unwanted by the recipient and desired harm self-inflicted by penitents or masochists; and between unlawful or unauthorized harm and harm inflicted in accordance with laws of the particular society in which it takes place, such as hangings or electrocutions.[52]

It turns out, however, that most such distinctions are largely beside the point when it comes to the effect on small children of exposure to violence. A three- or four-year-old is unlikely, in viewing a series of killings, to sort out the degree to which they are intended or to react differently depending on whether the killings are inflicted on animals or human beings or whether they are carried out by human beings or by animals, monsters, robots, or other creatures.

Cartoons generate especially frequent debates in this regard. Should it *count* as violence when, for instance, Donald Duck is dropped off a mountaintop or flattened by a rock, only to recover right away and be ready for new punishments? Such acts are counted as violent ones in a number of studies of children's programs, which then conclude that these are proportionately more saturated with violence than adult ones: that they contain more acts of overt, physical uses of power that hurt or kill and a higher percentage of characters engaging in such acts, as well as of victims, than prime time TV programs.[53]

These comparisons strike many as odd. Cartoon violence is, after all, meant to be humorous; and long before television, comic books and marionettes and theater groups offered similar fare to spectators. Such violence is therefore usually thought harmless by the adults who produce and present the programs and by many parents. But George Gerbner of the University of Pennsylvania's Annenberg School of Communication, who has conducted a number of comparative studies of TV violence, suggests that cartoon violence, presented hour after hour, does have cumulative demoralizing and desensitizing effects on the young children most frequently exposed to it and that humor becomes "a sugar coating that makes the pill of violence go down much more easily [so that] it gets integrated into one's framework of knowledge."[54]

Controversies of this nature are best resolved by looking with care at the evidence adduced for the harmful or innocuous effects of viewing such depictions of violence as compared to others. Too often, however, those who think that most cartoons contain nothing that should *count* as violence take such a disagreement over how to define its boundaries as proof that no further debate is possible. Here again, the fifth rationale usefully points to reasons for caution about problematic or disputed definitions, but when it is used to postpone debate until there is agreement on every definitional controversy, it functions also as a rationalization: both for those who simply wish to avoid considering the problem and for those who want to carry on with practices, such as the production or dissemination of especially violent TV programs, that might otherwise be targeted by a public debate.

6.   *It is too late to take action against violence on television, considering the plethora of video channels by which entertainment violence will soon be available in homes.*

This rationale, like the others, has a point. The task of curbing TV violence is daunting. Strong vested interests—commercial, cultural, and intellectual—guard against the slightest change in this regard. Violent programs, many of which are thought too raw for network television, are already transmitted through a growing number of TV and cable channels. If it has been so difficult to take action in the past, why should anyone imagine that such action will succeed in the future, when there will soon be so many more ways for violent programs to enter U.S. homes? The time for trying to stem the flow of violence into the lives of children may have already passed.

Yet the rationale offers but a flimsy basis for closing off the discussion of how and where to begin tackling this problem. It would be unconscionable to abandon the search for ways to cope with this problem, given its seriousness, merely on the grounds that there may come to be ever more numerous sources and channels of violent television. After all, air and water pollution, too, continue to spring from increasingly numerous sources and to spread in ways sometimes difficult to regulate, yet few propose giving up on measures to control them on such grounds. It is now more urgent than ever to consider how to act to stem the flow of televised violence and to set standards, establish precedents, and gain experience to use in protecting children before it becomes still more difficult to do so.

Data from other countries may be helpful in showing how they cope with a large part of the violent output possible by means of modern media and how they consider children's interests through a number of coordinated measures. Admittedly, no society will be able to anticipate every new avenue whereby children will be placed at risk. But many nations, including England, France, Australia, Germany, Sweden, and Canada, have controls in place that cut back substantially on the flood of violence that would otherwise be reaching young children.[55]

In Canada, the private television broadcasters have recently instituted a new, tougher TV violence code.[56] Undertaken on a voluntary basis in cooperation with the Canadian Radio-Television and Telecommunications Commission, it drew on "more than a year of intense discussions generated by growing public concern and the Commission's May 1992 release of two major reports on TV violence."[57] These discussions have included executives from the cable industry, pay-TV, and pay-per-view organizations, as well as representatives of Canada's Advertising Foundation, Teachers' Federation, Home and School and Parent-Teacher Federation, and other organizations. The commission has sponsored public colloquia and taken part in meetings in the United States, Mexico, France, and other nations to explore common problems.

The Canadian approach presents a model for other societies to study as they seek to respond to public concern and to facilitating widespread debate about public policy measures to deal with media violence.[58] It is a model, too, for proceeding with the work of building consensus and exploring alternative policies without being sidetracked by the rationales discussed in this chapter. With respect to the sixth rationale in particular, the Canadian approach shows the advantages of partial improvements over doing nothing: not only in cutting back substantially on the amount of violence reaching children but also in making possible broader changes once the societal burden of media violence is brought home to all who play a role in its production.

The United States' media may be the freest in the world of any government constraint on or regulation of their content. The combination of this lack of restraint with commercial financing of most television programming may have led to a particularly violent brand of TV.[59] The fact that the television networks are not the only avenues whereby violent television programs reach children is hardly sufficient to abandon the search for responses to the risk that such programs pose to children and to society.

7. *It should be up to parents, not the television industry, to monitor the programs that their children watch.*

A common argument against any form of public pressure or government control to cut back on television violence is that this addresses the problem at the wrong point: at the source rather than at the receiving end. Television commentator Jeff Greenfield put the argument as follows, at an August 1993 conference on TV violence: "Are we in fact saying that since parents—many—have abdicated their responsibility, we're going to ask the television programmers to do—replace the irreplaceable?"[60] Why should the television industry have to protect children against programs that might be corrupting or brutalizing, given that many adult viewers expressly want to see such programs and fear no harmful results for themselves? Why should this task not devolve directly on those who are responsible for their children's well-being—parents or other adults in a household? As Ted Herbert, president of the entertainment division of ABC, put it, adults can handle TV programs like NBC's *Between Love and Hate* that ends with a youth firing six bullets into his former lover, but children cannot: "This will sound like a paradox, but I don't believe we have to program the network and absolve parents of responsibility, as if it were our problem and not the parents' problem. Parents have to be responsible for what their kids watch."[61]

Here, too, the rationale has a point. It focuses attention on the genuine failure on the part of many parents to protect their children from the desensitizing and brutalizing effects of violence on TV. It is indeed their responsibility to do their best to protect their children thus, once they recognize the nature of these risks. Most parents would surely shield their children, to the extent they were able to, from witnessing actual murder, torture, rape, and other mayhem; but even when they are at home and able to control what their children watch from babyhood on up, it does not occur to large numbers of American parents to do the same with respect to the graphic violence their children observe on television.

The failure of many parents to exercise responsibility has been reinforced by lack of adequate information about the risks to children from violent TV. The same was once true with respect to the risks to children from lead paint, asbestos, or firecrackers. Not until recently has violent TV come to be mentioned as a factor in the growing public health hazard of societal, and in particular youth, violence. Rather, television has seemed a made-to-order baby-sitter for parents often tired from longer work hours than in the past and with less time to spare for children. Baby-sitters, in turn, rely heavily on TV to help entertain the children in their charge. Year by year, research has shown that the time parents spend with their children has been declining, from thirty hours a week twenty-five years ago to seventeen hours a week now.[62] The time that families currently do spend together, moreover, is often spent, precisely, in watching television.

Once the risks to children are clearly established and publicized, however, as is the case with lead paint, asbestos, and firecrackers and, as most would argue, is now the case with violent television and young children, it no longer makes sense for producers to claim that it is not up to them but only to parents to shield their children from the risks in question. True, parents have a strong responsibility, but toy manufacturers do not get far if they make such an argument about dangerous toys. And the drug industry is required to childproof packages of medicines children could otherwise accidentally ingest. In all such cases, claims that the whole burden of protecting children be put on parents would be quickly rejected.

In addition, although it is clear that it is part of the responsibility of parents to do what they can to protect their children from harm and that many parents do fail to do so, the fact is that many parents are not at home and therefore cannot do so during much of the time when their children watch television. Already in 1974, 50 percent of American children had no adult at home when school let out at 3 o'clock. By now, it is considerably higher.[63] And American children, unlike those in most other industrialized societies, are at school only 180 days a year. Too many American children, moreover, live in neighborhoods where it has become too dangerous for them to play out of doors. As one ten year-old put it:

> I used to hang out with my friends after school. Most of the time, we just acted stupid on the corner but that got dangerous and our moms said to quit it and come home. In this city, wear your hat the wrong way and you are dead. Now, I go home and watch TV and sleep. I get scared all by myself, even though Mom says there's nothing to be afraid of in the day.
>
> I would make a place for kids called My Father's Home. It would be a love place where there's no killing. They'd have stuff for me to do. Lift weights, eat snacks, play games. . . .
>
> I'd have beds at My Father's Home, like in a dormitory. Kids could sleep there in the summer when people go crazy on the streets. Last year, Mama and me slept on the floor, praying not to get shot.[64]

The reality of which this boy speaks exposes the specious nature of the seventh rationale. Fear, poverty, killings on the streets, and severe cutbacks in school, church, and community after-school programs make TV watching one of the few remaining "safe" activities for too many children. To be sure, it is right to urge parents, as do pediatricians, teachers, psychologists, and many others, to do much more to oversee the television programs that their children watch and to help children work through their responses to the violence they witness. To that extent, the rationale offers a legitimate reason for concern. But many parents are not in a position to do so, even with the best will in the world. As a result, to go further and to use the rationale to argue that no supplementary efforts are therefore needed on the part of the television industry or the public is to offer an unusually mindless rationalization.

A new technique could allow parents to block violent television programs even when they are not themselves at home. An inexpensive computer chip installed in the television set could be coded to respond to signals such as a V for programs rated violent. U.S. Representatives Edward J. Markey and Jack Fields have introduced legislation requiring that all new television sets sold in the United States contain what they call the "V-chip technology." Representatives of the television industry, however, are, so far, opposed to including a V for violence signal in the broadcast signals of shows rated violent. Representative Markey points out the irony in their stance: "For years parents have been told if they don't like what's on television they should turn it off. Now technology has made it possible to do just that—in an easy, effective targeted way and, most important, even when they are not there to pull the plug. Nevertheless, broadcasters remain unwilling to make it easier for parents to do their job."[65]

It is hard to know which element of the proposed legislation the industry fears most: the institution of ratings, long familiar for films, or the power that consumers would gain to shut certain types of programs out of their homes. The industry's opposition is inconsistent with the seventh rationale, placing the burden of responsibility on parents for what their children are allowed to see; as a result, broadcasters can hardly defend their stance by invoking that rationale. Instead they turn to yet another one. It condemns proposals such as that for the V-chip as constituting censorship and, as one source put it, representing interference with "the principles of a free society."[66]

8. *Any public policy to decrease TV violence constitutes censorship and represents an intolerable interference with free speech.*

This is not only the most frequently mentioned rationale on the part of industry representatives but the one with greatest appeal to journalists, however convinced some of them may be about the seriousness of the risks from present levels of TV violence. As a *Washington Post* editorial put it, in commenting on Attorney General Janet Reno's testimony before the Senate Commerce Committee (discussed at the beginning of this chapter): Reno "made a mistake the other day in encouraging Congress to regulate TV violence if the networks themselves don't do it pronto. The violence is terrible; the regulation would be worse."[67]

Journalists have every reason to be vigilant about free speech: it is always imperiled, and it does call for sacrifice. But when legitimate concern to defend free speech combines with poor press coverage of a problem such as that of TV violence, it plays into the hands of those whose primary aim is to silence debate. Too often, the First Amendment is wheeled out as a cannon from which to launch preemptive strikes against anyone challenging the levels of TV violence, regardless of whether censorship is in fact at issue.

Ironically, when the First Amendment is thus invoked, it serves to bludgeon the very principle it stands for: that of protecting free speech and free debate. Such appeals to the First Amendment are hard to reconcile with what Justice Hugo Black stated as its intended purpose in the Pentagon Papers case:

> In the First Amendment the Founding Fathers gave the free press the protection it must have to fulfill its essential role in our democracy. The press was to serve the governed, not the governors. The Government's power to censor the press was abolished so that the press would remain forever free to censor the Government. The press was protected so that it could bare the secrets of government and protect the people.[68]

Using the amendment to inhibit debate produces a chilling effect all its own, and often succeeds in achieving premature closure of all debate concerning the issue of violence on TV or elsewhere in the media. Once again, advocates wielding the First Amendment in this way shift the function of the rationale from that of a reason to proceed with caution when it comes to considering claims to harm from TV violence and proposals for how to limit it, to that of a rationalization for setting aside a difficult issue, not thinking it through with care, and not considering the children and others who have to suffer the consequences of one's inaction and for perpetuating every form of commercial and other exploitation of such violence.

The effects of this premature closure can be seen in many arenas. Intriguingly, most contemporary works *on* free speech and the First Amendment—such as Archibald Cox's *Freedom of Expression* and Anthony Lewis's *Make No Law*—hardly mention media violence, nor do they raise any questions with respect to its effects on children.[69] Indeed, children rarely figure in free speech analyses.[70] The resulting near-silence on the part of constitutional theoreticians regarding risks to children from

TV violence is the more problematic because the question of cumulative long-term risks from exposure to such violence is of such exceptional practical importance in our society. But even from a purely theoretical point of view, considering these risks would in fact also present scholars with an interesting theoretical challenge to the familiar First Amendment doctrine of "clear and present danger."[71]

Preemptive invocations of the First Amendment, moreover, often succeed in deflecting debate as to when it might and might not apply.[72] In so doing, they contribute to short-circuiting debate about what Mary Ann Glendon has called, in *Rights Talk,* the pervasiveness of the legal culture in American society, so that the rhetoric of absolute rights generates near-silence about responsibilities.[73] They bypass consideration of forms of government regulation, such as those taken up by Cass Sunstein in *The Partial Constitution,* which might "promote free speech and should not be treated as an abridgment at all."[74] Finally, they make it easier to dismiss instructive comparisons with how other countries deal with TV violence, on the grounds that these countries have nothing comparable to the First Amendment.

A further effect of the premature closure brought about by appeals to the First Amendment can be seen in the lumping together, as threatening censorship, of many measures to deal with TV violence that represent no censorship or other violation of the First Amendment at all. For instance, when Senator Paul Simon of Illinois, at an August 1993 conference on television violence, called for industry leaders to form an "advisory office on television violence" to review programs and report on them annually to the American public, Geoff Kowan, a producer and vice president of the National Council for Families and Television, is reported to have protested that such a panel could become a censorship body of its own.[75] Likewise, the print press in the United States has consistently blocked even the creation of a private press council.

The debate about the proposed V-chip legislation mentioned above is another case in point. To be sure, it would be important to consider what criteria would be used in rating TV programs with respect to their violence. Much can be learned from the practices of other nations in this respect, as from the long experience in our own country with movie ratings. But to dismiss such legislation as instituting a form of censorship represents either a misunderstanding of what constitutes censorship or an intentional effort to conjure it up indiscriminately for political purposes. In this regard, Newton Minow, former chairman of the Federal Communications Commission, has concluded that "anyone who proposes doing anything more to curb violence is almost certain to be shouted down as a censor," and that even many parents who think television violence is excessive are uncomfortable with judging speech:

They shouldn't be. If we really cared about our children, invocations of the First Amendment would mark the beginning, not the end, of such discussions. . . .

Rating programs is not censorship—far from it. Indeed, when combined with lock-out technologies, a ratings system would actually extend the reach of free expression on television, allowing adults to watch whatever suited them while effectively eliminating children from the audience.

It is time we used the First Amendment to protect and nurture our children, rather than as an excuse to ignore them.[76]

All eight rationales, in sum, do point to important considerations, but when advanced to short-circuit or stifle debate they contribute to the continued neglect of issues urgently in need of public policy debate. Many in the press are on their guard against unthinking adoption of similarly simplistic rationales when it comes to, for example, policy debates about the public health risks posed by firearms or tobacco. Journalists assume that it matters to examine not only the rationales advanced in such debates but also the special interests of the gun and tobacco lobbies in gaining widespread acceptance for some of these rationales. Why, then, should the press not devote the same attention to the rationales used in the debate regarding TV violence and to the special interests with the most to gain from their acceptance? What, more generally, are the special difficulties and challenges for the U.S. press in sorting out what its role should be in covering violence and in the debates concerning how to lessen its sway?

The Role of the Press

Journalists frequently find themselves in a double bind when it comes to covering particular stories involving violence. How can they treat such stories accurately without being accused of adding to the level of violence in society? They are criticized when they appear to sensationalize violent acts or glamorize violent persons, yet they know that honest reporting of brutal acts may influence public opinion in these directions.

Even the choice of what facts to report may present similar dilemmas. For example, both *Time* and *Newsweek* ran cover stories on young people and violence during the same week in August 1993: "Big Shots: An Inside Look at the Deadly Love Affair Between America's Kids and Their Guns" and "Teen Violence: Wild in the Streets," respectively.[77] Both sets of articles did a service in highlighting the unprecedented scale of the crisis such violence presents for young people and the entire society. Both explored the interlocking influences on young people of the easy availability of firearms, poverty, peer models, TV violence, and other cultural factors. Some of the material used, and in particular the lead-in paragraphs of the *Newsweek* coverage, were extraordinarily and graphically brutal. These stories were not gratuitous because they were closely related to the topic of teen violence under discussion; nor did they in any sense glamorize the young people described. Yet many would nevertheless regard the stories as sensationalistic with regard to what was singled out and suspect commercial motives behind such selectiveness. But how else, in that case, might the topic of teen violence be treated so as to inform the public and analyze the problems, yet not in any sense exploit the public's fascination with stories involving violence?

The sense of double bind stems, in part, from the frequently noted inherent conflict between the commercial and the public service functions of the press. If journalists are to cover practices and incidents of violence in such a way as to help curb or at least not exacerbate societal violence, they have to study the ways in which this conflict expresses itself in the context of violence. To what extent is it true that violence sells? What are the existing limits on exploiting the public's fascination with violence for competitive or otherwise commercial motives? How influential are tie-ins between newspaper chains, magazines, and TV stations? What about the daily revenues, for magazines and newspapers, from advertisements of violent "action-adventure" films and TV programs? Might there be a link between such advertisements and inadequate press coverage of the debate about the effects of TV violence, similar to that claimed between tobacco advertisements and the failure on the part of magazines accepting such advertising to report on the effects of smoking?[78]

In part, however, the sense of double bind also stems from a second source of conflict within the public service function of the press: a conflict generated when there is tension between the mandate not to downplay or cover up risks to the public on the one hand, and its special interest to protect the freedom of speech against all threatened restrictions on the other. Our society is uniquely dependent on the press for taking the responsibility to protect free speech with the utmost seriousness, but this special interest, just as much as the commercial one, requires self-scrutiny on the part of the press. Both bring temptations to engage in biased or slipshod news coverage. Such coverage, inconsistent with the most basic standards of good journalism, does disservice to the public whether or not it is motivated in part by ideals of public service.

It will matter, therefore, for the press to scrutinize its own role in covering the debate over television and other forms of violence, to be on the lookout for rationales and rationalizations such as those discussed in this chapter, and to explore the obstacles that stand in the way of providing better coverage. On such a basis, it ought to be possible, when reporting on contributions to this debate by public interest groups, industry officials, officeholders, and others, not only to convey more thoroughly what is being said and done (something that would already represent a significant improvement) but to provide the type of analysis routinely offered with respect to other societal problems.

For an example of an imaginative and probing journalistic approach to the problem of film and TV violence, consider the article prepared by Ken Auletta for *The New Yorker* in the spring of 1993.[79] Auletta chose to ask "a cross-section of the managers and artists who decide what we watch" the same provocative question: "What won't you do?"[80] Was there anything these individuals would refuse to film or broadcast, and on what grounds? The answers were telling. Oliver Stone, the director of the film *JFK*, answered that, "Off the top of my head, I'd pretty much do anything. . . . I don't view ethics from the outside, only from the inside. What you would find shocking, I probably would not. For me, it's a question more of taste."[81]

When asked whether he agreed with President Clinton that Hollywood was too preoccupied with violence and sex, Stone retorted, in a familiar non sequitur related to the eighth rationale discussed above, that he didn't believe that government had the right to legislate art or censor it. Others responded to Auletta's question in a more modulated way, a few expressing the conflict they felt between doing what they wanted in film and recognizing that they would not want their children to see what they had produced. When some tried to evade his questions, Auletta pressed farther, concluding that "many Hollywood programmers lead two lives—a truth they avoid by complaining about government censorship."[82]

Another way in which the press can contribute to the debate is already being explored in a number of publications. It involves giving voice to the individuals with most at stake in the outcome of the violence debate—the children who know violence in their daily lives, the parents and neighborhood groups who struggle against sometimes overwhelming odds, the organizations mobilizing to combat violence, the pediatricians and social workers who work to help individuals overcome its consequences—and in this way to try to penetrate the resistance many in the public feel to even thinking about the human dimension of the problems linked to violence. What is not yet common, however, is to report in this personalized way on TV violence in its own right. The field is wide open to covering more extensively the research now available and to focusing on the plight of the young, the poor, the disadvantaged, and the vulnerable, who have been found to be most easily affected by such violence.

A special difficulty in this regard is that a growing proportion of young adults appear to perceive nothing problematic about TV violence. The March 1993 Times Mirror survey reveals this clearly: "There is a 'video violence' generation gap. Those under 30 are far more likely to be heavy consumers of violent programming and movies. [They] are far less bothered by violence on television, less likely to feel violence is harmful to society than are older Americans."[83]

This difference in attitudes on the part of young adults may be due in part to the fact that many of them have not yet had children themselves and so have not had reason to try to put themselves in the place of a child exposed to today's levels of entertainment violence. But the difference may result also from the desensitizing influence of TV, to which young adults, unlike many of their elders, have been massively exposed. In that case, the gap may well shift upwards in age as more and more cohorts of children grow up having been exposed to heavy doses of television violence. Unless the majority of Americans, who are now coming to greater realization of the risk from such violence, take it seriously enough to move the public policy debate ahead energetically, it may then be even harder to bring about the necessary reforms.

Taking this risk seriously from the point of view of public policy should not mean granting it some unique status as the one causal factor related to the crisis of violence in U.S. society. On the contrary, the policy debate about this crisis can only do justice to the complexity of the interlocking causal factors by looking at it as a national public health crisis of dimensions at least equivalent to those of, say, heart disease, cancer, and AIDS.

It will matter for the press, therefore, to address this crisis, as the others, with the same caution about avoiding oversimplification. Doing so will mean devoting the same attention to public education regarding violence as about the other problems. This, in turn, will call for careful analysis of alternative forms of prevention, of the pros and cons of different remedies suggested, and interlocking risk factors—much as is now done, for example, for diet, exercise, surgery, and medication when it comes to heart disease. It will call for substantive reporting of a comparative nature, showing where we stand in relation to other nations in combating violence, much as is now beginning to be done with respect to health care here and abroad. Such shifts in coverage are important in their own right; but they may also help the press in its efforts to overcome the conflicts and other obstacles to fuller reporting noted above and, in so doing, free itself to participate more fully in the public policy debate now so urgently needed regarding the interlocking factors contributing to violence in the United States.

Notes

1. Michael Wines, "Reno Chastises TV Executives over Violence," *New York Times,* October 21, 1993, pp. A1, B16.

2. *New York Times,* October 22, 1993. Three weeks earlier, on October 4, 1993, the *Los Angeles Times* had carried an op-ed piece signed by Jack Valenti, president of the Motion Picture Association of America, which employed the "heavy hand" metaphor. Entitled "Whose Children Are They, Anyway?" the piece stressed the responsibility of parents, and stated that "what frightens the industry and should chill the blood of every citizen is the heavy hand of government slowly, steadily, remorselessly intruding into the outer perimeter of the First Amendment."

3. Michael Gartner, "Warning to the Attorney General," *USA Today,* October 26, 1993, p. 13A.

4. *Chicago Tribune,* October 23, 1993, p. 22.

5. Ibid.

6. Michael Janofsky, "A Cable Network Fires Off a Rebuttal About Regulating Violence," *New York Times,* November 10, 1993, p. D18.

7. See, for evaluations of studies of the effects of television violence, David Barry, "Screen Violence: It's Killing Us," *Harvard Magazine* 96 (November/December 1993): 38–43; Canadian Radio-Television and Telecommunications Commission; George Comstock, *Television: The Key Studies* (Santa Monica, Calif.: Rand, 1975); George Comstock and Hae-Jung Paik, *Television and Children: A Review on Recent Research* (Syracuse, N.Y.: Syracuse University, 1987); Andrea Martinez, Canadian Radio-Television and Telecommunications Commission, 1991; Brandon S. Centerwall, "Television and Violence: The Scale of the Problem and Where to Go From Here," *Journal of the American Medical Association* 267 (June 10, 1992); Kate Moody, *Growing Up on Television* (New York: New York Times Books, 1980); Albert J. Reiss, Jr., and Jeffrey A. Roth, eds., *Understanding and Preventing Violence* (Washington, D.C.: National Academy Press, 1993), including a reference to an unpublished 1990 report by George Comstock and Hae-Jung Paik, "The Effects of Television Violence on Aggressive Behavior: A Meta-Analysis," commissioned by the National Academy of Sciences Panel on the Understanding and Control of Violent Behavior; Cathy Spatz Widom, "Does Violence Beget Violence? A Critical Examination of the Literature," *Psychological Bulletin* 106 (1989): 3–28, esp. 20–24.

8. Ron Slaby, ed., *Violence and Youth: Psychology's Response,* American Psychological Association, August 1993, Report of the American Psychological Association's Commission on Violence and Youth.

9. Slaby, ed., *Violence and Youth,* pp. 32–33.

10. Jeff Greenfield, moderator, Conference on Violence in TV Programming, sponsored by the National Council for Families and TV, Beverly Hills, August 2, 1993. Partial transcript available on C-Span. See also the transcript of a panel convened in 1992 by the editors of *TV GUIDE, Violence on Television.*

11. David A. Hamburg, *Today's Children* (New York: Times Books, 1992), p. 192.

12. A.C. Nielsen Company, *Nielsen Report on Television* (Northbrook, Ill.: Nielsen Media Research, 1989).

13. William H. Dietz and Victor C. Strasburger, "Children, Adolescents, and Television," *Current Problems in Pediatrics* 21, 1991, pp. 8–31.

14. *Newsday,* October 25, 26, 27, 31, 1993; *Boston Globe,* August 10, 1993, p. 1.

15. Times Mirror Center for the People and the Press, March 24, 1993, "TV Violence More Objectionable in Entertainment than in Newscasts," pp. 5–7. See, for a report on surveys in a number of countries, Atkinson and Gourdreau, *Summary and Analysis,* note 7, above.

16. David Lange, Robert K. Baker, and Sandra J. Ball, *Mass Media and Violence,* Vol. 11, *A Report to the National Commission on the Causes and Prevention of Violence* (Washington, D.C.: U.S. Government Printing Office, 1969), pp. 359, 378–379.

17. Ibid., pp. 378–379.

18. Reiss and Roth, eds., *Understanding and Preventing Violence:* citation of "an extensive meta-analysis prepared for the panel by Comstock and Paik," p. 371.

19. Ibid., pp. 327–352. On pp. 329–330, it is recommended that a series of

approaches to "reducing childhood aggressiveness in different subpopulations" be compared from the point of view of effectiveness. The approaches listed include "the promotion of television programs that encourage prosocial nonviolent behavior." No mention is made of programs with the reverse effect.

20. See *New York Times,* April 4, 1993.

21. David Barry, "Screen Violence: It's Killing Us," p. 40.

22. Ibid.

23. Centerwall, "Television and Violence"; Deborah Prothrow-Stith, *Deadly Consequences* (New York: HarperCollins, 1991); Mark L. Rosenberg and Mary Ann Fenley, eds., *Violence in America: A Public Health Approach* (New York: Oxford University Press, 1991).

24. I have discussed the concept of rationales in *Secrets: On the Ethics of Concealment and Revelation* (New York: Pantheon Books, 1982), pp. 119–124.

25. Jean-Claude Chesnais, "The History of Violence: Homicide and Suicide Through the Ages," *International Social Science Journal* (May 1992): 217–234, at 219. It should be noted that the ten to one proportion that Chesnais noted was not entirely accurate in 1993; for although the U.S. homicide rate has gone up since he wrote, others have as well (as in Canada, where a debate about the role of TV violence, much of it coming from the United States, is also under way). By 1993, it was more accurate to view the ratio as one of one to anywhere between five and ten.

26. Dane Archer and Rosemary Gartner, "Violent Acts and Violent Times: A Comparative Approach to Postwar Homicide Rates," *American Sociological Review* 41 (1976): 937–963.

27. Jerome Kagan, in *Unstable Ideas* (Cambridge, Mass.: Harvard University Press, 1989), p. 9, has pointed out that rationalizations about cruelty and aggression being out of our control is a cue that allows people to live with the amount of them we now witness in our society. He contrasts this attitude to that of the Japanese, who, believing that people can control their anger, have so much less violent a society.

28. Michael Mann, director of the television shows *Crime Story* and *Miami Vice,* quoted in *New York Times,* October 22, 1993, p. C3.

29. This rationale—in the form "Why focus on x when y (and/or z, etc.) are more important?"—is asked, as well, of anyone focusing on, say, substance abuse or inadequate policing or family breakdown as a risk factor for societal violence.

30. See works cited in note 23, above. See also the statement regarding violence made by Secretary of Health and Human Services Donna Shalala on December 10, 1993.

31. Sam Donaldson, *This Week with David Brinkley,* Sunday, November 7, 1993.

32. Deborah Prothrow-Stith, quoted in *TV GUIDE: Violence on Television,* p. 9.

33. Myriam Miedzian, *Boys Will Be Boys: Breaking the Link Between Masculinity and Violence* (New York: Doubleday, 1991), p. 215.

34. Quoted by Michael Janofsky, in "On Cigarettes, Health, and Lawyers," *New York Times,* Monday, December 6, 1993, p. D8.

35. The television industry has already taken seriously the need to curtail the glamorization of smoking and of drunk driving on its programs, without requiring absolute documentation of the causative links between TV viewing and higher incidence of such conduct.

36. Frederick Schauer, "Causation Theory and the Causes of Sexual Violence," *American Bar Foundation Research Journal* (Fall 1987) 737–770, at 753.

37. Centerwall, "Television and Violence," pp. 63–64.

38. Martin Rose, reporting on research cited at the August 2, 1993, Beverly Hills conference on television violence, in "A Call to Disarm," *Washington Post,* August 3, 1993, p. E4.

39. Amartya Sen, "Political Rights Versus Economic Needs?" forthcoming, *The New Republic.* See also Jean Dreze and Amartya Sen, *Hunger and Public Action* (Oxford: Oxford University Press, 1989).

40. Catherine S. Manegold, "New York City by TV: A Wasteland of Crime and More Crime," *New York Times,* June 14, 1992, p. 22.

41. Bernard Weinraub, "For This Movie Producer, Violence Pays," *New York Times,* June 14, 1992, p. H20.

42. Brandon S. Centerwall puts it as follows: "In the minds of such young children television is a source of entirely factual information regarding how the world works." "Television and Violent Crime," *The Public Interest* (Spring 1993): 56–71, at 58.

43. A. C. Nielsen Company, *Nielsen Report on Television.*

44. Neil Hickey, "How Much Violence on TV? A Lot Says TV Guide," *Ethics: Easier Said Than Done* 21 (April 1993): 53. One of the proposals by Peggy Charren, founder and president of Action for Children's Television, is that such advertisements and promotionals be kept off programs that children watch. See interview in Ellen Edwards, "The Kids' Crusader," *Washington Post,* August 2, 1993, p. B6.

45. See Kenneth D. Gadow and Joyce Sprafkin, "Television 'Violence' and Children With Emotional and Behavioral Disorders," *Journal of Educational and Behavioral Disorders* 1 (1991): 54–63, for an account of factors, such as limitations in social experiences and cognitive abilities and concentrated exposure to television, that limit older children's abilities to discriminate between fictional and real events on television.

46. Groves et al., "Silent Victims: Children Who Witness Violence," p. 262.

47. For examples of such crimes, see Charles S. Clark, "TV Violence: The Issues," *CQ Researcher* 3 (March 1993): 168–169; Miedzian, *Boys Will Be Boys,* p. 208.

48. Christina Robb, "Are We Hooked on Media Violence?" *Boston Globe,* July 8, 1991: interview with James F. Gilligan.

49. John D. Searle, *Speech Acts* (Cambridge: Cambridge University Press, 1970), p. 55.

50. *Oxford English Dictionary,* "Violence."

51. Studies of TV programming have in fact reported consistently high levels of violence and aggression, regardless of the measures used to define or assess violence. See Diane M. Zuckerman and Barry S. Zuckerman, "Television's Impact on Children," *Pediatrics* 75 (1985): 233–240, at 234, citing studies by N. Signorelli and colleagues.

52. See Sara Ruddick, "Violence and Non-Violence," in Lawrence C. Becker and Charlotte B. Becker, eds., *Encyclopedia of Ethics* (New York: Garland Publishing Co., 1992), Vol. 2, pp. 1273–1276, for a thoughtful discussion of central and less central cases of violence.

53. For the most recent figures by George Gerbner, see *Newsweek,* July 12, 1993, p. 64.

54. George Gerbner, testimony, Conference on Violence in TV Programming, sponsored by the National Council for Families and TV, Beverly Hills, California, August 2, 1993.

55. Atkinson and Gourdreau, *Summary and Analysis of Various Studies on Violence and Television,* discussing studies in Australia, New Zealand, Great

Britain, France, Canada, and the United States; Nic Nilsson, "Children and the Commercial Exploitation of Violence in Sweden," *Current Sweden* (October 1991).

56. Canadian Radio-Television and Telecommunications Commission, "Voluntary Code Regarding Violence in Television Programming," Public Notice CRTC 1993-149, Ottawa, October 28, 1993.

57. Ibid.

58. For an outline of measures taken, beginning early in 1990, by the Canadian Radio-Television and Telecommunications Commission, see CRTC Fact Sheet, TV1-10-93: "CRTC Initiatives Regarding Violence on Television."

59. See Elizabeth Fox, "TV Violence: An International Perspective," in *TV Violence: More Objectionable* (Washington, D.C.: Times Mirror Center for the People and the Press), p. 9.

60. Jeff Greenfield, moderator, Conference on Violence in TV Programming.

61. Ken Auletta, "What Won't They Do?" *The New Yorker,* May 17, 1993, pp. 45–55, at 53.

62. Martha Minow and Richard Weissbound, "Societal Movements for Children," *Daedalus* (Winter 1993): 1–30, at 5.

63. Stephen Klineberg, cited in "The Violence in Our Heads," *Newsweek,* August 2, 1993, p. 48.

64. Carnegie Corporation of New York, *A Matter of Time: Risk and Opportunity in the Non-School Hours* (1992), p. 30.

65. Edward J. Markey, "A Cheap, Easy Way to Chip Away at TV Violence," *Boston Globe,* August 28, 1993, p. 11.

66. Cited by Markey, "A Cheap, Easy Way."

67. Editorial, *Washington Post,* October 23, 1993, p. A22.

68. *New York Times Co. v. United States,* 403 U.S. 713,717 (1970).

69. Alexander Bickel, *The Morality of Consent* (New Haven, Conn.: Yale University Press, 1975); Archibald Cox, *Freedom of Expression* (Cambridge, Mass.: Harvard University Press, 1981); Anthony Lewis, *Make No Law* (New York: Random House, 1991). See also C. Edwin Baker, *Human Liberty and Freedom of Speech* (New York: Oxford University Press, 1989); Ronald Dworkin, *Taking Rights Seriously* (Cambridge, Mass.: Harvard University Press, 1977); Ronald Dworkin, *A Matter of Principle* (Cambridge, Mass.: Harvard University Press, 1985); Gerald Gunther, *Cases and Materials on Individual Rights in Constitutional Law* (Mineola, N.Y.: Foundations Press, 1989), chap. 6; Rodney Smolla, *Free Speech in an Open Society* (New York: Alfred A. Knopf, 1992); Thomas I. Emerson, *The System of Freedom of Expression* (New York: Random House, 1970). (A number of books on the First Amendment were published before the advent of TV or in its very early days, when few could have foreseen the role that it would come to play in the lives of even the youngest children and the amount of violent programming that would therefore come their way.)

70. The writings of Cass Sunstein provide an important exception with respect to considering television, children, and the effects of television violence on children in the context of the First Amendment: see *The Partial Constitution* (Cambridge, Mass.: Harvard University Press, 1993), and *Democracy and the Problem of Free Press* (New York: Free Press, 1993).

71. See Bickel, *The Morality of Consent,* pp. 64–74, for a discussion of the doctrine of clear and present danger that can be helpful in this respect, although it does not take up TV violence.

72. For discussions of problematical invocations of the First Amendment and the public's right to know, see Sissela Bok, *Secrets: On the Ethics of Concealment and Revelation,* 2nd ed. (New York: Vintage Press, 1989), chap. 16; Mary Ann

Glendon, *Rights Talk* (New York: Free Press, 1991); Frederick Schauer, "The First Amendment as Ideology," *William and Mary Law Review* 33 (Spring 1992); and Cass Sunstein, works cited in note 71.

73. Glendon, *Rights Talk*.

74. Sunstein, *The Partial Constitution*, p. 204.

75. Jeff Kramer, "Lawmaker Campaigns Against TV Violence," *Boston Globe*, August 3, 1993, p. 11.

76. Newton Minow, "How to Zap TV Violence," *Wall Street Journal*, August 3, 1993, p. A14.

77. Jon D. Hull, "A Boy and His Gun," *Time*, August 2, 1993, pp. 20–27; Richard Zoglin, "The Networks Run for Cover," pp. 52–54; *Newsweek*, August 2, 1993, pp. 40–49.

78. C. Edwin Barker, "Advertising and the Democratic Press," *University of Pennsylvania Law Review* 140, June 19, 1992, pp. 2097–2243.

79. Auletta, "What Won't They Do?" See also Ken Auletta, "The Electronic Parent," *The New Yorker*, November 8, 1993, pp. 68–75.

80. Ibid., "What Won't They Do?" p. 46.

81. Ibid., p. 47.

82. Ibid., p. 53.

83. Fox, "TV Violence," p. 1.

9

News Coverage of AIDS

Timothy Cook

In June 1981 a curious combination of opportunistic diseases striking otherwise healthy gay men had been noted in the *Morbidity and Mortality Weekly Report*. In the years since then, the epidemic known as acquired immune deficiency syndrome (AIDS) has become perhaps the most pressing public health crisis in the United States and the world. With the number of deaths in the United States alone having edged into six figures and the spread of immune disorders growing within populations heretofore less affected, with costly and not always readily available treatments that can only prolong the lives of those people living with AIDS, and with no cure or vaccine on the horizon, there is no medical quick fix in sight.

How has the United States responded to this health emergency? The public policy picture is not reassuring.[1] True, money galore is now being spent on AIDS, about as much as on either heart disease or cancer, but most of it has been devoted to the high-consensus domain of medical research. Bureaucracies were mobilized to suggest a viral cause, isolate a virus, and develop treatments against the virus and against the opportunistic infections that are among the major causes of death for persons living with AIDS. But other policy responses have been slow and confused, and the federal government's response and advance planning can still be characterized not only as poorly coordinated but as too little, too late.

In particular, without a fully effective treatment, education and prevention become key, but the federal government's efforts have been scattershot and incomplete. Perhaps more troubling yet, the health care delivery system lacks resources to treat effectively the mounting number of cases, and there are few proposals to deal with them adequately. Even the welcome action in Congress in 1990 to treat cities and states hard hit by AIDS as virtual disaster areas and to appropriate funds to those entities set forth broad aims with neither specific indications of what to do nor adequate appropriations.

For the first decade of the epidemic, AIDS produced the policy stalemate. Valuable time (not to mention lives) was lost from the first recognition of a new and deadly disease in 1981 until April 1, 1987, when President Reagan delivered his first speech on the epidemic and definitively legitimated its place as a permanent item on the political agenda. Decisionmakers have been playing catch-up ball ever since.

What accounted for this sluggish governmental response? Why did AIDS not rise more quickly on the political agenda? One possible key is provided by a central actor in policymaking on new health threats in the 1970s and early 1980s, whether swine flu, Legionnaire's disease, toxic shock syndrome, high cholesterol, or Tylenols laced with poison: the press. Although the news media do not set the political agenda single-handedly, they help to determine which private matters (such as disease) become defined as public events (such as epidemics). After all, none of us live in the macrosociety depicted by the news but in microsocieties with which we interact on a daily basis. Since we cannot fully judge the reach, scope, and gravity of public problems in our immediate environments, the media construct the public realities distinct from the private worlds that we otherwise inhabit and thereby provide "resources for discourse in public matters."[2]

The media's identification and definition of public problems affect not just mass audiences. Politicians, too, are highly attentive to news coverage, which often diverges from the specific choices or emphases they would prefer. Policymakers are more likely to respond to issues as their prominence in the media increases, even those that provoke considerable conflict, but largely in the context of the initial frame that the media have provided.[3] The media's construction of AIDS thus has influenced not merely how we as individuals will react, but also how we as a polity will respond.

This chapter will examine the coverage, both from my own impressions from newspaper and television accounts as well as the more systematic evidence of news content. The conclusion will suggest the limits of "responsible journalism" in adequately covering a medical disaster. To be sure, some journalists, notably those directly affected by the epidemic, pushed the story, just as others, restricted by homophobia or prudery, blocked it. But the defects of AIDS coverage were and are not largely due to individual failures of individual journalists. Instead, the tried-and-true responsible methods of journalism as an institution—the reliance on authoritative sources to suggest news, the downplaying of subjects that do not seem to affect the hypothetical mass audience, the use of venerable story lines to quickly grasp new occurrences, the concerns about being inflammatory, and the rapidity with which topics become old news—contributed to downplay the epidemic in its first four years and continue to favor only certain political slants on the AIDS epidemic. We cannot just say that journalists have to be more careful in practicing their profession because, at least in this case, applying the very definitions of good journalism has *contributed* to the inadequate depiction of the AIDS epidemic in the news.

The lessons that we can take from the first decade of AIDS coverage in the 1980s are not only apt for how journalists and officials should approach reporting the ongoing epidemic. In some ways, some of the concerns that I express here may no longer be applicable for a disease about which a great amount is now known and the future course of which may not—by now— be easily controlled. But if AIDS has taught us any one thing, it is that we are not in a world freed from new epidemics.

To appreciate the neglect of AIDS in the early years, all that one need do is compare it to earlier unexpected outbreaks of a fatal and seemingly new disorder. In 1976, several middle-aged, middle-class white male members of the American Legion sickened and died after attending a convention at the Bellevue Stratford Hotel in Philadelphia. The new and mysterious disease was promptly dubbed Legionnaire's disease. David Shaw of the *Los Angeles Times* has noted the contrast:

> Legionnaire's disease, which left 29 people dead and 182 ill, received far more press coverage in a few weeks in 1976 than did AIDS in the three years from mid-1981 to mid-1984—during which time several thousand people died of AIDS. The *New York Times,* for example, published 62 stories on Legionnaire's disease in August and September, 1976, 11 of them on page one. But the *New York Times* published only seven stories about AIDS in the first 19 months of the AIDS epidemic, and AIDS didn't make Page 1 of the *New York Times* for the 11th time until the epidemic was more than four years old—by which time there were more than 12,000 AIDS cases and more than 6,000 deaths.[4]

The *New York Times* may have been unusually slow on the AIDS story, but no news outlet was quick to pick it up, and when the media did at last begin reporting it, their interest was intermittent. By contrast with the geometric rise in both the number of identified cases of AIDS and in the medical interest in the epidemic, attention to AIDS was astonishingly sporadic in any medium: newspapers, news magazines, or network television.[5]

Figure 9.1 indicates the rise in newly reported AIDS cases across most of the decade. By contrast, Figure 9.2 shows the number of seconds devoted to stories on AIDS in the nightly network news broadcasts of ABC, CBS, and NBC from the discovery of a new malady in June 1981 to the International AIDS Conference in Montreal in June 1989. Apart from three peaks—in June 1983, after speculation in the *Journal of the American Medical Association* that pediatric AIDS might portend infection by casual contact; in August and September 1985, following the disclosure of the illness of actor Rock Hudson; and in the spring of 1987, after the potential of heterosexual transmission of the human immunodeficiency virus (HIV) had become clear—AIDS was simply not reported as a continuing story of

Figure 9.1   U.S. AIDS Cases, by Quarter and Case Definition

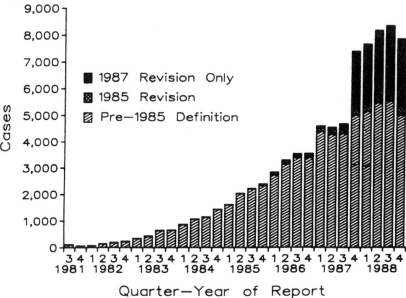

Source: Morbidity and Mortality Weekly Report, vol. 38, no. 14 (April 14, 1989), p. 230.

Figure 9.2   Seconds of U.S. Nightly News Time on AIDS, June 1981–December 1989

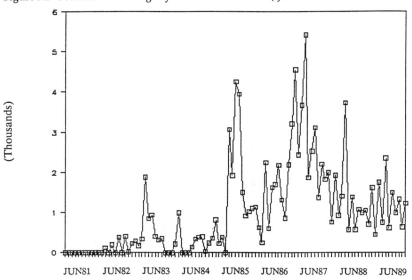

Source: Vanderbilt University Television News Abstracts and Index (1981–1989)

concern to the audience, even as the severity and reach of the epidemic dramatically worsened.

This pattern is curious, if one scholar is correct that "the epidemic known as acquired immune deficiency syndrome seemed tailor-made to the who, what, where and when ideology that often accounts for the content of stories which appear as the 'news.'"[6] Instead, I would argue that AIDS presented numerous problems for journalism as a whole—opportunities for sensational, dramatic, or moralizing news notwithstanding.

First, the earliest identified group at highest risk comprised gay men. The media would have to deal with individuals who had not attained journalistic standards for newsworthiness prior to 1981, in part because of concerns to maintain individual privacy.[7] The importance of this connection is best shown by the fact that the only newspaper to have increased its coverage of AIDS in 1984 over 1983 as numbers of cases inexorably climbed was the *San Francisco Chronicle*—the only newspaper to have, as of 1984, established the gay community as a newsbeat and thus as a subject of recurring newsworthiness.[8] Second, AIDS, mixing as it does references to blood, semen, sex, sexuality, and death, defied traditional notions of "taste." Although these considerations are strongest with television journalists anticipating the dinner hour of the nightly news, all reporters for a mass medium tend to take their audience into account by seeking out subjects that will affect the largest part of their audience, viewed as a collection of middle-class nuclear families, and that will not be offensive to such viewers and readers.[9] Those stories that do not seem to affect the stereotypical mass audience tend to be either avoided, euphemized, or quickly dropped.

Third, AIDS was a slow-moving disaster that did not easily meet the standard conventions for breaking news. The news media are better equipped to report dramatic, sudden disasters such as floods or earthquakes, as opposed to droughts and famines, even though the latter might be regarded as more important in terms of their effects on the world economy or the eventual loss of life. With no seeming beginning or end and little new change from day to day, journalists may simply not be alerted to a slow-moving disaster or consider it new enough until officials call it to their attention or impressive (usually visual) evidence is discovered.[10]

Finally, and perhaps most important, the media were in the unenviable position of seeking to raise public awareness without creating public panic. In introducing an early story (June 20, 1983) on ABC, anchor Max Robinson said, "As researchers attempt to conquer this disease called AIDS, public officials attempt to conquer the epidemic of fear," while in the report, Ken Kashiwahara added, "It is a delicate balancing act, raising the level of concern for the disease on the one hand, while reducing the level of panic on the other." Reporters take seriously their role to educate and alert, but they sense that they must also avoid being inflammatory or alarmist.[11] The reasons are simple. Public service includes protecting the public from information that might cause them harm. But in addition, insofar as journalists visualize themselves as reflecting, not meddling, in politics, any indication that they have either provoked or aggravated a problem can touch off criticism that can affect their legitimacy. In either case, journalists would end up shying away from topics that present the possibility of raising alarm or to report them so as to reassure rather than to worry.

Consequently, journalists spent little time investigating AIDS as a topic. Instead, they awaited particular authoritative sources to provide events that could become news stories. So despite the growing severity of AIDS and increasing attention in medical and scientific circles, reporters played up the epidemic, even after its mass-mediated discovery in mid-1983, less than they minimized its effect and threat. Only during the three peak periods was the process enterprising and topic-driven, with journalists seeking out new angles and aspects of the epidemic. To be sure, the quality of the news was not always enhanced during such saturation coverage. Especially in 1983 and 1987, coverage flipped from a reassuring portrait of the containment of AIDS to established risk-groups to an alarmist depiction that suggested, equally erroneously, that everybody was now at risk of contracting HIV. On television, there was frequent attention to the "epidemic of fear"—frightened responses to AIDS that, in their vividness and inaccuracy, only served to fuel rather than quell the fear. Little wonder that journalists often preferred, with seeming haste, to drop the story and move onto other matters.

When the news has been more routine than enterprising, it has unwittingly peddled unwarranted reassurance, especially prior to the revelation of Rock Hudson's illness in the summer of 1985. Only when authoritative sources—most often governmental officials and established scientists—created a news event that served as a peg for reporters would the epidemic become newsworthy. Of course, such a dependence on authoritative sources introduces bias only if doing so limits the diversity of perspectives represented. But governmental and scientific sources shared an interest in projecting an image of government and medicine coolly and gradually making progress against the epidemic, and they avoided calling journalists' attention to inaction and disappointing results. By contrast, those more likely to criticize the government's response had no newsbeat of their own, and all they could do was piggyback onto stories at established newsbeats, such as congressional hearings or medical meetings.

In science, news conferences are rarely called to announce a failed experiment, and the better the news, the more likely it is that prominent people will announce it. Thus, in 1989, Health and Human Services (HHS) Secretary Louis Sullivan appeared before the news media to announce the government's finding that the drug AZT worked to slow the reproduction of HIV among infected asymptomatic individuals; according to Sullivan's spokesman, had the news not been so upbeat, his boss would likely not have appeared.[12] Scientists and physicians have been no more disinterested than officials. Receiving credit for one's work is necessary for one to continue to do science; credit enables resources (e.g., grants, promotions) that can be reinvested in further research.[13] If publicity is now a device to build a career, it is only by playing down dead ends and stressing advances that the news media will cover.

With the government and the scientists dominating the coverage from mid-1983 to mid-1985, reporting on AIDS went back from alarming to soothing, suggesting that government, medicine, and science were slowly but inevitably progressing toward managing the epidemic. This approach was interrupted only by the revelation of Rock Hudson's illness in late July 1985, and, though journalists returned to routine event-driven coverage of AIDS after Hudson's death in October 1985, this post-Hudson coverage was less reassuring. On the nightly network news, for instance, the stories declined in number from the 1985 level but were more prominently presented, and the complete oversight of AIDS that occurred as recently as the month before Hudson flew to Paris would never be repeated.

With Hudson's illness certifying AIDS's newsworthiness, more approaches were brought to bear—not only medical and science correspondents, but also law reporters, political reporters (both foreign and domestic), and regional stringers who brought new angles and spoke to new sources. There was thus less consensus about how to cover the epidemic. The variety of story lines reinvigorated attention to the epidemic on numerous dimensions. Additional sources gained attention, and they were now in disagreement, unlike the pre-Hudson era when medical and political sources converged on a story line that reassuringly noted science and government doggedly at work.

Thus, from the fall of 1985 to the spring of 1987, the story of AIDS gradually built. With the internationalization of AIDS news, the media's discovery of roughly equal numbers of cases among men and women in Africa and the Caribbean, and the resurfacing of "epidemic of fear" stories, news coverage of AIDS built up to its highest point to date in 1987. Only when President Reagan gave his first speech on the epidemic on April 1, 1987, and when Vice President Bush, on behalf of the administration, presented policy recommendations to the International AIDS Conference in Washington did the upward spiral finally stop, and only then did AIDS become a permanently recurring part of the political agenda.

As with prior periods following the peaks, reporting since mid-1987 has slackened off.[14] Once again, it is routine and event-driven, focusing above all on prescheduled occasions like the annual international AIDS conferences that have taken place each June since 1985.[15] In the 1990s, the coverage of the HIV epidemic, though avoiding the extraordinary focuses of June 1983, September 1985, and the spring of 1987, should continue to be a relatively constant news item. There are some drawbacks to routine coverage, insofar as saturation of the airwaves may be necessary to keep individuals vigilant about proper prevention. But it avoids the on-again, off-again cycle of alarm and reassurance that proved so debilitating in the first decade of the epidemic.

We should not overlook the many benefits of the news coverage, including gradually raising the awareness of the American people as to what AIDS is and how HIV can and cannot be transmitted. Yet though AIDS had crossed the threshold of public awareness by mid-1983, the media did not push the urgency of the problem. The first public opinion polls on AIDS in 1983 showed relatively little concern that it would reach epidemic proportions; the issue had been seemingly contained, being defined as distant and not immediately threatening. Only after the summer of 1985 did the public at least begin to conceive of the disease as likely to affect their world—and only then would there be much pressure on the government to do something about the epidemic.[16]

There are many culprits in the continuing slow, confused response to the onset of AIDS; certainly, the media are not alone.[17] Yet some improvements can be worked into the fabric of U.S. journalism in preparation for the next epidemic, as well as the current one, without making undue demands upon the resources of news organizations and journalists or upon the attention and interest of audiences. All of these suggestions comprehend that journalists are performing a well nigh impossible task of getting all the news and that audiences cannot be expected to devote massive amounts of time to seeking out and consuming large quantities of news. The challenge of AIDS coverage is to provide a representative understanding of the disease and its possible implications for medicine, science, education, politics, and society to an audience (both among elites and in the public) that has many other competing activities besides attending to news but that must be involved in the crucial political decisions about AIDS that face us.

Realize that even the "general audience" can use—and be interested in— news that is neither about them nor reported from or toward their supposed perspective.

As we have seen, AIDS reporting was hampered by the presumption that, unlike Legionnaire's disease, swine flu, Alar sprayed on apples, or laced Tylenol capsules, the disease was unlikely to affect any and all of us in the general public. Yet as soon as science began to point toward a viral agent, the epidemiological emphasis upon high-risk *groups* was displaced by the virological concern with high-risk *behaviors* that could help to spread HIV. These behaviors were and are not restricted to members of those groups, but the concentration in marginalized segments of the population made it easier to think of AIDS as an isolated "outbreak" rather than an epidemic that could eventually reach all sectors of society.

AIDS, as do many other stories, reveals the presumption about the mass audience that makes reporting about minorities (whether racial, ethnic, or sexual) difficult. We have seen this response among journalists seeking to justify the media overkill on the story—later revealed to be a hoax engineered by her husband—that yuppie lawyer Carol Stuart was murdered by a black robber in Boston. Ed Siegel, television critic for the *Boston Globe,* wrote, "The media fell into public pandering. . . . The general, i.e, white, public wanted saturation coverage of the murder of a white couple and they got it. The general public does not want saturation coverage of the murder of a black person, unless it's a child, and they don't get it."[18]

But does the general public get just the news it wants? Not necessarily. First of all, this presumption may not be based in fact. Journalists have less constant contact with their mass audiences than with their peers, superiors, and sources whom they meet on a more systematic basis and who reinforce each other's ideas about what is and isn't news. Reporters tend to disdain audience research, since it would compromise what little autonomy they have left and complicate their already impossible task of managing their workload. Whether or not parts of the audience would respond favorably to stories that are not about them is an open question as long as they are not given the chance to do so.

Second, the presumption ignores the uses that the public could obtain from reporting from a variety of perspectives, given the multiplicity of communities to which individuals belong. Instead of the lowest-common-denominator approach that homogenizes the news and makes it apply to everybody and nobody, the media should start recognizing the diversity of its audience and the variety of its interests with an appropriate plethora of topics, story lines, sources, and conclusions. Because different individuals attend to the news for different reasons, it would seem to make not only journalistic sense but economic sense to do so.

Getting all sides of the story means that reporting cannot stop with experts. Experts have no lock on the truth, and one should not treat scientific and medical sources as Delphic oracles.

U.S. journalism necessarily depends upon sources to help provide it with information or create events that can become news; without such cooperation, newsgathering could no longer be economically viable. The more important problem is how sources are used and which sources are called upon.

Journalism has always had difficulty covering science. The media have been frequently criticized for oversimplifying, sensationalizing, and dramatizing science news.[19] Yet scientific inquiries become more technical and abstruse, policies become increasingly dependent on questions of technology, and audiences need information that can be readily understood in their own terms. Here, as elsewhere, reporters turn to accessible individuals who can encapsulate information, but scientific sources often comment in areas far from the purviews where they can best provide reliable evidence.[20] Thus, misleading conclusions about the possible spread of HIV through casual contact were legitimized by Harvard immunologist Dr. William Haseltine in the mid-1980s; sexologists William Masters and Virginia Johnson; and, more recently, by Dr. Lorraine Day, the head of orthopedic surgery at San Francisco General Hospital. All were discussing epidemiological or virological matters on which they were not expert.

Journalists and scientists also have different understandings of evidence. For the former, lone cases serve as undeniable evidence of a fact that is thereby shown to be true, whereas the latter, aware of anomalies and the overdetermination of any single case, generally require large batches of systematically gathered data. Even then, any single study must be regarded as tentative until it is joined by many others. The journalistic preference for clear-cut fact runs smack into the nuanced conclusions of science, and odd moments result when the media's consensus is turned upside-down. In the case of AIDS, recall the shift in news coverage from a portrait of an epidemic well away from the "general population" to a situation in which in the words of *Life* magazine's cover, "Now No One Is Safe from AIDS." The nuances of risk were obliterated at either stage.

Journalists covering science are often misled not only by lone studies—recall the reporting of cold fusion and of oat bran in 1989—but by lone cases that seem to be too good a story to pass up. On October 29, 1985, Tom Brokaw of NBC led off a story as follows: "There may be a dramatic breakthrough in the treatment of AIDS tonight. Maybe. Everybody is anxious for some encouraging news." Jim Bittermann's story on very preliminary results from Paris on the experimental treatment Cyclosporin-A was, for the most part, cautious about the results, yet the network presented what it knew was, at best, premature and, at worst, wrong. Brokaw noted, "Their research and testing have been very limited so skepticism as well as hope is running high tonight." Yet Bittermann's report concluded with unwarranted reassurance: "Still there is in this hospital tonight an AIDS victim up and walking around who the doctors say less than a week ago was only hours from death." This story was followed by one by science reporter Robert Bazell showing doubt among persons living with AIDS and health care workers about the treatment. But it too concluded on a positive note: "There is no question that the results from Paris will persuade many American researchers to try this new approach." In less than two weeks NBC had to report that two of the patients receiving the drug had died, one even before the initial story was reported. Although television, with its emphasis upon individual actors, is more prone to such errors, newspapers commit the same mistake. Witness Gina Kolata's 1989 *New York Times* front-page story that pointed to a lone case (the person died, apparently of unrelated causes) in which HIV disappeared from a man's body after a bone marrow transplant. Only later did it become clear that other attempts at this highly risky treatment had been unpublicized flops: "There are lots of us who haven't published our results because they've been so dismal."[21]

Some would prescribe that science journalists should painstakingly follow rules of science in deciding credibility: Has the source been designated by his or her colleagues as being in a position to provide reliable information, and can the lone study or lone case be backed up by other independent studies or cases? Such rules are necessary but not sufficient. Reporters must recognize that even the best science is intuitive, contingent, theory-driven, and altogether messy. The popular vision of science looks at the generation of indisputable facts that become bricks of the temple of knowledge. Yet starting with Thomas Kuhn's famous analysis of scientific revolutions, a clearer understanding of the scientific method shows its dependence upon the questions that are asked, a process further narrowed by an institutional structure that favors only particular questions and methods.[22]

These tendencies toward science as a social process are even more pronounced when we turn from the laboratory to what has been termed "public science," where scientists set forth "rhetoric, argument and polemic to persuade the public or influential sectors thereof that science . . . is worthy of receiving public attention, encouragement and financing."[23] News becomes a way to decide "who will speak for science"; to set research agendas; to establish careers; and to receive accolades, prizes, and grants. In short, scientists, like other sources, have axes to grind. Far from being outside of political and social processes, they are part of them.

Yet journalists do not generally approach scientific sources with much skepticism. Instead, reporters tend to be uncritical of the scientific facts with which they are provided. A reliance upon sources may be inevitable, but news cannot abandon the search for diversity in any realm in order to ensure an adequate understanding of what is going on. The early coverage of AIDS suggests limits on what experts, whether politicians or scientists, will provide, even though data suggesting that the epidemic was far from under control were readily available.

Likewise, different kinds of expertise should be brought to bear. For example, while journalists have covered, often respectfully, the demands of demonstrators in ACT UP (the AIDS Coalition to Unleash Power) at the international AIDS conferences, they have tended to cast these occasions as "science vs. politics," underestimating the degree of politics that infuses the scientific discussion as well as the degree of scientific knowledge among the demonstrators. The experience of the persons living with AIDS has only occasionally been tapped; they are allowed more to discuss their emotional state or their symptoms but rarely to offer commentary as informed experts about the epidemic, though nowadays they surely are that.[24] Reporters on any epidemic must cast their nets widely to ensure that they have not prematurely closed off public debate and to allow different kinds of expertise to inform that discussion.

Do not assume that telling "both sides" of the story is responsible journalism, particularly if one side is vivid and the other is not.

As journalists become increasingly aware that objectivity may be unattainable, recent journalism has begun to stress balanced accounts. Yet absolute balance may be as difficult to achieve as absolute objectivity, unless one is willing to assume that there are two sides to any given story. Even if there are two sides, journalists need to be more cautious about whether both sides deserve equal time.

As we have seen, AIDS reporting often fell prey to what a study of California earthquake coverage has termed an "alarm-and-reassurance pattern."[25] Stories led with dramatic worst-case scenarios that shaded the difference between "could" and "would," then turned to more reassuring indications of the low likelihood of calamity. At the very least, an alarm-and-reassurance pattern invites selective interpretation or confusion that restricts the potential to learn from the news.

More centrally, in such supposedly balanced stories, the vividness of alarm can easily predominate over the relatively bland reassurance, whether on television where upset individuals acted out or voiced fears that spread misinformation or in newspapers where the nuanced judgments of risk would not appear until several paragraphs into the story, often after the jump from the front page. Thus, during the heavily covered saga of Ryan White, a hemophiliac teenager with AIDS who sued to regain full access to public school in Kokomo, Indiana, stories routinely quoted worried parents pulling their children out of school and noting their concern about casual transmission in ways that science had virtually ruled out, such as by sneezing. Visual images of special protective outfits for prison guards or police officers who deal with persons living with AIDS inaccurately suggested that such reactions were legitimate. Although the stories also quoted experts to correct those misimpressions, the vividness of the allegations meant that stories, far from educating the public about the ways in which HIV could and could not be transmitted, often simply reinforced and authenticated viewers' doubts.

Nevertheless, caution in reporting the facts is not a good in itself. In the case of AIDS, such caution has contributed to the underreporting of AIDS and the misleadingly reassuring portrait of the epidemic. Nor is drama necessarily to be avoided; perhaps the best early report on television news was Geraldo Rivera's two-parter on *20/20* in May 1983. Similarly, risk-taking journalists such as Randy Shilts of the *San Francisco Chronicle* and Charles Ortleb of the *New York Native* attained complete and early reporting of the epidemic but also tripped into big mistakes.[26] *Newsweek,* for instance, was the first news magazine to do a cover story on AIDS in the spring of 1983, well before the first front-page story in the *New York Times* or the first lead story in network news; but that same commitment also pushed them to excerpt the flawed alarmism of Masters and Johnson in 1988. Perhaps errors about the unknown may have to be seen as the operational costs of aggressive journalism.

The dilemma for journalists is the difficulty with independently verifying the validity of the statements that sources proffer. If George Bush says X, and X turns out to be untrue, reporters can retrospectively defend their pursuit of factuality by saying that it was a fact that Bush indeed said X, regardless of whether X turned out to be true. Trying to check up on every fact in a breaking story is certainly impossible.

But in a long-range, continuing story, journalists can make judgments more easily; airing statements that are *known* beforehand to be misleading, and especially those that the reporter specifically wants to debunk, is simply irresponsible. A recent example occurred in Boston, where local television news and the tabloid *Boston Herald* gave prominent coverage to the fears of the patients of a gynecologist, Earl Gelman, who had been arrested for soliciting a prostitute who claimed to be HIV-positive. The *Herald* story could defend itself against charges of journalistic irresponsibility by pointing to their quoting experts that noted the infinitesimal possibility, particularly in these circumstances, of any transmission of HIV: "Police yesterday said they had no confirmation of the woman's claim, but some prostitutes have been known to tell police they have AIDS to prevent close body searches" and "Medical experts said it is extremely unlikely Gelman, if infected with the AIDS virus, could have passed the disease along to patients." But conveniently, these comments came after the jump; the headline, by contrast, was "Doc's Sex Arrest Ignites AIDS Fears,"[27] and by highlighting the clinic's offer of HIV tests, suggested this to be a reasonable response.

Resist the human interest temptation unless and until the political angles have been adequately covered.

Journalists have often responded to the AIDS epidemic, whether in print, radio, or television, by looking for the faces behind the statistics. One might think that the statistics are sobering enough, but the immediacy of the lives (and usually, the deaths) of persons living with AIDS is judged as providing a fuller and deeper sense of the extent of the epidemic. And indeed, distinguished journalism has emerged on the struggle of individual persons living with AIDS, particularly as their stories cast light on larger problems—the availability of treatments; discrimination; and support from lovers, families, and friends.[28]

Yet there are downsides to the human interest preoccupation. First, by focusing on individuals, the story may not provide a representative sample of persons living with AIDS or the population at risk. A story can be more vivid without being typical, and the conclusions drawn from one isolated case cannot be considered as anything more than suggestive. Yet such coverage does not come across as tentative. For example, the fall 1989 *AIDS Quarterly* program on PBS devoted a segment to the larger problem of the growing numbers of women with AIDS. But most of the segment was devoted to a woman who contracted HIV from her bisexual husband (himself interviewed with his back to the camera). The report left the sense that bisexual men were, in the phrase of the *New York Times,* an "AIDS specter for women,"[29] even though women are far more likely to contract HIV from a sexual partner who is an intravenous drug user.

A second and subtler problem occurs as human interest stories displace the attention from page one or the lead story. Feature stories occupy a different place for journalists and for the public. "Hard news" depicts ongoing events, allowing individuals to intercede in the continuing process. The first newspapers in the United States aimed at merchants; they provided news that could facilitate wise investments—a function for economic and political information that holds today. "Soft news," by contrast, became important parts of the newspaper as it aimed at a mass audience in the Jacksonian period. The tension between information-based and story-based journalism has continued since then, whether between or within news organizations.[30] Although journalists often like to think otherwise, the split between hard and soft news does not inhere in the content of what is being covered; they are no better at drawing a tangible border between hard news and soft news than they can demarcate news from nonnews.[31] Not merely the same subject matter but the same event could be fodder for hard news or soft news.

Sociologist Robert Park wrote fifty years ago in his introduction to Helen MacGill Hughes's classic analysis, *News and the Human Interest Story,* that human interest "gives the news the character of a story that will be read for its own sake, even when the reader is not at all concerned with it as news. . . . It is the ability to discover and interpret the human interest in the news that gives the reporter the character of a literary artist and the news story the character of literature."[32] As Hughes then said, the purpose of news thereby shifts from the instrumental emphasis of the front page to become expressive and contemplative. Audiences can certainly learn from such literary accounts. By freeing them from the necessity of having to get something done in the here-and-now, literature provides the opportunity to contemplate other experiences and derive conclusions and lessons.

But human interest stories downplay the role of intervention. Even more than breaking news, they make the audience into spectators rather than participants; to recall the dichotomy popular among mass communication scholars, they favor gratifications over uses. This tendency is exacerbated by the current preference for stories, particularly in television, in which individuals outside government are shown as generally helpless to alter the outcome.[33] Thus, network news has tended less to craft morality plays about persons living with AIDS than sadly to note that they couldn't help having been in the wrong place at the wrong time. Human interest stories about persons living with AIDS generally lead inevitably to their deaths, overlooking their frequently noble—and in a few cases so far, successful—fight to survive. These presumptions are best revealed when the story defies reporters' expectations. Take this front-page teaser in the *Sunday Boston Globe* in late 1989: "For the past year, *Globe* reporter Sally Jacobs and photographer Janet Knott have tracked the life of a 29-year-old woman with AIDS. But what was to have been a story of death became, instead, a story of life. Not even Mildred's doctors fully understand why she is still alive. In the *Boston Globe Magazine*."[34]

Even in breaking news stories on AIDS, the human interest preoccupation is never far away. In the process, they may present a distorted picture of the epidemic and of the political responses thereto. Sick, lost, or abandoned children—which Hughes identified fifty years ago as longtime favorites for human interest tearjerkers—have been prime subjects of AIDS coverage, reinforcing the notion that "innocent victims" are somehow worthier of attention from the media or from government. Thus, although President Bush and his wife made the historic step to meet with gay persons living with AIDS during a visit to the National Institutes of Health in late December 1989—a meeting that was open to the White House press corps and where photographers snapped away—virtually the only news coverage consisted of Bush with babies with AIDS, his next stop on his visit.[35]

When these human interest angles appear in breaking news, they draw attention either to popular cultural themes or individual story lines and away from analyses of policy problems.[36] When Veronica Prego, a doctor living with AIDS who claimed to have contracted HIV by being accidentally stuck with an infected needle, took the stand in New York in her suit alleging negligence on the part of the hospital where she worked, news accounts called attention to her impending death, alluded to in the courtroom above the sobs of her mother and sister. Even the august *New York Times* called attention to her "red silk dress, which only heightened her pallor."[37] The central dilemma for public policy that the Prego trial raises—how to protect health care workers from exposure and infection to HIV as the caseload grows—was obscured by the melodrama.

To cover AIDS adequately, journalists must find a way to enliven and communicate simply without reducing their accounts either to barren fact or to new variations on very old story lines. The human interest approach is worthwhile as long as it is only one approach out of many, and even there, special care should be taken to assure that the chosen individuals are representative of the larger population and of the larger political and scientific problems.

*Be constantly aware of the education that may best occur through the
media. Realizing this responsibility means that we must also realize that
we will be in for the long haul.*

Journalists are wary about embracing the role of education. After all, it compromises their autonomy and integrity, and it adds another task to news organizations already stretched to the breaking point. Sanford Socolow, former executive producer for CBS News, recently said, "It's not the news department's job to go out and promote the awareness of AIDS. It's their job to go out and look for stories about AIDS."[38]

The news media cling to the protections that the First Amendment offered to the vastly different (and much more self-consciously interventionist) press of the late eighteenth century. Nowadays, with increasing concentration of ownership and decreasing competition, the First Amendment protection only makes sense if the news media are performing their responsibility to the public. To be sure, there are many other institutions, public and private, political and otherwise, that need to play key parts in the public sphere. It is all too easy to blame the news media for many social phenomena, especially when, to recall the image of the media critic of the *Los Angeles Times,* "The press, contrary to common mythology, is rarely if ever a lone gunman. More often, it is society's accomplice."[39]

Nonetheless, the media have a crucial potential to affect the future course of the AIDS epidemic. Education on how to avoid infection is imperative. Although some individuals at risk, such as gay men, can be and have been reached effectively by private educational campaigns, others are not. Indeed, many populations in the United States are reached only through the mass media—such as those audiences at particular risk (the young, minorities, women) that are also heavy consumers of television. For example, children identify television as the chief way in which they found out about AIDS, during the decisive gap between when they have cognitively matured enough to understand what AIDS is but before they have engaged in high-risk behavior.[40]

To fulfill this educational function, traditional assumptions about what is old news must shift. One of the reasons that people garner so little from the news is that reinforcement necessary for learning is lost to the constant rise and fall in issues that disappear from the news even as they fail to be fully explained.[41] The search for the new prevails over the continuing commitment to following pressing issues to which they return on a routine basis. But the hallmark of news has always been allowing us to intervene in an ongoing process whose end we cannot know. If this is the case, the roller-coaster ride of AIDS coverage makes no sense when the situation worsens by the day.

The problem with AIDS coverage has been not merely the long valleys of unwarranted reassurance but also the heights, especially in 1983 and 1987, when the public would have been better served by more dispassionate coverage that did not wax hot and cold. Such commitment to the long term gains special urgency as the epidemic shifts away from gay men, who make up a fairly well-organized constituency, to other marginalized but less easily mobilizable populations—intravenous drug users and, primarily through them, into urban minority communities and to women. Again, if journalists are to play a virtuous part in the fight against the HIV epidemic, they will have to go beyond the elite sources upon whom they customarily rely and reflect a diversity of voices.

Above all, acknowledging the long haul means not declaring a premature end to AIDS. It is difficult to know what the future course of the HIV epidemic will be, but suffice it to say that even if starting today, no new individuals were infected, we would still be involved in an enormous international public health emergency, as we try to grapple with the huge numbers of cases that are infected and unaware, with a health care delivery system that is ill-prepared to provide the long-term treatment to those who are HIV-positive as well as those with AIDS-related complex or AIDS, and the burgeoning "pattern two" epidemic in Africa and the Caribbean with equivalent numbers of infected men and women. In effect, the recommendations I have made here may be too late to affect fully the future course of AIDS. But if they enable us to avoid the mistakes of this epidemic when the next epidemic hits, they will have served their purpose.

Notes

Editor's Note: This chapter, concerned with the early media coverage of the AIDS crisis and the initial government response, was completed in the early 1990s, before some of the more recent developments in AIDS prevention and treatment. The focus is therefore how new epidemics move into the policy arena and the role of the media in this agenda-setting process.

1. See, among others, Sandra Panem, *The AIDS Bureaucracy* (Cambridge, Mass.: Harvard University Press, 1988); and Charles Perrow and Mauro Guillén, *The AIDS Disaster: The Failure of Organizations in New York and the Nation* (New Haven, Conn.: Yale University Press, 1990).

2. Harvey Molotch and Marilyn Lester, "News as Purposive Behavior: On the Strategic Use of Routine Events, Accidents and Scandals," *American Sociological Review* 39 (1974): 101–112, at 103. For a good review of agenda-setting literature, see Everett M. Rogers and James W. Dearing, "Agenda-Setting Research: Where Has It Been, Where Is It Going?" in James A. Anderson, ed., *Communication Yearbook,* vol. 11 (Newbury Park, Calif.: Sage Publications, 1988), pp. 555–594.

3. For a fuller discussion of the media's role in elite agenda-setting, see Timothy E. Cook, *Making Laws and Making News: Media Strategies in the U.S. House of Representatives* (Washington, D.C.: Brookings Institution, 1989), chap. 6.

4. David Shaw, "Coverage of AIDS Story: A Slow Start," *Los Angeles Times,* December 20, 1987, pp. 39–40.

5. This section is based on a number of published studies of news content. My own interpretation of television news content can be found in two studies coauthored with David C. Colby: "Epidemics and Agendas: The Politics of Nightly News Coverage of AIDS," *Journal of Health Policy, Politics and Law* (Summer 1991), and "The Mass-Mediated Epidemic: AIDS on the Nightly Network News," in Elizabeth Fee and Daniel Fox, eds., *AIDS: The Makings of a Chronic Disease* (Berkeley: University of California Press, 1991). Those focusing on print media include Edward Albert, "Illness and Deviance: The Response of the Press to AIDS," and Andrea Baker, "The Portrayal of AIDS in the Media: An Analysis of Articles in the *New York Times,*" both in Douglas A. Feldman and Thomas M. Johnson, eds., *The Social Dimension of AIDS: Method and Theory* (New York: Praeger, 1986), pp. 163–194; William A. Check, "Beyond the Political Model of Reporting: Nonspecific Symptoms in Media Communication about AIDS," *Reviews of Infectious Diseases* 9 (1987): 987–1000; and Panem, *AIDS Bureaucracy,* chap. 8.

6. Edward Albert, "Acquired Immune Deficiency Syndrome: The Victim and the Press," *Studies in Communications* 3 (1986): 135–158, at 136.

7. Ransdall Pierson, "Uptight about Gay News," *Columbia Journalism Review* (March/April 1982): 25–33. These concerns about maintaining individual privacy have recently surfaced again with the controversy about "outing," in the news—publicly revealing the sexual orientation of a famous person.

8. Shaw, "Coverage of AIDS Story," p. 38. Impressionistic evidence suggests that those media outlets that were most inclined to cover homosexuality were also those that reported AIDS earliest and most thoroughly—NBC more than CBS and ABC; *Newsweek* and *Time* more than *U.S. News and World Report;* the *Los Angeles Times* more than the *New York Times.*

9. Herbert J. Gans, *Deciding What's News* (New York: Vintage, 1979), chap. 7.

10. A good example is Christopher J. Bosso, "Setting the Agenda: Mass Media and the Discovery of Famine in Ethiopia," in Michael Margolis and Gary A. Mauser, eds., *Manipulating Public Opinion: Essays on Public Opinion as a Dependent Variable* (Pacific Grove, Calif.: Brooks/Cole, 1989), pp. 153–174.

11. See, for example, David Paletz and Robert Dunn, "Press Coverage of Civil Disorders: A Case Study of Winston-Salem, 1967," *Public Opinion Quarterly* 33 (1969): 328–345.

12. Robert Schmermund, comments in panel, "NIH Announces AZT," at the Harvard School of Public Health, April 1990.

13. See, especially, Bruno Latour and Steve Woolgar, *Laboratory Life: The Construction of Scientific Facts,* 2nd ed. (Princeton, N.J.: Princeton University Press, 1986), chap. 7.

14. A search of the Nexis database showed that the number of newspaper stories were halved from 1987 to 1989; Larry Thompson, "Commentary: With No Magic Cure in Sight, Dramatic Epidemic Loses Luster as News Story," *Washington Post,* June 13, 1989, health section, p. 7.

15. The downside to the concentration on the international AIDS conferences may be that as research progresses, there will be far less breaking news to report and, eventually, the news devoted to AIDS will wane. The 1989 Montreal confer-

ence was virtually pushed out of the news altogether by the Tiananmen Square massacre in China and its aftermath, and the only news that network reporters were able to squeeze on often referred to news that was not news at all, such as women being at particular risk or the possibility of treating AIDS as a chronic condition much as one treats diabetes. The 1990 San Francisco conference received considerable attention, but mostly from the "science-versus-politics" angle. The 1991 Florence conference was far less visible than either one—though in a comparatively slow news week—with the principal angles being repeats of the "no breakthrough" narrative from Montreal and the "science-versus-politics" story from San Francisco.

16. A useful sample of poll results is Eleanor Singer, Theresa F. Rogers, and Mary Corcoran, "The Polls—A Report: AIDS," *Public Opinion Quarterly* 51 (1987): 580–595.

17. For the most inclusive (some would say excessive) list, see Randy Shilts, *And the Band Played On: People, Politics and the AIDS Epidemic* (New York: St. Martin's Press, 1986).

18. Ed Siegel, "Who Calls the Tune? The Public, Not the Media," *Boston Globe*, January 10, 1990, p. 69.

19. See, for example, Dorothy Nelkin, *Selling Science: How the Press Covers Science and Technology* (San Francisco: W. H. Freeman, 1986); and John C. Burnham, *How Superstition Won and Science Lost: Popularizing Science and Health in the United States* (New Brunswick, N.J.: Rutgers University Press, 1987). For a highly useful critique of this position, see Christopher Dornan, "Some Problems in Conceptualizing the Issue of 'Science and the Media,'" *Critical Studies in Mass Communication* 7 (1990): 48–71.

20. Sharon Dunwoody and Michael Ryan, "The Credible Scientific Source," *Journalism Quarterly* 64 (1987): 21–27.

21. Ronald Mitsuyasu of UCLA quoted in the *Boston Globe*, December 22, 1989, p. 15. Cf. Gina Kolata, "Physicians Rid a Man's Body of AIDS Virus in Experiment," *New York Times*, December 19, 1989, p. A1.

22. For a key introduction to recent trends in the sociology of science, see Karin D. Knorr-Cetina and Michael Mulkay, eds., *Science Observed: Perspectives on the Social Study of Science* (Beverly Hills, Calif.: Sage Publications, 1983).

23. Frank M. Turner, "Public Science in Britain, 1880–1919," *Isis* 71 (1980): 589–608. For an excellent extension of Turner's concept, see Thomas F. Gieryn, George M. Bevins, and Stephen C. Zehr, "Professionalization of American Scientists: Public Science in the Creation/Evolution Trials," *American Sociological Review* 50 (1985): 392–409.

24. Recently, there have been some interesting exceptions. Kimberly Bergalis, the first person known to have acquired HIV from a dentist, released a text of a letter condemning state and local policymakers that was widely republished. That example of middlebrow Americana, the Sunday magazine supplement *Parade*, on July 7, 1991, published a lengthy interview with a seventeen-year-old hemophiliac with AIDS, Henry Nicols, who noted, "I am considered an 'innocent' victim. Of course, there are no 'guilty' victims" (p. 6). And on a *Nightline* program on April 30, 1991, that discussed doctors with AIDS, several persons living with AIDS were treated as authoritative sources in the opening segment, providing their informed opinions along with physicians and lawyers.

25. Ralph H. Turner, Joanne M. Nigg, and Denise Heller Paz, *Waiting for Disaster: Earthquake Watch in California* (Berkeley: University of California Press, 1986), p. 58.

26. See James Kinsella, *Covering the Plague: AIDS and the American Media* (New Brunswick, N.J.: Rutgers University Press, 1989), chaps. 2 and 8.

27. David Armstrong and Helen Kennedy, "Doc's Sex Arrest Ignites AIDS Fears," *Boston Herald,* June 25, 1991, p. 1.

28. Three outstanding examples following the life of a person with AIDS (PWA) were Jean Blake's profile of PWA Paul Cronan on WBZ-TV in Boston; Patricia Nayman's recurring series on Archie Harrison on National Public Radio's *All Things Considered;* and Steve Sternberg, "When AIDS Comes Home: The Life and Death of Tom Fox," *Atlanta Journal and Constitution,* August 20, 1989, Section E.

29. Jon Nordheimer, "AIDS Specter for Women: The Bisexual Man," *New York Times,* April 3, 1987, p. A1. Even more tellingly, the headline after the jump was "For Many Women, Fear of AIDS Lies in the Shadows of Male Bisexuality."

30. See especially Michael Schudson, *Discovering the News: A Social History of American Newspapers* (New York: Basic Books, 1978).

31. See Gaye Tuchman, "Making News by Doing Work: Routinizing the Unexpected," *American Journal of Sociology* 79 (1973): 110–131.

32. Robert E. Park, "Introduction," to Helen MacGill Hughes, *News and the Human Interest Story* (Chicago: University of Chicago Press, 1940), p. xxi.

33. Grace Ferrari Levine showed helplessness to be a theme in over 70 percent of the television stories she analyzed, both nationally and in New York. Such portrayals of helplessness tended to be heaviest in stories about the general public. See her "Learned Helplessness and the Evening News," *Journal of Communication* (Autumn 1977): 100–105, and "Learned Helplessness in Local TV News," *Journalism Quarterly* 63 (1986): 12–18, 23.

34. *Boston Sunday Globe,* October 29, 1989, p. A1.

35. From an interview with Dr. Anthony Fauci, reported in Lou Chibbaro, Jr., "Bush Meets Gay Men with AIDS During NIH Visit," *Washington Blade,* January 5, 1990, p. 9.

36. In their ongoing research on how the public learns from news accounts in different media, Russell Neuman, Marion Just, and Ann Crigler noted that, out of five issues, AIDS was the only one where the audiences learned significantly less from television news stories than from news magazines and newspapers. Apparently, their subjects were distracted by the focus upon individual human interest stories and away from the larger issues. See Neuman, Just, and Crigler, "Knowledge, Opinion and the News: The Calculus of Political Learning," paper prepared for delivery at the annual meeting of the American Political Science Association, Washington, D.C., September 1988.

37. Marvine Howe, "A Teary Doctor Tells of AIDS from a Needle," *New York Times,* January 11, 1990, p. B1.

38. JSB Center Brown Bag Presentation, September 1989.

39. Thomas Rosenstiel, in the *Los Angeles Times,* calendar section, November 27, 1988, p. 28.

40. Myron Belfer, presentation at Harvard AIDS Institute, AIDS in the 1990s, Boston, December 1989.

41. The classic statement of the volatility of news attention is G. Ray Funkhouser, "The Issues of the Sixties: An Exploratory Study of the Dynamics of Public Opinion," *Public Opinion Quarterly* 37 (1973): 62–75. If anything, of course, matters have become considerably more fast-forwarded than the years that Funkhouser studied.

10

Live from the Battlefield

Barrie Dunsmore

It is 1999. In a move reminiscent of Hitler's pact with Stalin on the eve of World War II, Iraqi President Saddam Hussein and the clerics of Iran form an unholy alliance. Iraq's Republican Guard is soon rolling into Kuwait, with Iranian air support, and it does not stop at the border with Saudi Arabia. This time the goal is not only Kuwait's oil fields but the bulk of Saudi Arabia's oil reserves as well. The U.S. president faces the same challenge President George Bush faced in 1990, except the stakes are now even higher. The industrialized nations will not tolerate having the lion's share of the world's oil supplies in the hostile hands of Iraq and Iran. Thus, the scene is set for Gulf War II.

At first glance, the situation looks much as it did nine years earlier. The issues, the combatants, and the battlefields are pretty much the same. But this time, weapons of mass destruction may be used—and importantly for this chapter, advanced technology will have changed more than just the weapons of war. In the first Gulf War, Forrest Sawyer of ABC News and Bob McKeowan of CBS News (with much help from their courageous and enterprising crews) brought us the liberation of Kuwait "live." Sawyer went in with a team of seven. They needed four trucks to carry their equipment: a flyaway portable ground station with 6-foot-wide dish, a generator to provide power, a tank truck to carry gasoline to run the generator, a camera, lights, and sound equipment—quite literally, well over a ton of stuff.

By Gulf War II, a two-person team will be able to go to war with a digital camera, a wideband cellular phone to uplink to the satellite, and a laptop computer to coordinate the transmission. The equipment will fit into two cases and weigh about 100 pounds. "Live from the battlefield" will no longer be primitive and cumbersome. As a technological feat, it will be routine.

Access to Coverage

The possibility of live television coverage from the battlefield raises major security, political, and journalistic questions. What are its likely military consequences? Does it actually threaten operational security? Could it affect or change the outcome of a battle or even the war? What are its political consequences? What would be the impact of the scenes of carnage on the American people, especially in terms of their support for a given foreign policy or a given war? Could a mistake in a live broadcast, which cost U.S. lives, cause such a public backlash that people might be willing to sacrifice some democratic freedoms in order to curb the networks? With so much at risk, should the U.S. military and the four major U.S. networks negotiate guidelines that would set conditions for live coverage? What might those guidelines be?

In this chapter I attempt to answer these questions by addressing them to the key people who have made the coverage decisions in past wars and will decide what we see of wars of the future. Generals such as Colin Powell, John Shalikashvili, and Norman Schwarzkopf have talked at length of their concerns about live coverage; network anchors Tom Brokaw, Peter Jennings, Ted Koppel, Dan Rather, and Bernard Shaw have revealed their feelings about its possible consequences. I have also interviewed battlefield commanders, high-level present and former government officials, and senior network news executives.

As one would expect, these people hold varying views on the subject, but there was one point on which they were nearly unanimous—live television coverage of future wars is inevitable. It will be done because it can be done. That does not imply approval. Indeed there are lots of misgivings, including among television people. Ted Koppel, the anchorman of *ABC News Nightline,* is one of those adamantly against the very idea of live coverage from the battlefield, when the United States is truly at war.

> [When] you have a declared war in which the United States of America is engaged presumably for either its survival or the survival of interests— you simply cannot have that co-existing with an unedited rendition of what is going on in the battlefield, knowing full well that everything that is sent out is going to be made available to the enemy. . . . During a war, there just has to be a certain application of common sense here. The essence of journalism lies in the editing process, not in training a camera on an event. That is not journalism.[1]

Pete Williams, who is now a correspondent for NBC News but is better known for his role as assistant secretary of defense for public affairs and Pentagon spokesman during the Gulf War, is more cynical about TV news. "I suppose there are purists who would argue that sending back a live picture isn't journalism. . . . It may not be journalism, but it is television, and that is a fact of life.[2]

Dan Rather, the anchorman and managing editor of the *CBS Evening News,* takes strong issue with both Koppel and Williams.

> Live coverage, when directed and carried out by professional journalists of experience, is journalism and can be very good journalism. I don't agree that it isn't journalism. I don't agree with "Well it's just television." Live coverage of the four dark days in Dallas during the Kennedy assassination—that was television. It also was a lot of damn good journalism.[3]

Those of us who were glued to our television sets for those dark days in 1963 would not quarrel with Rather, who played a major role in that coverage. But the issue before us is live television coverage—from the battlefield.[4] Among decisionmakers, there are obvious differences of opinion about the desirability of such coverage and more than a little trepidation about its consequences, as this chapter will reflect.

The extent of live television coverage from the battlefield is ultimately going to depend on what kind of war and what kind of battlefield. If it were to be a repeat of the Gulf War, the military would again have near-total control of access. The First Amendment guarantees freedom of the press, but there is nothing in the Constitution that compels the military to allow journalists to run free on a battlefield (or to get onto most military bases or even into the Pentagon, for that matter). If, however, the action was in circumstances similar to Haiti, where several hundred journalists were already on the scene with live cameras poised to bring you "The American Invasion—Live," the U.S. military would have much less control over what got on the air.

In terms of its ability to control access, the Pentagon appears to believe that its operations in the foreseeable future are more likely to follow the Haitian rather than the Gulf model. And General John Shalikashvili, chairman of the Joint Chiefs of Staff, and his military planners are already calculating the impact of live coverage as a potential threat to operational security.

> Any kind of involvement of U.S. military forces, whether it's for the most benign assistance in a humanitarian operation here or abroad, to an all-out war. . . . They all seem to be newsworthy so there will be live coverage.
> From my position as the chairman, the most immediate issue is how live coverage might adversely impact on the safety of troops and the security of this and on future operations. That's my main concern.[5]

It is important to note that operational security and the safety of U.S. troops are also concerns of network journalists and executives. Tom

Brokaw, the anchorman and managing editor of *NBC Nightly News,* is very sensitive to the problem.

> We will bring to bear on our judgments all the experiences that we've had and we'll err on the side of caution rather than on recklessness. God, the last thing I want on my personal conscience or my professional resume is that he caused the death of one, say nothing of 100 or 1,000 or 2,000 American lives because in his zeal to get on the air, he spilled secrets.[6]

Actually there is more common ground among military, government, and television news people on the subject of live coverage than I expected to find. Part of this can be attributed to people telling me what they think I want to hear. But I believe that much of it is genuine.[7] This is consistent with a major poll published in September 1995 by the Freedom Forum First Amendment Center.[8] The survey went to more than 2,000 military officers and 351 selected news media members who had been or were likely to be involved in covering military operations. Among its more encouraging findings: 82 percent of the military agreed with the statement, "The news media are just as necessary to maintaining U.S. freedom as the military." And 93 percent of the news media disagreed with the statement, "Members of the military are more interested in their own image than in the good of the country." But some old points of tension die hard. Sixty-four percent of the military officers still believe strongly, or somewhat strongly, that news media coverage of events in Vietnam harmed the war effort.[9]

The good news, however, is that the so-called Vietnam Syndrome, while not dead, is becoming less evident among top officers and public affairs people in the Pentagon. White House press secretary Michael McCurry says the Pentagon people he deals with are in full agreement with a policy of openness.

> This president and this administration have said we ought to have user-friendly rules for the press when it comes to coverage of military action. We need the support of the American people. . . . And much to my delight—the public affairs professionals I've worked with at the Pentagon—that is basically their attitude too. They have very sophisticated people doing public affairs activities there now.[10]

This sense that military attitudes are changing in the Pentagon is shared by David Gergen, who handled communications for President Ronald Reagan, and as an adviser to President Bill Clinton oversaw negotiations for television coverage of the Haiti landings.

> I'm much more optimistic than I was ten years ago. Certainly, having gone through the experience of Grenada and then going through it again on Haiti, I thought both sides were much more enlightened about the needs of the other side.

> In Grenada ten years ago, the Vietnam Syndrome was still very strong in the military and the distrust of the press was very strong.[11]

Actually, it is not the Vietnam War but the Gulf War that is the source of most of the current friction between the media and the military. A great deal has been written on the subject that need not be repeated in detail here.[12] Because attitudes toward future coverage will have been shaped, in part, by the Gulf experience, it bears mentioning. In a review of Gulf War coverage, a group of Washington bureau chiefs representing major news organizations concluded that "the combination of security review and the use of the pool system as a form of censorship made the Gulf War the most uncovered major conflict in modern American history."[13] Although some may see this as an overstatement, very few people remember that the ground war lasted only 100 hours and the coverage of that was very sparse. Many Americans were left with the impression that the Marines liberated Kuwait because the Marines encouraged news coverage. Actually, the Marine role was minor compared to that of the Seventh Army Corps, which did most of the fighting, but because it shunned reporters it got much less coverage or credit.

In a letter to then Defense Secretary Richard Cheney, the bureau chiefs wrote:

> Our sense is that virtually all major news organizations agree that the flow of information to the public was blocked, impeded or diminished by the policies and practices of the Department of Defense. Pools did not work. Stories and pictures were late or lost. Access to the men and women in the field was interfered with by a needless system of military escorts and copy review. These conditions meant we could not tell the public the full story of those who fought the nation's battle.[14]

There was not a lot of sympathy in the Pentagon for these complaints. As Secretary Cheney said later in an interview, "It upsets my friends in the press corps when I say it was the best-covered war in history. They don't like this at all. They fundamentally disagree because they felt managed and controlled."[15]

Adding to the news media's frustration was an American public that did not at all feel cheated; quite the contrary. According to a poll taken by the Times Mirror Center for the People and the Press published just after the war,[16] eight out of ten Americans described the news coverage of the war as excellent or good, with 45 percent rating it excellent. Nevertheless, news organizations were determined that having been frozen out of Grenada, patronized in Panama, and now burned in the Gulf, there must be a new statement of principles to govern future arrangements for news coverage of the U.S. military in combat. A proposed set of ten guidelines was sent to Cheney in June 1991.

There was nothing very radical in what was proposed. The thrust of it was that independent reporting should be the "principal means of coverage" and that pools should be limited to "the very first stages of deployment—the initial twenty-four to thirty-six hours—and should then be rapidly disbanded." It was the pools that infuriated most news organizations because they saw them as the military's insidious instruments of control.[17] There was, however, one point in the proposed principles that, not surprisingly, became a major stumbling block. It read, "News material—words and pictures—will not be subject to prior military security review." This was an issue on which the military was absolutely unwilling to yield. And so, on March 11, 1992, a nine-point "Statement of Principles for News Coverage of Combat" was jointly adopted by the news media and the Pentagon. Most of the points were essentially what the news media had suggested. On that tenth point, however, prior security review, the two sides could only agree to disagree. Although live TV coverage is not mentioned explicitly in the statement of principles, the military's refusal to bend on the question of prior security review suggests it wants to maintain this instrument to control such coverage. On the face of it, prior security review would appear to preclude live coverage. How do you censor a live report when the action is ongoing, the correspondent is ad-libbing, and no one knows the outcome of the event?

There is one final point before I proceed to look at the potential consequences of telecasting live from the battlefield and the prospects for sensible guidelines. Live TV coverage of war is, of course, not the exclusive purview of the U.S. television networks. In fact, nowadays a major international event draws camera crews from the networks of dozens of countries, some friends of the United States, some not. The internationalization of the news media is certain to increase. When someone launches their own cable news network, who knows what alliances they might form and what allegiances they will feel? For the U.S. military, this seriously complicates the issue of press access. It is a complex issue and would certainly be a worthy subject for another study. But for purposes of this chapter, I am focusing only on the U.S. networks: ABC, CBS, CNN, and NBC. At least for the next decade, in time of war they would be the sources of any live coverage for the vast majority of Americans. And any guidelines or accommodations to which the U.S. networks might agree would certainly be imposed on foreigners by the U.S. military, if it could impose conditions.

Possible Consequences—the Military View

The Gulf War of 1991 was the first war in history in which live television cameras were able to capture some scenes or elements of the actual battle. As noted earlier, the technology was cumbersome and relatively primitive compared to what will be possible in the next few years. Still, people all over the world were able to sit at home and watch bombs landing in Baghdad, Scud missiles hitting in Israel and Saudi Arabia, Egyptian troops crossing into Kuwait on the first day of the ground war, and the liberation of Kuwait City as these events were actually happening. This introduced a new element to warfare in which the impact of television coverage was exponentially enhanced. As one who has spent his entire adult life as a television news correspondent, during which I have covered a few wars, I was struck by the power of the live picture from the battlefield. Twenty-four years earlier, I had been present at a historic moment on a battlefield, but then the presence of the television camera was barely noticed.

I was with the first group of Israeli soldiers to reach the Suez Canal during the June 1967 Middle East War, early on a Friday. The film had to be driven back through a tank-and-body-littered Sinai up to Tel Aviv. There was no satellite ground station in Israel at that time, so it next had to be put on a plane to Rome, where it would then be processed and edited. After all that, it finally got on the air—Sunday night. By that time, there was a cease-fire, people had read all about the capture of the Suez in the Saturday and Sunday papers, and my big scoop was, at best, a little footnote to history.

I am willing to admit to a trace of envy as I watched my ABC News colleague Forrest Sawyer telecasting live from Kuwait City as U.S. troops arrived. But I was also genuinely concerned about the potential conse-quences of this technological breakthrough. Among the questions that came to mind was, "What would have happened had there been live television coverage of D-Day?" My own sense then was that it would have been a dis-aster. The U.S. commander for Operation Desert Storm, General Norman Schwarzkopf, was also thinking about such consequences, and he was not happy about such prospects. To the extent that he could control access, Schwarzkopf tried to make sure that his mission was not threatened by such coverage.

Later I was interested to see Schwarzkopf being quoted as saying that had there been live television coverage of D-Day, "there would have been no D-Day plus two." In other words, in his view, the Normandy landings would have failed. That conformed to my own analysis and in our interview for this chapter that was the first thing I asked him about.

Schwarzkopf replied that, "frankly, the early hours of D-Day were a debacle. But more importantly, the German reaction was that the invasion was still coming at the Pas de Calais. As a result they never committed their reserves into the D-day area until it was too late. I think most military his-torians agree that had the Germans committed all their reserves immediate-ly into the D-Day area, that we would never have gained a foothold at Normandy."

Question: So you anticipate that live TV cameras would have told the Germans that without any question Normandy was the spot?

Answer: Absolutely. The record is replete with indications that some of the commanders were calling back trying to describe what was happening and general headquarters just disregarded it all as—these guys are overreacting and this is a feint. But I think the magnitude of the effort there, had it been seen by the German general staff, it would have been very obvious to them that this was the main invasion.[18]

General Colin Powell, former chairman of the Joint Chiefs of Staff, was equally adamant that live television would have turned D-Day into an Allied defeat. It is his position that live television simply cannot be allowed during operations such as D-Day.

> The thing speaks for itself. If there was live coverage of D-Day and Hitler could sit in Germany in Berlin and listen to the network anchors describing the confusion on the beach . . . there would have been no D-day plus one. Anything that gives away an advantage, an operational advantage to the enemy, has to be looked at most carefully, and I am sure that D-Day would have been a censored operation. It would have to be a censored operation. You could take all the pictures you want, but they wouldn't have been released in real time.[19]

On its face, this would appear to be a pretty compelling argument against live coverage. No television journalist or executive would like to be held responsible for a U.S. military defeat of those proportions. But not all military historians agree. General Bernard Trainor, who is a former *New York Times* military correspondent, says that a TV camera would only have been able to show a small segment of the battlefield and that anyway the German High Command knew full well that this was the real landing. The problem, says Trainor, was Hitler. "What deluded Hitler was his conviction that it was a feint, and his lack of understanding of naval and amphibious matters. [He believed] you could have a feint like that and very quickly shift your forces, which you can't."[20]

Several people, including ABC News anchor Peter Jennings, took exception to the D-Day analogy on the grounds that you can't just insert one element of 1990s technology (live TV) into a 1940s situation and draw conclusions with any validity. That's a little like asking what would have happened at Gettysburg if the Confederacy had air power? The question has to be: What would the Normandy landings be like with 1990s technology across the board and on both sides? White House press secretary Michael McCurry made a similar point. "D-Day would not have been D-Day [as we know it] had CNN been reporting live, because factoring in CNN reporting into the mission is now a given part of military planning. They do planning exercises in which Christiane Amanpour showing up for CNN is part of the exercise."[21]

Even if we concede those arguments, there is another problem that live television might have created on D-Day, a problem that seems certain to arise with live cameras covering future major U.S. military offensives. Schwarzkopf says that if people back at headquarters in Washington had been watching the action in Normandy, the armchair quarterbacks would have had a field day, which could have caused Eisenhower to consider pulling back.

> Even Eisenhower in the very early hours was troubled by what went on. I think it [live coverage] could very easily have caused people to start second guessing very early in the game as to whether or not we should continue with the invasion of the beaches we had selected. And if we had been kicked off the beaches it probably would have been a minimum of a year and by most estimates two years before we could have launched another invasion.[22]

NBC's Tom Brokaw expanded on that, predicting that the problem of the second guessers would have gone far beyond the staff officer–critics in the Pentagon.

> Not just the folks in Washington. All the talk shows. There would be armchair strategists on all our programs. *Nightline* would have devoted a special to it. We would all be on the air [saying], "The price has been very high, we've only gotten halfway up the beach, we're stuck there for two days now."
>   I think there are consequences to that.[23]

According to General Colin Powell, one consequence is that television, particularly when it involves the anchors, has a way of setting the agenda, which can have a negative impact on the operation. "In today's environment, the television anchors essentially are almost keeping a death watch on an operation and I think it would have been very difficult to have that hour by hour coverage of something like D-Day."[24] Powell, a few weeks into the NATO operation in Bosnia, was scornful of the television coverage there, particularly the attention given to the building of the pontoon bridge across the Sava River, which apparently took longer to construct than the military originally said it would.

> It's been sort of fun to sit here and watch Bosnia. That goddamn bridge. This was not news but it was made news because all those anchors were over there waiting and since we didn't accommodate them by having a casualty early on, they watched the bridge. And so it was, "Well, it's snowing here, boy it's cold, it's going to be hard, and this bridge just isn't going in."

And here's a picture of a humvee [the jeep's successor] spinning its wheels in the mud, which I saw every hour on the hour for almost a day. What's that got to do with anything? Humvees have been spinning their wheels forever. But now it's an international event because Rather, Jennings, and all the rest of them are there and they are going to get on the evening news, not because there's news, but because they're anchors. . . . The fact that bridges have trouble with high water would have meant nothing to anybody if it hadn't been covered by television.[25]

General Powell is also concerned that when television makes a huge issue over something like that pontoon bridge, everyone from the president on down gets caught up in it. And so, instead of planning grand strategy, the chairman of the Joint Chiefs becomes swamped with a daily barrage of questions from the White House, the Congress, and the press about when that bridge will be ready. I spoke to the current Joint Chiefs' chairman, General John Shalikashvili, before U.S. troops went to Bosnia but when contingency plans were being made for the Bosnia operation. He anticipated there would be some live coverage and he too was concerned about the impact of Washington "second guessers" on his commanders.

Maybe there's some good in the fact that commanders know there is going to be live coverage, and they will work their tails off to ensure there isn't a debacle. The bad aspect is . . . they're going to become timid because they know mistakes happen. They know the more active you are, proactive you are, the more mistakes are probably going to happen. And because none of us wants to become the subject of ridicule, we will grow up a group of leaders who will prefer to be timid, because they don't want to be second guessed back here.[26]

Timidity is really just the beginning of what military commanders worry about when they contemplate live coverage from the battlefield. Schwarzkopf recounts an incident reported live on one of the networks that could have cost him the strategic surprise of the Gulf War. That surprise was the "left hook" maneuver, according to which the U.S. Seventh Army Corps started west of Kuwait, went north into Iraq, curved around to the east and then came in behind the Iraqi forces who were dug in to repel a direct frontal assault on their positions in Kuwait.

According to Schwarzkopf, if the Iraqis had been carefully watching U.S. television, they would have picked up a vital clue as to his strategy for the ground war.

It was reported that at this time, right now, we are witnessing an artillery duel between the 82nd Airborne Division and the Iraqis. If they [the Iraqis] had any kind of halfway decent intelligence, they would have made note of the time . . . and through their intelligence network they would have pinpointed the location of the 82nd Airborne. Until that time everything they ever saw of the 82nd was on the east coast. All of a sudden they would have found the 82nd way to the west and it would certainly have telegraphed something to them.[27]

Fortunately for the United States, the Iraqis did not have "halfway decent intelligence," and they did not pick up this information that should have told them that U.S. troops were massing 200 miles west of Kuwait City. Therefore, they took no steps to prepare for that major flanking maneuver.

Schwarzkopf went on to explain why knowledge about the "Order of Battle" is so important. It is the job of military intelligence to collect information about all of the various enemy units on the battlefield and to determine the type, size, equipment, and capabilities of each unit. Then, if they can establish the location of these units on the battlefield, they can calculate the other side's probable plan of action. His concern was that those little details that are crucial to military intelligence are precisely the kinds of things that a reporter might inadvertently disclose, especially if that reporter had limited military experience. And the information would be even more valuable if it was broadcast live because then it would be information fixed to a specific time. That would make it much more useful for intelligence analysts in determining what the opponent was planning to do next.[28]

There are other inadvertent errors that when made on live television cannot be edited or taken back and so pose a potential threat to operational security. At least twice during the Gulf War, once in Israel and once in Saudi Arabia, television correspondents reported live precisely where a Scud missile had landed. I was more than a little vexed when one of my colleagues went on the air and, in effect, told the Iraqis that a Scud had just missed our hotel in downtown Riyadh by about a block. We journalists were not the target, of course, but we were directly across the street from General Schwarzkopf's command post, which presumably the Iraqis would have been delighted to hit.

As it happens, the Iraqi Scuds were notoriously inaccurate. But Scud missiles aside, even in a simple artillery exchange, any artillery officer will tell you that it would be extremely helpful to know where shells are landing. Artillery people want to know if they have done any damage and if they have inflicted any casualties. That's why they send out forward artillery observers. Live TV might do that job for them. Likewise, if the camera were to be showing a bombing raid, bomb damage assessment is an extremely useful tool in determining the effectiveness of a given raid. If the opponents can see on television what damage has been done, they can decide whether or not to revisit the target. Those things may appear to be obvious. But there are even seemingly harmless scenes a live camera might show that would be helpful to an enemy.

I remember having a run-in with the Israeli censors during the 1973 Middle East War. I had just returned from the Sinai Desert and was preparing my report for that evening's news. Among the pictures we had taken that day were a few shots of an Israeli convoy, just sitting on the road in Sinai, waiting to move closer toward the Egyptian front. The censor said, "You can't show that." I asked, "Why not?" He replied, "That convoy includes trucks carrying bridging equipment." I knew that, but I didn't consider it a huge military secret that the Israelis might be planning to cross the Suez Canal (which they did, a few days later). Whether or not the Israelis considered it a big secret, they censored my report that night.

In retrospect, I can certainly see that if this had been an uncensored live report, I would have inadvertently told the Egyptians that Israel was planning to cross the canal. They probably would be assuming the same thing, but I would have also revealed that at a specific time that day, Israel had that capability, already on trucks, somewhere deep in the Sinai Desert. I'm not suggesting this would have changed the course of the war, but I use the example to illustrate that even something as apparently benign as a camera pan of a convoy just sitting on the road might show the other side a few helpful things. These are some of the pitfalls of live coverage.

Whatever potential problems Schwarzkopf may have had with such coverage, he minimized them by setting up military roadblocks and closing off access to the battlefield. He was able to do that because the Gulf War was fought in a Middle Eastern desert in which the U.S. military could exercise almost complete control. It could keep journalists out of the country and, for the most part, away from the front lines. ABC's Peter Jennings does not find this surprising.

> I'm sure military men will tell you the contrary, but I don't believe them. The military would prefer to fight a war in secret. They would prefer that we were not there, except utterly and totally under their control, because it is the nature of military campaigns to have as much under control as you can. . . . If I were a military commander, the last thing I would ever want is the risk that one body . . . should be allowed to be exploited by people who are opposed to either the administration or the particular engagement.[29]

But the Gulf War may have been an exception in terms of the military's ability to impose strict control over a journalist's access to the front. Today's military leadership expects that future involvements of U.S. forces are much more likely to occur in places such as Haiti, Somalia, or Bosnia. Such actions are also more apt to be so-called military contingencies, as opposed to all-out wars.

Common to all these places is the fact that they are accessible to the international news media, and the U.S. military will be in no position to tightly control access to the battlefield, a battlefield that could be any street in Port-au-Prince or Sarajevo. For the military, that creates a whole new set of problems. Admiral Paul David Miller, the former commander in chief of

U.S. Atlantic Forces and the commander of the Haiti "contingency," made dealing with the issue of live coverage one of his top priorities.

[The Haiti] contingency was laced with media coverage from the very beginning all the way through the build-up to the crescendo of it [almost] happening, when we were just hours away from it being displayed on international television—live. . . . I put the media coverage right at the top block of my operational planning. And it was factored into everything I did, so much so that in my control room I even had a large screen TV, split on the major channels and CNN, to make sure that I was factoring that real time coverage in on what we were thinking about.[30]

One of Admiral Miller's principal problems was that, with 400 reporters and dozens of live cameras spread throughout the country, there was no way the United States could sneak into Haiti. "What I needed was tactical surprise. . . . It's going to become more and more difficult to achieve strategic surprise. And the commanders have to establish a relationship with the media for tactical surprise. . . . You want to be able to say, 'For the first 15 minutes, the first 30 minutes, pick a time, that you don't want this covered [live].'"[31]

Because the whole world knew the United States was about to invade Haiti, the tactical surprise Miller wanted was to be able to invade at a time and place of his choosing, without the Haitian military being able to watch it all happening on CNN. As things turned out, of course, there was no invasion as such, but if there had been, the U.S. networks appear to have been willing to grant Miller a chance for that tactical surprise. The way in which the military, the government, and the television media interacted over Haiti may well be a model for the future, which I will examine in greater detail in the section on "Guidelines."

Although it was never a major military problem, Haiti was a useful learning experience for the military, a lesson not lost on the Joint Chiefs' chairman. General Shalikashvili appears to have concluded that maneuvers such as General Schwarzkopf's strategic surprise in the Gulf War, which require strict secrecy, may not be possible when there are live television cameras on the battlefield. "When he was worrying about how he was going to hide the fact that he was doing a left hook . . . if he knew that he could not keep [live cameras out] and in future, I submit you will not be able to, then he would have not been able to do this maneuver. He would have had to develop his plan differently."[32] Schwarzkopf's reaction puts a heavy burden on proponents of live coverage because he says if he lost his element of surprise there would have been higher U.S. casualties.

Certainly, the Gulf War was one where if there had been live television coverage, I think, if we had telegraphed the plan to the Iraqis, I think they would have redeployed their troops in such a way, that the outcome would have been the same but the casualty figures I think, would have been higher. . . . We would have paid a much higher price in lives of the troops.[33]

Shalikashvili takes a more philosophical position, suggesting, as did Admiral Miller, that in the future military planners will need to be much more conscious of the possibility of live television coverage when they are developing their battle plans.

> From a military perspective it's unfortunate, because it's enough that you have to worry about the enemy, you have to worry about the weather, you have to worry about how much support you have, and you have to consider the tides. Now you have the press.[34] . . .
> Just as you cannot change the tides, although you wish that you could if you were MacArthur as you went into Inchon, you have to play with whatever you were dealt with. To the extent you've got to say, I've got this open press, so I've got to figure out how I am going to do this and still be successful, so [live TV] becomes somewhat like the tides.[35]

These, then, are some of the potential military consequences of live television coverage from the battlefield and some thoughts by former and present military leaders about such consequences and how to cope with or alleviate them. One thing that was notable, but not surprising, about the interviews for this chapter was that the military appears to have given a lot more thought to the issue of live coverage from the battlefield than have the people in television news. This will give the military an advantage when the issue becomes full blown, which some day, in the not too distant future, it inevitably will. The military people also have some tricks in their bag and options that they don't want to discuss publicly. We explore these in the following section about the perspective of the television networks.

Possible Consequences—the Television View

For people who work in the television industry, "live" is fundamentally different from all other forms of broadcasting. Those not accustomed to being on television discover that going "live" rather than being recorded on tape or film hyper-stimulates their "fight or flight" hormones. As the adrenaline level shoots up, the heart begins to race, the mouth goes dry, the muscles become taut, and all of the senses are heightened. For those who appear on television regularly, the symptoms are not so acute, but there is still a measurable physical change. Those who are successful on television are able to focus this energy into an enhanced performance. Most people are just plain scared—and it shows. The viewer senses all of this, admires the skillful performer, feels sorry for the poor sap who can't cope, and probably without even realizing it is energized too by the fact that the performance is live.

Walter Porges, the former ABC News vice president for news practices (the news division's legal and ethics watchdog), expressed a widely held view among television people about the world of difference between live and taped reports.

> There are two huge differences. One: the impact is much greater when you can say, "This is happening as we speak folks." The other thing is, "We don't know how this will end." We go on the air with the hijacking in the desert for instance. There are these planes. We don't know what's going to happen next. Are they going to blow up the planes? Are they going to kill people? . . . I think that "live-versus-this happened a few hours ago" makes a tremendous psychological difference.[36]

It is this psychological difference that has made "live from the battle-field" the dream of many people in television news, going back to the early days of the Vietnam War. The Vietnam War is now remembered as the United States' first television war. Today's conventional wisdom also has it that by bringing the war into their living rooms, television caused the American people to lose faith in the war effort and to demand that it be brought to an end. No one would dispute that the infamous television pictures of U.S. soldiers using Zippo lighters to torch a Vietnamese village—"in order to save it"—were lasting images burned into the American psyche. And it seems reasonable to assume that the daily drumbeat of pictures of the horrors of war would weaken the resolve of the American people.

It is worth noting, however, that there was an active U.S. military presence in Vietnam for some fourteen years—more than three times as long as the U.S. involvement in World War II. It can also be argued that it was the number of U.S. dead and wounded that finally turned the American people against the war; also there was the feeling that the reasons for fighting the war and the way in which it was being fought ultimately did not make any sense. By this I do not mean to minimize the impact of television. My argument is simply that the impact was less than it would have been had there been live coverage.

Local newscasts throughout the United States have been making much of their "live" coverage for a number of years, apparently in the belief that viewers would be attracted and ratings would rise. The networks later got on the bandwagon, *Prime Time—Live* on ABC being perhaps the most inauspicious example. Many of these efforts have been unsuccessful because of the technological problems involved in such broadcasts. However, as noted earlier in this chapter, in three to five years live coverage will available almost anywhere on the globe, which sets up a whole new series of dilemmas for the networks. Now that they're on the brink of having the technological capability to transmit live from the battlefield, some key people in the networks, such as Ted Koppel, are openly questioning the very idea.

Answer: I realize that I'm speaking heresy here as a journalist, but why do we have to have live coverage of a war?

Question: Because it's there?

Answer: All kinds of things are there. You know, the secret files of the CIA are there. The president going to the bathroom is there. We apply taste and common sense in other areas, why can't we apply it here?[37]

Dan Rather, however, makes the case that live television is an important new instrument for quickly getting the best available information to the people, which, he says, is an essential element of U.S. democracy.

> I will bet every time on giving individual citizens the most, best possible information, believing that in the main and in most circumstances, given that, they will make the right decisions about what the country's policies should be, and that includes the policy about war. . . . That's why I say that live television is another tool for getting the best available information to individual citizens in a fast manner. It isn't always orderly.[38]

Cheryl Gould, vice president of NBC News and former senior producer of the *Nightly News,* says networks go live on some occasions because not doing so would be withholding information from the American people, which the networks have no right to do. In this area of the people's right to know, she suggests, live battlefield coverage might be analogous to election night coverage. "When we have the ability to know right after or before the polls are even closed what the outcome is going to be with some precision, because the technology is there, polling technology, not to mention broadcast technology, we as an industry have always claimed it's the public's right to know."[39] Her argument is that if you have live pictures of a battle coming into your control room and if things are going badly for the United States, you have no right to withhold that information from your viewers any more than you have the right to keep the outcome of the election a secret.

This argument is regularly challenged by network television critics who counter that by broadcasting only a small portion of the information gathered each day, the networks are withholding information from the people all the time. In this case, Pete Williams, also of NBC News (although clearly reflecting his years at the Pentagon), is unmoved by the arguments in favor of live coverage and tends to agree with network critics who say live coverage is not a public's-right-to-know issue. "I just think it's hard to articulate a sound national reason that will get applause outside the

National Press Club for live coverage of the battlefield. . . . It's hard to stake a claim that live coverage has to be there for any reason other than the fact that we can do it and it would sure be neat."[40]

Bernard Shaw, a principal anchor at CNN, is one of the few TV journalists who has ever reported "live" from a battlefield. In his case, the battlefield was downtown Baghdad as U.S. bombs fell on the Iraqi capital in the opening hours of the Gulf War. As an experienced practitioner, Shaw too has serious reservations about live coverage of war.

> I would be worried about lack of perspective, because no matter where you were, you would be operating with no overview of what was going on. And by your mere presence and what is happening to your senses, what you're hearing, what you're feeling, indeed what you're smelling, I would be afraid would cloud your judgment. And it might find you exaggerating, however accurately you were reporting, exaggerating what you were seeing.[41]

What Shaw is getting at is the fear factor. Very few people who have been in combat have not felt this emotion, and he is obviously concerned that, in a live broadcast situation, this fear could and probably would color the judgment of even seasoned reporters. It is one thing to be shot at and write about it after the fact. It is quite another thing to talk about it to a million or more viewers as the shooting or bombing is actually taking place. Some people would do this better than others, but the emotional strain on the reporter is obviously one of the potential weaknesses of live coverage of war.

Another concern among network officials was voiced by Paul Friedman, the executive vice president of ABC News. As the man responsible for running ABC News on a day-to-day basis, Friedman worries about what would happen if his news team and their live capability equipment should fall into the hands of the enemy.

> What would I do if some of my people were taken by an enemy group, and they said, "Put us on live on the ABC television network or your people will die. We have not been able to tell the world our story. And we would like to show you pictures of what American forces have done to our country earlier in the conflict. And we want to do that in our own way, in our own time, and you do that or your people will die." That's not a decision I look forward to.[42]

Although this is a hypothetical case, Friedman has already made a real life decision along those lines. In June of 1985 a hijacked TWA plane was on the ground in Beirut. At the time, Friedman was the head of ABC News overseas coverage, based in London. What he calls some "eager beaver" in New York telephoned the technicians in London to find out if it would be possible to get a live picture from Beirut, by bouncing a microwave signal to Cyprus and from there via satellite to New York. Before hearing the real answer, Friedman decided to say it could not be done.

> They came to me with that question and I said, "I don't want to know what the truth is, but tell those people back in New York that it can't be done." I didn't want to be in a position of having, in that case Charlie Glass, taken and his captors saying to him, "Put us on the air live or you will die." That would have been a piece of cake for them to do. So I ducked it, essentially, by pretending that technologically it could not be done. But in fact, it could have been done.[43]

Friedman was the only TV executive to raise that particular problem, but the television people with whom I spoke seemed generally to see more liabilities in live coverage than benefits.

One overriding concern among all is the possibility of divulging information during a live broadcast that might lead to the deaths of U.S. troops. Tom Johnson, the president of CNN, fully expects that his network will provide live battlefield coverage, but he concedes he's worried about it.

> I think it is definitely a danger; there is no doubt it's a danger. Whenever battlefield conditions occur, that is live battlefield conditions, there will be almost of necessity some types of coordination [with the U.S. military] so that in no way would we jeopardize movements of troops, movements of ships, anything that would endanger the lives of troops on any side. . . . I think you would have in the Congress and God knows where-else, you'd have a firestorm if "live" led to loss of lives.[44]

Firestorm was also a word used by Tom Brokaw when he considered the consequences of a network blunder that cost U.S. lives. "I think that the networks are fat, dumb targets and if they do something as venal as giving away secrets, however accidental it may be, then they would have to stand what I think would be a withering firestorm of criticism coming in. And I don't know what the long-term consequences for the First Amendment would be."[45] The question of how a public backlash might threaten the First Amendment was one I posed to everyone. Brokaw's feeling that it would depend on how serious the mistake had been was typical.

> Certainly, there would be a lot of legislation right out of the box, and people would say, "We're going to change this. You're not going to be able to broadcast live when this nation goes to war. As an instrument of national policy the networks will not be able to broadcast." I mean, there will be a bill. You can count on it, just like that. Whether it will be successful or not I can't say. I think it depends on the magnitude of the blunder.[46]

I should say that the issue of a public backlash that could threaten the First Amendment has not been given much thought by people in television news, in government, or in the military. When it is raised, almost everyone sees it as a potential problem; but as they say in the military, it is not on anyone's radar at the moment.

One issue that was on the radar screens of people in television had to do with what steps they felt the military might be prepared to take in order to preserve its operational security and all that phrase implies. Ted Koppel, like most of his television colleagues, is skeptical about the military's willingness to cooperate in live coverage.

> If there is a war and if indeed the Pentagon permits live coverage, they will do so only until the first disaster happens and then they're going to cut it off immediately. I think it makes more sense to anticipate that's going to happen, rather than say, "Oh goody, the military is going to let us cover everything live." You know damn well that the first time that the enemy derives intelligence from that live coverage and comes back and kills a number of American service people, that's going to end. And it's inevitable that would happen.[47]

Peter Jennings goes even further, suggesting the military would be quite prepared to take extreme measures if it feels live TV has become a threat.

> My sense is that on the battlefield, the military holds all the cards and all the weapons. So it seems to me that in a situation in which the military was utterly determined to dominate, there is no negotiation. If the military is absolutely determined to prevail, it can suggest, stop or we'll shoot.[48]

Hodding Carter, the State Department spokesman during the Carter administration (and a former Marine), is quite sure the military is capable of coercive or even drastic action.

> There has never been any time I can think of, in which the forces in the field actually allowed the press to do something they thought was going to endanger their lives. They will prevent—they will do whatever they have to do to prevent—because they are in a life and death situation as they define it.[49]

For his part, CNN's Shaw, who covered the war in Vietnam, feels any television journalist the military considered a threat could easily become the victim of so-called friendly fire.

> There is no civility on a battlefield. There is no civility in war. So anything is possible. We certainly know of instances in Vietnam, when American troops fragged [used fragmentation-grenades against] their officers, their senior noncoms and one another. What's to prevent that from happening to journalists? We usually are not perceived as being great supporters.[50]

When I raised the possibility with General Schwarzkopf that he might be willing to take physical action, such as shooting out the tires of a TV vehicle to prevent a security breach, he laughed at the suggestion. But the military was a lot more frank when it was briefing television news executives on the Haiti contingency operation. CNN's president, Tom Johnson, remembers that the networks were warned, very bluntly, as to what would happen if lights were turned on during the expected U.S. landings.

> General Sheehan, Jack Sheehan [Admiral Paul Miller's successor as commander in chief of U.S. Atlantic Forces] said that if necessary, the choppers could take out the lights if we put lights on troopers coming down the streets. And they told me this, I mean, this is not hearsay, . . . that rules of engagement permitted taking out lights. Well I could have gotten a lot of people in the media killed [if CNN had insisted on using lights].[51]

General Powell completely agreed that the military had every right to take such action. He recalled that he had actually "giggled" at the live television coverage of Somalia landings. He thought turning the lights on the Navy Seals was silly, but he calculated that the sight of these heavily armed men emerging from the ocean would scare the Somalis. However, he added, if the Seals had been threatened, the situation would have quickly changed. "If those Seals had come under fire, I can assure you they would have shot everyone in sight, including the light holders. Those lights would not have stayed on if those Seals felt they were in danger. . . . If they had blown the lights away that would just have been one of the costs of being in a conflict area."[52]

Walter Porges remembered an occasion when he had assigned an ABC News crew to get pictures of the Sixth Fleet, which was on maneuvers in the Mediterranean. When the civilian plane carrying the crew neared the fleet, it was told to move immediately or it would be shot down. This would have been legal under provisions of international law defining military airspace. Nevertheless, it is another reminder to the networks that the military can play rough if they think they are being threatened.

General Powell pulled absolutely no punches about what steps he would take to keep live television from jeopardizing any mission he was commanding. He would lock the TV people up.

> We never hit a situation like that in Desert Storm because there was never any part of the operation that was in such real time that what you see would have caused us much operational problem. If we had been losing the battle, in Desert Storm let's say, and the manner in which we were losing it was immediately known to the enemy, I'd have locked all of you up and you could have taken me to every court in the land. And guess who would have won that battle? I mean the American people would have stripped your skin off.[53]

Short of such drastic steps, the military has another option that it is generally reluctant to talk about but that television people just assume could happen to them—namely, electronic jamming of their live television signal.

The top-level military officers I interviewed would concede nothing on this point. But Dennis Boxx, formerly the Pentagon spokesperson and now spokesperson of the CIA, told me that when the Haiti contingency was being planned, jamming was considered if the networks would not agree to hold off on live coverage for the first few hours after the U.S. landings.

Answer: It [jamming] was discussed. You know, if the networks wouldn't agree to the blackout. . . . I think we had discussed, not with the networks but among ourselves, a four-hour blackout. And if they wouldn't agree to that, which we knew they wouldn't, then perhaps jamming was an option. But that was immediately abandoned as, I guess, a pretty silly idea.

Question: Why would that not be a serious option?

Answer: I think it would be operationally. Politically, I think it's a non-starter. I don't see many administrations being willing to stand up to the heat that would generate.[54]

But Boxx may be overestimating the political costs of deliberately interfering with network transmissions. In poll after poll, the military shows up miles ahead of the networks in terms of public respect and confidence. There may actually be a political benefit to an administration taking on those powerful networks. Margaret Tutwiler, the State Department spokesperson during the Bush administration and longtime adviser to former Secretary of State James A. Baker III, feels strongly that the public would support putting limits on network coverage. "I think Joe Six-Pack sitting out in his home in Sioux City—his first reaction is going to be, 'Screw the press.' If a military general stands up and says, 'This [live coverage] is an interference, it's putting young men's lives in harm's way,' the networks are going to lose that battle."[55]

It is hard to believe that the military itself is unaware of such sentiment and that it would not be willing to exploit it. Cliff Bernath, who is currently the senior deputy assistant secretary of defense for public affairs, left no doubt in my mind that electronic jamming of live television transmissions remains a viable military option. "As the media deal with the ethics of live coverage, we have to deal with the ethics of protecting the operation, and how far and what means we have available to do that. One means is jamming. Is it legal? I don't know. I'll probably go to jail for saying it, but it's one of the tools that's available."[56] It seems unlikely that Bernath will be sent to jail for stating the obvious. The networks are certainly aware of that option and will not be surprised if it is used.

To sum up, among senior television news people, live coverage from the battlefield carries with it a host of potentially negative consequences. Then why do it? The answer is quite simple: competition. In every TV executive suite, there are banks of television screens showing what every major channel is carrying. The sound is always turned down, but the pictures never stop flickering. If, during the next war, one of those screens lights up with "live from the battlefield" coverage, the pressure to duplicate it will be virtually irresistible. No matter all the academic and philosophical arguments against doing so, the nature of the business is such that if one goes, they all go, and there is always an enormous temptation to be the one to go first. There are differing theories as to why this is the case. The most benign, and the one I lean toward, is that this is a very competitive business. Every good reporter in any medium longs for the big scoop. It is often how reputations are made and how salaries are calculated. A less charitable explanation (which doesn't negate the first) is that the networks are in a dog-eat-dog fight for commercial revenue and they will stoop to anything to improve their ratings. Colin Powell is one who takes this view, and he says the situation will get worse if, as now seems likely, there are several all-news channels.

> I believe that commercial competitive pressures of an increasing number of all-day-long news programs that require advertising to remain on the air will make it much more difficult to display the kind of seasoned news judgment that might be appropriate. . . . We [the military] should always be suspicious that the media will break a secret just for the purpose of getting a commercial advantage.[57]

Television news executives bridle at such a charge. At the same time, the potential consequences of live coverage of war is not a subject of enormous contemplation among them at this point. I suspect they might very well welcome some limits on live coverage. Among other things, it would relieve them of some of the burden of having to decide when to go live. I explore some of these possibilities, such as the Haitian model and other approaches, in the section of this chapter on "Guidelines."

Possible Consequences—the Political View

The impact of television pictures on diplomacy and policy is a subject of great interest to diplomats, journalists, and scholars and thus has been the subject of many books and studies. It is not my intention to replow that ground. However, any analysis of the consequences of live television coverage from the battlefield cannot ignore the political implications of such coverage.

Senator John McCain, (R-Arizona) knows more than a little bit about war, having been decorated in Vietnam and having spent many years as a prisoner of war there. In a CNN interview on the subject of how television pictures from various trouble spots can drive diplomacy and shape policy, McCain readily agreed that television was, if somewhat erratically, setting the foreign policy agenda. And what's more, he seemed to think this was just fine. "We are very selective in our morality because it is driven by the television cameras, and it's not all bad by the way. I still believe that World War I wouldn't have lasted three months if people had known what was going on in that conflict."[58] What the senator is saying is that if television had been able to show people the futility of trench warfare, public support for the war would have been quickly withdrawn. But as Ted Koppel countered, there is a danger in that situation because democracies are rarely, if ever, at war with other democracies. They have wars with dictatorships where the same rules do not apply to both sides.

> The problem that is implicit in that, is that a democracy will always be at a terrible disadvantage in a war with a totalitarian government, because the totalitarian government will not permit the transmission of live pictures, and might not permit the transmission of any pictures. So what would have happened in the First World War, if indeed live pictures had been shown in the United States, in France, in the United Kingdom—but not in Germany? Guess who would have given up?[59]

Like the argument over how live television would have changed the nature of D-Day, speculation about television's hypothetical impact on World War I depends on many assumptions. But Senator McCain's assertion does raise a fundamental question. Do we really want our policies shaped by the heated emotions that can be created by grisly television pictures? At the beginning of this chapter I raised a more neutral question. What would be the impact of scenes of carnage on the American people in terms of their support for a given foreign policy or war?

What happened in Mogadishu, Somalia, provides a good answer to that question. The pictures of a dead U.S. Ranger being dragged through the streets of the Somali capital created such a political furor in this country that President Bill Clinton was compelled to withdraw U.S. troops much sooner than had been planned. It was an embarrassing retreat that inevitably caused friend and foe alike to question U.S. reliability and resolve.

General Shalikashvili, who had just been designated Joint Chiefs' chairman at the time of that incident, is troubled by it. He is also worried about its broader implications, namely that the U.S. public often seems unable or unwilling to accept the reality of casualties during military operations.

> If I look at how many casualties the French have had in Bosnia, it hasn't affected their operation one bit. Great Britain, every country that has sent people to Bosnia for a total of over 200 now killed—they haven't had debates like we've had over Mogadishu. . . . We [the military] would not have left Mogadishu if we [the U.S.] had reacted differently to the killing of those American Rangers. We would not have. Things would have run totally different. So this is a real issue. This isn't some imaginary issue.[60]

Shalikashvili went on to suggest that the problem of casualties was not so much with the U.S. public as it was with the Congress, which he implied was motivated by partisan politics.

> I submit to you that it is not necessarily a national debate that we're having on this issue [of casualties]. It is a congressional issue. To what degree it is a politically motivated debate, I won't comment. But it is more a congressional issue than something that is being debated in the press. And it has a most significant impact on what we do or don't do.[61]

Shalikashvili is obviously concerned that there are some members of Congress who are playing politics with the casualty issue by exploiting public outrage after an incident like Mogadishu, as a way of promoting their own agendas.

As a general proposition, graphic television pictures involving U.S. casualties are bad for policymakers. Live graphic pictures will be even worse and will inevitably add fuel to the emotional issue of casualties. It should come as no surprise that some politicians will play on these emotions for their own ends. I found it very interesting, therefore, to get a very different interpretation of what Mogadishu meant, from none other than President Clinton's spokesperson, Michael McCurry. "That did in fact lead to a collapse of support for the mission. But that's because the mission was very hard to explain and justify to begin with. So in a sense, the reporting serves as a good lever against those missions that are not very well defined or don't have the support of the American people."[62]

In words that could easily come back to haunt the White House if things were to turn nasty for U.S. soldiers in Bosnia, McCurry went on to make a case that live coverage could play a positive role in shaping policy.

> I think the capacity for the American people to endure the pain of casualties is directly related to the popular support for the mission that's under way. I think the American people will have the stomach if they think that the cause is just, the mission is right and it's being effectively commanded by the president. If they don't believe those things then those pictures will be horrible for the Pentagon, horrible for the president. But they will

ultimately force a reckoning with the policy. And I think in a democracy that's not a bad thing.[63]

To reiterate Ted Koppel's last point, this puts democracies at a disadvantage when they are at war with a dictator who can totally control what pictures his or her people can see. Our future political leaders are going to have to take this into account when they consider the use of U.S. military forces.

The one man among the interviewees who may be a future political leader actually takes an optimistic view about what the American people will tolerate in terms of carnage and casualties. Although General Powell is quite prepared to censor live pictures to preserve operational security, he seems to be less concerned about the political impact of such pictures. He said that the burden on policymakers was to have a policy that was understandable and justifiable enough to "sustain carnage."

> They're [the American people] prepared to take casualties. And even if they see them on live television it will make them madder. Even if they see them on live television, as long as they believe it's for a solid purpose and for a cause that's understandable and for a cause that has something to do with an interest of ours. They will not understand it, if it can't be explained, which is the point I have made consistently over the years. If you can't explain it to the parents who are sending their kids, you'd better think twice about it.[64]

At several points in our interview Powell talked about the U.S. public being "very smart," "very sophisticated," when it came to dealing with wartime casualties. "They've handled it throughout our history," he said. "We went south in Vietnam because you couldn't explain it anymore."[65]

General Powell's belief that a sound, explainable policy can survive gory television pictures is not widely shared. The far more common view among those interviewed for this chapter is that such pictures do have political consequences in that they make it much more difficult to conduct and defend a policy, even when that policy may indeed be in the country's best interests.

Guidelines

Given these developments, do we need new guidelines for the media? The problem with guidelines is that most people have very different notions as to what "guidelines" actually are. Here are two examples. McCurry said he didn't approve of guidelines because he thinks they're a waste of time.

> We've seen this happen where that leads to endless, tedious, hypothetical negotiations between journalists and government and no situation will

ever fit in with the guidelines because each situation has its own contours. . . . I would prefer to start with a general rule and tailor it only as necessary to protect lives. The United States government has a responsibility to report in a timely way to the American people, through news organizations, significant military actions that put U.S. soldiers in harm's way. And we have a responsibility to do that immediately.[66]

Ed Fouhy, director of the Pew Center for Civic Journalism, has held senior management positions with all three networks and is a former Marine. He is leery of guidelines because he thinks they would limit the networks' reasonable options. "The thing that concerns me about guidelines is that the media give away their freedoms too quickly in return for logistical support. There's no question there's going to have to be some kind of accommodation . . . but I hope we don't start with guidelines.[67]

I infer that McCurry and Fouhy have very different perceptions of what guidelines would be in this case. And I found this to be generally true among most of the interviewees. Some saw guidelines as a set of rules that would have to be hammered out in negotiations and then would have to be "enforced." The military tended to take that view. Others saw them as a set of general principles that might be nice to follow but probably would carry no real weight. This was more or less the position of people in television.

So, long before there could be any discussions on specific guidelines for live coverage from the battlefield, there was a fundamental split over the very definition of "guidelines." My instincts told me that it might be wise to set aside the question of guidelines and try to approach the problem from a different direction. The role of a mediator is to find the common ground among the parties in a dispute. Although I do not presume to be performing such a role, I certainly found, in the course of the interviews, a good deal of common ground on which to build. For instance, among all the players there is a bedrock position that no one wants live television coverage from the battlefield to endanger U.S. forces. That being the case, there is a basis for discussions on how the military can fulfill its role and how the networks can do their jobs without risking the lives of U.S. troops.

Here, the Haiti contingency may be a useful model in terms of how the military, the government, and the networks tried to achieve an accommodation by which the security of the operation was protected without damage to the First Amendment. As noted earlier, Haiti represented a very different set of problems for the military. They could not keep reporters out; there were already hundreds there. Some form of live coverage was very likely because the networks all had such capability in place. In addition, the U.S. government had made a policy decision to tell the Haitian leadership that an invasion was imminent.

Having decided that there was no acceptable way to prevent live coverage of that invasion, the administration moved to try to shape the coverage. David Gergen, then a senior adviser to President Clinton, organized a

Pentagon meeting to include the Washington bureau chiefs of the four networks—Robin Sproul of ABC, Barbara Cochrane of CBS, Bill Headline of CNN, and Tim Russert of NBC; the then director of operations for the Joint Chiefs of Staff, Marine General Jack Sheehan; Dennis Boxx, the Pentagon spokesperson at the time; and Gergen and one or two others from the White House. Senior executives from the network head offices were listening in on speaker phones.

As Gergen explained, the purpose of this meeting was to give the military a chance to lay out its plans and its concerns about the potential impact of live coverage of the event. "The primary issue was whether the troops could go in and maintain an element of surprise, should an order have gone forth, to go in."[68] In order to achieve that tactical surprise the administration asked the networks not to go on the air live with the departure of U.S. planes from U.S. bases, which would signal the beginning of the invasion. To do so would give the Haitians a three-hour warning. The other request was for a television blackout in the initial stages of the troop landings.

Some wildly optimistic civilians in the White House thought this blackout should last for several hours. Gergen says that, realistically, he hoped for about an hour, so that the Haitians would not know precisely when or where the landings were taking place.

> Once it hit, it was understood that they [the networks] were going to move to simultaneous reporting pretty fast, because the other side would already know we were there. There was no point in not telling the American people if the other side was already engaged. So really, the essential issue was one of surprise. And I must say that to the credit of those people engaged on the network side, they all agreed with that.[69]

At that meeting, the military also requested that no lights be shone on paratroopers and helicopters. As discussed earlier, there may have been an element of intimidation in this "request" that lights not be used. But it is also true that those who recalled the infamous Somalia landings, when some of the networks did use lights on the first U.S. troops to come ashore, were determined not to do that again. Although General Powell just thought it was silly, there is a broad consensus that the coverage of those landings was an embarrassing fiasco for both the networks and the military.

Gergen felt very pleased with how that Pentagon meeting went, and he believed it might well represent a model for how things might be handled in the future.

> I felt very good walking out of the room. I felt we had gone a long way in understanding each other about what the relative needs were, respectful of the needs of the press and respectful of protecting American soldiers. . . . I found the networks to be extremely reasonable. . . . What has evolved in this, in my judgment, is that the military has become much, much more reasonable about this issue.[70]

Meanwhile, there was another track that Gergen and the White House were developing. CNN has worldwide distribution and thus deserved special attention, as it will in most cases in the future. McCurry told me that the Pentagon's operations chief said at the time, "Cedras [Haiti's then military ruler] is watching CNN. So long as Wolf Blitzer [CNN's White House correspondent] doesn't have it, we're basically okay."

According to CNN president Tom Johnson, his first discussion with the Clinton administration on Haiti coverage was a conference call with White House officials, which he thinks David Gergen initiated. Johnson said that this conversation led to what he described as "frequent discussions with Admiral Miller [the commander of the Haiti operation] throughout." "It was their view [the White House] that if at my level and at his [Miller's] level, if we could just communicate on it, that probably we could do our jobs responsibly and they could do theirs. He was not going to put in any kind of draconian pool arrangements and we were going to respect their need for operational secrecy."[71]

We have already covered the extent to which Admiral Miller considered the possibility of live coverage in his planning. CNN was a major concern. Miller confirms this and the fact that he worked directly with Johnson. "Tom Johnson might have told you that they were set to cover this one live. I mean, they were clearly set to cover it. And so, knowing that, how does a commander factor that into what he does? I worked with him in factoring that in."[72]

Neither the admiral nor Johnson went into detail about their contacts beyond confirming they talked regularly throughout the critical moments of the Haitian contingency. It is evident, however, that both men believe that dialogue was useful. Johnson, of course, is concerned that this kind of collaboration not be misconstrued. "My gut concern on the one side is that we become some arm of the military or arm of the government. We must not. We can not. On the other hand, I don't want to jeopardize lives of people coming ashore by inadvertently turning on live cameras."[73] In spite of Johnson's uneasiness that CNN might be perceived as being in the government's pocket, it appears he would do it again. "I think that type of communication can be helpful, and I'll tell you, everywhere along the line, I asked myself, how's this going to look if it's on the front page of tomorrow's *Washington Post?* We're as tough and as competitive here and dedicated to getting the story out as anybody. But I do think that type of communication is helpful."[74]

The Haitian model is essentially built, then, on high-level communications between senior military and senior network officials. Actually, Chairman Shalikashvili feels that in the case of Haiti, the consultations should have started earlier.

> I submit to you that had we brought in the very senior leadership of the major networks [earlier], we would have even more support. This is where

my fellow uniformed guys will probably turn over in their graves, but as you start planning a military operation, you become aware of factors which shape your plan. One of the factors today is this open, instant reporting, particularly live coverage. So now you need to shape your plan knowing that this exists.[75]

It should be stressed that Tom Johnson of CNN is not the only network executive who does not wish to be seen doing the bidding of any administration or the Pentagon. And that is probably one of the reasons high-level contact takes place only rarely.

Another reason is that television executives live in a twenty-four-hour news cycle, in which news organizations expend enormous energy each day reinventing themselves and their product. There are network people responsible for long-term planning. But the main decisionmakers do not spend any appreciable time on strategic and future matters. As it is in the nature of military people to plan ahead, it is in the nature of television news people to be happy to get through the events of the day. Therefore, it is apparent that senior television executives could derive considerable benefit from periodic discussions with high-level military people, if only so that when the next crisis occurs, they are not making decisions in a vacuum.

Of course, not all contacts between military and television people need necessarily be at the highest level. In fact, General Bernard Trainor believes that it is the relationships in the field that can be the most productive. Trainor says that reporters who expect to be doing live coverage must get to know the local unit commanders and, if they do, they are much less likely to make costly mistakes.

With reasonable association with the unit you're with, and with a certain amount of trust and openness and exchange between the television journalist and the military command he's covering, the dangers even of the inadvertent disclosure of something that would violate security are very low. That's because the military guy is going to be able to tell you, "In your reporting—make sure you don't do this or [make sure you] do that."[76]

General Trainor cites the example of General Dwight Eisenhower, on the eve of D-Day, telling reporters he knew and trusted how the operation would be conducted. "The journalists were told, 'So you understand what's going on around you, here is what we're going to do.' And the journalists armed with that, then covered the thing and were discreet. There's no reason why television journalists can't do the same thing."[77] Without the World War II censorship system protecting Eisenhower, it is fair to ask how much secret strategy a unit or battle commander might be willing to confide in today's television reporter.

Still, one such reporter, the legendary Peter Arnett, now with CNN, has many times gained the confidence of the military people he has covered, from Vietnam to the Gulf to Bosnia. Arnett says that the secret of his success and survival is that he always plays by the rules set down by the people he is with. "I've always looked at it this way. That if you're traveling with an organization or institution, if you're the guest of the Serbian army, the FMLN in Central America, or HAMAS or the U.S. military, you play by their rules. If you don't, you're going to get your throat cut."[78]

Forrest Sawyer was able to get into Kuwait to cover the liberation "live," but not because of any deals cut by the ABC News brass in New York or Washington. He was able to persuade a series of unit commanders, Saudi Arabian, Egyptian, and U.S., that he was serious and could be trusted. And then he was true to his word.

> I found that the closer I got to the front, and the further away I got from the rear echelon guys, the better off I was. I could say, "Here I am, this is what I want to do. You tell me what you need and I'll work with you and I'll make it right." A Special Forces colonel that I met turned out to be just aces. The same with the Kuwaiti resistance guys. There was no problem whatsoever. The problems all existed back at Dhahran [headquarters].[79]

There is another approach, in lieu of guidelines, worth mentioning. On many occasions, network people will be willing to trade off live capability in exchange for going in with the troops, some logistical help, and the ability to get the story out and on the air in a timely manner. This can almost always be negotiated and might ease some fears about live coverage.

Finally, for all the talk about going live, when they really stop to think about it, television people such as Peter Jennings are very ambivalent about the prospects of live coverage from the battlefield. When they are handling live coverage, Jennings and his fellow anchors are known, and think of themselves, as gatekeepers. They have a major role in deciding who and what gets on.

> I tend to be inclined against live coverage of events like this, basically because I think technology is making it difficult for us to think and contemplate what's going on. [The American people] are not all that well served by the new technology. I think there is a general tendency to slow down, when you have this option for live pictures on the battlefield. I think I will say to myself, Why? Why do they have to be live? Why can't they wait until tomorrow? Why can't we wait until six o'clock?[80]

Jennings does not speak for the entire television industry. The pressure of competition (journalistic or commercial) may force a decision to go live, even when people such as Peter or Ted and Dan, Tom, or Bernard have serious reservations about doing it. But it could be that this reluctance to go live, and the growing awareness of its potential consequences, may be more effective than any guidelines in reducing the downside of live coverage.

Conclusion

Drawing conclusions about something that has yet to happen may be a very questionable exercise, but it seems to me there are some answers to the questions posed at the beginning of this chapter.

Just because live television coverage from the battlefield is possible, is it desirable?

Probably not, but it is going to happen in any case. The phrase "we do things because we can," used repeatedly by people in television, is hardly unique to that industry. It can more properly be applied to the way in which the human species normally behaves. Historically, we begin to use those technologies that are at hand long before we have any understanding of their implications. Thus there will likely be some live television coverage of future wars, because it's possible.

What are its likely consequences in terms of operational security, and might it even affect the outcome of a battle or war?

There is no doubt that it has the potential to threaten operational security. There will always be a problem with inadvertent disclosure of information that will be of use to the other side. As General Schwarzkopf was able to explain, even a seemingly trivial piece of information regarding the order of battle, such as identifying the location of a given unit at a precise moment, can be extremely helpful to even modestly competent intelligence analysts. Fewer and fewer people in television having any military background at all also adds to the chances that television will inadvertently disclose useful information to the enemy. Whether that information is likely to change the outcome of a battle or a war is a much different question. I think that probability is much lower.

General Trainor says one of the most egregious examples of the press breaching security occurred three days before the first major battle of the Civil War when the *New York Times* published the Order of Battle and the battle plan of the Union Army. That may be a factor in the army's historical mistrust of the press, but as we know it did not change the outcome of the Civil War.

At the same time, it does appear that the existence of live television may change the way certain battles will be fought in the future. I was struck by General Shalikashvili's suggestion that live TV might preclude future strategic surprises such as General Schwarzkopf's famous "left hook" maneuver in the Gulf War. I was also impressed by Schwarzkopf's analysis that in future wars, live television coverage will have to be factored into the overall planning, just like the tides, the weather, and other problems that are not controllable. However, I fully expect that in the event of a major battle or war in which live coverage is seen as a threat, the U.S. military will, as General Powell suggested, lock up the TV people or close down the live television operations, one way or another. This reality leads me to conclude that a battle or war will not be lost because of live coverage.

Could a mistake in live broadcast that led to the loss of American lives cause such a public backlash that democratic freedoms might be threatened?

There was nearly unanimous opinion among those interviewed for this chapter that such a mistake would cause a public outcry and that there would be some political demagogues who would demand legislation to curb the power of the networks. But most people didn't think this would actually lead to limitations on the First Amendment. It is worth noting that after the United States went to war in 1917, Congress passed the Espionage and Sedition Acts, designed to suppress obstruction or criticism of the war effort. Dozens of journalists and other citizens were prosecuted and jailed as a result. Until that time, very little attention had been paid to the First Amendment, and there was no great opposition to the idea of setting limits during wartime. Given the body of First Amendment legal precedent set in this century, attempts to place such limits today would quickly be challenged in the courts, with the likelihood that any specific limits to the First Amendment itself would eventually be struck down. Still, the networks are vulnerable to government pressure. They have little popular support, and they have to be concerned that on issues such as broadcast licensing or regulation, they could be directly targeted by a Congress urged on by an angry public.

This raises another issue. In this chapter I assume that the U.S. television networks will maintain the integrity of their news departments and, within the bounds of genuine national security, will want to push the envelope for as much coverage as possible. I hope that assumption continues to hold true. I think that as long as the present leadership of the network news divisions is in place, it will. But as each network becomes part of an ever-growing poly-glomerate—huge corporations with no history, experience, or commitment to news—one should not assume network news coverage will remain aggressive.

One does not have to be a conspiracy theorist to visualize a situation in which companies with worldwide holdings and any number of interests subject to government regulation would not want to go out of their way to antagonize a given government or administration. When corporate lawyers have the final decision about news coverage based primarily on the fear of potential lawsuits, that is a danger signal. Could there come a time when the networks would be only too willing to bend to the wishes of the government and ban all live battlefield coverage in order to ingratiate themselves for future business benefit? Frankly, I don't know, but it bears watching.

What about guidelines?

I don't see prospects for a formal set of rules for live coverage, negotiated in advance between the government and the networks. There appears to be merit in an ad hoc approach, in which, in a specific crisis, very senior military people bring very senior television people into the planning process and work out the ways television can operate so that it will not jeopardize the mission. Having periodic meetings at high levels could also be useful. The military is thinking about this issue. By and large the networks aren't, but occasional high-level discussions might help to focus their attention. I also foresee many occasions when the networks will be willing to forgo live coverage in return for good access and a way to transmit uncensored material some reasonable time after the fact. Also, as noted, some of the best guidelines can be evolved by the people in the field themselves, journalists and unit commanders, who have developed a degree of mutual trust.

What about the political consequences of the American people watching coverage of U.S. soldiers being killed—live and in color?

There will definitely be consequences. If it were a war of survival, such as World War II, one would imagine that public toleration for such scenes would be greater than if it were some less important police action. But in either case, it will place a heavy burden on the political leadership to keep public support from flagging.

In spite of General Powell's faith in the people, in recent years Americans have been conditioned to believe that it is possible to fight wars and not sustain any casualties. Presidents of both parties, the Pentagon, Congress, and the news media share the blame for this. Although no one wants to see Americans killed or wounded in some meaningless military campaign, U.S. policymakers must not be precluded from choosing the best policy option for the country's interests just because that option could involve casualties. To the extent that there is live coverage from the battlefield, that issue will be greatly magnified. This suggests to me that in the case of a future war in which U.S. vital interests were at stake, the government of the day might well have to take steps to severely limit live coverage, or to ban it in some circumstances, as a way of preserving the national will. This is as crucial as protecting operational security.

I do not believe such steps would be appropriate for peacekeeping missions or contingency operations such as Bosnia or Haiti. It would have to be something of the magnitude of a U.S. land war with China or North

Korea or perhaps a new Gulf war, which I suppose are the most obvious battlefields one could imagine for the next decade or two. In that event, I believe there would be strong public support for limitations on live coverage, and I expect there would only be perfunctory protests on the part of the networks. In the final analysis, live coverage from the battlefield is not protected by the First Amendment. Nor is it synonymous with the public's right to know. Live television can be, in some circumstances, an interesting tool, but it is not an essential one to the practice of good television journalism. And in my view, it is good journalism that is the best protection of freedom of the press and the American people's right to know.

Notes

1. Ted Koppel, telephone interview, October 2, 1995.
2. Pete Williams, telephone interview, October 13, 1995.
3. Dan Rather, telephone interview, November 8, 1995.
4. What is or is not journalism may seem like an academic debate among journalists with no practical meaning to outsiders. However, when it is being debated by a Dan Rather or a Ted Koppel, it does have a practical implication because both men have enormous influence over what is or is not seen on CBS or ABC News programs.
5. General John Shalikashvili, personal interview, October 10, 1995.
6. Tom Brokaw, personal interview, October 25, 1995.
7. For the most part, the interviewees are either friends, acquaintances, or people with whom I have had professional contact over a period of time. After four decades as a reporter I feel confident that I can tell when someone I know is dissembling.
8. Frank Aukofer and William P. Lawrence, *America's Team: The Odd Couple* (Nashville, Tenn.: The Freedom Forum First Amendment Center, 1995), p. viii.
9. Polls are often skewed when respondents say what they think they should say rather than what they really feel. This should be taken into account when reading polls about how the military feels about the media and vice versa. My experience has been that there are very few senior officers who served in Vietnam who do not feel a degree of antipathy toward journalists. And most journalists who covered Vietnam remain highly suspicious of the Pentagon.
10. Michael McCurry, personal interview, September 29, 1995.
11. David Gergen, telephone interview, October 19, 1995.
12. There are numerous books and studies done in the wake of the Gulf War that were researched in the preparation of this chapter. The Powell and the Schwarzkopf memoirs devote substantial space to how the war was won and a little to relations with the news media. Not surprisingly, as they tightly controlled it, they were generally happy with the news coverage.

The Frank Aukofer–William P. Lawrence study, *America's Team: The Odd Couple*, is a major analysis of press coverage of the Gulf War. It includes new polling on military and media attitudes toward each other and extensive interviews with more than eighty high-ranking military and government officials and numerous top journalists who examine coverage of the war in great detail.

John Fialka's *Hotel Warriors: Covering the Gulf War* (Washington, D.C.:

Woodrow Wilson Center Press, 1991), is an excellent account of the tribulations and frustrations of most of the journalists who tried to cover that war. As one of them, I can vouch for its verisimilitude.

13. Washington Bureau Chiefs, "Covering the Persian Gulf War" (unpublished report), May 30, 1991.

14. Washington Bureau Chiefs, letter to Defense Secretary Richard Cheney, April 29, 1991.

15. Aukofer and Lawrence, *America's Team*, p. 10.

16. Times Mirror Center for the People and the Press, *The People, the Press and the War in the Gulf, Part II* (Washington, D.C.: March 25, 1991), p. 1.

17. Any time journalists submit to a pool, they are surrendering a degree of independence and accepting some level of exclusion. There was a time when the networks fought furiously against any pool, any time. However, it is clear that there are many occasions when pool arrangements become necessary. For instance, you can't fit twenty-five television crews into the Oval Office to watch the president sign something. Nowadays, White House pools are routine and the networks actually encourage them in some cases because it helps keep costs down.

The Department of Defense National Media Pool System was created as a kind of journalistic "quick reaction force" to be put into place at the outset of any war or conflict involving U.S. military forces. The DOD pool includes representatives of major media organizations, although its size can vary depending on the available transport, logistical requirements, and the size and location of the battlefield. In theory, this pool is only to function at the beginning of a conflict or operation, after which open coverage is to be established.

Smaller news organizations inevitably get squeezed out when such pools are invoked, but large organizations too are often unhappy if there is space for only one of their people when many of their stars may be on the scene.

One of the biggest media complaints in the Gulf War was that pool coverage became the norm instead of the exception, as the military used pools routinely as a way of dealing with the large number of reporters covering the war. Under the new principles agreed to by the media and the Pentagon in March 1992, that is not supposed to happen in the future.

18. General Norman Schwarzkopf, telephone interview, October 24, 1995.

19. General Colin Powell, telephone interview, January 3, 1996.

20. General Bernard Trainor, personal interview, September 19, 1995.

21. McCurry, interview.

22. Schwarzkopf, interview.

23. Brokaw, interview.

24. Powell, interview.

25. Ibid.

26. Shalikashvili, interview.

27. Schwarzkopf, interview.

28. This would also seem to be the perfect situation for the military to use live television to put out false information to confuse the enemy. I do not believe the networks would be willing parties to such a deception campaign because it would destroy their credibility. But inexperienced reporters would be likely candidates to be fed disinformation and, frankly, even experienced reporters can sometimes be taken in.

Although the military denies it would do such a thing, such denials can be taken with more than a grain of salt. During the Gulf War, the presence of U.S. Marines offshore prompted a number of stories that there would be an amphibious assault on Kuwait once the ground war began. Schwarzkopf told me he was delighted with these reports, but he denies he ever told reporters that such a landing was planned. Powell later said that there was contingency planning for such a landing, but it was never implemented. Powell added that as the Iraqis themselves could see the marine buildup, the press was not needed to bolster the story. Nevertheless, both generals admitted that in raising the prospect of a marine assault, the press had done the military a favor.

29. Peter Jennings, personal interview, October 25, 1995.

30. Admiral Paul David Miller, telephone interview, November 6, 1995.

31. Ibid.

32. Shalikashvili, interview.

33. Schwarzkopf, interview.

34. My interview with the chairman was very specifically to discuss the implications of live television coverage of the battlefield. He understood that and all of my questions were directly related to such coverage. However, from time to time in the interview he used "live television" and "the press" interchangeably.

35. Shalikashvili, interview.

36. Walter Porges, telephone interview, October 18, 1995.

37. Koppel, interview.

38. Rather, interview.

39. Cheryl Gould, personal interview, October 25, 1995.

40. Williams, interview.

41. Bernard Shaw, telephone interview, October 13, 1995.

42. Paul Friedman, personal interview, October 27, 1995.

43. Ibid.

44. Tom Johnson, telephone interview, November 1, 1995.

45. Brokaw, interview.

46. Ibid.

47. Koppel, interview.

48. Jennings, interview.

49. Hodding Carter, telephone interview, October 10, 1995.

50. Shaw, interview.

51. Johnson, interview.

52. Powell, interview.

53. Ibid.

54. Dennis Boxx, telephone interview, October 6, 1995.

55. Margaret Tutwiler, telephone interview, October 17, 1995.

56. Cliff Bernath, personal interview, October 26, 1995.

57. Powell, interview.

58. Senator John McCain, interview, *Crossfire*, CNN, October 14, 1993.

59. Koppel, interview.

60. Shalikashvili, interview.

61. Ibid.

62. McCurry, interview.

63. Ibid.

64. Powell, interview.

65. Ibid.

66. McCurry, interview.

67. Ed Fouhy, telephone interview, October 12, 1995.

68. Gergen, interview.

69. Ibid.

70. Ibid.

71. Johnson, interview.

72. Miller, interview.
73. Johnson, interview.
74. Ibid.
75. Shalikashvili, interview.
76. Trainor, interview.
77. Ibid.
78. Peter Arnett, telephone interview, October 4, 1995.
79. Forrest Sawyer, telephone interview, October 19, 1995.
80. Jennings, interview.

11

News of the World

Pippa Norris

Understanding mass communications through the concept of framing has become increasingly common, whether in the fields of social psychology, public opinion, or media studies.[1] The idea of "news frames" refers to interpretive structures that set particular events within their broader context. Information processing research suggests that people have cognitive schema that organize their thinking, linking substantive beliefs, attitudes, and values.[2] For journalists and readers, these frames guide the selection, interpretation, and evaluation of new information by slotting the new into familiar categories.

A growing literature has explored the nature of news frames, whether in coverage of election campaigns, foreign policy, or social conflict. Yet remarkably little attention has focused on how news frames alter over time in response to external events. The central aim of this chapter is to understand how dominant news frames evolve, change, and adapt, by focusing on U.S. network news coverage of international affairs after the end of the Cold War. Just as with the far-reaching structural and organizational changes in the Pentagon, CIA, and NATO, the question is how far and how fast routine network coverage of international news adapted to reflect the realities of the new geopolitical world.

Theoretical Framework

The concept of framing is complex and elusive, so first we need to clarify our terms. The theory of framing suggests that journalists commonly work with news "frames" to simplify, prioritize, and structure the narrative flow of events. News frames bundle key concepts, stock phrases, and stereotyped images to reinforce certain common ways of interpreting developments. The essence of framing is selection to prioritize some facts, events, or developments over others, thereby promoting a particular interpretation.[3]

Reporters can "tell it like it is" within sixty seconds, rapidly sorting key events from surrounding trivia, by drawing on reservoirs of familiar stories to cue readers. New developments are understood within regular patterns. Frames represent stereotypes, which slot particular events into broader interpretive categories that may, or may not, be appropriate. Because news frames can be expected to reflect broader social norms, political minorities challenging the dominant culture are likely to prove most critical of such treatment.

There are numerous examples of framing that we can recognize. To take just a few: within the election campaign the familiar "horse race" frame (who is ahead, who is behind) dominates coverage of the primaries.[4] In reporting complex acts of "terrorist" violence the victim-perpetrator frame simplifies the attribution of responsibility.[5] The black-white "racial conflict" frame can shape coverage of riots, whether appropriate or not.[6] The campaign associated with the New World Information Order (NWIO) has long criticized the framing of Western news from developing countries only in terms of "coups, earthquakes and disasters."[7] Alternative social movements such as feminists and anti-nuclear groups may be framed in ways that they judge inappropriate.[8] Framing has also been applied to how we evaluate government responsibility for issues such as the Gulf War, crime, poverty, and Iran-Contra.[9] Dominant frames are so widespread within a journalistic culture that they come to be seen as natural and inevitable, with contradictory information discounted as failing to fit preexisting views. Like paradigms guiding scientific understanding, dominant news frames can be seen as "journalism as usual." Yet just like paradigms, at times long-established schema break down, producing a period of confusing rivalry between alternative interpretations of the news narrative.

Like the development of all-pervasive social stereotypes, it is often difficult to study the origins and gradual evolution of frames. It is like trying to see the air around us. Yet periods of sharp change—like the end of the Cold War—highlight awareness of frames that come to be seen as out of touch with social reality. From 1945 to 1989 the Cold War frame prevailed in U.S. foreign policy, providing a cultural prism to explain complex political and military events in countries from Hungary to Vietnam, Cuba, Angola, Afghanistan, and Nicaragua. Since the fall of the Berlin Wall, old stereotypes of friends and enemies have had to be rapidly recast.

The Cold War frame functioned to highlight certain events as international problems, identified their source, offered normative judgments, and recommended particular policy solutions. Specifically, the familiar Cold War frame depicted international events in terms of rivalry between two major superpowers and ranged other countries into friends and enemies of these superpowers. Events in Vietnam, Angola, Nicaragua, or Afghanistan could be interpreted as internal power struggles, provoked by religious, ethnic, or regional civil wars that toppled unstable regimes. Or these conflicts could be seen in terms of international rivalry for global ascendancy, thereby involving vital U.S. interests. During the Cold War the United States' interests were defined in large part by virtue of opposition to Soviet allies. This led to a policy framework in which U.S. involvement in the Middle East, Latin America, or Southeast Asia was justified by a policy of containment.

The frame for the mainstream U.S. media can be expected to reflect and reinforce the dominant frame in U.S. culture. This has certain significant consequences for the presentation of news in terms of the priority given to international news, regional coverage, and thematic coverage. In particular, the Cold War frame could be expected to have an agenda-setting effect by prioritizing the selection of certain events and countries as newsworthy. International conflicts perceived to affect U.S. interests can be expected to be given greater priority in news coverage than global events that are unrelated. If armed conflict, ethnic rivalry, violations of human rights, or civil unrest in countries like Algeria, Liberia, or Burma is not perceived as affecting vital U.S. military or economic interests, we might expect little network news coverage of these events. The end of the Cold War may also be expected to influence the regions and countries that are regarded as newsworthy, notably with a decline in coverage of the countries of the former Soviet bloc. Moreover, we might expect a significant change in the themes of international news stories, with a shift away from stories about military conflict, and greater attention given to a more diverse range of social, economic, and political issues, including those about competition and cooperation in the global economy. Therefore, the end of the Cold War frame does not simply affect the way news stories are interpreted, although this is one important component. The pace at which the frame changed can also be gauged by trends in the priority given to international or domestic news stories; trends in the coverage of the Soviet Union/Russia compared with other regions; and trends in whether international news stories about the global economy have overtaken traditional concerns about military conflict. In this sense, the breakdown of a dominant frame can be expected to determine not only how journalists interpret events but also what events they choose to interpret.

Of course we should not exaggerate. The Cold War frame was never the only schema in U.S. news of international affairs, even in the 1950s and 1960s. The "North-South" frame has commonly been evoked in covering disasters like famines or floods in developing countries. The "dictatorship-democracy" frame was often evident in reports of political struggles such as those in Chile, Argentina, Greece, and Spain. Nevertheless, the Cold War frame ran like a red thread through most coverage of international news in the past because it dominated U.S. foreign policy. The schema simplified and prioritized coverage of international news by providing certainties about friends and enemies.

The task of reporting international politics became increasingly complex following the breakdown of the Cold War.[10] This raises certain central issues considered in this chapter that help us to understand the framing process: how fast U.S. network news abandoned the dominant Cold War frame in response to events in Eastern and Central Europe; how far this frame was replaced by alternative schema; and, in conclusion, what the consequences were for U.S. television coverage of international affairs. To consider these issues we can turn to a content analysis of a sample of routine network news from 1973 to 1995.

Data and Methods

To consider the most appropriate research design for a new study of framing, we can draw a distinction, as William Adams suggests, between three lines of inquiry.[11] Production research looks at how journalists' values and news-gathering structures shape news frames. Contents research—the focus here—analyzes the characteristics of news frames. Effects research examines the impact of news frames on the public's interpretation of events.

Content analysis has commonly focused on the framing of particular events. This includes conflict in Vietnam,[12] the Middle East,[13] Nicaragua,[14] and the Gulf War,[15] and international disasters such as Bhopal, the 1973 oil crisis, Chernobyl, the *Exxon Valdez* oil spill, and international terrorism.[16] Some have looked at framing of a specific foreign policy decision, such as U.S. withdrawal from the United Nations Educational, Scientific, and Cultural Organization (UNESCO) in 1985,[17] or reaction to the KAL and Iran Air incidents[18] and Iran-Contra.[19] Yet, by definition, it is difficult to generalize from the framing of major wars, specific decisions, and dramatic disasters to the more typical, day-to-day framing of international news on the major U.S. networks, as this chapter tries to do. Moreover, events-driven research is in itself a product of the dominant foreign policy frame, because it focuses on events deemed important to U.S. interests. In this respect, there is a systemic bias similar to the problem faced by decision analysis of power elites. Just as certain decisions may never be discussed due to a "mobilization of bias," so we need to study "nonevents" in foreign policy as well as events where the United States did intervene. A comparison of the events deemed newsworthy on the BBC World Service and U.S. television news suggests that if the networks do not cover events like human rights abuses in East Timor or political struggles in Nigeria, this may be as significant for understanding the dominant international news frame as the way they did cover the Gulf War or Panama.

The focus of this chapter is to analyze framing in routine U.S. television network news. Coverage of international news has been analyzed in a range of media outlets in the United States, including the *New York Times* and CNN.[20] There have been a number of previous studies of foreign and international news coverage on U.S. television network newscasts. James Larson provided the most systematic content analysis of network news, based on a random sample of programs from 1972 to 1981.[21] This has subsequently been updated by others, with the most recent analysis by William Gonzenbach, David Arant, and Robert Stevenson covering the period from 1972 until 1989, just prior to the end of the Cold War.[22]

To investigate how far and how fast international news frames on television changed in response to the end of the Cold War, a structured random sample of 2,228 ABC and CBS network news television programs was drawn at annual intervals from 1973 to 1995. Previous studies have found no significant difference in international coverage between the major networks (excluding CNN),[23] and this was confirmed in our results; hence it was felt that it was not necessary to include NBC in the sample. Each year's sample included between 59 and 125 stories. The sample of stories was drawn from broadcasts on a constant day (every Monday) during one constant month per annum (February). One coder was used to classify all stories, to avoid problems of intercoder reliability. Replicating previous studies, data were derived from the *Television News Index and Abstracts* from the Vanderbilt Archive,[24] which has provided short abstracts of the evening new broadcasts of the three major networks since 1972. The *Index* has been widely used in previous research and found to provide a highly reliable source of data about international news coverage.[25] For analysis of the geographic coverage, these data produced an insufficient number of cases to run a reliable trend analysis. Accordingly, the data were supplemented by a keyword search to identify network news stories in the Vanderbilt abstracts that were indexed under the "USSR" or "Russia" during a constant month (February) during the last decade (1985–1995). This process identified 956 stories to analyze trends over time in coverage of the USSR/Russia.

The study focuses on trends from 1973 to 1995, subdivided into three periods (1973–1988, 1989–1991, 1992–1995) to analyze the dynamics of change. The period 1973–1988 is treated as representing the late Cold War years (N stories = 1,663). In contrast, 1989–1991 is regarded as the watershed transition (N stories = 254). There is obviously room for argument about the appropriate categorization of this process. In 1988 Hungary began the process of transition to a multiparty system. By 1989 radical change became contagious, as a noncommunist government swept into power in Poland and communist regimes collapsed in East Germany, Czechoslovakia, and Romania. In November 1989 the Berlin Wall fell to the tune of Beethoven's "Ode to Joy." In 1990 even the most diehard communist regimes were shifting, and the old Soviet Union broke up in 1991. Following these dramatic events in Central and Eastern Europe, the period

1992–1995 is seen as representing the early years of the post–Cold War era (N stories = 309). International news coverage was compared over two decades to analyze consistent trends because coverage of particular countries may vary substantially from one year to the next.

Content analysis reveals what countries, issues, and themes are considered newsworthy by the press. Previous studies, including the most recent, have often emphasized the continuity over time in the pattern of international coverage by the networks. Gonzenbach, Arant, and Stevenson say, "In conclusion, the study suggests that network TV coverage of the world at the end of the 1980s did not differ substantially from the TV world at the beginning of the 1970s."[26] Following the end of the Cold War, as discussed earlier, we might expect major changes in network news to occur in the *priority* given to international news, the *geographic coverage* of countries and regions, and the *thematic* focus of stories.

First, the priority of coverage can be measured by the number of stories, their length, and the story order. Previous studies have found that domestic news dominated the networks, but that international coverage remained significant. Adnan Almaney's review of network newscasts in 1969 found that 37 percent of all stories were about foreign and international news.[27] This estimate received further confirmation in later studies by Larson and by Gonzenbach, Arant, and Stevenson,[28] who report that 40 percent of network news dealt with foreign or international news. Other · studies found that foreign news (defined more narrowly as news reported from outside the United States) represented about one-quarter of network news time.[29] Measures based on the number of stories and their length provide slightly different estimates mainly because many financial and economic items are relatively brief (e.g., stock market reports). The first hypothesis for this study is that the breakdown of the Cold War and the dramatic events in Central and Eastern Europe would stimulate a dramatic increase in international news during the transition period (1989–1991). Thereafter we might expect that the amount of international coverage would either (1) return to the levels of the Cold War period, or (2) perhaps would fall even lower, if the complexities of the "new world order" proved difficult for television journalism to convey without the structure of the Cold War frame. There are theoretical reasons to find both equally plausible hypotheses. The length of international news stories and their order in the program may be expected to follow similar patterns.

Second, we might expect changes in which countries and regions were considered newsworthy. Most previous studies have focused on the question of news flows between countries, in particular Western dominance of the news. Interest in this issue was expressed as early as the 1920s by Walter Lippmann,[30] with the first systematic research by William Schramm in the 1960s, and in a major debate over the New World Information Order prompted by UNESCO in the 1980s.[31] This generated a series of studies comparing the volume and direction of news flows across different countries, including newspaper coverage,[32] television,[33] and wire services.[34] Although studies commonly report an imbalance in news flows across countries, there is no consensus about the extent of the imbalance, still less the implications for news frames.

The pattern of news flows might be expected to change in recent years. The end of the Cold War era brought about a major realignment of U.S. interests. The story changed from the NATO region versus the Warsaw Pact countries toward a diverse series of engagements in Bosnia, Somalia, and the Gulf. Therefore, in the transition period we would expect considerable attention to the dramatic events in Central and Eastern Europe (the "Dan Rather here by the Berlin Wall" phenomenon). Thereafter we would expect to see a diminution of interest in the old Soviet bloc and a wider range of international concerns, with perhaps a tilt from the developed to the developing world.

Last, we might expect that the themes of news stories would also have changed in recent years. Previous studies found overall coverage often depicted the world as a dangerous and conflictual place, with the greatest attention (39 percent of stories) given to military-defense issues,[35] although this proportion dropped after the end of the Vietnam War.[36] Following the end of the Cold War period, we might anticipate concern to shift from defense to the international economy, such as the North American Free Trade Agreement (NAFTA) among the United States, Mexico, and Canada; the trade gap with Japan; and threats to the stability of the dollar. We might also expect stories about Russia to shift from a concern about military strength toward more diverse stories about Russian politics, economics, and society.

Amount of International News

Given the deep cultural roots of news frames, the first question concerns how far and how fast the priority given to international events changed on network news during these years. During the last twenty years most network news programs covered about eleven stories every evening, including about four international and seven domestic items. The results confirm the expectation that there have been certain significant fluctuations over time in the total number of international stories on network news (see Figure 11.1). During the Cold War period, about a third of news stories could be classified as international, with peaks in 1980 and 1986. In contrast, during the transition period the number of international news stories grew sharply, reflecting the momentous events during these years, including the fall of the Berlin Wall; the breakup of the old Soviet empire; the first free elections in Eastern and Central Europe; developments in the Middle East,

Figure 11.1   **Amount of International News, 1973–1995**

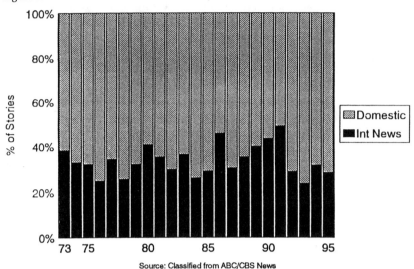

Source: Classified from ABC/CBS News

China, and Panama; and the Gulf War. During the transition period, about 44 percent of all news stories were international, with coverage that spiked in 1991. This was followed by a sharp fall in the post–Cold War period, (1992–1995) down to 29 percent of stories. Network news turned back again toward the predominant domestic agenda, returning to a position similar or slightly lower than that during the Cold War period. The average number of international news stories fell dramatically from five stories every evening in 1991 down to two per night in 1993, before recovering slightly to three per night in 1995. The transition period therefore represented a marked peak of interest, as expected, with lower coverage in both the Cold War and post–Cold War period.

Length of Stories

The amount of time devoted to international news displays similar trends over time. The last two decades experienced a sharp decline in the time spent on international coverage, from 45 percent of news bulletins in 1973 down to just 27 percent in 1995. In the average twenty minutes of news per program (after ads) coverage of developments around the world fell from about ten to five minutes per night. The length of stories remained brief but showed no clear shrinkage; the average story lasted 1.7 minutes. As is shown in Figure 11.2, there were different patterns in the periods under comparison. In the Cold War, and particularly in the transition period,

Figure 11.2   Length of News Stories, 1973–1995

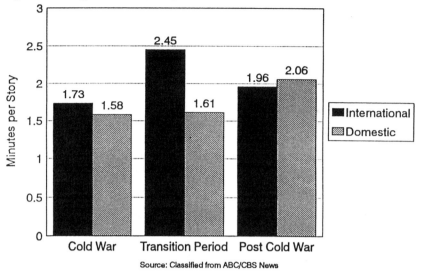

Source: Classified from ABC/CBS News

Figure 11.3   Priority in Headline News, 1973–1995

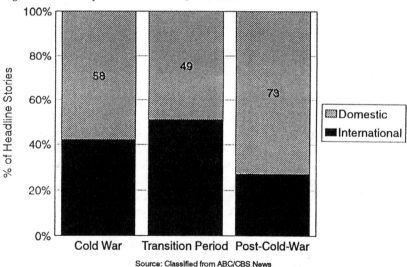

Source: Classified from ABC/CBS News

international stories were longer than domestic items. This pattern was reversed in the post–Cold War period.

Running Order

The last indicator of editorial priority concerns the running order of stories and what is given headline treatment. "Headlines" in this study are defined by the first three stories in the news. As Figure 11.3 shows, during the Cold War period domestic stories were given the greatest priority. During the transition period this was reversed, with U.S. events and international developments given roughly equal treatment in the headlines. Lastly, in the post–Cold War period domestic stories overwhelmingly topped the headline news.

Trends in Geographic Coverage

The end of the Cold War may also be expected to influence the regions and countries that are regarded as newsworthy. During the first period, we would expect U.S. news to reflect the structural and cultural Cold War framework with considerable attention toward the Soviet bloc. The transitional years should increase attention in Central and Eastern Europe. In the post–Cold War period we might expect more diverse country coverage, with greater attention to regional and ethnic disputes such as Rwanda, Somalia, and Bosnia and a decline in interest in Russian affairs.

The content analysis produced only a limited number of cases for most countries, which was supplemented by a keyword search for stories in the Vanderbilt abstracts that referred to either the USSR or Russia. The sample was drawn from a contract month (February) every year during the last decade. The results suggest that coverage of the USSR and Russia fluctuated considerably during this period. As shown in Figure 11.4, coverage of the USSR peaked in 1987, during the first evidence of Mikhail Gorbachev's reforms in the Soviet Union, before rising again sharply in the year of transition (1990), then falling sharply during the post–Cold War period. As expected, with the fading of its superpower status, coverage of the region during the post–Cold War period is about half that during the Cold War years.

Changes in the Themes of News Stories

The breakdown of the Cold War frame may also be expected to change the predominant balance of international stories. In particular, the number of international stories about war, civil unrest, and the military may be overtaken by greater emphasis on international relations through economic cooperation, with the development of important trading agreements such as

Figure 11.4   Coverage of the USSR/Russia, 1985–1995

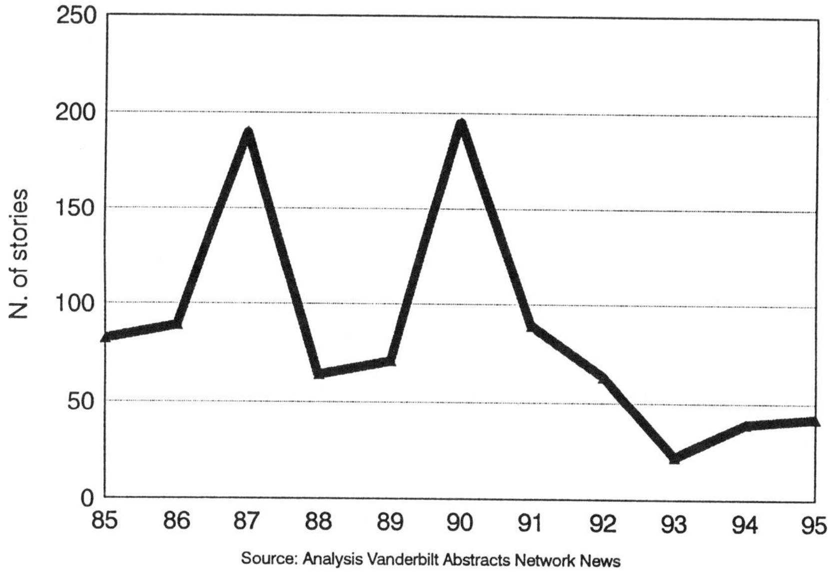

Source: Analysis Vanderbilt Abstracts Network News

the General Agreement on Tariffs and Trade (GATT), NAFTA, and the European Union (EU). Stories were classified replicating the twelve major categories developed by Larson.[37] The result of analyzing the main themes of stories covered during these periods (see Figure 11.5) shows that the focus on security and defense issues expanded during the transition period and remained high during the post–Cold War years. Contrary to expectations, coverage of economic stories remained fairly low, while coverage of political events declined sharply in recent years.

Conclusion

This chapter suggests that the end of the Cold War has had significant consequences for how U.S. network news has framed world news. To recapitulate, the transition period experienced a peak in network news coverage of international affairs, whether measured by the number of stories, their average duration, or their position in the headlines. The end of the Cold War was clearly treated as major news. By 1995, however, there were fewer international news stories than a few years before. Those shown were shorter and further down the running order. The most decisive evidence for a shift in priorities is shown in the substantial decline in coverage of Russia.

Figure 11.5   Themes of International Stories, 1973–1993

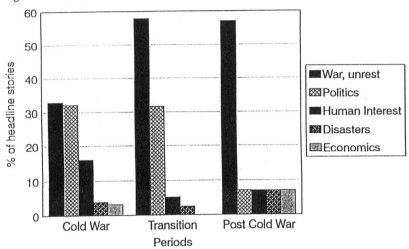

With the notable exceptions of a few foreign stories, such as coverage of Somalia, Haiti, and Bosnia, in the mid-1990s American viewers have far more opportunities to learn about domestic stories, ranging from O.J. Simpson's murder trial to the health care debate and crime, than they have to learn about, say, the Mexican, French, or Italian elections, debates over integration in the European Union, or problems of economic development in Africa. Over the last two decades there have been significant fluctuations in the priority given to international news, coverage of different regions, and the themes of international stories that are judged newsworthy, although given the limited period since the fall of the Berlin Wall, it is probably premature to draw lessons from this about future trends. Events such as the election of more hard-line nationalist forces in Russia could revive U.S. security concerns and media interest in the region. Despite the significance of the Cold War frame as a way of understanding U.S. foreign policy in the 1970s and early 1980s, the study suggests that network news adapted fairly rapidly to the new geopolitical realities.

Nevertheless we can speculate that television news, without a new framework, may have far greater problems in explaining the United States' role in the world and in making sense of international developments for viewers who lack familiar benchmarks to distinguish friends from enemies. Since the fall of the Berlin Wall, U.S. foreign policy has been searching for an appropriate role to mediate complex ethnic, regional, and religious conflicts in Bosnia, Haiti, and the Middle East. Rapid change in South Africa, Russia, or Japan has received brief attention on U.S. network news during moments of sudden tension, but the revolving laser of attention quickly moves to the next crisis elsewhere. New leaders or political developments in these countries are often highlighted with bewildering speed, without much background information to provide an understandable framework for viewers. In Walter Lippmann's words, "The press . . . is like the beam of a searchlight that moves restlessly about, bringing one episode and then another out of darkness into vision. Men cannot do the work of the world by this light alone. They cannot govern society by episodes, incidents, and eruptions."[38]

The end of the Cold War frame has exacerbated this tendency. Global developments produce complex issues for the press to explain: policies such as economic negotiations over GATT, NAFTA, and the European Monetary System (EMS), or issues of environmental regulations agreed at the Rio de Janeiro summit. Although quality newspapers like the *New York Times* and the *Financial Times* can cover these issues on a regular basis in some depth, the lack of a simple frame identifiable for journalists and viewers makes it difficult to encapsulate these events into brief stories suitable for television news.

Because of technological developments, more information than ever before is instantly available, such as pictures transmitted live from Tiananmen Square, the tanks outside the Moscow White House, or the bomb damage in Sarajevo. Moreover, the links created by network coverage allow faster interconnection between political leaders, so that proposals originating in Geneva can be reported, along with simultaneous reactions to camera, from Tel Aviv, Moscow, London, and Washington, D.C.

The growth of picture-driven television information has been accompanied, some suggest, by a simultaneous loss of contextual analysis by the press.[39] Organizational changes in news gathering, driven by budgetary constraints, have reduced the number of foreign correspondents who are able to provide expert commentary, in-depth analysis, and contextual background. In 1945 U.S. newspapers had about 2,500 reporters abroad. By 1969 Larson suggests the number had dropped to under 600, with a further decline to 500 by the mid-1970s,[40] although there is some disagreement about these figures, and other estimates suggest a subsequent increase in the 1990s.[41] U.S. television networks each established about fifteen foreign bureaus in cities like Moscow, Paris, and London, but often during an international crisis film coverage is provided by special reporters flown in for particular assignments. "Parachute" journalists jet from crisis to crisis, crisscrossing the globe, replacing the resident correspondents or veteran stringers with a lifetime experience in a region.[42] The lower costs of overseas video footage means that local television stations can now afford to cover international stories, with commentary provided by the local anchors. There are fewer experienced foreign correspondents who have spent years absorbing the politics and culture of a region, like the BBC's Mark Tully in

India or CNN's Peter Arnett in Southeast Asia. The growth of parachute journalism may therefore provide viewers with a more confusing, disjointed, and violent image of the world, rather than an informed and balanced understanding of international events.

During the last decade the rapid pace of change in international politics in the post–Cold War period, the technological expansion of global news and transnational television, and changes in news-gathering organizations have combined to raise questions about the ability of U.S. network television to cover the world. No single factor is critical but their interaction, many believe, has transformed the role of international news. Perhaps without the familiar Cold War frame, viewers have information available about a wide range of countries. Whether they thereby understand the world better remains an open question.

Notes

1. Robert M. Entman, "Framing: Towards Clarification of a Fractured Paradigm," *Journal of Communication* 43, no. 4 (1993); Entman, "Framing US Coverage of International News," *Journal of Communication* 41, no. 4 (1991): 6–28.

2. William Gamson, *Talking Politics* (New York: Cambridge University Press, 1991).

3. Entman, "Framing."

4. Daniel Hallin, "Sound-bite News," in *Blurring the Lines,* ed. Gary Orren (New York: Free Press, 1990).

5. Akiba A. Cohen and Gadi Wolfsfeld, eds., *Framing the Intifada: People and Media* (Norwood, N.J.: Ablex Publishing, 1993).

6. Erna Smith, *Transmitting Race,* Joan Shorenstein Center Research Paper R-11, Cambridge, Massachusetts, 1994.

7. Hamid Mowlana, *International Flow of Information: Global Report and Analysis* (Paris: UNESCO, 1985).

8. Regarding feminists, see Pamela J. Creedon, "Framing Feminism—a Feminist Primer for the Mass Media," *Media Studies Journal* 7, no. 1 (1993): 68–81; regarding antinuclear groups, see Robert Entman, "Freezing Out the Public: Elite and Media Framing of the US Anti-Nuclear Movement," *Political Communication* 10, no. 2 (1993): 155–173.

9. Shanto Iyengar, *Is Anyone Responsible? How Television Frames Political Issues* (Chicago: University of Chicago Press, 1994).

10. For a discussion of this, see "Global News After the Cold War," a special issue of *Media Studies Journal* (Fall 1993).

11. William Adams and Fay Schreibman, eds., *Television Network News: Issues in Content Research* (Washington, D.C.: School of Public and International Affairs, George Washington University, 1978).

12. On the war in Vietnam, see George Bailey, "Television Wars: Trends in Network Coverage of Vietnam, 1965–70," *Journal of Broadcasting* 20, no. 1 (1976): 147–158; Bailey, "Interpretive Reporting of the Vietnam War by Anchormen," *Journalism Quarterly* 53, no. 2 (1976): 319–324; Frank Russo, "A Study of Bias in TV Coverage of the Vietnam War: 1969 and 1970," *Public Opinion Quarterly* 35, no. 4 (1971): 539–543.

13. On the Middle East, see William Adams, ed., *Television Coverage of the Middle East* (Norwood, N.J.: Ablex, 1981); V. M. Mishra, "News from the Middle East in Five US Media," *Journalism Quarterly* 59 (1979): 374–378.

14. On Nicaragua, see Joshua Muravchik, *News Coverage of the Sandinista Revolution* (Washington, D.C.: American Enterprise Institute, 1988).

15. On the Gulf War, see Robert Wiener, *Live from Baghdad* (New York: Doubleday, 1992); Bradley Greenberg and Walter Gantz, eds., *Desert Storm and the Mass Media* (New Jersey: Hampton Press, 1993); Philip M. Taylor, *War and the Media: Propaganda and Persuasion in the Gulf War* (Manchester: Manchester University Press, 1992); James P. Winter, *Common Cents: Media Portrayals of the Gulf War and Other Events* (Montreal: Black Rose Books, 1992); Everett E. Dennis, *The Media at War: The Press and the Persian Gulf Conflict* (New York: Gannett Foundation, 1991); John Mueller, *Policy and Opinion in the Gulf War* (Chicago: University of Chicago Press, 1994).

16. On international disasters, see Lynne Masel Walter, Lee Wilkins, and Tim Wates, *Bad Tidings* (Hillsdale, N.J.: Lawrence Erlbaum Associates, 1989); Leonard J. Theberge, ed., *TV Coverage of the Oil Crisis: How Well Was the Public Served?* (Washington, D.C.: The Media Institute, 1982).

17. On UNESCO, see William Preston, Edward S. Herman, and Herbert I. Schiller, *Hope and Folly: The United States and UNESCO 1945–1985* (Minneapolis: University of Minnesota Press, 1989).

18. Regarding the KAL and Iran Air incidents, see Entman, "Framing."

19. Regarding Iran-Contra, see Richard Sobel, *Public Opinion in US Foreign Policy: The Controversy over Contra Aid* (Maryland: Rowman and Littlefield, 1993).

20. On the *New York Times,* see Nicholas O. Berry, *Foreign Policy and the Press: An Analysis of the New York Times Coverage of US Foreign Policy* (New York: Greenwood Press, 1990); and George Gerber and George Marvanyi, "The Many Worlds of the World's Press," *Journal of Communication* 27, no. 4 (1977): 55–60. On CNN, see Hank Whittemore, *CNN: The Inside Story* (Boston: Little, Brown and Company, 1990).

21. James F. Larson, *Television's Window on the Word: International Affairs Coverage on the US Networks* (Norwood, N.J.: Ablex, 1984).

22. See Albert Hester, "Five Years of Foreign News on US Evening Newscasts," *Gazette* 24 (1978): 86–95; James B. Weaver, Christopher J. Porter, and Margaret E. Evans, "Patterns in Foreign News Coverage on US Network TV: A 10-year Analysis," *Gazette* 84 (1984): 356–363; William J. Gonzenbach, David Arant, and Robert L. Stevenson, "The World of US Network News: Eighteen Years of International and Foreign News Coverage," *Gazette* 50, no. 1 (1992): 53–72.

23. Larson, *Television's Window.*

24. *Television News Index and Abstracts* (Nashville, Tenn.: Vanderbilt Television News Archive, 1972–1992).

25. Larson checked the reliability of the coding in the *Index* against an independent coding of thirty-two newscasts and found intercoder reliability was .89 or higher for all content categories. See James F. Larson, *Television's Window,* pp. 34–35.

26. Gonzenbach, Arant, and Stevenson, "The World of US Network News."

27. Adnan Almaney, "International and Foreign Affairs on Network Television News," *Journal of Broadcasting* 14, no. 4 (1970): 499–509.

28. See James Larson and Andy Hardy, "International Affairs Coverage on Network Television News," *Gazette* 234 (1977): 241–251; Larson, *Television's Window;* Gonzenbach, Arant, and Stevenson, "The World of US Network News."

29. Hester, "Five Years of Foreign News"; Weaver, Porter, and Evans, "Patterns in Foreign News Coverage."

30. Walter Lippmann, *Public Opinion* (New York: Macmillan, 1922).

31. See Mowlana, *International Flow of Information;* Hamid Mowlana, "Towards a NWICO for the Twenty-First Century," *Journal of International Affairs* 47, no. 1 (1993): 59–72; Annabelle Sreberny-Mohammadi, *Foreign News in the Media: International Reporting in Twenty-Nine Countries,* Reports and Papers on Mass Communications 93 (Paris: UNESCO, 1984); Robert L. Stevenson and Donald Lewis Shaw, eds., *Foreign News and the New World Information Order* (Ames, Iowa: Iowa State University Press, 1984); K. Kyloon Hur, "A Critical Analysis of International News Flow Research," *Critical Studies in Mass Communication* 1 (1984): 365–378.

32. On newspaper coverage, see Jacques Kayser, *One Week's News: Comparative Study of 17 Major Dailies for a Seven Day Period* (Paris: UNESCO, 1953); Wilbur Schramm, *One Day in the World's Press* (Stanford, Calif.: Stanford University Press, 1960); Schramm, *Mass Media and National Development* (Stanford, Calif.: Stanford University Press, 1964).

33. On television, see Francois Heinderyckx, "Television News Programmes in Western Europe: A Comparative Study," *European Journal of Communication* 8 (1993): 425–450; Kaarle Nordenstreng and Tapio Varis, *Television Traffic: A One Way Street,* Reports and Papers on Mass Communication 70 (Paris: UNESCO, 1974); Tapio Varis, "The International Flow of Television Programs," *Journal of Communication* 34, no. 1 (1984): 143–152.

34. On the wire services, see Scott M. Cutlip, "Content and Flow of AP News—from Trunk to TTs to Reader," *Journalism Quarterly* 31 (1954): 434–446.

35. Hester, "Five Years of Foreign News."

36. Weaver, Porter, and Evans, "Patterns in Foreign News Coverage."

37. Larson and Hardy, "International Affairs Coverage."

38. Walter Lippman, *Drift and Mastery: An Attempt to Diagnose the Current Unrest* (Englewood Cliffs, N.J.: Prentice-Hall, 1961).

39. See William Hachen, *The World News Prism: Changing Media of International Communication* (Ames, Iowa: Iowa State University Press, 1992); John Merrill, ed., *Global Journalism* (New York: Longman, 1991); Ralph Negrine and S. Papathanassopoulas, *The Internationalization of Television* (London: Pinter Publishers, 1990).

40. See Larson, *Television's Window;* Bill Carter, "Networks Reduce Foreign Coverage," *New York Times,* June 10, 1992; Lewis A. Friedland, *Covering the World: International Television News Services* (New York: Twentieth Century Fund, 1992).

41. Ralph Kliesch, quoted in Mort Rosenblum, *Who Stole the News?* (New York: John Wiley, 1993), p. 18.

42. See Robert J. Donovan and Ray Scherer, *The Unsilent Revolution* (New York: Cambridge University Press, 1992); Bernard Kalb, "In the Days of Carrier-Pigeon Journalism," *Media Studies Journal* 7, no. 4 (1993).

12

Beyond the "CNN Effect": The Media–Foreign Policy Dynamic

Steven Livingston

In recent years, observers of international affairs have raised the concern that the media have expanded their ability to affect the conduct of U.S. diplomacy and foreign policy. Dubbed the "CNN effect" (or "CNN curve" or "CNN factor"), the impact of these new global, real-time media is typically regarded as substantial, if not profound.

Two key factors have joined to bring this about. One is the end of the Cold War. With its passing the United States lacks an evident rationale in fashioning its foreign policy.[1] The other factor is technological. Advances in communication technology have created a capacity to broadcast live from anywhere on earth. As a result, the vacuum left by the end of the Cold War has been filled by a foreign policy of media-specified crisis management.

Compared to William Randolph Hearst's *New York Journal* and Joseph Pulitzer's *World*, which may have created the climate for war with Spain in 1898, the extent, depth, and speed of the new global media have created a new species of effects. It is this global, real-time quality of contemporary media that separates the CNN effect from earlier media effects on foreign policy. Yet exactly what those effects are, when they are likely to be seen, and even whether they exist at all is the subject of intense debate.

Despite numerous symposia, books, articles, and research fellowships devoted to unraveling the CNN effect, success at clarifying it—this chapter will argue—has been minimal. In part, this may be due to the imprecise use of the term "CNN effect." Writers too often and too easily slip back and forth between related but otherwise conceptually distinct understandings of the effect or effects in question. The first objective of this chapter is to clarify exactly what is meant by the CNN effect. The second objective concerns policy. Just as we must speak more precisely regarding the *type of effect* we might expect to find as a result of media coverage, so too must we speak more precisely about *foreign policy*. Rather than treat foreign policy as an undifferentiated monolith, we need to discriminate between different foreign *policies,* each with its own objectives, means, potential and actual costs (measured in dollars, lives, and political prestige), and sensitivities to media and public pressures. We must develop, in other words, a greater appreciation for the possibility that different foreign policy objectives will present different types and levels of sensitivity to different types of media. A typology of policy-media effects will be developed in the last half of this chapter that demonstrates several different potential consequences for policy, some harmful, some salubrious, depending upon the nature of the policy objectives and media content. A matrix of media effects, policy types, and objectives is offered last.

Differentiating Several CNN Effects

For many journalists, policymakers, and scholars, there is little doubt that the media profoundly affect the foreign policy process. Former Defense Secretary James Schlesinger, for example, argues that in the post–Cold War era the United States has come to make foreign policy in response to "impulse and image": "In this age image means television, and policies seem increasingly subject, especially in democracies, to the images flickering across the television screen."[2] A commonly cited example is the Clinton administration's response to the mortar attack on a Sarajevo market in February 1994 that killed sixty-eight people.[3]

Despite the frequency, volume, and intuitive appeal of this argument, a growing number of scholars and commentators have begun to question whether the media actually do have the ability to affect the foreign policy process as presumed.[4] The key variable in the media's effect on foreign policy is not the presence or absence of cameras but rather the presence or absence of political leadership. James Hoge, Jr., editor of *Foreign Affairs,* for example, argues that although a CNN effect of some sort may have once existed immediately following the end of the Cold War, it no longer does, or at least not to the same extent.

> It seems to me that about two years ago we reached the high-water mark on standing in awe over the potential CNN effect on things. Since then, there have been a lot of conferences and things written that have essentially gotten us to where we are today, which is that television news has a tactical effect from time to time, but not a strategic one; that it operates more when humanitarian issues are at hand than when actual security issues are.[5]

Hoge's point is important. Whether his specific assertions are correct is less important than the approach he takes to the question. He is suggesting that effects on policy are conditional and specific to policy types and objectives.

A reading of the growing literature suggests at least three conceptually distinct and analytically useful understandings of the media's effect on the foreign policy process (see Table 12.1).

Table 12.1 Conceptual Variations of CNN Effects

Accelerant	Media shortens decisionmaking response time. Television diplomacy evident. During time of war, live global television offers potential security-intelligence risks. But media may also be a force multiplier, method of sending signals. Evident in most foreign policy issues to receive media attention.
Impediment	Two types: (1.) Emotional, grisly coverage may undermine morale. Government attempts to sanitize war (emphasis on video game war), limit access to the battlefield. (2.) Global, real-time media constitute a threat to operational security.
Agenda-Setting Agency	Emotional, compelling coverage of atrocities or humanitarian crises reorder foreign policy priorities. Somalia, Bosnia, and Haiti said to be examples.

We may speak of the CNN effect as (1) a *policy agenda-setting agent,* (2) an *accelerant* to policy decisionmaking, and (3) an *impediment* to the achievement of desired policy goals. Each roughly corresponds to various stages of the useful, though slightly contrived, notion of a linear policy process. The initial formulation of policy corresponds with concerns that media are policy agenda-setting agents. Second, policy implementation corresponds with concerns that media may serve as accelerants of the process or impediments to the achievement of policy objectives. (Table 12.1 provides an outline of these effects.)

It is important to keep in mind that each of these possible effects may be evident over time—sometimes a very short time—on a single policy issue. It is possible, for example, that the media as "policy agenda-setters" may raise the prominence of an issue, placing it before higher-level policymakers. It may then shorten the time those policymakers have to deal with or resolve the issue (accelerant). Finally, it may then—with coverage of some traumatic event or disclosure of tactically important information, impede the development or implementation of policy meant to address the problem. U.S. policy in Somalia, in some measure, fits this mold. These are, nevertheless, analytically distinct effects, and as I will argue later, each is likely to be associated with different types of policy. I take up the media as accelerent, then the media as impediment, and finally the media as agenda setter.[6]

The Media as Accelerant

One of the potential effects of global, real-time media is the shortening of response time for decisionmaking. Decisions are made in haste, sometimes dangerously so. Policymakers "decry the absence of quiet time to deliberate choices, reach private agreements, and mold the public's understanding."[7] "Instantaneous reporting of events," remarks State Department spokesperson Nicholas Burns, "often demands instant analysis by governments. . . . In our day, as events unfold half a world away, it is not unusual for CNN State Department correspondent Steve Hurst to ask me for a reaction before we've had a chance to receive a more detailed report from our embassy and consider carefully our options."[8]

Former Secretary of State James A. Baker III highlights this understanding of the CNN effect. "The one thing it does," he says, "is to drive policymakers to have a policy position. I would have to articulate it very quickly. You are in a real-time mode. You don't have time to reflect."[9] His adviser and former press secretary, Margaret Tutwiler, echoes his assessment: "Time for reaction is compressed. Analysis and intelligence gathering is out" in the new world of global media.[10]

Richard Haass, former member of the National Security Council and one of President George Bush's closest advisers during the Persian Gulf conflict, also notes this effect, saying that CNN has changed the concept of a daily news cycle. "We no longer have the old rhythms, everything is telescoped. So, if he [Saddam Hussein] was going to get out there at 4:00 or 5:00 in the afternoon, we had to get out by 4:30 or 5:00 in order to make sure that the evening news was not a disaster or that people in the Middle East some seven or eight hours ahead didn't go to sleep thinking that somehow Saddam had made some great new offer, when in fact he really hadn't."[11]

Understood as an accelerant to the policy process, the CNN effect has also had an effect on the operation of the foreign policy bureaucracy, particularly intelligence agencies and desk officers in the State Department. Former presidential press secretary Marlin Fitzwater remarks, "In most of these kinds of international crises now, we virtually cut out the State Department and the desk officers. . . . Their reports are still important, but they don't get here in time for the basic decisions to be made."[12] Intelligence agencies now must compete with news organizations, thus speeding up their assessments, and be prepared to defend their assessments against the evidence presented on television or other real-time media, such as the Internet and telephone.

Although global, real-time television is often treated as a detriment to good policy, Haass argues that its availability can just as well be considered an asset. "People are looking at the media's impact as a downer, . . . a problem for policymakers to cope with. That is true. But it was also an opportunity. One of the things about the 'CNN effect' for people like me at the time [of the Gulf War] was it gave you some real opportunities. One was to penetration. CNN gave you tremendous access to markets that normally you couldn't get to." Besides TV's use in the Middle East, it helped, says Haass, in "sending signals into Europe. And it gave us a real capacity to reach people at home. The media which brought information in instantaneously also gave us the chance to respond and to get our message out instantaneously." This had consequences, in Haass's view, but not of the sort supposed by those lamenting the CNN effect. "We felt we could manage public opinion in this country and that we could manage the alliance, or the coalition dimensions of the war, as well as get to the Iraqi people and the Arab world. Much of the time, global, real-time media offered opportunities for a policymaker, rather than only presenting problems."[13] This more inclusive understanding of the CNN effect was evident even at the dawn of the global reach of media over thirty years ago.

During the Cuban missile crisis in 1962, the Kennedy administration had several days during which the public knew nothing of the threat looming over the horizon. According to historian Michael Beschloss, Kennedy's successors might well look back longingly at the episode, for "Kennedy had the luxury of operating in what they would probably consider to be the halcyon age before modern television news coverage."[14] Kennedy used the first six days of the crisis to convene his advisers and rationally consider the options "in quiet, without public hysteria."[15]

What is often overlooked, however, is the constructive role played by the "real-time, global media," such as they were in 1962, in ending the crisis. At the time, government-to-government communication between Moscow and Washington was so primitive, according to Beschloss, it took six to eight hours to send and translate messages. In an attempt to overcome this barrier, and to sidestep the KGB and Soviet military, Nikita Khrushchev began sending messages to the U.S. leadership via Radio Moscow, which he knew was constantly monitored by the United States. Robert McNamara recalls that on Sunday, October 28, the day the crisis was finally defused,

> He [Khrushchev] instructed that the public radio transmitter in Moscow be held open for his message. And his message was sent over that so that it would avoid the long interval of coding and decoding. . . . It was to eliminate that time gap of six or eight hours that Khrushchev insisted that the final message be transmitted immediately, because he feared that we were engaged at that moment in time in initiating military action.

Meanwhile, CBS News Moscow correspondent Marvin Kalb, having anticipated Khrushchev's announcement, secured a line to New York to coincide with the key Radio Moscow broadcast that morning. As Kalb simultaneously translated the Radio Moscow announcement, President Kennedy and his advisers listened in the White House.[16]

Ironically, it seems, the preglobal television "halcyon age" included a scramble to find a means to achieve what is today one of the chief characteristics of the CNN effect: accelerated, real-time diplomacy. Today, the instantaneous transmission of diplomatic signals via global media is routine. Tutwiler points out that other governments watched her briefings with great care, looking for nuanced policy shifts. Consequently, the State Department would use this to its advantage to inform its counterparts overseas of U.S. reactions or intentions.[17] State Department spokesperson Nicholas Burns does the same thing. "I sometimes read carefully calibrated statements to communicate with those governments with which we have no diplomatic relations—Iraq, Iran, Libya and North Korea. . . . Given the concentration of journalists in Washington and our position in the world, the US is uniquely situated to use television to our best advantage, with our friends as well as our adversaries."[18] Although the new environment constitutes a significant change from the slower, more deliberate processes of yesteryear, it is less clear whether this is necessarily injurious to sound policymaking. A resourceful diplomat may just as well find global, real-time media an asset rather than a liability.

The Media as Impediment

There are at least two types of media-related policy impediments. One is rooted in the inhibiting effects of emotional coverage and operates through the agency of public opinion, both actual and latent. The other is rooted in the potential for global, real-time media to compromise operational security, the veil of secrecy especially needed with some types of military operations. We will take up each of these types in order.

The media as emotional inhibitor. Following the decisive U.S. military victory in the Persian Gulf, President Bush enthusiastically remarked, "By God, we've kicked the Vietnam syndrome once and for all."[19] At the heart of the Vietnam Syndrome was the concern that media coverage of military operations had the potential to undermine public support for an operation and erode troop morale on the ground. As such, perceived U.S. credibility and resolve in the world was undermined.

Yet two years later, in October 1993, pictures of a dead U.S. soldier being dragged through the streets of Mogadishu revived some of the same fears and concerns evoked by Vietnam. The Clinton administration's decision to withdraw U.S. troops from Somalia as soon as possible was the more immediate result.[20] As the *New York Times* put it, the recent fighting "crystallized American public opinion on an issue that previously was not particularly pressing to the average citizen. And the pictures of a dead American soldier being dragged through the streets of Mogadishu seem to have made it all but impossible for Mr. Clinton to change many minds." Indeed, public opinion polls found that more than half the respondents did not approve of President Bill Clinton's handling of the situation in Somalia.[21]

During the Gulf War, fear of an unsanitized presentation of the carnage of battle was perhaps central to the military's efforts to control the media through the use of press pools and military escorts. John J. Fialka, a *Wall Street Journal* correspondent, remarks, "We were escorted away from most of the violence because the bodies of the dead chopped up by artillery, pulverized by B-52 raids, or lacerated by friendly fire don't play well, politically."[22] Military planners insisted, however, that they were motivated by a legitimate concern for operational security as well as a concern for the well-being of the journalists. They further pointed to the logistical difficulties encountered in accommodating the large number of journalists who wanted to cover the war.

But for many the impression remained that at the heart of the military's concern was the capacity of media to undermine public and political support for an operation involving casualties. Ted Koppel, speaking of the Gulf War, remarks, "I'm not sure the public's interest is served by seeing what seems to have been such a painless war, when 50,000 to 100,000 people may have died on the other side. Obviously this was done so they could maintain the closest possible control over public opinion, to increase support for the war."[23]

Control of the reporter was a central component of the military's effort to limit the potential for public relations damage. Just before the ground war there were twenty-five to thirty pool reporters to cover six army and two marine divisions near the Kuwaiti border. No reporter from the *New York Times* bureau in Saudi Arabia was given official access to a pool slot before February 10, 1991.[24]

Use of officially sanctioned pools had a particularly pronounced effect on the availability of pictures during combat. One editor at the time was quoted as remarking, "The pictures coming out of pool arrangements are quite ordinary. There are no negative aspects to the war."[25]

Tomorrow's wars will most likely look more like the conflicts in Somalia, Bosnia, and Haiti and less like the Gulf War. In such circumstances, journalists will already be in the zone of conflict, making their control far more difficult for military planners. Yet, in the long run, pictures may not matter as much as context and leadership. The key variable may be the presence of a clearly articulated policy and a public sense that the policy is "worth it." General Colin Powell expresses this point:

> They're [the American people] prepared to take casualties. And even if they see them on live television it will make them madder. Even if they see them on live television, as long as they believe it's for a solid purpose

and for a cause that is understandable and for a cause that has something
to do with an interest of ours. They will not understand it, if it can't be
explained, which is the point I have made consistently over the years. If
you can't explain it to the parents who are sending their kids, you'd better
think twice about it.[26]

Media scholars suggest that government officials and agencies are
becoming more sophisticated in their efforts to offer the sort of credible
"explanations" referred to by Powell and that in most circumstances they
are assisted in their efforts by the U.S. media.[27] For example, political scientist W. Lance Bennett finds that the media closely "index" their coverage
to the contours of official debate and controversy.[28] That is, the levels of
criticism directed at government policy rise and fall in accordance with the
intensity of criticisms emanating out of other institutionally based official
sources. As Bennett and political scientist Jarol Manheim put it, "As a practical matter, news organizations routinely leave policy framing and issue
emphasis to political elites (generally, government officials)."[29]

The media as threat to operational security.   While it may still be an open
question whether media content, live or otherwise, has the ability to hinder
the pursuit of desired policy goals because of their emotional freight, the
fact remains that some operations are extremely sensitive to media exposure. Maintaining operational security during conventional war and tactical
operations, such as antiterrorism operations, is essential. In these circumstances, the media have the technological capacity to hinder some types of
operations simply by exposing them.

This is true, for example, in conventional warfare. As communication
equipment becomes more mobile and global in its reach and real-time
reporting of all types becomes more pervasive, the danger to operational
security will become more pronounced. "It isn't like World War II, when
George Patton would sit around in his tent with six or seven reporters and
muse," with the results "transcribed and reviewed" before being released,
remarks Powell. If a commander "in Desert Shield sat around in his tent
and mused with a few CNN guys and pool guys and other guys, it's in 105
capitals a minute later."[30] In the process of covering an operation, news
organizations may reveal information that leads to unnecessary casualties
and even the possible failure of a mission. This is not to say that journalists
will seek (or have sought) to deliberately expose operations. The disclo-
sures are inadvertent. Retired General Norman Schwarzkopf has told of
such a case.

It was reported [by a U.S. television network] that at this time, right now,
we are witnessing an artillery duel between the 82nd Airborne Division
and the Iraqis. If they [the Iraqis] had any kind of halfway decent intelligence, they would have made note of the time . . . and through their intel-

ligence network they would have pinpointed the location of the 82nd Airborne. Until that time everything they ever saw of the 82nd was on the east coast. All of a sudden they would have found the 82nd way to the west and it would certainly have telegraphed something to them.[31]

Shortcomings in Iraqi military intelligence meant they were not able to take advantage of a key piece of information that would have informed them the U.S. military was massing 200 miles west of Kuwait City.

In summary, there are two understandings of media effect as policy impediment. One is psychological and concerns the corrosive effect some types of media content may have on public opinion, particularly public support for war. The seriousness of this potential effect is open to question. As Colin Powell remarked, pictures of dead U.S. soldiers, as one example, may just make the American public "madder." The other, and potentially far more profound effect involves violations of operational security, as we have just reviewed.

The Media as Agenda-Setting Agents

Of the presumed media effects on foreign policy, perhaps the most disturbing is the suggestion that the U.S. foreign policy agenda itself is at times merely a reflection of news content. This is not to say that issues are necessarily created ex nihilo by media content but rather that priorities are reordered by coverage.[32] What would have been handled by mid-level officials in a routine fashion instead becomes the focus of high-level decision-making. Former Secretary of State James Baker makes the point this way:

> All too often, television is what determines what is a crisis. Television concluded the break-up of the former Yugoslavia and the fighting in the Balkans was a crisis, and they began to cover it and cover it. And so the Clinton administration [was left] to find a way to do something. [Yet] they didn't do that in Rwanda where the excesses were every bit as bad, if not worse. And so, you have to ask yourself, does that mean you should do foreign policy by television? Are we going to define crises according to what is covered, by what the editors decide to cover? I don't think we should do that.[33]

This has been a constant theme of criticism since the end of the Cold War. James Schlesinger argues this when he remarks, "National policy is determined by the plight of the Kurds or starvation in Somalia, as it appears on the screen." Jessica Mathews agrees, "The process by which a particular human tragedy becomes a crisis demanding a response is less the result of a rational weighing of need or of what is remediable than it is of what gets on nightly news shows."[34]

Most of the post–Cold War interventions—Somalia, Haiti, and Bosnia—have been done in the name of humanitarianism, what Michael Mandelbaum refers to as "the foreign policy of Mother Teresa" or foreign policy as "a branch of social work."[35] In his view, foreign policy as social work, particularly during the Clinton administration, has tended to be about peripheral issues. It is intended, he says, "to relieve the suffering caused by ethnic cleansing in Bosnia, starvation in Somalia, and oppression in Haiti. Historically the foreign policy of the United States has centered on American interests, defined as developments that could affect the lives of American citizens. Nothing that occurred in these three countries fit that criterion."[36]

It is debatable whether this is a fair criticism of the Clinton administration's foreign policy. In particular, Mandelbaum's reliance on a traditional values/national interests dichotomy is problematic, as Stanley Hoffmann pointed out in his response to the argument.[37] National interests are not self-evident, but are instead constructs—the choices and preferences made by national leaders. Because the selections are often controversial, "those who support them cover them with the mantle of the national interest, and those who do not back them argue, like Mandelbaum, that they deal with developments that 'could [not] affect the lives of . . . citizens' and thus are not in the national interest."[38]

Whatever its shortcomings, Mandelbaum's argument does point us to the fact that of all the humanitarian crises found at any given point in time, the inclination will be to address those that happen to be featured on television, rather than those that are the more severe or those with the greatest likelihood of successful redress by outside intervention. To put it another way, proponents of the media-as-agenda-setting-agent view argue that the choices and selections of national interests are too heavily weighted in favor of what happens to get covered by CNN or other media.

These are important considerations, for clearly the conditions that have given rise to humanitarian interventions by the United States in the past are only likely to grow more severe in the future. According to a 1996 study by the United States Mission to the United Nations, regional conflicts in the mid-1990s have put 42 million people around the world at risk of disease and starvation.[39] If media coverage of crises has had an effect on U.S. foreign policy in the past, as some argue, then the potential for similar effects in the future are great.

Television, for a variety of commercial and professional reasons, is drawn to the dramatic visuals found in most—*but not all*—humanitarian emergencies. The pitched battles between gun-toting teenagers in the streets of some hitherto unheard-of place, massive flows of refugees, the pathos of a starving child, all make for compelling television. Once engaged, once the U.S. foreign policy priorities align themselves with media coverage, the other two manifestations of the CNN effect may come into play. Decisionmaking may be accelerated and rash. Events may cascade out of control, leading to confrontations for which the public and policymakers themselves are psychologically unprepared. "Vivid imagery," in such a scenario, drives both ends of policy. First there is the politics of "humanitarian intervention and then of disillusioned withdrawal."[40]

Although this version of the CNN effect has the most profound potential consequences, it is also the most problematic for several reasons. First, what few empirical investigations exist have not borne out the contention. Andrew Natsios, the Bush administration official who headed up the relief effort in Somalia, has argued that if one examines the record of U.S. policy involvement in overseas humanitarian crises, one comes away with the conclusion that "the so-called CNN effect has taken on more importance than it deserves as an explanation for responses emanating from the policymaking process in Washington."[41]

The majority of humanitarian operations are conducted without media attention. In 1991, for example, the United States Agency for International Development's Office of Foreign Disaster Assistance and Food for Peace Program shipped some 12,000 tons of food to Somalia. This was well before the news media discovered the crisis there in August of the following year.[42] Furthermore, the eventual media coverage itself was the *consequence* of official actions. Specifically, it resulted from the efforts of one part of the foreign policy community (Office of Foreign Disaster Assistance and its allies in Congress and portions of the State Department) to persuade other elements of the foreign policy community (primarily senior decision-makers in the White House) to sign on to desired policy goals. The media were used by some officials to get the attention of other officials, a tried and true practice of bureaucratic politics that predates CNN by many years.[43] The great majority of Somalia coverage followed rather than preceded official action (see Figures 12.1 and 12.2).

Of the events noted on the timeline presented in Figures 12.1 and 12.2, the White House's August 14 announcement (point designation "D") that it would use U.S. aircraft to send relief supplies precipitated the first wave of U.S. news media attention to Somalia, which jumped five-fold almost overnight. As an executive at NBC said at the time, "With the international relief effort growing, the Somalia situation is likely to be examined more often by the network news shows in the coming weeks. We're going to cover it more."[44] The announcement of the planned deployment of troops two months later (point designation "H") caused a second expansion of coverage. In both instances, media attention *followed* official actions.

This trend was even more pronounced with CNN coverage (see Figure 12.2). CNN coverage of Somalia prior to the announcement of the airlift of emergency food and medicine in August (notation "E") was sporadic to nonexistent. By logical necessity, it is difficult to conceive how media could be the cause of policy developments in Somalia in 1992.[45] Media were doing as they have for generations: they followed the troops.

Figure 12.1 Network News Coverage of Somalia

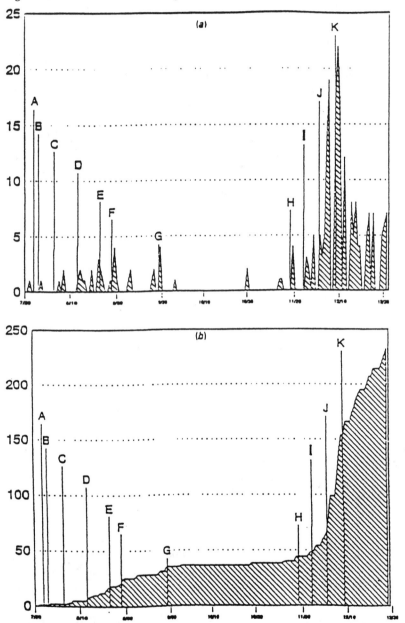

Network news coverage: (a) Daily story count; (b) Cumulative story count. A, UN secretary general's report to Security Council; B, UN Security Council's report on Somalia; C, OFDA press conference, Washington, D.C.; D, White House announces relief effort; E, U.S. airlift commences; F, first flights into Somalia; G, President Bush advocates use of security forces; H, Bush approves 28,000 U.S. troops; I, secretary of state tells UN that United States will send troops; J, UN Security Council authorizes troops; K, first U.S. troops go ashore in Somalia

Figure 12.2 Daily Coverage of Somalia by CNN

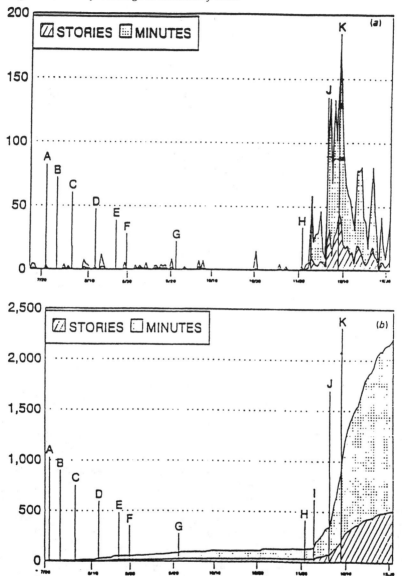

News coverage by CNN: (a) Daily story count; (b) Cumulative story count. A, UN secretary general's report to Security Council; B, UN Security Council's report on Somalia; C, OFDA press conference, Washington, D.C.; D, White House announces relief effort; E, U.S. airlift commences; F, first flights into Somalia; G, President Bush advocates use of security forces; H, Bush approves 28,000 U.S. troops; I, secretary of state tells UN that United States will send troops; J, UN Security Council authorizes troops; K, first U.S. troops go ashore in Somalia

Although disease and starvation are commonly seen by U.S. journalists in Africa and elsewhere in the developing world,[46] they are not common news stories. In fact, it may be that journalists tend to dismiss humanitarian crises because they are so much a part of the landscape in some regions of the world. In 1993, when approximately 50,000 people were killed in political fighting between Hutus and Tutsis in Burundi, U.S. broadcast television networks ignored the story. When regional leaders met in Dar es Salaam in April 1994 in an attempt to reach a regional peace accord, only CNN mentioned the meeting. Yet a more sophisticated analysis of events in Rwanda that same month required understanding that fear of successful peace talks encouraged Hutu extremists in Rwanda to launch their campaign of carnage against Tutsis and Hutu moderates who favored accommodation.

Overall, the lack of media coverage of humanitarian emergencies is most striking.[47] Table 12.2 presents the percentage of mentions of all thirteen of the most severe humanitarian emergencies combined and total individual mentions in the *New York Times, Washington Post,* ABC News programming, CNN news programming, and NPR's *All Things Considered* and *Morning Edition* from January 1995 to mid-May 1996.

Table 12.2   Proportion at Risk and News Coverage (percent)[a]

Country	Percentage of Mentions (millions at risk)	N.Y. Times %	N	Washington Post %	N	ABC News %	N	CNN %	N	NPR %	N
Afghanistan	14 (4)	4.7	(274)	4.8	(225)	1.5	(19)	1.2	(57)	2.9	(57)
Sudan	14 (4)	3.3	(190)	3.5	(166)	0.6	(8)	1.1	(54)	1.5	(31)
Bosnia	13 (3.7)	45.8	(2,633)	43.7	(2,046)	66.0	(833)	66.7	(3,062)	61.3	(1,204)
Ethiopia	11 (3–4)	0.2	(15)	0.2	(10)	0	(0)	0	(3)	0.3	(6)
Angola	9 (2.5)	2.0	(120)	3.0	(144)	0.7	(9)	0.4	(22)	1.7	(34)
Rwanda	9 (2.5)	6.9	(401)	5.9	(277)	3.9	(49)	9.8	(150)	6.0	(118)
Sierra Leone	6 (1.8)	1.0	(63)	1.6	(78)	0.3	(4)	0.5	(26)	1.0	(20)
Liberia	5 (1.5)	2.8	(164)	3.2	(150)	2.5	(32)	1.0	(49)	2.3	(46)
Iraq	5 (1.3–<4)	14.6	(839)	14.5	(679)	11.9	(150)	11.7	(540)	10.2	(201)
Haiti	3 (0.9–1.3)	11.3	(654)	11.1	(522)	7.0	(89)	6.8	(316)	6.7	(132)
Eritrea	4 (1)	0.4	(28)	0.4	(21)	0	(0)	0	(3)	0.2	(4)
Somalia	14 (4)	5.4	(312)	6.6	(309)	5.5	(69)	6.4	(294)	5.1	(102)
Tajikistan	5 (1)	0.7	(45)	1.1	(52)	0	(0)	0.2	(13)	0.4	(9)
Totals	100 (28.2)[b]	99.1	(5,738)	99.6	(4,679)	99.9	(1,262)	99.2	(4,589)	99.6	(1,964)

Notes: a. Due to rounding, percentages do not necessarily add to 100 percent for any given column.
b. Calculated with low-end figures where a range has been given in the total estimated at risk.

Table 12.2, of course, does not capture changes in news coverage over time, as Figures 12.1 and 12.2 did regarding Somalia, but it does clearly indicate the tendency of the U.S. news media to give uneven attention to humanitarian crises. This is seen in the cases of Liberia and Sierra Leone.

Next to Tajikistan, they each received the least attention by the news organizations represented here.[48] Afghanistan and the Sudan have more people at risk than Bosnia, but together they received only 12 percent of the total media coverage devoted to Bosnia alone. Tajikistan, with 1 million people at risk, has a little over 1 percent of the media coverage devoted to Bosnia alone. Put another way, of all news stories between January 1995 and May 1996 concerning the thirteen worst humanitarian crises in the world—affecting nearly 30 million people—nearly half were devoted to the plight of the 3.7 million people of Bosnia.[49] This is not to dismiss their condition but only to make the point that media coverage of humanitarian crises is not uniform and, more importantly, is typically triggered by official actions associated with the presence of U.S. troops.

The second reason the CNN effect may have "taken on more importance than it deserves," to use Natsios's characterization, is that if one looks more closely at some of the more prominent post–Cold War U.S. "humanitarian" interventions, one is likely to find equally compelling geostrategic reasons for the intervention. This was certainly true of the response to the Kurdish refugee crises along the Iraqi border with Turkey following the Gulf War in the spring of 1991.

President Bush's national security adviser, Brent Scowcroft, emphatically makes this point: "We were actually quite cynical about media's impact. Media are too fickle [to have an impact]." Media attention to any given crisis could therefore be ridden out by policymakers. Geopolitical factors, in Scowcroft's view, were more important concerning the implementation of Operation Provide Comfort. "Without Turkey factored in, with just television pictures, I don't know what our response would have been. We were very sensitive to Turkey's anxiety about allowing the Kurds to stay. That was fundamentally what motivated us."[50] Turkey, a staunch U.S. ally and a member of NATO, has been in a long and bloody guerrilla war with elements of its own Kurdish population in eastern Turkey. The idea that thousands of Kurdish refugees from Iraq might become permanently located on or near the border was anathema to the Turkish government.

James Baker made the same point, "Once they [the Iraqi Kurdish refugees] all went into Turkey, it was important to get them back to Iraq."[51] When Saddam Hussein's surviving forces ruthlessly crushed first the Shiite rebellion in the south and then the Kurdish rebellion in the north in March 1991, the policy of the United States was to let the rebellions fail, despite the gruesome pictures coming out of northern Iraq at the time. When asked if it was accurate to suggest that U.S. policy at the time was not to get involved, regardless of what the pictures showed, Baker responded, "That's right. I think that is an accurate description. It would have been a mistake to be involved."[52] For geopolitical reasons, the United States allowed the rebellions to fail and implemented a policy designed to resettle the Kurdish refugees back in their towns and villages in northern Iraq. This was not done because of pictures. It was done because Turkey needed it done for its stability and for the stability of the entire region.

Third, the CNN effect may be overstated because the formal policy requirements put into place following events in Somalia in 1993 may limit it. Under the provisions of Presidential Decision Directive 25 (PDD 25), issued in May 1994, approval of the use of U.S. forces for humanitarian relief missions became more difficult. Before forces may be used, a series of strict conditions must be met, including a clear statement of U.S. interests at stake in the operation, the approval of Congress, the availability of funding for the operation, a fixed date of withdrawal of U.S. forces, and an agreed-upon command and control structure.[53]

The first application of PDD 25 was in Rwanda. The U.S. representative to the UN, Madeleine Albright, insisted it would have been "folly" for a UN force to venture into the "maelstrom" of killing.[54] Despite the biblical proportions of the bloodshed, the United States did not intervene until later, when Hutu refugees in camps in Zaire—some of whom were the perpetrators of the massacre in the first place—began dying from the effects of dehydration, malnutrition, and disease. But "feeding and watering," as it is sometimes called in the Pentagon and what we will call a "consensual humanitarian operation" in this chapter, is a considerably different policy objective than shooting and pacifying, as would have been necessary to stop the bloodshed and possibly avoid the exodus of refugees. It would have involved far higher risks and potential costs, measured on several scales.

The debate regarding the effect(s) the media have on foreign policy and diplomacy has run aground on the shoals of its own conceptual ambiguity. To advance the argument requires a clarification of the hypothesis at hand. There are at least three understandings of the CNN effect: media as an accelerant to the process, as an impediment, and as an agenda setter. The next step is to clarify further the relationship among these various possible effects and different policy types.

Types of Intervention

Eight types of military interventions and their possible relation with one or another of the media effects outlined previously will be reviewed next. The objective is simply to illustrate the thesis, not to offer a comprehensive review of potential media effects on all policy types. It is intended to stimulate thought anchored in a more refined understanding of media and policy interaction. The policy types reviewed are conventional warfare, strategic deterrence, tactical deterrence, special operations and low-intensity conflict (SOLIC), peacemaking, peacekeeping, imposed humanitarian operations, and consensual humanitarian operations.[55]

As one moves from top to bottom of Table 12.3, one sees reduced potential costs resulting from failure, measured in money and lives, and—less precisely—in political prestige, international standing, and confidence felt by alliance partners. Beginning with peacemaking, as one moves toward the bottom of Table 12.3 one finds policies designed to respond to crises stemming from war or other human-created conditions. Failed states or civil wars such as in Somalia, the Sudan, and Zaire offer examples.

Conventional Warfare

The stakes are highest in conventional warfare, which also generates the greatest media and public interest. Reprising the difficulties found between the military and the media in wartime is not necessary here.[56] Experience in recent wars indicates that when and where possible, the military will attempt to control the movements of journalists and the content of their reports, behavior rooted in the two concerns outlined above: fear that the "wrong" pictures will undermine public or congressional support for the effort and, second, that journalists will inadvertently disclose tactical or strategic information to the enemy.

Pool systems, prior clearance of dispatches, and other forms of censorship will continue to be a part of military planning for conventional warfare. At the same time, high public interest and the journalists' ambition and sense of independent professionalism will lead to efforts to avoid and undermine the military's attempts to control them. The media will be assisted in these efforts by the greater mobility provided to them by smaller, light-weight equipment capable of point-to-point transmissions from anywhere to anywhere on earth.

In conventional warfare, the media are most likely to serve as accelerants and impediments in the policy process. It is highly unlikely that media content *alone* might in some fashion lead the United States into a conventional war. The degree to which the media serve as accelerants to decision-making in war and the degree to which this is necessarily injurious cannot be answered in the abstract. The answer depends on the circumstances and the resourcefulness of the policymakers. The same is true of the possibility that pictures may undermine public support for the war. As Colin Powell remarked, pictures may just as well make people "madder."

The media effect of greatest concern to the military in conventional warfare is their ability to provide adversaries with sensitive information. In an era of highly mobile, decentralized, global, real-time media, the risks to operational security are considerable.

Strategic Deterrence

Deterrence may be defined as "the persuasion of one's opponent that the costs and/or risks of a given course of action he might take outweigh its

Table 12.3 Intervention Types and Media Considerations

	Policy Goals and Objectives	Likely Media Interest	Government Media Policy	Likely Media Effects	Public Opinion
Use of Force					
Conventional Warfare	Destruction of enemy and its war-fighting capability.	Extremely high.	High degree of attempted media control. "Indexed" news.	Accelerant, impediment (both types).	High public interest and attentiveness to it.
Strategic Deterrence	Maintain status quo. Example: Cold War, Korean peninsula.	Moderate to high interest. Routinized coverage.	Routine news interaction. White House, DOD, State briefings, etc.	During stability, little effect. Accelerant during periods of instability.	Scrutiny only by attentive public. Expansion of base during instability.
Tactical Deterrence	Meet challenge to status quo. Example: Desert Shield, PRC-Taiwan, March 1996.	Moderate to high interest but episodic.	Controlled but cooperative. Force multiplier.	All three effects, but not necessarily injurious.	Attentive public scrutiny. Latent public opinion a concern to policymakers.
SOLIC	Counterterrorism, hostage rescue, specialized operations.	High interest, particularly hostage situations, some terrorism.	Secrecy. Barring of all access.	Impediment (operational security risk).	Little to no public awareness in most cases.
Peacemaking	Third party imposition of political solution by force of arms. Example: late Somalia, Yugoslavia.	High interest at initial stages of operation. Variation afterward dependent on level of stability.	Volatile conditions. Danger in reporting. Access with risk.	Impediment (both types).	Attentive public scrutiny. Latent public opinion a concern to policymakers.
Peacekeeping	Bolster an accepted political solution by presence of third party.	Moderate interest unless accord is destabilized.	Generally unrestricted access to theater of operation.	Impediment (emotional impediment most likely).	Attentive public scrutiny. Latent public opinion a concern to policymakers.
Imposed Humanitarian Operations	Forceful, apolitical aid policy.	Low/moderate interest unless violence ensues.	Volatile conditions. Reporting risky.	Impediment (emotional impediment most likely).	Attentive public scrutiny. Latent public opinion a concern to policymakers.
Consensual Humanitarian Operations	Agreed humanitarian assistance.	Initial operation met by moderate to low interest.	Unrestricted, even encouraged media coverage.	Media effect unlikely.	Attentive public scrutiny.
Operations Other than War					

Source: Adapted from Richard Haass, *Intervention: The Use of American Military Force in the Post–Cold War World* (Washington, D.C.: Carnegie Endowment Book, 1995).

benefits."[57] Persuasion, of course, involves communication. The idea is to communicate a willingness to use force with the hope that, ironically, it will negate the necessity to do so. The movement of force and a projected willingness to use it is an important component of deterrence. It can take the form of a long-term deployment, such as was the case in Western Europe during the Cold War, the continued positioning of forces on the Korean peninsula, the more recent stationing of U.S. troops in Macedonia, and the stationing of mostly U.S. Air Force units in southern Turkey. The objective is to maintain the status quo.[58]

Typically, media coverage of strategic deterrence operations during times of relative stability will be highly routinized. Regular correspondents assigned to institutional settings such as the State Department, Defense Department, and White House and foreign correspondents in the regions of the operation will monitor usually incremental developments over an extended time. The level of media and public interest will vary according to the perceived stability of the situation, that is, according to the perceived effectiveness of deterrence. Signs of instability, such as the rash of North Korean incursions into the demilitarized zone between the two Koreas in 1996, will spark an increase in attention. The likely media effect is subtle. Elite debate and dialogue in columns and opinion journals regarding the best way to maintain (or perhaps dissolve) the status quo is most common. Except during times of crisis, foreign policy debate of this sort is commonly left to the "attentive public" and policy elite. Television, with a few exceptions, does not dwell on such matters, again except during times of instability, such as when the Eastern bloc and Soviet Union collapsed.

Tactical Deterrence

Deterrence may also come in the form of a rapid response to tactical developments, such as the deployment of a Navy carrier group or rapid reaction force to some trouble spot in the world. In these circumstances media interest is likely to be extremely high, as is almost always the case with troop deployments in circumstances of potential conflict.

With tactical deterrence, global media are often important and valuable *assets* to the military, particularly when time is short and conditions are critical. Admiral Kendal Pease, chief of information for the U.S. Navy, has called global media in such circumstances a "force multiplier." After showing a CNN video clip of carrier-based U.S. fighter-bombers taking off on a practice bombing run against an implied Iraqi target during Desert Shield, Pease explained that the Navy had arranged for a CNN crew to be aboard the carrier to film the "hardware in use" and to "send a message to Saddam Hussein." The Iraqis, the Navy realized and counted on, monitored CNN.[59] "The same thing is going on now," said Pease, "in Taiwan."[60] Prior to Taiwan's March 1996 elections, which China opposed and threatened to stop with military force if necessary, the Clinton administration sent two aircraft carrier groups to the seas off Taiwan. Television crews accompanying the Navy ships sent pictures of the U.S. defenders to the Chinese and the rest of the world.

By using the media as a "force multiplier" in conjunction with deterrent force, U.S. policymakers are, in effect, attempting to create a "CNN effect" in the policymaking of a potential or actual adversary. As Richard Haass noted at the beginning of this chapter, global, real-time media should not be regarded solely as an impediment or obstacle to policymakers. They may just as well be assets.

SOLIC

Special operations and low-intensity conflict is a general term applied to an array of military missions employing highly trained and specialized commando forces. Navy Seals, Army Rangers, special operations wings of the air force, and the Delta Force offer examples of units typically involved in SOLIC. SOLIC missions include counterterrorism operations, hostage rescue, and, during conventional warfare, infiltration into enemy territory. During the Gulf War, many of the Scud missile batteries in Iraq were destroyed by special operations units, rather than by airstrikes.

SOLIC operations take place in hostile environments, are usually limited in scope, and are conducted in an envelope of extreme secrecy. In fact, for years the most elite of the U.S. military units involved in counterterrorism/hostage rescue operations, Delta Force, was not publicly acknowledged. The necessity for secrecy makes SOLIC operations the most sensitive to media coverage. The disclosure of an operation would, in all likelihood, lead to its termination. It is unlikely other forms of media effects would be associated with SOLIC, though it is conceivable that special operations units may be activated, for example, in response to some highly publicized situation involving hostages.

Peacemaking

With peacemaking operations we begin a discussion of several "nontraditional" military missions, each differentiated by subtle but important features. Peacemaking, also sometimes referred to as "robust peacekeeping" and "aggravated peacekeeping," presupposes that one or more parties to a conflict are not interested in peace and do not agree to the presence of outsider peacekeepers. Ergo, such an outside force is heavily armed. However, while there is little or no peace in a peacemaking environment, there is considerable restraint in the use of force. Peacekeeping is distinguished from conventional war by its objectives in using violence, if necessary. In war, the objective is to inflict massive destruction on an enemy. In peacemaking, the goal is to create the conditions necessary for the implementation of an accord. In a sense, the goal of *peacemaking* is to create the environment required for *peacekeeping* operations discussed below.

The hostile, unstable nature of the peacemaking environment means media and public interest is likely to be extremely high, at least initially. As with peacekeeping, if and when a sense of stability is established, media interest will diminish accordingly. Also as with peacekeeping, the most likely potential media effect with peacemaking is that it will create an emotional impediment. Casualties may undermine public and elite support for the operation. Knowing this, opponents of peace may deliberately target peacemaking forces. Due to the hostile nature of the environment and the potential for open conflict between the peacemakers and one or more of the hostile forces in the war, operational security is also a concern. Descriptions of peacemaker capabilities may serve as a "force multiplier," but if they are too detailed they may just as well suggest vulnerabilities of the peacemaking force. Furthermore, it is feasible that in highly unstable, fluid situations, media content may accelerate decisionmaking. Finally, it seems unlikely, particularly after implementation of PDD 25, that media content *alone* will lead to U.S. involvement in risky peacemaking operations.

Peacekeeping

In peacekeeping missions, lightly armed forces are deployed in a "permissive environment" to bolster a fragile peace. A permissive environment is one in which the outside military force is welcome in sufficient measure by all combatants to allow for relatively safe operation. Haass describes peacekeeping as the deployment of force "in a largely consensual framework in which there are at most only periodic, relatively isolated, and small-scale breakdowns of the peace."[61] The role of troops is relatively passive.

As with all U.S. troop deployments, the news media will show considerable interest in peacekeeping operations, though after a period of apparent stability, media interest is likely to flag. U.S. peacekeeping forces in Macedonia offer an example. Coverage, to the degree there is any, will be limited to the elite press, such as the *New York Times*. Television, at best, will pay only passing interest. Media interest will rise in direct proportion to the sense of potential instability. Put another way, the more fragile the peace that the peacekeepers are there to protect, the greater will be media and public interest. If the situation appears unstable, and political leaders have not made the case that U.S. national interests are involved in preserving the peace, media coverage of casualties may quickly undermine support for the mission. Here the media effect is an emotional impediment. Operational security, though a concern, is not central. Peacekeeping missions are often "transparent" in any case, an openness in operations that is meant to suggest evenhandedness.

Imposed Humanitarian Interventions

As the title implies, imposed humanitarian interventions differ from peace-keeping operations in that the scope of their objectives is more limited. Examples of imposed humanitarian interventions are Somalia after December 1992 but before the summer of 1993, Iraq since April 1991, and in and around Sarajevo in 1994. The objectives are limited to providing food; medicine; clean, safe water; and a secure but limited geographical location.[62] Whereas the mission of a peacekeeping operation is to maintain a fragile status quo (peace), and the mission of a peacemaking operation is to impose a political solution, by force of arms if necessary, on one or more sides to a conflict, the mission of an imposed humanitarian intervention is to feed and care for a population in need.

In large measure, in these circumstances the military is used for its technical capabilities, such as water purification; field medicine; and, most importantly, logistical capabilities. The U.S. military is unmatched in its ability to move massive amounts of cargo great distances to almost any sort of terrain.

Media interest is likely to be quite high, particularly at the beginning with the introduction of U.S. troops, as discussed earlier. This will be particularly true if correspondents can operate safely in the secure zone established by the military. One of the very legitimate and understandable reasons so little coverage was given to the massacres in Rwanda prior to the Goma refugee coverage was the inability of journalists to move about safely in Rwanda.[63]

Though media content alone is not likely to lead to an imposed humanitarian intervention, it cannot be ruled out. The media effect of greatest potential in imposed humanitarian missions is as an impediment. The argument for continuation of a policy with possibly little or no direct U.S. interest would be difficult to sustain in the face of pictures of injured and dead Americans.

Consensual Humanitarian Interventions

Consensual humanitarian interventions, as the name implies, involve the use of the military in addressing the urgent needs of a distressed population. As with imposed humanitarian interventions, consensual humanitarian interventions are intended to save lives, not alter political circumstances on the ground through the use of force.[64] The U.S. response to a devastating cyclone that hit Bangladesh on May 3, 1991, offers an example. In the midst of Operation Provide Comfort in northern Iraq, the U.S. military sent military teams to assist the survivors. U.S. assistance to refugees in Goma, Zaire, in 1994 is another example of a consensual humanitarian intervention.

Consensual humanitarian interventions are relatively low-cost, not only in material resources but also in terms of the potential political capital at stake. Because U.S. soldiers are working in a relatively permissive environment, political leaders face relatively little risk in deploying them on such a mission. What risk there is may be found in a general sense of unease that pervades such missions, at least with some, over the possibility that "mission creep" will lead to a deeper involvement, as happened in Somalia. If involvement is truly consensual and remains so, there will probably be little sustained media interest in the story.

Shifts in Media-Policy Effects

Each operation outlined above tends to have different sensitivities to media content. Further, the potential effects in question are interactive. Shifts in policy will produce changes in media coverage, just as media coverage may change policy. U.S. policy in Somalia offers an example of the dynamic interactive nature of foreign policy making and media coverage.

From late 1991 to about July 1992, the U.S. policy response to the worsening conditions in Somalia was nonmilitary in nature, with relief operations working through the auspices of nongovernmental organizations, the Office of Foreign Disaster Assistance, the International Committee of the Red Cross, and UN agencies. As noted above, during this time there was practically no media attention to Somalia.[65] In August 1992, the Bush administration undertook a *consensual humanitarian intervention,* transporting relief supplies to Somalia using military cargo planes. A small contingent of security and other support personnel were also involved. With Todd Eachus, I have argued elsewhere that media content had no effect on this decision, contrary to popular belief. Instead, it resulted from a number of bureaucratic and domestic political (presidential campaign) considerations.[66] That is not to say that media did not play a role in the unfolding policy developments. With the introduction of U.S. military personnel in August, media coverage of Somalia skyrocketed, not because conditions had worsened but because Americans were there.

The continued fighting and banditry in Somalia made the environment there something less than consensual; not all of the players on the ground agreed that giving food and other forms of aid to those in need was necessarily a good idea. As a result, in December the Bush administration sent in marines to provide security. At that point the policy changed, for the third time, and became an *imposed humanitarian intervention.* Media attention, as Figures 12.1 and 12.2 indicate, rose accordingly.

Then, by the summer of 1993, the Clinton administration and its counterparts in the UN allowed the mission in Somalia to become something else again. It drifted into becoming a *peacemaking* operation. The problem the administration created for itself in the process was found in the fact that it had not put an appropriate force structure on the ground—the troops and equipment necessary to achieve the new political mission. Whereas humanitarian missions, strictly speaking, do not pursue political objectives, at least not in theory, peacemaking missions do. More importantly, the Clinton administration failed to build the political support with Congress, opinion leaders, and the American public necessary for sustaining a more demanding political mission in Somalia. As a result, the policy was derailed in October 1993, as is often said, with the pictures of a dead American body on macabre display in Mogadishu. Different policies with different types and levels of media scrutiny produced different results.

Conclusion

Each policy outlined above obviously has different objectives, actual and potential costs, and operational requirements. As a result, the level of interest the media have and the potential consequence of that interest vary substantially. Before we can make theoretical and empirical progress in understanding the effects of the media on foreign policy, we must refine the debate to meaningful terms. The grand, interesting, and often heated debate about the "CNN effect" will continue to fail us unless we distill it into its constituent parts. That means speaking more precisely about the likely effects relative to specific policies.

Notes

1. James Schlesinger, "Quest for a Post–Cold War Foreign Policy," *Foreign Affairs* (Winter 1992), on-line without pagination. See also Richard N. Haass, "Paradigm Lost," *Foreign Affairs* (Winter 1995), on-line without pagination.

2. James Schlesinger, "Quest for a Post–Cold War Foreign Policy." See also Richard N. Haass, "Paradigm Lost"; and James F. Hoge, Jr., "Media Pervasiveness," *Foreign Affairs* (Summer 1994), on-line without pagination.

3. Charles Krauthammer, "Intervention Lite: Foreign Policy by CNN," *Washington Post,* February 18, 1994, p 25.

4. Nik Gowing, "Real-Time Television Coverage of Armed Conflicts and Diplomatic Crises: Does It Pressure or Distort Foreign Policy Decision Making?" Working Paper 94-1, The Joan Shorenstein Center on the Press, Politics and Public Policy, John F. Kennedy School of Government, Harvard University, p. 9. See also Johanna Neuman, *Lights, Camera, War: Is Technology Driving International Politics?* (New York: St. Martin's Press, 1995); Warren Strobel, "The CNN Effect," *American Journalism Review* (May 1996): 32; and Hearing Before the Committee on Foreign Affairs, U.S. House of Representatives, 103rd Congress, second session, April 26, 1994, p. 5. See also "For the Record," *Washington Post,* April 27, 1994, p. A22.

5. James Hoge, Jr., speaking at the Robert R. McCormick Tribune

Foundation–George Washington University conference on Military, Media, and Humanitarian Crises; held on the campus of George Washington University, May 5, 1995.

6. This does not exhaust the possibilities, of course. Murray Edelman pointed out in several important works (*Constructing the Political Spectacle, Political Language*) that the policy process often acts in reverse of what has just been implied. At times, particular policy goals are first identified by officials. Second, a problem of sufficient emotional or symbolic importance is then offered as a justification for adopting a set of favored solutions.

For example, reducing Iraq's ability to conduct hostile actions against its neighbors was a policy goal of the Bush administration in the fall and winter of 1990. The administration needed to find ways to frame U.S. interests there as something more compelling than protecting oil. Secretary of State James A. Baker's "It's jobs, jobs, jobs" just didn't do the trick. Instead, the administration and its allies at Hill and Knowlton, a Washington public relations firm, were able to cast Saddam Hussein as Adolf Hitler and create emotionally compelling but factually unsound stories about Iraqi soldiers removing Kuwaiti babies from incubators. See William A. Dorman and Steven Livingston, "News and Historical Content: The Establishing Phase of the Persian Gulf Policy Debate," in *Taken by Storm: The Media, Public Opinion, and U.S. Foreign Policy in the Gulf War,* W. Lance Bennett and David L. Paletz (eds.) (Chicago: University of Chicago Press, 1994). Desired policy was achieved by creating compelling news stories and frames.

I do not mean to suggest that the analytical framework offered here explains more than a portion of the foreign policy process. Not all policy is the result of media content. There are many sources of policy, and just as often as media influences policy, media themselves are the instruments of policymakers. If we assume some portion of policy and policy outcomes are the result of media content (knowing also that media content is itself often a reflection of policy), what might those effects be?

7. James F. Hoge, Jr., "Media Pervasiveness."

8. Nicholas Burns, "Talking to the World About American Foreign Policy," *The Harvard International Journal of Press/Politics* 1(4), Fall 1996, pp. 10–14.

9. Author interview with James A. Baker III, Houston, Texas, May 13, 1996. See also James A. Baker III, *The Politics of Diplomacy: Revolution, War and Peace, 1989–92* (New York: G. P. Putnam's Sons, 1995), p. 103.

10. Author interview with Margaret Tutwiler, Alexandria, Virginia, March 29, 1996.

11. Richard Haass, speaking at the Robert R. McCormick Tribune Foundation–George Washington University conference on Military, Media, and Humanitarian Crises.

12. Frank J. Stech, "Winning CNN Wars," *Parameters* (Autumn 1994): 38.

13. Haass, the Robert R. McCormick Tribune Foundation–George Washington University conference on Military, Media, and Humanitarian Crises.

14. Michael R. Beschloss, "Presidents, Television, and Foreign Crises" (Washington, D.C.: The Annenberg Washington Program, 1993), p. 9.

15. Beschloss, "Presidents, Television, and Foreign Crises," p. 10.

16. Author interview with Marvin Kalb, Joan Shorenstein Center on Press, Politics and Public Policy, Harvard University, May 29, 1996.

17. Author interview with Tutwiler. See also Baker, *Politics of Diplomacy,* p. 34.

18. Burns, "Talking to the World."

19. Maureen Dowd, "War Introduces a Tougher Bush to the Nation," *New*

York Times, March 2, 1991. How much this has proven to be the case is an open question.

More recently, Thomas Friedman wryly remarked that if the Vietnam Syndrome was eliminated in 1991, then it has been replaced by the "Gulf War syndrome." The Gulf War Syndrome "says that the US will engage in military operations abroad only if they take place in a desert with nowhere for the enemy to hide, if the fighting can be guaranteed to last no more than five days, if casualties can be counted on one hand, if both oil and nuclear weapons are at stake, if the enemy is a madman who will not accept any compromise, and if the whole operation will be paid for by Germany and Japan." Thomas Friedman, "Global Mandate," *New York Times,* March 5, 1995, p. 15.

On a more general level, the role of public opinion in U.S. foreign policy has been the subject of considerable debate. See Donald L. Jordan and Benjamin I. Page, "Shaping Foreign Policy Opinion: The Role of Television," *Journal of Conflict Resolution* (June 1992): 227–241; Philip J. Powlick, "The Sources of Public Opinion for American Foreign Policy Officials," *International Studies Quarterly* 39 (1995): 427–451.

20. See B. Drummond Ayers, Jr., "A Common Cry Across the US: It's Time to Exit," *New York Times,* October 9, 1993, p. 1.

21. Ibid. It may well have been the case that once the October battle occurred the Clinton administration seized the opportunity to extricate itself from a situation not of its choosing. The pictures were less an impediment and more an opportunity.

22. John J. Fialka, *Hotel Warriors: Covering the Gulf War* (Washington, D.C.: Woodrow Wilson Center Press, 1991), p. 2.

23. Ibid., p. 1.

24. R. W. Apple, "Correspondents Protest Pool System," *New York Times,* February 12, 1991, p. 14.

25. "Editors Criticize Picture Limits," *New York Times,* February 21, 1991, p 14.

26. Barrie Dunsmore, *The Next War: Live?* The Joan Shorenstein Center on Press, Politics and Public Policy, Harvard University, March 1996, p. 9. Edward N. Luttwak has questioned whether television plays a role at all in creating an intolerance of casualties, suggesting it is a "superficial explanation." He noted that the Soviets demonstrated such an intolerance, despite the fact that Soviet television was not allowed to show the sort of gruesome pictures that are of concern to some policymakers in the United States. He instead suggested that the smaller average size of families in contemporary postindustrial society has concentrated emotional familial capital into fewer children, therefore raising the level of sacrifice in war to intolerable levels. Edward N. Luttwak, "Where Are the Great Powers? At Home with the Kids," *Foreign Affairs* (Summer 1994), on-line without pagination.

27. Jarol B. Manheim, "Managing Kuwait's Image During the Gulf Conflict," and Dorman and Livingston, "News and Historical Content," in W. Lance Bennett and David L. Paletz (eds.), *Taken by Storm: The Media, Public Opinion, and U.S. Foreign Policy in the Gulf War* (Chicago: University of Chicago Press, 1994). See also Jarol B. Manheim, *Strategic Public Diplomacy and American Foreign Policy: The Evolution of Influence* (Oxford: Oxford University Press, 1994).

28. W. Lance Bennett, "Marginalizing the Majority: Conditioning Public Opinion to Accept Managerial Democracy," in Michael Margolis and Gary Mauser (eds.), *Manipulating Public Opinion* (Pacific Grove, Calif.:Brooks/Cole, 1989), pp. 320–361.

29. W. Lance Bennett and Jarol B. Manheim, "Taking the Media by Storm:

Information, Cuing, and the Democratic Process in the Gulf Conflict," *Political Communication* 10: 331–351.

30. Jason DeParle, "Long Series of Military Decisions Led to Gulf War News Censorship," *New York Times,* May 5, 1991, p. 1.

31. Barrie Dunsmore, *The Next War: Live?* p. 9.

32. Thanks to Jonathan Moore of the Kennedy School at Harvard for helping me appreciate this important distinction.

33. Author interview with James A Baker III, Houston, Texas, May 14, 1996.

34. Jessica Mathews, "Policy Vs. TV," *Washington Post,* March 8, 1994, p. A19.

35. Michael Mandelbaum, "Foreign Policy as Social Work," *Foreign Affairs* (January 1996), on-line without pagination.

36. Ibid.

37. Stanley Hoffmann, "In Defense of Mother Teresa: Morality in Foreign Policy," *Foreign Affairs* (March 1996), on-line without pagination.

38. Ibid.

39. United States Mission to the United Nations, *Global Humanitarian Emergencies,* 1996, p. 1.

40. David C. Unger, "Taking Haiti," *New York Times Magazine,* October 23, 1994, p. 50. Jim Hoagland has also noted this "whipsaw effect" of media coverage. "A wave of emotion roiled up by horrific images that demand immediate action" is "pushed back by new sets of heart-rending images. A government initially lambasted for callousness is suddenly vulnerable to accusations of being foolhardy. This whipsaw effect is the politician's nightmare." Hoagland's larger point, however, is that this is a condition created by the lack of a clearly articulated foreign policy. (Jim Hoagland, "Don't Blame CNN," *Washington Post,* March 3, 1994, p. 29.)

41. Andrew Natsios, "Illusions of Influence: The CNN Effect in Complex Emergencies," in *From Massacres to Genocide: The Media, Public Policy, and Humanitarian Crises,* Robert I. Rotberg and Thomas G. Weiss (eds.) (Washington, D.C.: Brookings Institution, 1996), p. 150.

42. Steven Livingston and Todd Eachus, "Humanitarian Crises and US Foreign Policy: Somalia and the CNN Effect Reconsidered," *Political Communication* 12 (1995): 417.

43. Ibid.

44. Ibid., p. 426.

45. Events in 1993 presented another story. CNN-as-impediment almost certainly explains the withdrawal of U.S. troops from Somalia. My only point here is that CNN-as-agenda-setter does not serve as an acceptable explanation for the intervention in Somalia in 1992.

46. A point made clear to me in interviews of foreign correspondents in Nairobi, Kenya, in May 1994.

47. Steven Livingston, "Suffering in Silence: Media Coverage of War and Famine in the Sudan," in *From Massacres to Genocide,* pp. 68–89. See also Howard Adelman and Astri Suhrke, "Early Warning and Conflict Management," *The International Response to Conflict and Genocide: Lessons from the Rwanda Experience* (York, Ontario: Centre for Refugee Studies, York University), pp. 46–48.

48. The figures for Liberia are even more pronounced when one takes into consideration that most of the print news items, and nearly all of the broadcast news items, occurred in April and May 1996, at a time of heavy combat and U.S. evacuation missions to the stricken capital of Monrovia. For the *New York Times,* 43 percent (71 of 164) of the news items to mention Liberia between January 1995 and

mid-May 1996 were found in April and half of May 1996. For ABC News, nearly 88 percent (28 of 32) of its reports from Liberia came in April and half of May 1996.

49. Why Bosnia in 1995 and 1996? To address this question well would require another study. But certainly high on the list of reasons for the coverage would be NATO's involvement and the deployment of U.S. troops there (as in Somalia).

50. Author interview with Brent Scowcroft, Washington, D.C., March 27, 1996.

51. Author interview with Baker.

52. Ibid.

53. Larry Minear and Thomas G. Weiss, *Humanitarian Policies* (Headline Series, Foreign Policy Association, 1995), p. 36.

54. Douglas Jehl, "US Is Showing a New Caution on UN Peacekeeping Mission," *New York Times,* May 18, 1994, p. 1.

55. Each intervention type has been adapted from Richard Haass's *Intervention: The Use of American Military Force in the Post–Cold War World* (Washington, D.C.: Carnegie Endowment Book, 1994).

56. See Nancy Ethiel (ed.), *Reporting the Next War* (Chicago: The Robert R. McMormick Tribune Foundation, 1992), and *The Military and the Media: The Continuing Dialogue* (Chicago: The Robert R. McMormick Tribune Foundation, 1993).

57. Alexander L. George and Richard Smoke, *Deterrence in American Foreign Policy: Theory and Practice* (New York: Columbia University Press, 1974), p. 11.

58. Even the Reagan Doctrine's claim to rolling back communist control was careful not to risk the total destabilization of Europe. All-out war on the European continent was not an objective.

59. Author interview with Admiral Kendal Pease, Pentagon, September 1995.

60. Author telephone interview with Admiral Kendal Pease, March 12, 1996.

61. Richard N. Haass, *Intervention,* p. 57.

62. Ibid., p. 62.

63. I was in Nairobi during this time and saw firsthand the attempts made by correspondents such as Terry Leonard of the Associated Press to get into Rwanda. It was simply too dangerous.

64. Of course, this formulation might be criticized as missing the point that saving lives in political conflict is not apolitical in nature. Certainly in the case of the efforts to save the lives of largely Hutu refugees in Goma and elsewhere in Zaire, the results were not politically neutral. Some of these very refugees were responsible for the massacre of Tutsi and Hutu moderates in the weeks before.

65. Steven Livingston, "Suffering in Silence"; Roger Wallis and Stanley Baran, *The Known World of Broadcast News: International News and the Electronic Media* (London: Routledge, 1990); Mort Rosenblum, *Coups and Earthquakes: Reporting the World to America* (New York: Harper Colophon Books, 1979).

66. Livingston and Eachus, "Humanitarian Crises and US Foreign Policy," p. 417.

The Contributors

Sissela Bok is a philosopher and fellow at the Harvard Center for Population and Development Studies, and author of many books including *Entertainment Violence, Lying,* and *Secrets.*

Justin Brown was a graduate research assistant at the University of Massachusetts/Boston at the time this research was conducted.

Alison Carper was a journalist for thirteen years, most recently with *Newsday* in New York City. Her reporting focused on social issues, particularly problems afflicting the urban poor. She is currently a doctoral student at Adelphi University.

Michael X. Delli Carpini is associate professor of political science at Barnard College. He has published *What Americans Know About Politics and Why It Matters* (with Scott Keeter) and *Stability and Change in American Politics.*

Timothy E. Cook is professor of political science at Williams College. His books include *Crosstalk: Citizens, Candidates, and the Media in a Presidential Campaign* (coauthor) and *Making Laws and Making News: Media Strategies in the U.S. House of Representatives.*

Barrie Dunsmore was foreign and diplomatic correspondent for ABC News for more than thirty years. He covered nearly all the major international events from 1965 to 1995.

Marion Just is professor of political science at Wellesley College. She has held visiting fellowships at Harvard University and the Massachusetts Institute of Technology. Her books include *Crosstalk: Citizens, Candidates, and the Media in a Presidential Campaign; Common Knowledge: News* *and the Construction of Political Meaning;* and *Coping in a Troubled Society;* she has also published journal articles and book chapters on political communications and electoral behavior.

Scott Keeter is professor of political science at Virginia Commonwealth University. His most recent book, with Delli Carpini, is *What Americans Know About Politics and Why It Matters.*

Montague Kern is associate professor of communications at Rutgers University. She is the author of *Thirty-Second Politics,* and is coauthor of *The Kennedy Crisis* and *Crosstalk: Citizens, Candidates, and the Media in a Presidential Campaign.*

Steven Livingston is associate professor of political communication and international affairs at George Washington University. His research focuses on media and foreign policy processes, as well as the role of the media in U.S. domestic politics. Among other publications, he is author of *The Terrorism Spectacle.*

Michael Milburn is professor of psychology at the University of Massachusetts/Boston. He is the author of *Persuasion and Politics: The Social Psychology of Public Opinion* and *The Politics of Denial.*

Pippa Norris is associate director (research) of the Joan Shorenstein Center on the Press, Politics and Public Policy and teaches at the Kennedy School of Government, Harvard University. Her books include *Electoral Change Since 1945; Britain Votes 1997; Passages to Power; Comparing Democracies; Women, Media and Politics; Political Recruitment; British By-elections; Politics and Sexual Equality; Women and Politics; Different Voices, Different Lives; Gender and Party Politics;* and the *British Elections and Parties Yearbooks.* She coedits *The Harvard International Journal of Press/Politics.*

Richard Parker is senior fellow at the Joan Shorenstein Center, Kennedy School of Government, Harvard University. He teaches at the Kennedy School of Government and Tufts University. An economist by training, he is a graduate of Dartmouth University and Oxford University. He has published three books, including *Mixed Signals: The Prospects for Global Television News, The Myth of the Middle Class,* and *Economics and Democracy,* as well as numerous articles. For several years a journalist as well, he cofounded the monthly *Mother Jones,* which won three National Magazine Awards during his tenure.

Jorge Quiroga has been a television journalist for twenty years. In 1974 he was hired by WCVB in Boston to create and produce *Aqui,* a weekly program for and about the Hispanic community. Three years later he moved to the newsroom, becoming a reporter for *NewsCenter Five,* the highest-rated TV news organization in the Boston market.

Pearl Stewart, former editor of the *Oakland Tribune,* was the first African American woman editor of a major U.S. daily newspaper. She was also a Freedom Forum journalist-in-residence at Howard University and Xavier University of Louisiana.

Sharon Webb was a graduate student in the School of Mass Communications, Virginia Commonwealth University, at the time this research was conducted.

Index

ABC, 4, 6, 13, 106, 165, 203, 219, 221, 237, 244, 251, 253, 256, 263, 266, 279, 304; broadcast revenues, 43*n12; Prime Time*, 251; *World News Tonight*, 97

Action for Children's Television, 214*n45*

ACT UP, 227

Advertisements, 180*n7;* "Ad Police," 166; Adwatch features in, 12, 165–180; affective messages in, 11; analysis of, 126–129; campaign, 165–180; content, 12; deconstructing, 168; emotional, 125, 165, 166; exposure to, 26, 165; factual correctness, 168; global, 22; image, 165, 166; income from, 32; influence on voters, 165, 178; infomercials, 169; issue-based, 125, 165–166; misleading, 168; negative, 11, 132, 136–139, 166; newspaper, 45; paid, 12; peripheral cues in, 167, 175; political, 126, 165–180; positive character, 125; press coverage, 167–168; resistance to, 166; role in campaigns, 121–141; stimuli in, 124–126, 125*tab;* talking head, 125; television, 25, 27, 32, 33–34*tab,* 35

Adwatch, 12, 165–180; and attitude change, 171, 175, 177; effects on voters, 170–178; gender differences, 172, 173, 174, 177; and issue-orientation, 174–175; journalist reaction to, 167–170; recommendations for, 169

Affirmative action, 10, 69, 77, 78, 81, 82, 82*tab,* 83, 84, 125, 126, 137, 140

Afghanistan, 304*tab,* 305

Africa: per capita incomes, 31; television in, 30*tab,* 31, 32, 33*tab*

African-Americans, employment in journalism, 67–88

AIDS: Coalition to Unleash Power (ACT UP), 227; erroneous information on, 225–228; governmental response to, 217, 218; human interest stories of, 229–232; initial neglect of, 219–222; internalization of, 223; media coverage of, 14, 217–233; public opinion on, 224; television coverage, 230

Ailes, Roger, 166

Albania, 30*tab*

Albright, Madeleine, 306

Algeria, 30*tab*

Amanpour, Christiane, 245

American Newspaper Publishers Association, 48

American Psychological Association, 186, 187, 188

American Society of Newspaper Editors, 48, 54, 56, 62, 67, 70, 71, 72, 75, 78, 81, 83, 88*n14*

Angola, 30*tab,* 304*tab*

Argentina: programming costs, 30*tab;* television in, 23, 34*tab,* 277

Arkansas Gazette, 47

Arnett, Peter, 265, 288

Arocha, Zita, 103, 106

Aruba, 30*tab*

About the Book

Politics and the Press not only examines how journalists define the news; it also explores the role of the media in elections and the shaping of public opinion, as well as the reportage of the news on policy issues.

This important work presents original research by a unique team of visiting scholars, journalists, and industry leaders at the Joan Shorenstein Center at Harvard University. Norris and the contributors pay particular attention to the influence of the press on the policy apparatus of government, and the impact of economics and changes in communications technology on news reporting. Included in the book are perspectives on minorities and women as members of the news industry.

Pippa Norris is associate director of the Joan Shorenstein Center on the Press, Politics and Public Policy at the John F. Kennedy School of Government, Harvard University.